# A Court
# Without Justice

# A Court Without Justice

## Administrative Law, the Constitution, and Me

BROOK CHAMBERY

A Court Without Justice
Administrative Law, The Constitution, and Me

Library of Congress Control Number: 2020911570

ISBN: 978-1-7350272-0-3 (Paperback)
ISBN: 978-1-7350272-2-7 (eBook)

Printed in the United States

Edited by Alan Axelrod
Design by Carol Norton
Cover images by icedmocha/Shutterstock and Jack R. Perry/Shutterstock

For further information or to contact the author,
please go to www.BrookChambery.com.

"I BELIEVE THERE ARE MORE INSTANCES OF
THE ABRIDGMENT OF THE FREEDOM OF
THE PEOPLE BY GRADUAL AND SILENT
ENCROACHMENTS OF THOSE IN POWER THAN
BY VIOLENT AND SUDDEN USURPATIONS."

—JAMES MADISON,

*Speech in the Virginia Ratifying Convention on Control of the Military,
June 16, 1788*

# CONTENTS

# The Lengthening Shadow

O n June 23, 1999, with the TV cameras rolling, I made my way into the hearing room for an unprecedented administrative "proceeding" that was being staged against me. It was initiated by the New York State Department of Health, and its objective was to revoke my license to operate Beechwood Restorative Care Center. Although authorized under NYS law, such a hearing was contrary to standard protocol. In fact, it had never been done before.

Normally, there are safeguards in place when an agency such as DOH contemplates putting someone or something out of business. Normally, DOH would prepare its case and take it to the state Attorney General (AG). If the AG determined the case had merit, the AG would prosecute it in a court of law. But in this instance, since DOH was bringing a case without a shred of evidence, there was no point in taking it to the AG. It would never get beyond his office. So, DOH officials chose to use their own arena in a process euphemistically termed "quasi-judicial." The "quasi" part described a procedure without any constitutionally guaranteed protections of due process. True, it was staged in the United States of America, but, depending on how you want to translate it into the dimension of space, the entire process was conducted above, below, or beside the law.

Both the hearing officer, who is given the quasi-judicial title of Administrative Law Judge (ALJ), and the prosecutors are employees of DOH. After hearing the case, the ALJ makes a recommendation to the Commissioner of Health, who is the head of DOH. He or she is the ultimate decision maker. It is a hermetically sealed process, the outcome of which is judged by DOH based on the work of DOH prosecutors and finalized by the person at the top of DOH. In the olden days of absolute monarchs, kings could at will bypass parliaments and regular courts by acting on their own "prerogative power." They would issue a command via royal proclamation or decree, which they could enforce not through pesky courts of law but their own prerogative courts, with names like the King's Council, Star Chamber, or High Commission. Whereas ordinary judges passed judgments independently of the king and could even issue judgments that ran counter to the king's will, in cases of the exercise of prerogative power, kings tried cases in their own prerogative courts to which the regular judicial courts and judges slavishly deferred. Processes under today's administrative law are medieval, far more closely resembling England prior to the signing of the Magna Carta on June 15, 1215 than the United States on June 21, 1788, after the Constitution was ratified.

What swirled through this closed quasi-judicial loop were false charges and false testimony in a case preplanned and thoroughly scripted by the prosecutors. Including the investigations leading up to it, the hearing amounted to a huge fraud and abuse of power perpetrated against Beechwood, everyone connected with it—me, my professional staff, my mostly elderly, mostly vulnerable patients, and the public.

We were shocked that there was a provision in law allowing an administrative proceeding to impose, with so little due process, a sanction of such magnitude. We were shocked that DOH had blown the dust off the law and employed it in conflict with federal contractual obligations, or that the federal authorities were allowing it. Most of all, we were shocked that this could happen in the United States. But we had no choice other than to show up, put on our defense, and preserve our legal standing for future court appeals.

As my attorneys prepared for the opening of the hearing, I scanned the cast of dim and nefarious opponents across the room. With the outcome of this proceeding preordained, I resigned myself to losing this round but resolved that I would win the final one.

The *fact* was that this hearing was nothing more than an empty formality. The real damage had already been done. Beechwood Restorative Care Center had been founded in 1955, by my parents, as Beechwood Nursing Home. By 1999, it had been serving the community in and around Rochester, New York, for forty-four years. In the hyper-compressed span of the two months preceding the hearing, the facility had been decertified from Medicaid/Medicare, payments had been shut off, patients were told they would be relocated against their will, and the DOH public relations apparatus, like the compactor on a garbage truck, relentlessly trashed my reputation as well as the reputations of my professional staff—doctors and nurses—and the facility itself.

New York State Assemblywomen Susan John attended a meeting at Beechwood where, according to a DOH email, "visibly distraught" patients and their families were "learning of the imminent closure and need to transfer" to other facilities. She called it a "nightmare." John Darling, a DOH attorney, used very different language, congratulating the DOH PR operation for doing "a fine job through the press of sullying Beechwood, and the Chamberys' good name." One reporter confided to me that DOH PR was doing everything short of sending her flowers to get her to cover events from *their* perspective.

The hearing that pulled my operating license was a culminating formality but not the last step. There was still the high-dollar value of the physical plant that housed what was generally acknowledged to be a state-of-the-art facility. The DOH legal staff had wielded this fact as a cudgel intended to force me to sign an agreement that I would never again work in healthcare in New York State. When I would not give them that satisfaction, Hank Greenberg, DOH Director of the Division of Legal Affairs, took it upon himself to rule that the physical plant could not be sold to anyone else for use as a nursing home. This prompted Russel Altone, Director of the Bureau of Hearings, to gloat that now "Chambery has nothing but bricks and mortar to sell." As it turned out, Beechwood, purpose-built to DOH specifications for nursing home use, could not be sold for any other use, not even for the cost of its bricks and mortar. DOH officials had managed to destroy every last dollar of value.

The vindictive insanity of all this was apparent to everyone except the federal court in which I sought an injunction, hoping to put the brakes on the juggernaut of devastation. The federal judge had the power to grant my injunction but felt that case law prevented his doing so. He opined that the administrative proceedings would offer ample opportunity for Beechwood to defend itself and air any and all grievances. As in the medieval epoch of absolute monarchy, it seemed, a federal judge felt obliged to defer to an administrative prerogative "court."

As you are about to read, Beechwood, the work of forty-four years, was destroyed in the blink of an administrator's eye. But I fought on, beyond the destruction, irreversible as I knew it was. I fought on until I could get a hearing in a real court before a jury, as guaranteed by the Constitution. Getting there took thirteen years, the span of the narrative you are about to read.

*Insanity* is not a word I use lightly. But understand DOH, the department bent on destroying Beechwood, had, earlier in the year published its own quality data that put Beechwood at 68% above the norm, placing it among the top two or three of the 670 facilities in New York. Medicare data demonstrated that Beechwood was also one of the most efficient and effectively run facilities in the state, if not the nation. It was on the cutting edge of rehabilitation services and use of computerized medical records. A good share of its staff had been there for decades. It was the facility of choice for staff and patients. A remarkable 80 percent of its revenues came from private, insurance, and Medicare business—clients who vote on satisfaction with their patronage. Achievements of this magnitude are not easily obtained, and the goal of continual quality improvement had become ingrained in Beechwood's culture.

Yet here my staff and I stood accused of doing such widespread harm to patients that we needed to be shut down in a matter of days. In his closing argument to a jury thirteen years after the destruction, one of my attorneys, David Rothenberg, put my situation this way: it "absolutely makes no sense," he said, that "Beechwood would suddenly and for no apparent reason completely fall apart, or that there was lurking somewhere within Beechwood, a secret bad facility. A bad facility that apparently nobody knew about but could only be detected by this crew of surveyors, spearheaded by secret agent 00710." DOH inspectors are called "surveyors," and the "secret agent" among them was Susan Baker, Western New York Director of Long-Term Care, surveyor number 00710.

Kevin Cooman, another of my attorneys—for it took several of them to make my case—eloquently summarized in his opening remarks to that federal jury just what had been destroyed without a shred of evidence:

> Herbert and Olive Chambery jointly owned and operated Beechwood for a period of 37 years. It was their life, it was their passion. And when Brook's father, Herbert, died in 1993, Brook took over the day-to-day operation and direction of the home in partnership with his mother, Olive.
>
> Brook had grown up knowing the business over the kitchen table, and I mean that literally. Brook from childhood had watched and learned how a nursing home was to be run. When his parents had opened the nursing home in the 1950s on Culver Road, it was actually in their own home back at that time. That's the way nursing homes were established and operated. And in the

facility the Chamberys themselves lived with the residents. So, Brook observed and internalized all of these values that his parents had with respect to how you cared for and demonstrated concern for elderly people, vulnerable people.

After he obtained his college degree in 1972, Brook came back home, he obtained a nursing home license, administrator's license, and he joined his father in building and opening in 1974 the new and expanded Beechwood facility, a three-story facility, on Culver Road. And that new facility was able to accommodate 82 residents.

Brook also continued his studies, he went to the University of Rochester and obtained a master's in business administration, MBA, in 1976. Brook then spent a considerable portion of the next 20 years learning and immersing himself in every aspect of the nursing home business. He learned all the things about staffing, about care delivery, about food service, finances, facility management, maintenance and compliance with the Department of Health and federal regulations, which govern how it was that a nursing home had to operate.

The Beechwood staff members who will be here to testify will tell you that Brook was an inspirational leader. He was the best boss that they had ever had before or since because he was intent on leading them through this exciting evolution in nursing home care to meet the changes that were occurring in the healthcare delivery system and the patients' demands and needs as they became consumers of healthcare services. He set out to build upon, expand upon what his parents had already created because Brook understood in a way that few others did back in the late 1990s that nursing homes had to change the way they were delivering care. He envisioned improving quality of care and life for the traditional long-term residents, making even the declining end years of somebody's life as meaningful and comfortable as they could possibly be. In addition, Brook understood that nursing homes were no longer going to be solely viewed as a place for end-of-life care where you simply went and stayed and then endured until the end, but they were becoming—to the extent possible—places for rehabilitation, places that you moved through on the way back to more independent living, whether that be at home or some sort of assisted living.

How is it that Brook accomplished this? With tremendous foresight. You're going to hear that he understood that truly excellent healthcare required coordination among all the different disciplines, all the different kind of caregivers that are within a nursing home. And he understood this was going to best be made possible through the use of technology. You don't replace the caring people. You can't do that. But you put in their hands tools that they've never had before. So, Brook and his brother Dale created from scratch a comprehensive electronic medical records system—what we refer to by shorthand as an EMR, electronic medical record, for use in the nursing home environment. And he installed and implemented it at Beechwood as the flagship site. He developed this software in a companion business to the nursing home. Appropriately enough, it was named Beechwood Software. The EMR software was the first system approved in the United States by the federal government for use in reporting patient assessment data from the database that was created with respect to each of the residents. Brook became a speaker at national conventions and seminars. Nursing home administrators from around the country came to Beechwood to see how this was implemented and to see Beechwood in action.

By the time of the DOH hearing, what had taken decades to build had been destroyed in a few chaotic weeks. Tens of millions of dollars in assets along with lives and livelihoods, reputations, and future plans—all were devastated in an administrative scorched-earth attack.

What emboldened these government officials to use the regulatory framework to make false claims and take drastic measures? A body of regulation called administrative law.

What motivated them? Retaliation.

As Kevin Cooman put it in a seminar he conducted about the case, I was "bright, highly creative, analytical," and didn't "suffer fools easily." I don't know how bright it was, but when DOH officials interfered with my business or needlessly got in the way of innovation, I pushed back, as the Constitution entitles me to do. Because I was driving quality, I always challenged improper survey outcomes—and I did so at the federal level, through the Healthcare Financing Administration (HCFA), which had ultimate responsibility in these matters. Repeatedly going to the feds did not make the state happy.

As an owner-operator who was on the cutting edge of innovative nursing home services that exposed a number of regulatory issues, I "barraged"—to use Cooman's term—both state and federal officials with letters that Cooman described as "careful expositions" of regulations and statutes. I pointed out internal conflicts within them and pressed the urgent need for reform. I made suggestions for fixing, changing, and resolving the conflicts. Almost always unwelcome by the state officials, these suggestions wound their way through DOH, to the governor's office, and to HCFA. When all else failed, I took the state to court. One lawsuit resulted in the DOH stipulating that it would change its regulations, which, as Cooman noted, "enraged regulators." Well, they do hate to lose. "Imagine them having to send out the 'Dear Administrator' letter to all the facilities," Cooman told his seminar attendees, "notifying them that they would be changing procedures and regulations due to the Beechwood case."

Kevin Cooman titled his seminar "The Long Road to Justice and $25 Million." That road is the subject of much of this book. But before we can begin to travel it, we must understand that a long stretch of it is patched and potted by administrative law, which I will describe to you in as tight a nutshell as I can manage.

The Fifth Amendment to the Constitution guarantees that no person shall be deprived of life, liberty, or property without due process of law—namely, the protections offered by our judicial system. The Fourteenth Amendment forbids states from abridging any constitutional right or denying any person within its jurisdiction equal protection of the laws.

We depend on these rights, and we assume they are legally absolute and inviolable. But as I discovered, this is a mistaken assumption. Very few Americans understand that legislators have created certain laws that interfere with these Fifth and Fourteenth Amendment rights, that work around them, and that even abridge them. The most important law that does this is the federal Administrative Procedures Act (APA; Pub. L. 79-404). The product of a contentious legislative debate in 1946, the APA was followed by similar legislation enacted by numerous state legislatures. Along with agency-specific regulations, the APA and its state-based progeny guide rulemaking, enforcement, and adjudication by government agencies. This, along with a body of court decisions made pursuant to or in connection with these actions, is what is meant by "administrative law."

As the size and reach of the American regulatory state have grown, so have the legal structures to support it, including the breathtaking power of enforcement actions and sanctions. The APA defines "sanctions" as any "prohibition, requirement, limitation, or other condition affecting the freedom of any person." The problem is that, without establishing any boundaries, it allows these government agencies to bypass the court, when legislatively authorized, and use their own quasi-judicial processes to charge, try, pass judgment, and apply sanctions. To add insult to injury, the APA then dictates how the constitutionally established courts are to deal with appeals of these administrative actions.

How *do* they deal with them? In a word, *deferentially*.

We think of the Constitution as bedrock. It surely appears to be just that.

It offers but two avenues of legally binding power in the United States. One is paved with acts of Congress. The other with the decisions of the courts. The nation's founders and constitutional framers failed to anticipate the emergence of a third "avenue." Indeed, how could they have begun to imagine the kind of back alley, byway, dim detour by which our constitutional guarantees are skirted, and in my case, a prospering family business destroyed? How could they have foreseen the creation, let alone the abuses, administrative law enables?

Administrative law manifests itself wherever and whenever the legislative branch and the judicial branch delegate their Constitutional powers to unelected and unaccountable executive agencies at the federal and state levels. These bodies, these unelected men and women, are empowered to create administrative acts, which have all the force of constitutionally legislated law without any of law's constitutional protections. Administrative acts can and do deprive Americans of liberty, property, livelihood, and even life itself, all without due process.

Law professor Philip Hamburger explains that administrative law "is commonly defended as a new sort of power, a product of the 19th and the 20th centuries that developed to deal with the problems of modern society in all its complexity." The thought is that as American society became more technologically and economically complex, specialized expertise was increasingly in demand for the crafting of laws; therefore, Congress turned to civil servants, administrators, and technocrats who supposedly had the necessary expertise to create very detailed rules and regulations. These were not legislative acts of Congress. They were acts of an extra-constitutional regulatory state. Nevertheless, because Congress had legislated that "state" into existence, the rules and regulations carried all the force of law without any of the restraints and checks and balances governing constitutionally sanctioned, congressionally legislated laws.

Regulatory and administrative agencies have their own quasi-judicial administrative proceedings to enforce their rules and regulations. These are presided over by departmental hearing officers and prosecuted by departmental attorneys who enjoy absolute immunity from civil suits arising from their actions. The hearing officers are often referred to as Administrative Law Judges (ALJs), a title that puts a fig leaf on the "quasi" part of *quasi-judicial*. It lends an air of credibility for the benefit of the public, obscuring the fact that the ALJs are not members of the federal or state judiciaries. As for agency investigators and administrative officials, who are personally instrumental in putting charges together and deciding on the sanctions to be applied, they have qualified immunity, shielding them from suit unless it is proved that they knowingly violated the few clearly established laws that even the regulatory state cannot evade.

An administrative proceeding can be initiated either by the agency imposing a sanction or through a formal appeal by the entity being sanctioned. Depending on a given agency's rules—and these rules vary from agency to agency—notice of hearing and statement of charges may be a mere 15 days and still be deemed "reasonable." Discovery—the exchange of evidence and legal information by all parties in a case, an indispensable feature of pretrial procedure in normal civil and criminal law—is not provided for in administrative proceedings. No aid is available to facilitate preparation of a proper defense. Also, in contrast to regular judicial courts, the rules of evidence for an administrative proceeding are by design quite lax. Subpoenas are issued only reluctantly, and compliance and timeliness of response cannot be relied upon. Indeed, if the issue of a subpoena was calculated to reveal any improper motive or procedure, the agency or agencies involved routinely respond with defiant, even arrogant resistance, including claims of privilege and steadfast lack of compliance.

Although there are various provisions in the state and federal statutes governing the conduct of hearings in an impartial manner and maintaining the independence of the hearing officers, impartiality and independence are impossible in practice because everyone involved on the agency side is an employee of the agency. There are no legal, ethical, or moral firewalls. In fact, there are many affirmative *restrictions* on the independence of the proceeding, including the fact that the hearing officer—the so-called administrative law *judge*—is charged only with making the initial determination. The final determination, the actual *judgment,* is reserved for the agency commissioner, some other agency designee, or an internal appeal board. The administrative law "judge" has no authority to change the sanctions sought by the commissioner's office. Nor is the "judge" empowered to hear, let alone rule upon, claims of improper procedure or motives. In fact, unless a monetary penalty is involved, the ALJ avoids ruling on the scope and severity of the alleged violations and whether these justify whatever penalty is fixed.

*Independence? Impartiality?* These qualities descend from illusion to delusion. For ALJs often solicit aid and advice from agency staff in making their decisions. They may even enlist agency staff in the writing of them. While it is true that those agency personnel who were directly involved in the case in question as investigators or prosecutors are barred from such collaborative contacts with the ALJ, this prohibition leaves ample wiggle room for interpretation. Moreover, any attempt the defendant makes to find out just who was involved in the decision making, and for what reason, is routinely stonewalled with a claim of "deliberative process privilege."

*Independence? Impartiality?* In New York State, the record considered in decision making can either be the entire record or whatever portion of the record has been cited by either party in their proposed findings of fact and conclusions, which are submitted *after* the hearing. This makes it possible for the ALJ to base the initial determination—the recommendation sent to the commissioner—solely on the proposed findings of his or her own agency.

It does not take much calculation or imagination to understand that one's odds of prevailing in an administrative hearing are vanishingly small. Appeal is an option, but the prospects of prevailing don't improve. The APA standard is that the actions, findings, or conclusions of an ALJ may be set aside or the agency determination be held unlawful only if the court on appeal finds that the decisions made and actions taken were arbitrary and capricious, an abuse of discretion, or unsupported by substantial evidence. But the APA also states that, in adjudicating an appeal, a court may ignore the whole record and take only such portions of it as may be cited by either party. It is quite possible that a court will use only the agency's determination in deciding the merits of an appeal. Because the agency's determination may have come directly from the proposed findings of its own prosecutors, the bar is set so low as to be nearly subterranean, and courts almost automatically dismiss any and all appeals in deference to the agency and its discretion (granted by law, under the APA) to carry out its legislated authority, including the interpretation of statutes and regulations. True, there is language in the APA that says that nothing in the act shall be construed to diminish the constitutional rights of any person in a proceeding. Yet it is equally true that such diminishment is precisely what happens. In short, almost invariably, the appellant loses.

I walked upon what I took to be the bedrock of constitutional law only to discover that, in places, it was the thinnest of crusts. Having broken through, I lived thirteen years of my life, from 1999 to 2012, beneath the surface of a system so many other Americans continued to glide upon, blithely unaware of what was at work under the familiar realm of law they took for granted.

Read my story, and I am certain you will conclude that the level of indifference to private constitutional rights shown by the regulatory state is profoundly disturbing. I hope so, because it *should* disturb you. But if, like me, you are ever targeted and ensnared by that shadow government, you will be far more than disturbed. You will find yourself fallen into a nightmare, and you will be very fortunate to escape serious loss if not total devastation.

Bureaucratic agencies are not immune from organizational problems. Agency decisions are not always expert or rational, let alone just. Investigative and prosecutorial staff can make honest mistakes, dishonest mistakes, or mistakes that flow unintentionally from a superabundance of zeal. Personalities may conflict, so that normal regulatory tensions escalate and lead to unintended consequences. Supervisors and managers can be too heavy handed in the sanctions they ask for and apply.

The framers of the Constitution recognized that human beings are capable of a wide range of actions, from the noblest and wisest to the most craven and impulsive. For this reason, they sought to build a government of checks and balances. They understood that, for reasons of nature—both bureaucratic nature and human nature—it is far too easy for problems to occur and situations to spin out of control. They designed the judicial system to recognize that an independent and de novo review of the entire record of a case is often needed to avoid wrongful prosecutions, unjust verdicts, and inappropriate or unconstitutional sanctions.

But agency officials can easily imagine that they are above the law because an act of Congress, the APA, puts them above or beyond or simply beside the law. Power unrestrained leads to abuses of authority and violation of the rights of those being regulated. This is not a radical proposition, and it is certainly not news. The English barons forced King John to sign the Magna Carta in 1215 explicitly to restrain royal prerogative power, John Adams wrote the Constitution of the State of Massachusetts in 1780 expressly to establish "a government of laws and not of men," and John Dalberg-Acton, 1st Baron Acton, famously wrote in a letter of 1887 that "Power tends to corrupt, and absolute power corrupts absolutely."

To unrestrained power add improper motives and unconstitutional actions by government officials, and the nullification of constitutional rights takes on additional levels of complexity. An unconstitutional administrative process can be used to cover up an underlying unconstitutional offense. In these cases, a separate suit must be filed seeking damages for the violations of constitutional rights, but courts generally require that the legal remedies afforded in the administrative process be exhausted before the court will consider constitutional claims. Because the administrative appeal process does not allow damages, the courts regard any constitutional case brought before them as an illegitimate end run around the administrative case. The judicial courts try, therefore, to dispose of such cases accordingly. Often, this includes allowing the outcome of the administrative proceeding to influence their decision to dismiss the case.

As this typical course makes apparent, administrative law is not merely independent of constitutionally sanctioned law, it can bleed into and contaminate the judicial system. In a constitutional case, agency officials must be specifically and personally named. But the courts have a great aversion to claims leveled against government officials. Much less are they inclined to award damages against them. The courts dislike even more strongly accusations of widespread abuse within an agency or allegations that officials from multiple agencies may have been involved. Over decades of accumulated case law, the courts have afforded government officials ever-increasing protection from liability even as agencies have been legislatively tasked with—or simply assumed—more and more regulatory functions. The legal theory behind this accumulation of protections is that if agency officers are obliged to make tougher and inherently more contentious decisions as regulators serving the public welfare, they must be protected from liability for their decisions lest the public be endangered by that regulator's reluctance to make personally risky regulatory calls. Into this legal rationale, the possibility that some may abuse their authority simply does not enter. And so, a growing mountain of case law has established stratospherically high burdens for any plaintiff who seeks to move forward with a constitutional challenge.

## THE PURPOSE OF THIS BOOK

I have written this book to provide a concrete example of administrative law and the unfettered regulatory power it puts into the hands of unelected and largely unaccountable federal and state bureaucrats. I want to show you what I saw and felt, namely power that can readily be abused to turn white into black, to violate public trust, and to trample constitutional rights—all without consequence for the perpetrators. I intend to illustrate just how audacious and arrogant agency officials can be at abusing their regulatory authority and how difficult—even unfeasible or downright impossible—it is for the typical individual or small business to fight such administrative action. Finally, I want my readers to understand why, despite all the complaints of administrative overreach and retribution, little is ever proven and, thus, little is ever learned.

My book is based on one case, that of Beechwood Restorative Care Center. Beechwood was a healthcare facility, but it could just as easily have been a manufacturing plant subject to EPA inspections and Department of Labor actions, or a financial firm regulated by the SEC. The lessons apply generally, no matter the industry or regulatory agency involved.

The fact is that our state and federal regulator agencies are out of control, as witnessed by the depth of the political agenda now driving the management of such agencies as the Department of State, the Department of Justice, the FBI, and IRS. Even Congress has difficulty reigning in the administrative agencies of the Executive Branch, which is among its chief constitutional responsibilities.

Congress has loosed upon us freewheeling behemoths that set standards, investigate, regulate, and control just about everything. This has resulted in a sprawling chaos, armed and protected by the APA, with neither internal nor external checks and balances. No wonder the regulatory state proceeds as if it is not subject to any laws. What happened to Beechwood and what is going on in Washington and elsewhere must be seen as part and parcel of the same problem. Agency managers do not feel the need to answer to anyone for their actions. This perception, combined with authorized agency power, makes it extremely easy for administrators to act on personal agendas or vendettas. When the APA directs the courts to provide a high level of deference to actions undertaken by agency personnel, faulty, false, or fraudulent cases can readily be built, exculpatory information hidden, and lies made to the courts. Normally, these are all crimes—grave felonies, to be precise. But in the realm of administrative law, they are almost all without consequence. And the sinkhole sinks deeper. For "public officers laws" dictate that, at government expense, defense be provided these individuals precisely when prosecution is called for. What Beechwood was forced to endure illustrates why Congress is having trouble controlling what it created back in 1946 with passage of the APA.

This book narrates a thirteen-year war involving millions of dollars in legal expenses and seemingly endless battles on many administrative and judicial fronts to find justice to counter unconstitutional bureaucratic actions. It was a war that no American should be forced to fight—not with the constitutional protections we are guaranteed, and which took a very rare combination of resources, dedication, tenacity and courage to win. It was a war that would never have broken out if the agencies involved had been obliged, like the rest of us, to prepare their case for presentation in courts of law and nowhere else.

I have carefully documented the Beechwood case to bring to light for Americans the realities of administrative law. I hope my story will be a catalyst for change. It has it all: a valuable business, ranked at the top of its class in quality and innovative services, yet forced out of business and turned worthless because an owner *irritated* government officials; a plaintiff who survived the administrative and judicial processes forced upon him, fought for the needed evidence to prove retaliation, and after thirteen years, obtained a measure of vindication.

There may not be another case that so succinctly presents such an in-depth perspective on the subject. This is not surprising, given the dismal chances of success, the sheer legal complexity, personal hardship, expense, and emotional toll that accompany these battles. Those who support the current administrative law structure admit that abuses will take place but argue that these need to be tolerated for a broader public interest. The regulatory actions brought against Beechwood not only violated my constitutional rights and those of the business, but the rights of all those connected with it, including the staff and patients. Protecting the public welfare means, first and foremost, protecting the constitutional rights of every member of the public.

Thirteen years is a long time. It represents approximately thirty percent of a typical working career. In my case, it ended that career just as I was entering my most productive years. When the ordeal started in 1999, I was 49, my son was in seventh grade, and Google consisted of a couple of people working out of their garage. By the time it was done, I was 62, my son was through college, graduate school, and the first year of marriage. Google? It was a multibillion-dollar technological and cultural enterprise. As I drove to my office in the suburbs, I would often observe a new housing development being built, and it would strike me how a whole subdivision could be raised in the time it would take to research and write one legal brief. The sense of waste and lack of productivity was pervasive, oppressive. While my life was on hold, dealing with the aftermath of the events that unfolded in 1999, the world marched on.

Throughout my long ordeal, I witnessed the breathtaking boldness of a set of administrators in pursuing their agenda and protecting their interests. They did so without flinching, no matter what investigations of agency corruption were ongoing, no matter what warning was given them by counsel or admonition by the courts, and, most of all, no matter what toll it took on others. They rested comfortably, knowing that their defense and indemnification were ensured by the public officer laws. They were boundlessly confident of the legal shield the current system of administrative law provided. It is not hyperbole to point out that they smiled and joked all the way through depositions and trial. The incentive to create such reckless, heedless, and needless havoc must end. Constitutional protections must be restored to protect us all from a shadow government whose shadow continues to lengthen.

PART I

# Absolute Power: 1999

CHAPTER 1

# Raid

A pril 15, 1999. I was busy working on the rate to be inserted in a contract with one of the two major health insurers in the area, and which would be a game changer in the industry nationally. It was the final piece that I wanted in place before embarking on a long-planned, long prepared-for expansion of our healthcare operations. Twenty-five years of experience and everything I had worked for were coming together.

Many elements had been put in place to ensure this expansion plan would be a success. First and foremost, there was Beechwood Restorative Care Center, our showcase facility. In the past five years, Beechwood had evolved from exclusively providing traditional nursing home services, to devoting half of its beds to rehabilitation. We were very successful at this endeavor and were now on track to dedicating the entire facility to restorative and other innovative levels of care. Beechwood was among a handful of leaders nationwide that had worked to demonstrate that rehabilitation services could be efficiently and effectively provided outside the hospital setting. Now, we were moving beyond that.

Crucial to our endeavor to create meaningful innovation in the industry were the high standards Beechwood had always set for its staff and the quality of care they delivered. Thanks to the benchmark quality of its services, the innovation of its programs, and its cutting-edge use of computer technology, Beechwood was the facility of choice for those looking for challenging professional employment, as well as those looking for nursing home services. Eighty percent of its revenues came from private patients and insurers. Most of our patients *chose* us, and they were in a financial position to choose anyplace they wanted. Even the government attested to our excellence. Official state data showed that, as of January 1999, the quality of care indicators or outcomes Beechwood achieved were 68% above the norm. This placed us in the top three of the 670 facilities in New York State. Had this data been weighted by the level of care provided, Beechwood would likely have been rated number one. Such results were not achieved by accident, luck, or overnight. They were the product of a long-term special focus on continuous quality improvement which began in 1994—a year in which Beechwood was already 20% over the norm.

The establishment of our rehabilitation program had gone remarkably well. In 1998, measured by our 330 discharges to home or adult homes, Beechwood had already created one of the largest and most successful rehabilitation programs in the state. The program had been expanding at an average growth rate of 70% over the preceding five years, and it was on track for 100% growth in 1999. We took on some of the most challenging sub-acute cases but nevertheless achieved the state's third lowest average length of stay—at 24 days—and the fourth lowest cost per stay.

Health insurers loved us. Seventy percent of our 1998 discharges left us having achieved total independence in what the profession calls "activities of daily living" (ADLs). This means that they were capable of performing the basic activities necessary for independent living at home or in the community. Another twenty percent of those who had completed rehabilitation with us only needed some oversight or limited assistance, which translated into a very low level of need for homecare services. A representative of Preferred Care, Molly Kelly, who was negotiating the contract with Beechwood, later testified that no matter how difficult the case, "there was never a question" that every aspect of care "would have been appropriately managed." Beechwood's "outcomes were beyond belief," and the facility ranked "at the very top, absolutely" of the 70 facilities in her nine county area, she said.

She further explained that Beechwood's capabilities were so far above the other facilities in the area that Preferred Care's medical panel chose it as the "exclusive" contractor for a new and innovative program the company was launching to provide coverage for "those folks who presented at an emergency room and were stabilized," yet still had an "acute problem that really did not require the intensity of service that was available in a hospital setting." The benefit to both the insurer and the patient was that they would receive the same "high acute level of care at a much more cost-effective price, … and not have to stay in a hospital." To accomplish this, the panel needed "a facility where there was medical coverage and around-the-clock nursing care that was of very high quality." In other words, we would be admitting patients around the clock, for stays that might be as brief as a day or two, and have the appropriate medical, nursing, and other staff to deal with them. Beechwood had not only achieved success at rehabilitation, we were using this expertise to move into a totally new level of care that had never been witnessed nationally.

That mid-April day in 1999 found me proud to be leading a facility that had proved itself an extraordinary resource for the community and that was well on its way to becoming even more valuable. There were three main reasons for our high level of performance: management, staff, and computerized operations. More than innovative, our use of computerized operations was defining the cutting edge in an era still on the cusp of a digital transformation.

Daily administrative duties were in the capable hands of Paul Kesselring, and my mother, Olive Chambery. Paul had dedicated twenty-six years of his professional life to Beechwood, and my mother had been involved in managing the facility since its doors opened in 1955. As for our department heads and unit supervisors, all were highly experienced, as was the entire staff. In 1999, 25% of our staff had worked at Beechwood for more than ten years, and half of this group for more than twenty. Overall, the average length of employment was about eight years. Everyone on our staff was eminently qualified and intensely dedicated, professionals all, who functioned as members of a cohesive team. As we grew, we worked hard to ensure that all new hires met our very exacting standards.

The management ideas and technology incorporated in the computer system were highly advanced in 1999, and in many aspects, remain so today. The software was not something bought off the shelf, largely because it could not have been bought off the shelf back then. What we wanted simply did not exist, and so my brother, Dale, and I designed and built it. I designed the management concepts behind the system. My brother designed the structure of the system and headed up the programming at a sister company, Beechwood Software, Inc. The applications we designed were for micro-computers and consisted of both financial and medical records systems. As early as 1992, Beechwood had a fully functioning electronic medical record (EMR) system thoroughly networked throughout the facility with complete staff access in every department.

Without doubt, Beechwood had made bold strides into digital technology, and we did so during an era in which "EMR"—electronic medical records—was only slowly and painfully making its way into very large hospitals. In smaller facilities, such as ours, and private practices, EMR was gaining almost no traction at all, even though, as early as 1991, the Institute of Medicine, an affiliate of the National Academies of Science, had issued a recommendation that every physician should be using computers to improve patient care by 2000. It was 2009 before President Obama signed into law the American Recovery and Reinvestment Act, which provided incentives for facilities that demonstrated "meaningful use" of EMR. By that time, Beechwood, the innovator, had been shuttered for an entire decade.

As CEO of Beechwood Software, Inc., I frequently conducted medical records seminars for various healthcare industry associations, and it was not at all unusual for healthcare executives and practitioners from all over the nation to fly into Rochester to see our system in full operation. We sold Beechwood Software to a multibillion-dollar corporation in the spring of 1998 because we wanted to focus on our core business, the delivery of healthcare services. But since the software concepts were integral to our management philosophy and thus crucial to our goals for expanded operations, we negotiated a sale contract allowing us to use the software in up to fifty facilities at minimal charge.

We were on course, moving forward. We had the software tools, the staff, the management, the reputation, and the profits to keep driving forward with more facilities. We had proven ourselves on many fronts, there was just one more step before unfolding a major expansion. We needed to get that contract signed with Preferred Care. As Molly Kelly testified, the "terms of the program" had already been negotiated, and "the contract was literally at the point of signature pending a rate."

-------

*April 15, 1999, late afternoon.* Donna Richardson, our director of nursing (DON) came into my office. She looked worried. She told me that surveyors (as New York State Department of Health healthcare facility inspectors were called) were in the facility doing a "complaint survey."

Surveys—inspections—are the primary vehicles for the regulation of nursing home operations. Every facility is subject to annual certification surveys, plus abbreviated surveys that may be made at any time, typically in response to a change in operations or a complaint. Surveys are a fact of life in the nursing home industry. They are part of the routine, but the underlying stakes are always high, and no operator looks forward to them. Ultimately, it is the surveys that determine a facility's eligibility for Medicaid (MD) and Medicare (MR) payments. Surveys are also the basis of the certification required to maintain a state operating license. The annual certification survey is done by a team of Department of Health (DOH) surveyors representing a cross-section of disciplines. Collectively, their responsibility is to enforce every line of a surprisingly subjective code that is byzantine in its complexity. The abbreviated "complaint" survey is usually carried out by a single surveyor, who typically focuses on a specific concern or area of the code.

Most of the time, an abbreviated survey is triggered by a complaint made to DOH. Complaints, which may be submitted anonymously, range from someone upset over how they were billed for co-insurance to an allegation of physical abuse at the hands of a staff member. In my experience, a complaint survey is quickly over and done with. The surveyor first meets with the appropriate facility manager and discusses why he or she is there. After performing the survey, the surveyor meets with the manager again in an "exit conference" to identify the problem or set of problems (if he or she determines that problems exist). Rarely does the complaint survey lead to a more comprehensive survey. One possible consequence of either an abbreviated or a full survey is a "deficiency." Any deficiency means that your facility is out-of-compliance, and its certification is therefore in peril.

Donna was a very capable DON and experienced nurse, who was not easily flustered. In the past, almost always, she handled conferences with surveyors herself, on her own. Now she stood in my office doorway, telling me that she needed my help with the exit conference. She explained that, this time, the surveyors—there were two, not the usual one—were behaving very strangely. They requested information she had no way of knowing how to provide.

In view of this appeal, I did not hesitate to follow Donna into her office. As soon as I walked in, it was apparent that the surveyors, Cynthia Francis and Elizabeth Rich, were indeed acting out-of-character. I knew them both to be highly experienced, and yet they were now bizarrely unfocused. They were downright unable or unwilling to voice any specific concerns. As for their requests for information, these were so vague that it was simply impossible to provide answers, let alone documents.

Within seconds, I understood why Donna was so upset. I was upset. The whole meeting was utterly frustrating. Dealing with DOH was often unpleasant and tinged with hostility. But this encounter resembled nothing I had experienced in my twenty-seven years interacting with the department. I saw before me whole banks of caution lights flashing.

I had become accustomed to dealing with contentious surveys. They had been taking on a harder and ever more heated edge since 1996, when I began confronting the department on a number of significant regulatory issues and even found it necessary take DOH to court. The thing is, because regulators are given so much autonomy from constitutionally mandated legal processes, it is all too easy for surveys and the deficiencies that may result from them to be influenced and shaped by retaliatory motives. So, I began to take a proactive approach. When survey issues arose that I felt were improper and therefore could not be adequately resolved within the New York State DOH, I began making it a practice to appeal to federal authorities at the Healthcare Financing Administration. Today known as the Centers for Medicare & Medicaid Services (CMS), the HFCA had ultimate responsibility for the work done by state departments of health. I looked upon the federal agency as a check and balance against the largely autonomous state DOH regulators.

At first, informally appealing to the HFCA prompted common sense and reason to prevail. The contentious matters were satisfactorily resolved—until the next time. We were going on three straight years of what seemed deliberately hostile surveys when I finally asked the HCFA in January 1999 to conduct a formal investigation of DOH moves against Beechwood—and, quite frankly, against me. This did not sit well with Sanford Rubin, at the time the director of the Rochester office of DOH, who had recently received the title of Acting Director of the Western Region.

It soon became apparent that relations between the Acting Director and Beechwood—more to the point, between Rubin and me—had come to a rolling boil. Moreover, the ill will toward me was now also emanating from the central DOH office at Albany, the state capital.

The entire timeline of deteriorating relations went like this: Back in 1994, Beechwood first challenged DOH when it denied the facility short-term beds for respite care and then attempted to force our agreement to constraints on admissions as a condition for granting approval of two respite beds. Bridling at the coercion, I brought suit in state court on behalf of Beechwood, and no sooner was our petition filed than DOH relented, backed down, and folded, conceding the case. The next year, 1995, DOH surveyors alleged two "D-level" deficiencies, the lowest level there is. I challenged these through an informal dispute resolution process afforded by the federal regulatory code. Once again, DOH backed down by rescinding the deficiencies.

In 1996, I sued again when DOH failed to abide by federal law. The federal Omnibus Budget Reconciliation Act (OBRA) prescribed a set of procedures governing hearings to resolve disputed nursing home resident discharges. The New York State DOH disregarded these, we sued, and the action ended with DOH stipulating that it would change its regulations to comply with federal regulations. Clearly, yielding to the feds like this had to have infuriated Albany officials, as well as Rubin, a party specifically named in the suit. Nevertheless, I was right. Beechwood was operating within the law. The state had strayed outside of it.

From 1996 to 1998, I sent what the federal district court later described as "a 'voluminous' series of letters and other papers to DOH and other state officials protesting various aspects of DOH's policies and practices, and advocating a number of changes." As the Assistant Attorney General for Medicaid Fraud dryly commented, "Brook Chambery's relationship with the NYSDOH can be described as rocky at best." This was not a subjective judgment. The facts were that, before 1995, Beechwood rarely received deficiencies as a result of DOH surveys. From 1995 through 1998, the facility received a handful of them. The Assistant AG observed that these "were not out of line with the results of other homes in the region. However, unlike other homes, Chambery almost always disputed the survey's findings."

True. From 1995 through 1998, I exercised my First Amendment right—a right Beechwood also enjoyed—and my right under specific federal laws to challenge each deficiency through the Informal Dispute Resolution (IDR) process. And then I sent the letter to HCFA requesting a formal investigation into the practices and procedures employed by DOH's Western Regional Office.

Why did I do all this?

In part, I wanted the state to comply with federal requirements by instituting appropriate regulatory changes. Doubtless, my impatience with state DOH stonewalling fueled the fire boiling the pot. But I had a business to operate and could not operate it optimally in a state regulatory environment at odds with federal regulation.

Why didn't other nursing homes have my kind of problems with the state? Was it just me? Well, I was willing to stand up and challenge regulatory stupidity. My competitors in the industry were not. They went along to get along.

But there were more basic issues involved than a conflict of personalities. From 1995 to 1998, DOH surveyors struggled to comprehend, let alone use, our advanced EMR during surveys. We offered them special training sessions, but the old guard simply dug in, refusing to recognize the new system. Resistance to innovation was reflexive among the regulators. And it was not just resistance to the EMR. Beechwood's rapidly evolving rehabilitation business put our focus on short-term care but did so within what the state classified as a nursing home. This put our business at odds with an increasingly obsolescent regulatory framework that contemplated nothing other than long-term care in a nursing home environment. The treatment objective of rehabilitation is to resolve medical problems altogether or to transition the patient to a level at which he or she can live as independently as possible. Whether the objective is total resolution or achieving a high level of independence, the aim is to reach these ends as quickly as possible. Thus, rehabilitation is a world removed from the long-term care mentality that assumes patients are invariably "residents," who will be in the facility for the rest of their lives.

Rehabilitation is an expensive, fast-moving environment. It deals with other providers and insurers who are intolerant of mistakes and desire the best outcomes at the lowest costs. It is also a business environment with a dichotomy inherent in its outcomes. In fixing the patient's problems, you create a problem for the facility. A successful outcome for the patient means an empty bed that must be filled again. Today, it is generally expected that "nursing" facilities provide some level of rehabilitative services, but in the mid-1990s this was a rarity. It took a real passion to enter this world, to train and hire staff accordingly, and to deal with the liability concerns and regulatory problems that come with being on the cutting edge.

So, frustrated and alarmed as I was by the vague, provocative, and unsettling meeting on April 15, I was not taken by surprise. A few weeks earlier, on Monday, March 8, another incident aroused my suspicion that ulterior motives were behind recent DOH actions. It was about ten in the morning, and the City of Rochester had just lifted the state of emergency that had been declared four days earlier, late Friday afternoon, after the city was so deeply buried in snow that the National Guard had to be deployed to help the hospitals. As a private nursing home, we were not eligible for this public aid. The staff on duty Monday was basically the staff that had been on duty since Friday. They were exhausted. I was outside with Paul Kesselring and two maintenance men. Together, we were trying to clear away approximately four feet of drifted snow, so that the driveway and sidewalk could be used. The snowbanks created by our efforts were enormous, but, over them, I somehow caught a glimpse of something I will never forget. As one of the maintenance men was coming down the sidewalk blowing snow, I saw two surveyors following right behind him, as if he were clearing the way expressly for them. To say that I was totally flabbergasted would be a complete understatement.

The surveyors came up to me and said they were on a complaint investigation.

What kind of complaint could be sufficiently urgent to bring two surveyors in on the tail end of a State of Emergency snowstorm? Well, not *this* complaint. Filed thirty days earlier, it qualified as a golden oldie. At issue was the amount of co-insurance we had billed a Medicare resident for a rehab visit. Not only was it far from urgent—DOH having sat on it for a month—it was unlikely to amount to anything. But here's the point, and the surveyors knew it as well as I. Once surveyors are present in the facility, everything is fair game for investigation. They were prospecting for a deficiency.

The pair stayed most of the day. Despite what we had been through that weekend, they were not finding any problems. Finally, at 2:15 p.m., one of them observed a newly hired aide helping a patient to the bathroom. The patient had an infection, for which Beechwood had a special procedure that this aide was not following. Even though the surveyors returned two days later, on the tenth, for further investigation, they found no one else violating this or any other policy. Nevertheless, they issued a deficiency over the single incident.

Yet this deficiency posed a significant problem for the regulators. Although the employee had violated a Beechwood policy, our policy exceeded state and federal standards. By the regulators' own definition, therefore, no standard had been violated, so no deficiency existed. But the regulators inhabited the far side of Alice's looking glass. No deficiency existed, yet a deficiency had been issued. The issuance obligated us to develop a plan of correction (POC)—for a non-existent deficiency. Applying the through-the-looking-glass logic of the situation, we devised a plan that consisted of lowering Beechwood's standard to be less restrictive and therefore more in line with state and federal expectations.

What victory had the surveyors won? They had driven Beechwood to diminish a standard of care. This sort of pettiness, while surreal, was not unusual. But it was beginning to get worrisome.

On March 19, another investigation was launched. This one was based on an anonymous complaint concerning a rehab patient who had decided to go home the afternoon of the snowstorm. The facility was cited for low-level "D" deficiency for having failed to do proper discharge planning. We appealed, whereupon DOH rescinded the deficiency because the investigator had never bothered to check with the patient, who later told surveyors that she had decided on her own to go home and did not notify Beechwood. She had been on an outpatient visit to a hospital, heard about the imminent snowstorm, and instructed her driver to take her home instead of back to Beechwood.

It was abundantly clear that the local DOH office was stalking us, looking for the least chance to pounce. I was unaware, however, that the agency's objective had ratcheted up from employing the survey process to hassle and harass us, to using it to not just to put Beechwood out of business, but to destroy my reputation and thereby keep me out of the industry permanently. I was also unaware that the operation went beyond the local office and embraced DOH headquarters in Albany. I had no inkling that it involved lobbying efforts aimed at gaining the support of federal HCFA officials in what was being plotted out as an illegal, fraudulent, scorched-earth offensive.

———————————

*April 19, 1999. Midday, Monday.* Donna Richardson came into my office again. This time she was crying. If I rarely saw her worried, I had never seen her in tears. I asked her what the matter was.

The surveyors were back, she said. And, this time, they were accompanied by Susan Baker. As we both knew, Baker was the regional director of Long-Term Care from the Buffalo office. Whatever was going on, it was not good.

I followed Donna into the conference room. Baker's arm was already in motion, waving a list of patient records she demanded to see—*by the end of the day*. Before I could respond, she warned me that she would request that HCFA terminate Beechwood as a Medicare/Medicaid provider if I failed to comply.

As regional Long-Term Care director, Susan Baker had considerable authority. But, in my experience, people confident of their power seldom resort to threats, let alone preemptively lead with one. To my ear, this signaled someone in full-on defensive mode, who, despite the bluster, felt herself to be on thin ice. In any case, I had no intention of denying her the patient records she wanted, but you don't just fetch them and hand them over to anyone who asks or demands, no matter how powerful. The records had to be copied, so that the originals could remain where they belonged, in the files of Beechwood. While I would not deny Baker access to the records, I asked her to wait, and I walked out of the conference room and back into my office, where I looked up federal regulations.

In the few minutes it took me to confirm what I believed, that no regulation required us to make copies of records on demand, and return to the conference room, Baker's boss, Sharon Carlo, arrived. She was the regional director of Continuing Care, also from the Buffalo office. No doubt about it. The presence on site of Carlo and Baker, boss and underboss, combined with the extensive record copying demanded and the almost theatrical declamation of threats, was hardly part of a normal survey. Something was seriously wrong, and it was not going to end well for Beechwood.

But years of dealing with DOH had taught me the value of maintaining an impassive poker face. As deeply worried as I was, I calmly informed Sharon Baker that the code did not require us to do any record copying. Nevertheless, I continued, as a courtesy, we would make our copy machine available for their use.

Baker was having none of it. She phoned the feds, a brief conversation ensued, her set-jaw grimace turned to a frown, and I knew that whoever was on the other end of the line had told her that I was right. She and her boss stalked off to begin the tedious labor of copying a small mountain of records.

The pair commandeered the business office and the copy machine all that afternoon. In the meantime, the surveyors roamed the nursing floors, looking through more charts and printing off information directly from the computers at the nursing stations. That and the frenzied copying activity resumed into the next day, which put the regulators behind their own by-end-of-the-day deadline. Moreover, the busy work left no time for actual investigation or analysis. Each day, however, ended with an exit conference, as regulations dictated. The upshot was that DOH was in the same position they had been on April 15. They were talking about "potential deficiencies," nothing more, nothing less.

I did not know—had no way of knowing—that while one of the surveyors, Cynthia Francis, was out on the nursing floor on April 20, she remarked to Beechwood nurse Gwen Westbrook that "there has been a problem between Brook [Chambery] and Sandy [Rubin]" and went on to explain that "Brook had sued Sandy and the Department of Health; and that they [DOH and Rubin] were going to get him for it." By "him," Francis meant *me*.

*April 22, 1999, Thursday.* The situation escalated sharply as Sandy Rubin himself joined Carlo, Baker, Francis, and fellow surveyor Elizabeth Rich for the "final" exit conference. His appearance was the loud, dissonant chord in what had been a crescendo of escalation up the ladder of regulatory authority. As acting director, Rubin was responsible for supervising all health care within a seventeen-county area, hospital care included.

Rubin announced that his people anticipated citing Beechwood for "widespread immediate jeopardy." Immediate jeopardy (IJ) was an official term for any situation that posed a clear and present danger to patients. An IJ meant that patients were imperiled. Lives were at stake. There wasn't a moment to be wasted. That the IJ was also "widespread," well, that pretty much branded us a snake pit.

Given the urgency of the situation, Rubin said that the next step was applying sanctions, to include a fast-track (twenty-three-day) termination, a directed plan of correction (DPOC), and monitoring visits to assess the effectiveness of correction efforts. Deficiencies are graded based on the severity of the findings cited and how widespread the problem. In the past, we were hassled with low, D-level, deficiencies. Now we were being cited for the highest possible level of deficiency. It was the regulatory equivalent of capital punishment.

---

Finding yourself the target of horrendous accusations—nothing less than endangering the health, welfare, and the very lives of patients entrusted to your care— evokes a dark storm cloud of emotion. There is outrage, disbelief, fear, and panic. The adrenalin starts pumping. It is fight or flight.

Whatever else I was feeling at the moment, I could envision no alternative to fighting.

Intellectually, I knew that the charges were unfounded. I knew that retribution, no actual deficiency, was their basis. I responded as calmly as I could, telling them what they already knew all too well. They were levying serious accusations, which could ruin our business. I was, I said, "very concerned."

Rubin and his entourage threw out some random "facts" to support an unsupportable set of conclusions. It was all so flimsy that I simply could not begin to fathom how they were going to even try to put their allegations in writing, let alone make them withstand even the most cursory scrutiny. It seemed absurd.

But I also knew how serious this matter was—for the simple, awful, unavoidable reason that they had hold of all the strings. Administrative law hardly contemplated that surveyors and their bosses would make egregious errors. Far less did it consider that they would set out purposely to put someone out of business because they were a thorn in the regulatory side or a pain in the bureaucratic bottom. It was clear to me that our business was at stake.

We knew we had done nothing wrong. That a facility the government had just weeks earlier rated at or near the very top of all those in the state would suddenly be revealed as a place so dreadful that only immediate termination could cure it was, on its very face, absurd. But we also knew that federal survey regulations left no wiggle room. Once a deficiency is issued claiming at least the potential for more than minimal harm, the facility cited has no alternative but to assemble and submit a plan of correction (POC), even if it disagrees with and challenges the deficiency. Once cited, you are not permitted even to assert your innocence without first admitting your guilt by creating and presenting a POC, which is ipso facto a plea of guilt. DOH would review this document and then return to the facility at a scheduled time to assess its compliance. The POC itself is intended to give DOH a means of judging the likelihood that the facility will achieve compliance. But only compliance itself can serve as the basis for certifying the facility to continue doing business.

Despite our certainty that we were victims of vengeance, we immediately got to work after the exit conference combing minutely through the patient records. We needed to understand the issues, bogus though they were, so that we could assemble some credible plan of correction, despite the manifest fact that there was nothing to correct.

CHAPTER 2

# Beyond Legal

T he raid on Beechwood was followed by a scorched-earth campaign culminating in the procedural equivalent of the nuclear option. In addition
to overkill, it was a sneak attack. Had the intention of the regulators been
simply to cripple a nursing home sufficiently to destroy it, they would have
brought forward a "normal" federal decertification process to prevent Beechwood from serving Medicare and Medicaid patients. Instead, they convened a
full-on administrative hearing aimed at nothing less than revoking our operating license. We would receive no warning of this phase of the assault until fifteen
days before the relevant hearing was set to begin. It was a sneak attack. Was there
anyone with the elected or judicially appointed authority to stop it?

No, there was not. Not willing to, anyway.

On *Tuesday, April 27,* five days after the final exit conference at the conclusion
of the survey, the whole Department of Health (DOH) team, including Sandy
Rubin, director of the Rochester DOH office, returned to Beechwood, a statement of deficiency (SOD) in hand. I don't know for a fact that hand delivery of
an SOD was unprecedented in the state, let alone hand delivery by a squad
that included regional-level officials, but in more than thirty years I had never
heard of it and, except for my own case, I haven't heard of it since. The kindest
interpretation I can attach to this was that it was a ham-handed show of force,
intended to send a message. Less charitably, it was the act of supposedly professional regulators taking extraordinary pleasure in personally embarking

41

on a punitive expedition.

The SOD itself was surprising in its unorthodox, even self-contradictory nature. It was presented as the result and product of an "abbreviated survey," which, as the name implies, involves abbreviated procedures, a much smaller survey team, and a singular focus. There were just two surveyors, but records revealed that continuing care director Sharon Carlo, DOH regional director of Long-Term Care Susan Baker, Laura Leeds, Deputy Director of the Office of Continuing Care in Albany, and central office staff were all engaged in a massive effort behind the scenes combing the copied medical records for things to write up, with multiple drafts, until they had what they wanted. It was a thirty-two-page diatribe (the first of three), which initiated a "survey" process in which surveyors swarmed over our facility day after day. Major FBI search warrants are not executed so elaborately.

The document expanded on—and often conflicted with—much that had already been delivered verbally. When I had first heard the surveyors' "findings" from their own lips, I genuinely struggled to imagine how any written case could possibly be made of it. "Nothing will come of nothing," King Lear tells Cordelia in Shakespeare's play, and what the surveyors had taken away from the raid was the thinnest of thin air. But now, their thirty-two pages before me, I had the answer.

They cited Beechwood for a *lack* of policies and procedures to prevent abuse or neglect (F224). Moreover, they cited this *lack* at the level of widespread "Immediate Jeopardy" (IJ), that official, formal term for any situation that posed a clear and present danger to patients. Yet the SOD did not cite a single instance of actual neglect or abuse (F223). So, no patient had actually been endangered or had been shown to be in imminent peril of such endangerment. But, then, the surveyors were asserting that the *absence* of policies and procedures in and of itself put everyone in immediate jeopardy. Nothing will come of nothing? According to the SOD, *everything* would come of nothing.

As the DOH regulators well knew, if your motive is to put a regulated health-care facility out of business—and not actually to identify, assess, and remedy a genuine deficiency or danger—it hardly mattered what the IJ label was being applied to. Something or nothing, it was all the same. The only phrase anyone would see, hear, and take away was "widespread IJ."

And it got even worse. The fact was that the citation of IJ was in blatant violation of survey regulations. This was beyond question. Rubin and his deputies, however, were not bothered by this detail and, for their purposes, they did not need to be. The target of an IJ, they well knew, would not get to make an appeal until after sanctions had been applied. In this case, the sanctions included the nuclear winter that comes with the annihilation of a thriving business performing a much needed and highly welcome service to the community. At this point, I was legally powerless to stop any unnecessary damage.

But just consider the fiction by which the destruction was taking place before our eyes. Not just the IJ but the entire SOD violated survey regulations in that not a single finding involved a *current* patient or an *actual* observation of care. The whole thirty-two-page report was based on reviews of the medical records of discharged patients. This was reason enough to invalidate the SOD. Add to it, however, that the findings grossly and deliberately misrepresented facts about patient conditions and the care that had actually been delivered. The findings contained ridiculous assumptions about the potential for harm or alternative outcomes—which, of course, had not happened and would never happen, since all the findings concerned discharged patients, who, no longer in our care, were no longer in a position to be either harmed or helped by us.

It was not that the SOD found a few items and blew them out of proportion in an effort to cobble together an action against Beechwood. The scale of the allegations was beyond anything I could have remotely envisioned possible.

I am neither naïve nor trusting by nature. I had long feared a DOH assault incoming by way of retribution for my frequent—but scrupulously legal—challenges to a system that warranted challenging. But I always managed to allay my fears by reminding myself that we lived in a nation of laws, and law was ultimately based on objective fact. Beechwood had objective fact on its side. A ton of it. Our reputation was based on years and years of data that demonstrated the highest possible level of quality of care. It was data. What is more, it was DOH data. It was not opinion. So, how could—and why would—these state regulators even attempt to make a case for poor patient care when all the data argued loudly and consistently against any such thing? Impossible! Beechwood was in absolutely no danger.

I was wrong.

As those promotional trailers for horror movies tell us, *Be afraid. Be very afraid.* I should have heeded my own healthy paranoia. Not only can white be turned into black simply by violating the public trust, abusing the power of an agency, and defrauding the system, there are people who think nothing of doing such things. What is more, they will commit these violations, these abuses, these frauds not even in response to the lure of some great material gain, but out of a desire for personal retribution against someone who gave them what they deemed a hard time. No wonder John Adams, back in 1780, when he drafted the constitution of his home state of Massachusetts, was so anxious to create what he called a "government of laws and not of men."

That the horrendous allegations of the DOH were dramatically contrary to Beechwood's reputation, past survey history, and official DOH quality indicator scores as of January demonstrated that the SOD was a product of "men," the "law" be damned. At the time of the charges, my staff and I were well aware that, as mentioned in the previous chapter, we ranked 68% above the norm in New York State. What we did not yet know is that this placed us within the top couple of facilities in the state. Attaining this level of performance, as measured by the regulators themselves, could hardly be dismissed by any objective authority as some aberration hiding a house of horrors. Achieving such a level of quantifiable excellence, especially as measured against other institutions, required consistent focus, effort, commitment, and competence over an extended period. Moreover, such measured performance could hardly be the product of a lack of policies and procedures. Could a facility of our sustained caliber suddenly—in fact, instantly—and completely fall apart? To imagine so stretches credibility far beyond the legal standard of reasonable doubt. It is, in fact, a virtual impossibility. No matter. Here was DOH making the case—and so very confidently.

Such boldness could only indicate that something was terribly wrong in the regulatory mechanism. But we had no time to sort that "something" out. Citation of IJ carries with it—in fact, dictates—a fast-track termination, which is defined as termination of Medicare/Medicaid certification within twenty-three days. For most nursing homes, loss of federal certification would be in itself an instant death blow. Beechwood's quality of care was so high, however, that we had long been a facility of choice. Patients who could afford to go anywhere came to us, which meant that some 80 percent of our patients paid privately, not through Medicare or Medicaid. But it was serious nonetheless because I knew it would severely damage Beechwood's reputation and, therefore, even its privately paid business. If the decertification were allowed to stand, it would also lead to the loss of our operating license. All this, of course, was no instance of collateral damage. I was certain that it was Sandy Rubin's objective.

Time was short, and time was of the essence, and the DOH had made certain to create a task that was supremely difficult for us. The very absurdity of the SOD worked *against* us. The document was long and loaded with inaccurate or incomplete facts as well as ridiculous and unsupported conclusions. A federal Health Care Finance Administration (HCFA) official who later reviewed the material commented that it was "hard to get a sense of the aspect or a sense of [the] neglect" that DOH was claiming. If this was not enough, it imposed a sanction called a directed plan of correction (DPOC). The DPOC included with the SOD demanded that we "complete an assessment of the causative factors that may have contributed to the issues identified on the SOD." In other words, they were not just asking us to propose remedies but to do the job that survey rules dictate *they* should have done, namely identify and assess the causes of the deficiencies they alleged. In short, the DOH demanded that we prove their unprovable case and, doubtless, hoped that we would succeed in implicating ourselves in the process.

Susan Baker stated in the cover letter accompanying the SOD that "If you disagree with this determination, you … may request a hearing before … the Department of Health and Human Services, Department Appeals Board," as set forth in 42 CFR 498.40. We immediately made this appeal to the feds, which obliged us to research facts alleged, document the facts left out, and submit a rebuttal report explaining how the findings were improper. The rebuttal material was due by May 7. At the same time, appeal or no appeal, we were obliged to comply with the DPOC, which dictated that we change policies and procedures, train the staff accordingly, and send to the DOH reports of changes in patient conditions—even though we naturally disagreed with everything in the SOD.

Whatever else the DOH wanted to result from our response—self-implication doubtless being at the top of their list—the demands all were calculated to create a massive amount of work. Most small businesses would have found the demands overwhelming and even impossible to comply with in the time allotted. The DOH doubtless realized this. What they did not realize was that our cutting-edge electronic medical record system—to which they had so often objected in various ways—proved critically important in rapidly supplying all the needed data. Donna Richardson, our Director of Nursing (DON), put in a mountain of overtime meeting the demands of the DPOC while I worked around the clock writing up the formal submissions for both the rebuttal and the DPOC. To say that this was daunting is a gross understatement. Just imagine the utter incongruity of having to figure out "causative factors" of problems not clearly identified—because they did not, in fact, exist. Then consider the absurdity of developing new policies and procedures and training staff accordingly to solve undefined and non-existent problems, the very problems that you are in the midst of explaining why they came about even as you seek to rebut their existence.

In connection with these labors, the names *Hercules, Sisyphus*, and *Kafka* come to mind, and if these brutal, mind-busting, and heartbreaking tasks were not burden enough, two surveyors haunted the facility at least every other day in an effort to find some semblance of "facts" to mold into deficiencies for future SODs. Their presence interfered with nursing care, created even more overtime, and ratcheted up the already nearly intolerable tension. Billed as "monitoring" visits, which are to assess compliance with a DPOC, they are not customarily done by surveyors. Well, it soon became apparent that the DOH had ulterior motives in the surveyor visits. Even under normal circumstances, Beechwood was a busy place, admitting and discharging two or three patients on a typical day since the average length of stay in our predominantly rehabilitative facility was just twenty-four days. This activity generated plenty of new medical charts, which the surveyors eyed as hopeful grist for their deficiencies mill.

The routine for each monitoring visit was deliberately grueling, After an initial brief conference with the DON, during which they would make it appear as if they were genuinely checking on the progress of DPOC compliance, one surveyor would go to each floor, and ask the nurses questions about new admissions, probing for any problems they encountered with anyone's care since the last monitoring visit. The answers became the shaky foundation for further fact finding. This done, the surveyor would then take over one of the computers at the nursing station and use it to review medical records. Since the nursing station is the core of activity on the floor, the surveyors were in position to review staff interactions, overhear discussions and reports, and get further insight on what to target. They spent enormous stretches of time watching staff provide care, yet without offering any reason for such constant observation. Obviously, this made for a very tense environment and impeded the staff's ability to get their work done. Overtime was crushing, and our staff was tiring. It was a war of attrition.

———————

At 2:45 on the afternoon of April 28, Sue Kelly, regional director of HCFA in New York City, called me. I knew that the federal and state regulators often had more of a competitive than a collaborative relationship, and I was hoping to use that to my advantage. What I did not know—because she did not tell me—was that Sharon Carlo and the Albany-based director of quality assurance, Anna Colello, were listening in on the call. Kelly warned me to take the situation seriously and get the DPOC done. I reminded her that Daniel Walsky, who was acting branch chief of the fed's Medicaid and State Operations, had told me that his agency was going to investigate the DOH. Kelly replied that Walsky was now gone, that she had been his supervisor, and that he never should have made such a commitment. Without breaking my stride, I alluded to our high-quality HFCA stats, which Kelly well knew. She admitted the quality data but then added that she "didn't like it" and "didn't put any weight on it." It became clear to me that she was delivering a message. The regulatory ground had shifted, and HCFA would be standing with DOH. My hope to divide federal authorities from state authorities faded with that call.

Nevertheless, we were working diligently to comply with the DPOC. Although we had received it late in the afternoon of April 27, by the morning of the 29th our director of nursing was already discussing proposed policy changes with regional director of Long-Term Care Baker and the surveyors. Baker duly noted specifics of the changes discussed and did not offer any criticism.

We pushed ahead, complying with every step of this outlandish exercise. Determined despite everything to conduct business as usual, on May 5, doubtless looking like death warmed over, I had a morning meeting with another major health insurer to sell them on our ideas for a new level of care. When I returned to Beechwood, DON Donna Richardson greeted me with the unsurprising news that the surveyors were in on a monitoring visit. What she said next, however, was refreshingly hopeful. She had handed them drafts of policy and procedure changes, to which they responded that the material indicated a lot of progress in the areas with which they were concerned. They told her they were going back to the office to review the drafts further and would let us know if the proposed changes were sufficient to lift the immediate jeopardy status. On the next day, Richardson, continuing to follow the DPOC, submitted the first weekly report of resident changes in condition and, on May 7, had Beechwood's Quality Assurance Subcommittee meet to review the new policies and procedures.

I was working around the clock. But it was clear to me that I would not be able to get all the DPOC material and SOD rebuttal completed by the deadline, 5 p.m. on Friday, May 7. I submitted all that I had completed and asked our attorney, Kevin Cooman, to request an extension to eight on Monday morning, May 10. To me, it seemed a reasonable request, especially since no DOH person would be reviewing documents over the weekend. Baker, however, not only rejected the request but recommended to HCFA that Beechwood be terminated as a Medicare/Medicaid provider for failing to meet the deadline. At 5:15 p.m. that Friday, we received a fax from Sue Kelly informing us that HFCA "accepted" the DOH termination recommendation. Beechwood's "Medicare provider agreement will terminate on May 15, 1999," the fax concluded. Nevertheless, on Monday, May 10, at 8 a.m. sharp, we hand-delivered the completed DPOC and rebuttal to DOH. On the next day, I augmented this material by faxing rebuttal statements from the physicians of the seven—former, discharged—patients specifically cited on the SOD. Each of the physicians completely disagreed with everything the DOH surveyors had written.

In the meantime, at 2:30 p.m. on May 10, surveyors Cynthia Francis and Elizabeth Rich made another monitoring visit. Later that afternoon, they asked the DON and me to stay until seven for an exit conference. Since we had heard no negative feedback from surveyors regarding any patient care issues or DPOC compliance efforts, we dared to be hopeful that the IJ status would be lifted. Instead, Francis and Rich relayed that other potential deficiencies were being discussed based on monitoring visit observations.

We were left to wonder just what we were facing. Well, we had not yet heard from Darcy Salisbury, a physician's assistant on duty on the second floor that day. She later reported in an affidavit: "it was crazy [on the floor] ... Francis was saying the facility was to be closed down on May 15th."

---

*May 12, 7:30 a.m.* The survey team returned for a survey revisit, its official purpose to check for correction and compliance status. But that was not happening.

Baker did talk with the DON and staff and even made notes on the compliance measures taken. But then, as it turned out, without making any negative comments verbally or in her notes, she simply recorded that *nothing was acceptable.* Again, the surveyors wreaked havoc on the nursing floors. I later heard from Charlene O'Connor, third-floor supervisor, that the surveyors "went through every chart." Even though "they [had already] been through every chart on the floor [during previous visits,] they kept zeroing in on the same patients." From the second floor, Gwen Westbrook stated that Francis told her, "You know, there are better places to work than this, if you value your license, you won't work here anymore."

On May 13, at 10 a.m., Baker and Francis returned for an exit conference. We had not yet seen Baker's notes or heard anything from the nursing floors, so we had reason to hope that, in the absence of negative feedback, the onslaught was finally over and that we would be formally designated as returned to compliance.

Instead, Baker and Francis told us that they would no longer cite an IJ situation, which did remove the May 15 termination date. However, we would now be cited for substandard quality of care (SQC). The DOH would further recommend to HCFA that it implement an immediate ban on payment for new Medicare and Medicaid admissions and that an early termination date of June 17 be put in place—if compliance were not obtained by then. Baker and Francis added that the DPOC and the monitoring visits would remain in effect because of the lack of correction.

It was a terrible development. A cutoff of funding for new admissions is accompanied by official notices to patient physicians, referring providers, and the public. *That* could be a swift death blow. The healthcare profession—and business—is all about confidence. Besides, private insurance companies mandate continuing Medicare certification. In a war of attrition, the objective is to wear the other side down. I felt worn out, all right, but I decided that there was no alternative but continue trying to follow instructions and get back into what even *they* would deem compliance.

But now the federal government added to the assault. HCFA placed a termination notice in the newspaper that very day, May 13: "Notice is hereby given that on May 15, 1999, the agreement between Beechwood Restorative Care Center and the Secretary of Health and Human Services will be terminated after determining that Beechwood is not in compliance." It was not until two days later, May 15, that a Notice of Retraction (M06474) was published: "The Health Care Financing Administration has determined that Beechwood Sanitarium is now in compliance with the Medicare requirements for long-term care facilities." It hardly repaired the damage done by the first notice, and even we were left wondering if we were now officially in compliance—despite what we were told at the exit conference.

------

On May 18 Beechwood received a letter from Baker rejecting every single aspect of the directed plan of correction I submitted on May 10. I responded on May 21: "This letter concerns the letter of May 18, 1999 stating that the POC for the survey of 4/22/99 is unacceptable.... This POC took a tremendous amount of work on our part.... To simply reject it in its entirety without comment is unreasonable, and leaves us not knowing where to turn.... Could you please provide us with more to go on?"

I never received a response.

On May 21, surveyor Francis hand-delivered a new thirty-page SOD alleging non-compliance at the substandard quality of care (SQC) level. In a covering letter, Baker officially informed us that they had recommended to HCFA that funding for new admissions be discontinued as of May 21 and that the termination date be rescheduled for June 17th if total compliance had not been obtained. The same day, Kelly directed her subordinate, Lee Pope, to fax Beechwood a letter:

> Based on a revisit to your facility on May 12, 1999, by the New York State Department of Health it was determined that the immediate jeopardy had been removed, and the termination action is being rescinded as of that date. However, please be advised that, due to the seriousness of the deficiencies still remaining, the termination of your Medicare provider agreement has been rescheduled for June 17, 1999, unless the deficiencies are corrected by that date. In addition, a ban on payment for new Medicare/Medicaid patients is being imposed as of the date of the receipt of this letter.

Acknowledging the fax, our attorney, Kevin Cooman, faxed Pope in return:

> As Beechwood representatives have repeatedly advised HCFA, Beechwood is not out of compliance, and is being wrongfully and maliciously targeted by regional DOH administrators and surveyors with erroneous and trumped-up

allegations of non-compliance.... HCFA's denial of payment for new admissions ... immediately triggers substantial accruing damages to the facility and its owners. Beechwood will be forced to seek recompense against the DOH employees responsible for this. We urge you in the strongest terms to retract immediately HCFA's ban on payment so that HCFA is not unwittingly made a party.

On the next day, May 21, Beechwood filed a formal request with HCFA for a hearing concerning the survey results and the sanctions. On May 24, we sent the April SOD and DPOC to Pope, requesting a review of the facts, pointing out that the outcomes Beechwood achieved clearly raised "serious questions as to how the State can come to the conclusions presented in the deficiency report.... Serious and irreparable damage will be done by a ban on new Medicare admissions.... Please give us a time extension to get this matter properly structured and reviewed." We followed this with a second letter to Pope on the same day:

URGENT. Under section 7506 B of the survey manual, it states that the facility must receive 15 days notice before any Denial of Payment can be made for new admissions. Since the facility does not meet the requirement for mandatory denial, it would appear that the notice provided from your office on Friday is invalid. Am I correct? ... If I am, please officially retract the notice of denial of payment."

On May 25, Cooman faxed Pope:

We are still awaiting your response to my letter of Friday, May 21, and Brook Chambery's two fax communications to you yesterday. It is imperative that we have HCFA's response to Beechwood's request for immediate (and retroactive) retraction of the ban on payment for new admissions in light of substantial flaws in the DOH's process, procedure and the 15 day advance notice requirement imposed by the survey manual.

On May 25, while on a monitoring visit, surveyor Rich made a curious remark to our third-floor supervisor Charlene O'Connor. "Remember," she said, "it is not over till it's over; we are just players in the greater scheme of things." On the very next day, I phoned Baker about her failure to respond to my letter of May 21. I needed help, I pleaded, explaining that creating the plan of correction had taken tremendous effort and had elicited zero feedback concerning the reason for its blanket rejection. When she remained unresponsive, two of our attorneys,

Kevin Cooman and Paul Barden, called later in the day. Our lawyers inquired about the DOH "agenda" in this matter. On the phone with Baker were her supervisor, Sharon Carlo, and Marie Shea, a DOH attorney. In a recording of the conversation, Carlo said that "the remedies are just that, to get the facility back in compliance, nothing would please us more than to have Beechwood up and running and back in compliance, there is no other agenda."

On May 27, attorney Cooman called Pope, who told him that it was not in anyone's interest to close Beechwood. The beds, he said, are needed. Cooman stressed the gravity of the matter, and that the ban on payment alone was costing $12,000 per day. In response, Pope promised to talk to Sandy Rubin and Sue Kelly. Hopefully, he said, this would be worked out, and soon. Chuckling, Pope said, "Let me talk to these people and find out what they're doing; I get faxes and reams of paper, but I am not there." He ended with "Let me see what I can do. I'll call you back."

There was never any return call.

---

On May 28, our attorney Paul Barden faxed Pope a letter: "Based on Beechwood's focus on rehabilitative care ... unless you immediately lift the ban, you have effectively shut down Beechwood.... We respectfully request that you exercise your power and immediately lift the ban on payments."

There was no response.

On June 3, our attorney Kevin Cooman called Pope, continuing to press for a decision on the payment ban. He responded that he had had no answer yet from Kelly or the DOH attorneys. I sent Pope a letter on the same day, telling him, "I am trying with all my might to work with DOH Officials and get back in compliance" but that "DOH has not responded to our requests to help evaluate our efforts and get back into compliance." I mentioned that our "attorneys stated that you indicated not having seen the new [May] report or my response. It was submitted June 1, 1999. Please get a copy and read it.... Please reverse the funding ban and remove the decertification threat for at least 90 days."

Surveyors were still in the facility at least every other day, exhausting our staff. With funding for new admissions cut off, empty beds were becoming more numerous, and termination was on everyone's mind. Yet Beechwood was getting no cooperation from either DOH or HCFA.

This, it soon became apparent, was not the worst of it. On June 7, while we were still under a DOH mandate to comply with the DPOC and achieve correction by June 17, the New York State Department of Health made unmistakably manifest that there was indeed "another agenda" at work. We were served a DOH Statement of Charges (SOC) and Notice of DOH Hearing. It was to begin in just fifteen days. The sanction sought was nothing less than revocation of Beechwood's state operating certificate.

Blindsided? This was numbing.

For one thing, a hearing of this kind was historic in that it had never before been convened in the state of New York. It was in direct conflict with the State Medicaid Plan under which DOH contracted to use the HCFA adjudicatory process to settle challenges to the survey outcomes—the process already offered to Beechwood and which Beechwood had formally requested. Moreover, a state hearing made no sense. Medicare/Medicaid certification was required to maintain an operating certificate. If certification were eventually denied, the operating certificate would automatically be in jeopardy. The hearing was at the very least premature and at most redundant. In a word, it was overkill.

The state charges served on us were essentially modified statement of deficiency (SOD) findings from the April and May surveys. New York *state* was now moving to adjudicate in its own hearing the findings from a *federal* survey process. The difference was that the state hearing would be free from the federal requirements under which the findings had been issued. This meant that if the operating certificate were revoked by the state but Beechwood subsequently succeeded in its federal recertification appeal, that success would be moot. A facility cannot be recertified if it no longer has a license to operate.

On June 9, I attended what was supposed to be an informal dispute resolution (IDR) conference regarding Beechwood's objections to the April survey report. With me were my attorneys Cooman and Barden. DOH was represented by Marie Shea. The DOH program representatives in attendance were Baker and Carlo. Because the Statement of Charges had already been served, Carlo and Baker refused to discuss Beechwood's rebuttal material, physician rebuttal statements, or the reasons for deeming the facility's POC to be totally inadequate. The IDR was thus concluded after fifteen minutes.

Before the day was over, Beechwood filed a Federal "§1983 Complaint," seeking an injunction or temporary restraining order against Rubin, Francis, Rich,

Baker, Carlo, Arlene Gray (a central office person), and four Jane Does (to cover central office officials yet unknown) for retribution due primarily to the exercise of our First Amendment Rights. Since the named individuals needed to be served, and Baker and Carlo were at the IDR meeting, we took the opportunity to serve them at the end of the meeting.

Carlo blanched white. Both she and Baker looked terrified and quickly retired to another room with Shea and other officials. It was the first time I had seen any chink in the state's armor.

---

During June 10-11, a final survey revisit took place, ostensibly to assess correction and compliance for Medicare/Medicaid certification. With DOH now in direct conflict of interest, having served a statement of charges, the chances that they would suddenly find the facility in compliance were exactly zero.

On June 11, Beechwood received a letter signed by Carlo (for Baker), rejecting our May plan of correction in toto. Next came a letter from Baker, stating that the June 9 IDR conference failed to result in any changes to the April SOD. Third, Beechwood was yet again blindsided by a court filing in which DOH was requesting an order that an involuntary Caretaker be installed at Beechwood. It was yet another action that had never been taken before in New York State.

The Caretaker petitioner was a new player in this tragic farce, Dennis Whalen, Acting Commissioner of the Department of Health. He claimed in his petition that "*there exist* operating deficiencies in Beechwood which show (a) conditions in substantial violation of the standards ... under federal or state law or regulations; and (b) a pattern or practice of habitual violation." The petition was accompanied by an affidavit from Laura Leeds, Deputy Director of the Office of Continuing Care in Albany, an official with whom I had often corresponded in the past regarding my regulatory concerns. The affidavit asserted that "*there are* serious deficiencies at Beechwood" and "*if not corrected*, Beechwood *will be* terminated." Leeds pointed out that the "Department has [already] commenced a proceeding to revoke ... based on these deficiencies." Damning on the face of it, this notation actually demonstrated a major inconsistency (which would be noted in later legal action): Whalen and Leeds were moving to revoke our operating license and apply for a caretaker *before* they had finished the survey cycle to assess correction. What is more, the ongoing survey was failing to find anything in "substantial violation." Surveyor Francis, who submitted an affidavit stating that the Petition was "true upon information and belief," testified years later at trial that she "didn't know if she understood the seriousness or gravity" of what she was signing.

An involuntary caretaker, also called a receiver, is a party chosen by DOH and ordered by the court to operate the facility even as the displaced operator, now rendered powerless, remains financially responsible, including for any operating losses incurred as a result of poor management. Does the DOH take care to install caretakers highly qualified in healthcare? Politics rather than operating experience plays a big part in the hiring decision. In our case, Whalen and Leeds chose an operator and wanted him "fully approved" by the Governor's Office even before they knew anything at all about his "past experience." The same day as Beechwood received the Caretaker Petition, we asked attorney Cooman to call Steven Steinhardt, an attorney at DOH, about the possibility of a voluntary receivership, which would allow us input as to the choice of receiver. Steinhardt replied that the only terms on which DOH would "ever" do a caretaker was with "full and unfettered authority to operate the facility" for "an unlimited period of time" while the license was in the process of being revoked. Moreover, he had full confidence that the license *would* be revoked. "The Department," he said, "had never lost a proceeding to revoke an operating certificate."

A Survey Exit Conference on June 14 came with yet another show of force. Attended by Rubin, Carlo, Baker, Francis, Rich, and another surveyor from the DOH, it also included Jerry Solomon and Neil Davis, both from the Medicaid Fraud Control Unit (MFCU), a unit of the New York State Attorney General's Office. The matter had suddenly escalated from the strictly civil and into the criminal realm.

Carlo did most of the talking, emphasizing the "tentative" nature of the findings under discussion. None of these findings were claimed to be at the level of immediate jeopardy (IJ) or substandard quality of care (SQC) level. That was clearly a strategic decision, since such charges would have to be defended in any future federal hearing as the grounds for termination. HCFA's previous letter in May had set the bar low, stating simply that the facility had to be in total compliance on the next visit. So, all DOH had to do now was claim any level of non-compliance. That would be sufficient grounds for termination—even though, as a matter of standard practice, in the absence of IJ, a facility would be automatically granted an additional 120 days to achieve compliance.

At the conclusion of the conference, Carlo remarked that "termination is an issue" and she and her colleagues "recognize the seriousness of the issue" for the facility, staff, residents, and the DOH. For this reason, they pledged to "look at this very, very carefully" and get an SOD out as soon as possible.

We were not about to throw ourselves on the tender mercies of Carlo and company. On June 15, we presented an oral argument in front of David Larimer, Senior United States District Judge of the United States District Court for the Western District of New York, in support of a request for an injunction to forestall what was for all intents and purposes the imminent demise of Beechwood Restorative Care Center. Even as the argument was being made, DOH issued a press release trumpeting "Serious Harm" to residents as grounds for its "petition … to appoint a caretaker to ensure the health, safety, and well-being of residents. … Based on these deficiencies, the Department seeks to permanently revoke the Chambery's operating certificate … HCFA has notified the (facility) that it no longer may accept new admissions … (and) termination … is under consideration."

On June 16 Judge Larimer announced his decision to deny Beechwood's request for an injunction. On that very day, the latest Statement of Deficiency was hand-delivered to Beechwood. It contained no claims of immediate jeopardy or substandard quality of care. It stated simply: "correction required."

## WHEN REASONABLENESS FAILS, ANARCHY AND CHAOS FOLLOW

As mentioned previously, Beechwood had been serving the community for 45 years. It was basically a private pay facility, a testament to the level of care it provided. It was known around the country as being very innovative in the application of electronic medical records (EMR) technology. It did not have a poor survey history—quite the opposite—and was not on any poor performance regulatory watch list. The Attorney General's Office had never initiated any suit against Beechwood, or against any of its staff for any abuse, neglect, or fraud.

Beechwood had just been through a full certification survey in January 1999, and had not only been found in full compliance, the quality data the surveyors collected at the time put the facility at the very top in the state. It had been through at least 25 annual Medicare/Medicaid certification surveys, and the facility's administration was very capable of handling such matters, including writing plans of correction (POCs) and submitting rebuttal materials to preserve appeal rights.

I had been directly involved with Beechwood for 27 years, and had been the CEO for the last six years, three of which had perfect surveys, a very rare achievement. There had also been no change in the management of any department for many years.

And yet DOH was claiming that a facility of this caliber suddenly had widespread immediate jeopardy (IJ) and other serious problems. Moreover, the DOH reported that we were incapable of writing a POC, were unwilling to work with the regulators, and that we could not be expected to improve in the future. In fact, DOH represented that conditions were so bad that it was imperative to decertify the facility within sixty days—33% of what was normally allowed—apply for a caretaker, and initiate a DOH hearing to revoke its operating license. Such actions had never been taken before, even against the worst of the worst. Oh, and all of this was based on an "abbreviated" survey.

The patients and their families were greatly distressed by the DOH allegations. They called their elected representatives and picketed in front of the state courthouse as well as at political events.

No wonder. It was inconceivable to any rational person that a facility of Beechwood's caliber simply fell apart within the last month or two and now couldn't or just wouldn't do anything to right the situation. It was equally unlikely that patients and their families, including those spending their own funds, did not know how to judge the care being provided—or that every personal physician of the patients cited was wrong in disagreeing with the survey findings. And it was downright bizarre to contemplate that such drastic and draconian enforcement actions needed to be taken at all, let alone so quickly.

Years later, when a quick thirty-minute overview of the charges, penalties sought, and timeframes involved was presented to a mock jury of ordinary citizens, they unanimously saw the DOH action as over-the-top and thus highly suspect. After the civil rights trial, jury members stated that they regarded the DOH actions as suspect after the department's opening statement.

With the filing of a request for an injunction, Judge Larimer knew that DOH had never taken such actions previously and that Beechwood was claiming a conspiracy against it. He knew that Beechwood had no previous record of adverse regulatory actions. He was well aware that, typically, the Attorney General's Office (AG), not the DOH, would bring an action in state court against a poor-performing facility and would do so only after a long period of trying to elicit improvements in care. Judge Larimer knew that if any staff member had been accused of patient abuse or neglect, the AG would need to bring an action in state court to obtain an order for any desired sanction. He knew that the combination of decertification, license revocation, and the surrounding publicity would mean irreparable damage to any healthcare business. Indeed, he knew it would mean total destruction—which was not only unfair to the business and its stakeholders, but that the total upheaval created would cause tremendous stress in the lives of patients, staff, and their families. He knew that patient lives were endangered and that staff careers would be thrown into turmoil and reputations damaged or ruined.

Judge Larimer also knew that "imminent danger" was a necessary element mandated by both federal (SSA Section 1819[c][2] & [h][4]) and state (PHL 2806-b) laws, and in many other legal contexts, as the basis for closing a facility and moving its patients. Yet he never stopped to inquire about whether there was any immediate jeopardy (IJ) present in the facility at the time of the injunction request, whether IJ had been confirmed by physicians, or anything else about the validity of the IJ claims. If he had, he might have found out that the claim of widespread IJ had been built using the records of discharged patients. When faced with this fact twelve years later in the second summary judgment motion requested by the DOH defendants, Larimer (p. 23) ruled on September 12, 2011 that discharged residents "could not be in immediate jeopardy."

Judge Larimer never inquired about documentation behind this horrendous enforcement action, who authorized it, for what reasons, or whether the enforcement actions being taken were statutorily mandated. Whalen had been very concerned about the Department's vulnerability here, and with good reason. A couple of days later, in the DOH hearing, and in response to Beechwood's request as to the statutory basis for the hearing, DOH attorney Marie Shea stated that it was voluntarily brought under PHL 2806-1.

In summary, these are the facts that were before Judge Larimer on the court date, June 15:

1. A facility without any past history of survey or regulatory problems was being forced to close in a mind-boggling 60-day timeframe and was

currently facing a mind-numbing and conflicting array of survey mandates and legal actions.

2.  Staff would be losing their jobs; and patients would have to move.

3.  Of the actions being taken,

    a) Termination hadn't been done in at least 12 years!

    b) License revocation had never been done before!

    c) A caretaker application under 2806-b had never been done before!

4.  There were no DOH policies, procedures or regulatory framework for this sort of enforcement action.

5.  The survey at issue was not even a full, comprehensive certification survey, and the revocation and caretaker actions had been filed before it was even completed, when Beechwood was still under a mandate to complete the directed plan of correction (DPOC).

6.  There were no longer any allegations of IJ or substandard quality of care (SQC) as of the DOH exit conference which was held the day before court.

7.  There were vague DOH assertions of abuse and neglect without specific citation on survey reports, without identification or allegation against individuals, or without having turned the matters over to the Medicare Fraud Control Unit (MFCU) for the required independent investigation.

8.  The MFCU of the Department of the Attorney General (DAG) would typically be bringing an action against a provider in court for such offences.

9.  If DOH actions were improper, as Beechwood was alleging, the DAG would have a conflict of interest given its duty to both investigate and defend DOH officials.

10. The facility would be closed, and the damages incurred before any of the allegations would have any sort of review administratively or judicially.


In short, everything was tremendously out of whack. DOH actions had the appearance of throwing as much as possible at the provider, both administratively and civilly, and in the shortest amount of time, to create a very complex legal environment and prevent the bigger agenda from shining through. Judge Larimer failed to inquire about the need for the "several state and federal proceedings" that he discussed, while ignoring his responsibility to weigh private interests and constitutional rights before allowing these agency actions to continue. He failed to subject DOH to any test or legal burden and allowed references to HCFA's actions to add an aura of validity to the whole affair.

What Judge Larimer did know was that DOH (with HCFA) was under intense public scrutiny for its actions against Beechwood, that DOH's reputation was at stake, and that this action had to have been authorized at the highest levels. He was not going to rock that boat.

## JUDGE LARIMER'S DECISION, JUNE 16, 1999

*Irrational burdens established by the court.* Following oral argument on June 15, 1999, Judge Larimer perceived:

1. Page 6: "conflicting evidence on the merits ... on the entire issue concerning patient care, and the reasons why the DOH got involved when it did, and to the extent it did,"

2. Page 23: "very serious issues ... have been raised by the plaintiffs"

And he knew:

3. Page 9: "We are obviously dealing here with some [regulatory] subjective component, and Courts have been concerned when that occurs especially if there is an objective standard here."

But he simply stated that:

1. Page 5: "A preliminary injunction for temporary relief is often described as an extraordinary and drastic remedy,"

2. Page 7: especially when moving to stop "several agencies—the state agency on two fronts and the federal government—from carrying on its statutorily imposed obligations,"

3. Page 8: "very drastic remedies."

He then established impossible burdens of persuasion for Beechwood to meet at this stage in order to get him to grant a temporary injunction:

1. Page 5: "The moving party must show irreparable harm should the injunction not be granted and a likelihood of success on the merits of the controversy."

2. Page 7: "The standard here is not whether the plaintiffs should have their day in Court, but whether they are likely to succeed"

3. Page 7: The plaintiff must establish "that the actions commenced by the State DOH were done in substantial part and motivating part to somehow punish or injure the operators and the facility."

In doing so, he stated:

1. Page 5: "I do not believe that plaintiffs have carried their burden and have failed to establish the necessary elements"

2. Page 6: "I simply am not persuaded there is a likelihood of success for plaintiffs to establish such a (First Amendment Retaliation) claim."

3. Page 7: "At this stage I simply do not believe that the evidence establishes that the plaintiffs have sufficiently" met their burden.

4. Page 9: "I think that the showing in the case before me in my view does not justify the relief that is requested here which is essentially complete relief to block the state agency from doing what they're doing here."

Judge Larimer continued (p. 9): "There are several other reasons why I think this Court must pause, and then deal with the matter raised by the federal defendant, and that is exhaustion, and the matter suggested and briefed to some extent by the state defendants, and that is the abstention issue."

Regarding the exhaustion issue, Judge Larimer stated that:

1. Page 10: "HCFA has commenced a proceeding to terminate."

2. Page 14: "Congress in its wisdom did not provide for a pre-deprivation proceeding, but rather a post-deprivation proceeding. ... Plaintiffs have requested a hearing and ... there is no indication one will not be provided."

3. Page 10: "In my view plaintiffs clearly seek to rescind the termination of its provider status and halt the suspension of Medicare payments. Clearly, such relief is administrative in nature even though the complaint here is framed in constitutional terms. I think it's clear that the constitutional claims are inextricably intertwined with the substantive claims relating to the entitlement to the provider status and the receipt of Medicare payments.

4. Page 11: Therefore, in my view, I believe plaintiffs must proceed to exhaust their administrative remedies."

Regarding the abstention issue, Judge Larimer stated that:

1. Page 17: He believed "a further reason for ... declining to grant injunctive relief here is that there is ample reason for this Court to stay its hand and

abstain and let the state issues which predominate be decided by the state administrative and judicial proceedings."

In doing this, he (p. 15) discusses the Younger doctrine and (p. 16) a Second Circuit case (*DeSario v. Thomas*, 139 F. 3rd 80 at 86), stating the "The Younger abstention doctrine requires that federal courts abstain from considering Section 1983 (retaliation) claims that are the subject of ongoing state criminal proceedings or civil proceedings which involve vital state interests when those proceedings provide an adequate opportunity to raise federal claims."

2. Page 18: He disagreed with Beechwood's argument that they would not be able to raise constitutional issues in the state hearing, and that "Surely, the bias and animus of those bringing the charges would always be a matter of defense and could be raised appropriately in these state proceedings."

Demonstrating his strong bias toward the administrative state, and administrative law principles yet ignoring the regulatory framework, Judge Larimer stated:

1. Page 20: "I think it's important simply to recognize and underscore the fact that the very reason for these state agencies is to guarantee and protect the safety and well-being of patients who are confined to facilities that may not be in the best position to protect themselves, so that great caution must be used by state agencies and also Courts that are asked to interfere and intrude into the process."

2. Page 20: "agencies do have broad discretion in the manner in which they undertake their tasks, and even though the Court may see a better way to do it, that does not necessarily mean that this Court is charged with some kind of a role of Ombudsman to oversee how the state agency carries out its very difficult tasks."

Demonstrating his unwavering confidence in the administrative process, Judge Larimer stated:

1. Page 7: "as the matter may proceed, ... the facts may develop such that plaintiffs may have a basis to proceed."

2. Page 18: "Surely, the bias and animus of those bringing the charges would always be a matter of defense and could be raised appropriately in these state proceedings."

3. Page 24: "This decision is not meant to chill or discourage those agencies charged with reviewing this or taking a very close look at the very serious charges that have been made here."

While paying little attention to private interests, and the plaintiff's claim that irreparable injury will occur:

> Page 22: "There is no doubt that some injury might occur here ..."

Judge Larimer chooses to avoid facing the magnitude of issue, namely that DOH is moving to close the facility, and dwells on the interim issues of whether a temporary caretaker might be appointed by Judge Affronti, and the remote possibility that Beechwood could prevail in the DOH hearing. Then, seemingly out of touch with reality, he makes the following contradictory sentence:

> Page 23: "There may be a diminution of earning power, but ... it is not clear that the business couldn't be resurrected and continued."

Judge Larimer makes absolutely no attempt to consider:

1. The validity of Beechwood's claims, and the enormous consequences for the business and all connected with it.
2. The stake that the agency has in the outcome of its own quasi-judicial process, and the potential bias that can be introduced.
3. The appropriateness of using a quasi-judicial hearing when constitutional issues and freedoms are at stake

Instead, leaving it all in the hands of the state agencies, he states:

> Page 24: "These are serious issues, and if, in fact, a state agency or its agent has decided to take action which is arbitrary and without factual basis to cause injury to a bona fide, long-established business, that is most troubling and reprehensible."

This seems like a stern warning to DOH, but Judge Larimer's actions here and in the future demonstrated that he was an agency guy, cared little about the extent of the damage being created, and was not going to do anything to give Beechwood a chance to pursue and prove its case. In fact, he became and remained quite hostile when the case kept coming back to his court.

## THE INJUNCTION DENIED, DOH MARCHES AHEAD

*The program termination.* On June 16, just 63 days into the ordeal, and without any IJ or SQC claims—and in a circumstance in which a facility is typically allowed 180 days to correct—Baker sent Beechwood a notice of federal Medicare/Medicaid program termination. It was an outcome that even she had never heard of happening in the state of New York, not in the thirteen years she had worked for the DOH. It left her unsure of "what the process [was] going forward."

DOH also issued a news release claiming "serious harm" at Beechwood, and announcing that this had prompted the department to file with the court for a caretaker to "ensure the health, safety and well-being of residents while it pursues a revocation action."

The next day, June 17, sixty-four days after the survey, Beechwood was terminated from the Medicare/Medicaid program. We also received a letter from Preferred Care stating: "Preferred Care has received notice from the NYS DOH that it has filed a petition ... to appoint a caretaker to ensure the health and safety of residents ... while it pursues a revocation action against the facility's operators. In light of this information Preferred Care has decided not to pursue a contract for post-stabilization services with your organization." The contract I had been pursuing for many months with this insurer was lost and, with it, my hope of proving that a nursing home could be used for services typically reserved for the hospital.

**DOH uses patients as poker chips.** On that June 17, Beechwood enlisted the services of Neil Murray, an attorney for the New York State Health Facilities Association (NYSHFA), to again discuss with DOH the possibility of a voluntary receiver so as to protect staff from the trauma of losing their jobs and patients from suffering the grave trauma and disruption of transfer to other facilities. The following day, Murray had a conversation with Anna Colello, whom Laura Leeds had recently named director of the Bureau for Long-Term Care. However, now that DOH was forcing the hand of HCFA in the matter of termination and with full confidence that there would be a license revocation, Colello took the position that there was no need for a voluntary receiver or caretaker. With or without official notice from HCFA, she said, the facility was terminated, and that meant the Medicare/Medicaid residents had to leave.

It was a position that demonstrated Colello's lack of any concern whatsoever for our patients. Sue Kelly at HCFA had not yet transmitted any termination confirmation. She had told Leeds that she would not terminate if a receivership was instituted. Moreover, Colello's draconian position was also against DOH policy. In her deposition years later, Colello admitted that a receiver is "generally an option to avoid termination," and use of a temporary manager to avoid termination "had to be part of the conversation [with HCFA] prior to the termination." DOH attorney Steinhardt further explained that a voluntary receivership was a mechanism expressly to avoid the necessity of revoking a license, adding that if a facility agreed to the "voluntary" route, the current owners/management would be given a voice in the selection of the receiver, which would ensure the continuity of facility operations and finances. Nevertheless, after giving the matter further thought, Colello decided to exercise her regulatory power to negotiate a better deal for DOH.

Murray reported receiving a call from Colello later on June 18. She had, he said, taken the position that DOH might be more flexible on the receivership terms if I agreed not to fight the revocation. On June 19, Murray reported that Colello, playing hardball, had even more stringent conditions for granting a voluntary receivership. She demanded our voluntary relinquishment of the operating certificate and a release or discontinuance of all claims against state officials for the actions being taken. This attempted extortion fell on deaf ears at Beechwood.

***Judge Affronti's refusal to allow the Involuntary receiver.*** On June 21, Judge Affronti refused to allow DOH the option of replacing me with an involuntary receiver at Beechwood. He stated (p. 7) that he was "extremely mindful" of the need for quality care and that the "proceeding was supremely significant" for him personally, but after expending "substantial time" reading the papers in detail, he discovered "seemingly inconsistent findings in the record as submitted" by DOH regarding compliance with the regulations governing patient care.

That same day we sent a fax to Kelly's subordinate, Lee Pope:

"Re: Termination of Certification and Funding Continuation. Urgent.

"We have not had notice, nor have we seen any public notice about this issue.... If you have not made a final determination yet, I want to bring to your attention Judge Affronti's comments this morning ... We urge you to review the facts behind this case before supporting the State's recommendations any further."

Pope circled the word urgent in the heading and sent a copy to Kelly. But we received no response from Pope or her boss. Judge Affronti's rebuff did not prompt DOH to change course in the slightest.

CHAPTER 3

# Going Nuclear

T he wheels of justice turn slowly," the old proverb begins. It does not apply to the "justice" meted out via administrative law. We had filed a complaint under the Civil Rights Act of 1871 (42 U.S.C. § 1983) claiming that "under color of" state law, our federal civil rights had been violated. On this basis, we sought an injunction to stay the summary execution of the Beechwood Restorative Care Center. On June 16, 1999, Federal District Judge David Larimer denied our injunction request, stating that he was "not persuaded" Beechwood would prevail on its claim and that he was not convinced of irreparable harm to Beechwood if the state agencies continued on their current path. Further citing the "broad discretion" the state and federal agencies have to protect patients, Judge Larimer decided that the administrative proceedings should continue. On June 23, therefore, just fifteen days after we received notice, the Department of Health Administrative Hearing to revoke our operating license commenced on the top floor of the Alliance Building at 183 East Main Street in downtown Rochester.

The "hearing room" was not a permanent DOH facility, and was anything but a formal courtroom. It was just a space rented for the occasion, which was a proceeding unprecedented in DOH history. There were judicial-looking props. Instead of a judge's bench, the ALJ sat behind a 4 x 8 table with a stackable plastic chair to his left for a witness stand. For some unknown reason, our attorneys addressed the ALJ as "your honor," but he wore no black judicial robe, and there was nothing at all honorable about the role he was playing in this barren, undignified court. I cringed each time he was addressed by the judicial title. The DOH

attorneys were less deferential to the ALJ, who was, after all, a departmental col-
league. They addressed him merely as "Judge." Neither was the process fair, it
was a kangaroo court.

The DOH had launched a major public relations assault on Beechwood,
which drew a level of media attention generally reserved for major criminal tri-
als. I had to fight my way through reporters and TV cameras just to get into the
building and to the elevator. As the doors opened, the top-floor lobby was also
jammed. Who knew that Western New York had so many journalists? I threaded
my way through the lobby and into the hearing room. I took my place with my
attorneys, and, as they were getting their papers organized and we waited for the
hearing to begin, I looked across the room at the DOH officials. They looked
confident, not to say smug. I realized they had good reason to feel this way. Their
case was being presented by their prosecutors in their "court" and being heard
by their Administrative Law Judge. I was pretty certain that I would lose this
round. But I was not despondent. I was, rather, resolved that I would triumph—
eventually.

The DOH ALJ was Marc Zylberberg, a DOH attorney who worked for the
Bureau of Adjudication within the Division of Legal Affairs (DLA). The prosecutors were DOH attorneys from the Bureau of Hearings, another division of
DLA. They were Russel Altone, Director of the Bureau of Hearings, and his side-
kick from Albany, David Abel, along with Marie Shea, an attorney from the DOH
Buffalo office. Shea, in fact, was introduced as the lead prosecutor for the hearing, even though she was a rookie lawyer, having received her degree a couple
of years earlier. My lawyers and I were stunned that DOH would anoint someone so inexperienced as the lead in a category of action the department had never
in its entire history taken before.

Her performance did not disappoint. In her opening statement, Shea claimed
that over the course of the investigation at Beechwood, not only were "serious
deficiencies ... found" but that "residents' conditions deteriorated, ... in some
cases to the point of death." It was an assertion by no means drawn from the
deficiency statements or the Statement of Charges, none of which alleged anything remotely so dire. Yet Shea exuded confidence in making these wildly false
claims. If this had been a real court—a state court, a federal court, or even a local
magistrate's court—she would likely have been courting major trouble. Instead,
she could assert pretty much whatever she wanted in the confidence that she

would be upheld within her own department's forum. Besides, the allegations made dramatic sound bites for the media, who were the jurists responsible for the court of public opinion. Shea might have been a rookie, but the DOH had its own PR guy, Joseph Rohm, on post in the hearing room, ready to capitalize on every syllable.

The attorneys representing Beechwood were Kevin Cooman and Paul Barden. In his opening statement, Barden responded to Shea's dramatic recitation by asking a question: "How is it possible that a facility that has been in continuous operation for 44 years, with a proven track record of quality care, can become so bad in the course of 60 days that we're now before you considering whether to close this facility's doors forever?"

---

DOH PR and other personnel had prepared the ground at least as thoroughly as they had their legal case. On June 23, just as the hearing began, Beechwood residents received a letter from Regional Director of Long-Term Care Sharon Carlo:

> I am writing to notify you that, effective June 17, 1999, Beechwood Restorative Care Center was terminated from participating in the Federal Title 18 Medicare program and the Title 19 Medicaid Program. This action is being taken by the US Department of Health and Human Services, Health Care Financing Administration, and the New York State Department of Health as a result of the facility's failure to correct serious deficiencies ... residents who rely on these insurance programs to pay for the care and services received at the home must be transferred to another location by July 17, 1999. I must also inform you that a separate but related action has been initiated ... to revoke the facility's license to operate this nursing home. If the Department prevails ... the remaining residents that pay privately ... would also be required to relocate.

This was followed two days later by a DOH press release stating that "planned transfers of Medicaid and Medicare residents ... are *mandated* by federal law and, equally important, are essential to protect vulnerable residents.... The facility's operators ... have adamantly refused to correct numerous and significant deficiencies ... The violations put Beechwood residents at risk of serious harm ... Based on continuing deficiencies, the nursing home has been terminated ... and reimbursement will end ... The termination action and the need to discharge residents, could have been avoided had the operators corrected the deficiencies.

However, they have been consistently unwilling or unable to do so."

That same day, during a break in the hearing, I met with patients, families, and staff. They were caught in a vortex of chaos. We did our best to explain something that was inexplicable, but we held nothing back. We told patients and families they would have to leave and that Beechwood would most likely be closing. On the 26th, the *Rochester Democrat & Chronicle* wrote about the meeting under the headline, "Beechwood Families Furious; meeting ends in shouting." This was accurate as far as it went. The environment was, in a word, insane. State and federal officials were subsequently in the facility virtually every day trying to transfer patients elsewhere. Under the best of circumstances, transferring elderly or disabled patients from one facility to another takes a toll on them. Our patients were suffering significant transfer trauma, damage exacerbated by the fact that they were being treated extraordinarily well at Beechwood. For many, it was as close as they could get to being at home. Most of our patients chose us—deliberately. Now, under the guise of rescue, they were being evicted.

Our staff did their best to keep patients calm and make the transfers as safe as possible while trying to hold Beechwood together. As for the nursing director and me, we were forced to be at the hearing every day throughout the chaos. The one gratifying thing about the whole nightmare is that patients' families and other concerned people in the community were inundating state and federal legislators with requests for intervention to save Beechwood. We likewise received hundreds of letters of support from throughout the community. In the court of public opinion, to be sure, the tables had turned dramatically. It was the DOH that was being blamed for putting patients in "immediate jeopardy." Public trust in their Department of Health was disintegrating. No matter. The juggernaut was in motion. Everybody with or without official power were equally powerless to do anything to stop it.

On June 26, Cooman wrote a letter to Health Care Financing Administration regional director Sue Kelly: "To date, Beechwood has received no further communication from HCFA with respect to whether either: (1) the payment ban has been lifted ... (2) or the termination of Beechwood's Medicare provider agreement is scheduled to occur." Two days later, on June 28, during an afternoon recess in the hearing, I called an established provider with the resources and political connections to quickly obtain from DOH a certificate of need (CON), an official endorsement required before new construction of a health-care facility or a change in its operations can proceed. I soon had a "Letter of Interest" to purchase the facility by July 1, 1999. A few weeks earlier, I would not have sold Beechwood for $25 million. Now the proposed purchase price was $6.3 to $7.6 million and was contingent on being granted 60 days for due diligence work and being able to get DOH to approve the purchaser as a receiver. These were not unreasonable contingencies, but at the rate events were moving they were simply impossible.

On June 29, we finally received a letter from Kelly regarding Medicare termination: "Based on another post-survey revisit conducted by the New York State Department of Health on June 14, 1999, it was determined that your facility had not achieved substantial compliance with Federal participation requirements for long-term care facilities and termination of your Medicare Provider Agreement is therefore effective June 17, 1999. A public notice of the termination will be published in the *Rochester Democrat & Chronicle*." On July 1, HCFA published the notice in the paper, and DOH issued a press release regarding the filing of "Additional Charges Against Beechwood Restorative Care Center." Kelly swooped in from Albany to provide media interviews in support of the HCFA termination and the actions taken by DOH. In the meantime, I occupied whatever spare hours I could find filing the plan of correction and rebuttal material for the June survey, which was necessary to receive a federal hearing regarding the survey outcome. In the meantime, these unadjudicated federal deficiencies had already become the basis for the additional charges in the state hearing.

––––––––––

Given the stakes involved, our adversarial administrative hearing was just as personally draining as a major trial in civil court. Days were consumed in the hearing, nights by review of testimony and supporting documents as we prepared for the next day's examination or case presentation. Business matters, especially for a business under lethal siege, also clamored for attention. Life began to blur. Undergoing the closure of a business I had known virtually my entire life— well, blur is not the best word for it; the fact is, there are no words to describe the environment that had been created.

The late Senator John McCain was fond of quoting a saying he misattributed to Mao Zedong: "It' always darkest before it gets pitch black." Jerry M. Solomon, regional director for the New York State Attorney General's Medicare Fraud

Control Unit (MFCU), made an appearance in the hearing room just before Sharon Carlo was to testify about meetings local DOH officials had with Solomon concerning his opening possible fraud investigations of Beechwood for its failure to deliver care.

The ALJ stopped the proceeding. "I want to make sure that none of [Carlo's] testimony will compromise any investigation your office is doing." Solomon responded: "I don't believe it will." Despite my resolve to ultimately triumph in this ordeal, I felt a shiver of panic as I was compelled to contemplate the sheer gravity of the forces now aligned against me. The mere presence of Solomon pushed the proceedings from the arena of administrative law and toward the possibility of a criminal case somehow being confected from the bogus civil administrative charges I was facing. Had it come to this? Not only was I losing my assets, reputation, and livelihood, I could lose my freedom as well.

I knew I could not afford the feelings that threatened to steal over me. I had to shake them off and move on to fight the hearing. What might be in the works certainly warranted fear—for myself and for my family—but these emotions had to be tamped down into the backmost part of my mind.

On July 7, I sent Kelly a letter accompanying our third plan of correction (POC) in response to the DOH "Post Remedy Revisit" Report of June 16. "It is incredible that HCFA could recommend decertification based upon this deficiency report," I wrote. "It is also incredible that decertification and wholesale destruction of a previously thriving business could be done in 60 days ... and without a hearing. Consider this POC and this covering letter to be my Credible Allegation that the facility is in compliance and hereby desires to be readmitted to the Medicare program immediately." The Chief of the Civil Remedies Division at HCFA notified us two days later that the federal hearing I had requested was assigned to ALJ Steven T. Kessel but docketed while the state proceeding was ongoing.

---

On July 13, a new "letter of interest" arrived. The proposed price to purchase Beechwood? $4.6 million—some $2 million less than what had been offered two weeks earlier—and with a fresh contingency stipulating that the buyer would not be responsible to fund more than $250,000 of operating losses. It was, of course, incredibly depressing—but hardly surprising, given the flow of poison from the DOH publicity machine and the ongoing forced march of patients from the facility.

On July 14, the prospective buyer went to Albany in quest of the necessary regulatory approvals. Anna Colello, the recently appointed Director of Long-Term Care, reiterated to him that transfer of ownership would require Beechwood's agreement to a "global settlement," which included giving up the hearing, relinquishing its operating certificate, and releasing all federal civil claims against named individuals. Her position was that if we continued to fight in the hearing, the operating certificate would be revoked—involuntarily, leaving nothing to transfer. The intensity of the state's hostility surprised the buyer, who nevertheless sent another letter of intent to purchase, which we received on July 16. The proposed price was $4.85 million—but with yet another contingency. There had to be at least twenty residents in the facility at time of transfer of operations. I could not accept Colello's "global settlement" terms, and there were no longer any residents in the facility. I called off the purchase negotiations.

On Friday, July 16, 1999, ninety-three days since the assault began, Beechwood Restorative Center stood closed, all residents having been transferred. After forty-five years, the doors were closed. We had not even begun to present our case in the hearing until the day before. So, we were shuttered, finished, without having had any opportunity to refute the survey findings or charges—in any forum, before any authority.

July 16 was the very day Kelly, with breathtaking deceit, answered the patients, families, and those in the public who had protested the lethal attack on Beechwood:

> HCFA generally views cancellation of the provider agreement as a last resort. … *In the most recent complaint investigation,* the NYS DOH found that resident health and safety were in immediate jeopardy and that the facility was providing substandard care. Opportunities to correct these situations were available to the facility's operators. However, the facility failed to do so. … [leaving] HCFA, and its authorized agents … had no alternatives but to pursue termination.

There was no time to mourn. The death of my business did not end my commitments at the hearing. When the proceedings had concluded for the day on July 16, I did walk Beechwood's empty hallways, shaking my head in disbelief at the atrocity. I had not even had a chance to say goodbye to the staff who so lovingly stayed until the very end, concerned for the welfare of the patients even as they knew they faced the loss of their employment. I would not see most of them again for thirteen years.

———————

On July 21, just three days into our presentation of Beechwood's case, we were on a mid-morning break in the hearing. We were, that is, off the record. That is when I overheard ALJ Zylberberg ask Marie Shea about compromising. He told her that he didn't understand what was going on. Beechwood, he said, was refuting everything. That same day, during the lunch break—so, again, off the record—Zylberberg dismissed everyone except the attorneys. He suggested that Shea call Henry Greenberg, Director of the DOH Division of Legal Affairs (DLA), to discuss this case. As our attorney, Kevin Cooman, related to me, ALJ Zylberberg told Shea that although he had yet to hear the DOH rebuttal, documents Beechwood submitted "significantly refute" many of the charges, and he didn't "understand what is going on here."

As I saw it, Zylberberg was warning Shea and the DOH that either he would not be able to support their case or he was afraid it would not hold up on appeal. Later that same afternoon, Russel Altone, Director of the Bureau of Hearings, told us that he would do his best to expedite transfer of the facility by the end of the year, provided that the facility, in return, accept "some" blame—and that we sign a release from all federal claims. As Colello had already attempted, Altone was in effect abusing regulatory power to attempt to preclude personal legal liability. Zylberberg had hinted at discontinuing his support for the DOH position, but Altone was aware that he did not have to take this threat seriously. No, the real threat to him and others in the DOH was personal liability for running a fraudulent sanction process. A measure of Altone's concern was that, even though I had already rejected such "global settlement" terms twice, he persisted in calling the potential buyer to renew interest in making a deal.

On July 22, Beechwood told Zylberberg that it still had "lots of questions" about the absence of email messages in response to the subpoena for documents we issued at the beginning of the hearing. Our attorneys asked the ALJ to remind DOH that it had a legal obligation to disclose. DOH senior attorney John Darling admitted that the department had not checked for deleted emails in response to the subpoena. Accordingly, we requested that a "thorough search" of emails be conducted by a system administrator to recover total emails sent and identify those relevant to the subpoena.

The following day saw the arrival of another "intent to purchase" letter, this one the result of Altone's persistent discussions with the interested purchaser. The proposed price was now lowered to $3.7 million, and still contingent on further due diligence as well as gaining all applicable government approvals. Since Altone's "global settlement" demands had not changed and the price offered was basically the minimum that the empty building and a Certificate of Need (CON) would fetch on the market, I again called off any settlement negotiation. On July 30, Beechwood concluded the presentation of its case. Less than a week later, on August 5, 1999, after three days of DOH rebuttal testimony, the hearing ended. It had consumed nineteen days and produced a transcript of more than 4,000 pages.

The next day, Darling wrote Greenberg and other central office attorneys that "The hearing was completed today on what can only be termed a high note for the Department":

> Ms Baker completed the Department's rebuttal establishing clearly and concisely that the Department made every effort to ensure a complete and fair review of Beechwood's practices during the period under review ... always aiming to bring Beechwood back into compliance for the sake of its residents. When that became unrealistic, the decision to close Beechwood was reluctantly made, again for the sake of those same residents. Ms. Baker also gave the ALJ a very plausible reason for the change in Beechwood performance. The staff, from administration to nursing to aides, was simply not adapting to the changing population that the Chamberys were trying to service; sub-acute and high demand rehabilitation cases ... The skills were just not there.

This "analysis" departed wildly from what Sandy Rubin, director of the Rochester DOH office had written on April 26: "Although the rehab protocols are followed, the facility is neglecting the other needs." The ALJ had complained that he didn't understand what was going on, and DOH officials themselves proved incapable of delivering a consistent message—"for the sake of the residents" or for the sake of truth and justice. Where was Beechwood in all this? Out of business.

Not that it was over. Now the work of assembling our proposed findings and conclusions for the hearing officer began. The document we would submit on

August 30 consisted of 1,211 individually numbered paragraphs of what we proposed as the correct findings and conclusions in this case. It was a task that consumed virtually my every waking moment since August 5. It was a mountain of work necessitated by retributive malfeasance of a handful of small people given disproportionate power. I have never been afraid of work. What I resented to my very core was the necessity of devoting so many hours to labor that served not a single one of our patients. That had been my business, my professional life.

CHAPTER 4

# Court Without Justice

H ow is it that a healthcare enterprise that had served Western New York
State for more than four decades, that was consistently rated—by the
state Department of Health—at the top among providers, that was
innovating restorative care in a "nursing home" setting, that was consistently a
provider of choice for its patients, could have been out of business by the very
department that had always rated it so highly? How was it that a quasi-judicial
proceeding could have been confected in a nation of law with essentially the
express purpose of putting one enterprise, Beechwood Restorative Care Center,
out of business?

The Administrative Procedure Act of 1946, as I have explained, created the
constitutional workaround that made this possible and put us all at risk. Yet,
as I have also acknowledged, the rationale for the APA has an arguable basis.
It is true that the nature of modern American civilization involves legislation
relating to many complex fields, professions, and industries that require levels
of sophistication and subject-area expertise beyond the compass of law makers. The fact is that we Americans count not only on the Constitution but on
the character and good faith of legislators as well as administrators and regulators, the integrity of both the elected and unelected government. When these
moral qualities are deficient or lacking entirely, we very quickly find ourselves
at the mercy of a government no longer of laws but of men—fallible human
beings quite capable of acting from base motives, the very basest of which is
retribution.

"Attorneys are responsible to a professional code of conduct," Tirone T.

Butler, Director of the New York State Department of Health Bureau of Adjudication, wrote in a March 2011 article written for the NYSALJ Association. He continued: "...and there are several model codes of conduct for administrative adjudication promulgated by the various national and specialty bar associations. However, these model codes have not been adopted into law in New York State, and therefore, are not binding upon the various state administrative entities that employ administrative adjudicators. Where does this leave the practitioner in the field?"

Where indeed?

Butler was Administrative Law Judge Marc Zylberberg's boss.

In responding to the "quasi-judicial" ALJ hearing that destroyed Beechwood, we identified and described twenty significant legal "issues"—for lack of a better word, the better word, I believe, being "travesties"—which drove the proceeding.

## THE HEARING WAS LEGALLY SUPERFLUOUS

New York State DOH controls the licensing of providers. Under the law, Medicaid and Medicare certification is a condition necessary to maintain an operating certificate. The certification is done through a federally defined survey process in which the states act as agents for the federal government. Medicare is a federal program, but Medicaid is a joint state/federal program. To maintain consistency during the survey process, the state may define and enforce any standards higher than the federal Medicare standards. Such standards must be identified in the state's contract with the Health Care Financing Administration (as it was known from 1977 to 2001; today, it is the Centers for Medicare and Medicaid Services), a contract that is referred to as the "state plan." The New York State Medicaid State Plan stipulated that its requirements were designed to "mirror" the federal requirements, and it therefore identified no higher standards than those of the federal government. Indeed, Susan Baker's covering letter accompanying the April statement of deficiencies (SOD) expressly stated that "All references to regulatory requirements contained in [the letter with the SOD] are found in Title 42, Code of Federal Regulations (CFR)." State surveyors have to be federally trained and tested to be certified, and all survey results and sanctions desired had to be certified to HCFA and concurred with by that agency to be considered official. The survey process is, therefore, partially federalized, and the state must agree to adhere to the appeal procedures that conform to federal regulation. New York State formally made such an agreement in its State Plan. Accordingly, Baker's covering letter instructed: "If you disagree with this [survey] determination, you and your legal representative may request a hearing before an administrative law judge of the Department of Health and Human Services, Department Appeals Board." Although Section 2806 of the NYS Public Health Law contained a decades-old provision allowing DOH to issue its own Statement of Charges (SOC) and run its own administrative hearing, this provision had never been used. The federalization of the survey process precluded it, and federal control only got stronger with a change in federal regulations made as part of the Omnibus Budget Reconciliation Act of 1987 (OBRA 87).

## THE HEARING WAS UNIQUE IN THE HISTORY OF THE NEW YORK STATE DEPARTMENT OF HEALTH

Beechwood was the target of an unprecedented hearing. While it is true that everything is unprecedented until it happens, never before in the history of New York State regulation had a skilled nursing facility (SNF) been subjected to the proceeding brought against us. This historical information came not from our research alone but was confirmed by the DOH in 2012 in response to our third request for admission before trial:

> Admit #8: DOH has never commenced any DOH administrative enforcement proceeding against an SNF seeking revocation of its operating certificate based on allegations of inadequate patient care resulting from a Title 18/19 (MR/MD) survey, other than that against Beechwood in 1999.

> Admit #9: Since the implementation of OBRA 87, DOH has never commenced such a proceeding while the facility was still federally certified as a Title 18/19 (MR/MD) provider, other than the 1999 proceeding against Beechwood.

Furthermore, Laura Leeds, the Deputy Director of the Office of Continuing Care in Albany admitted that the Office of Continuing Care (OCC) did not even have any enforcement policy regarding revocation of an operating license. Arlene Gray, who worked under Leeds in the OCC, testified that she did not even "know what the normal procedure" was for a revocation action. Clearly, in the fullest sense of the phrase possible, Beechwood had been singled out.

## THE NOTICE OF HEARING WAS IN CONFLICT

Not only had DOH never issued a Notice of Hearing (NOH) and accompanying Statement of Charges (SOC) such as the facility received on June 7, 1999, these documents were in conflict with the fact that Beechwood was still under a mandate to comply with the DOH Directed Plan of Correction (DPOC) and DOH had not yet returned to Beechwood for the final survey to assess compliance. The NOH and SOC also conflicted with our right to a federal hearing, which DOH itself had previously offered and Beechwood requested.

Thus, the issuance of an NOH and SOC created a mind-numbing set of legal questions to be dealt with, beginning with whether even to legitimatize the hearing by showing up and defending against the charges. And it wasn't as if we had plenty of time for careful reflection. Everything had be sorted out and decided within the fifteen-day notification period—even as a similarly mind-numbing battery of regulatory activity was ongoing.

The free rein government officials have to misuse their regulatory power to eliminate any effective opposition was on shameless display here. On June 7, when we received the DOH notice of administrative hearing, we were not only working furiously to comply with the DPOC and avoid a pending termination on June 17, Beechwood had already suffered a DOH-recommended sanction cutting off Medicaid and Medicare funding for new admissions as of May 21. This meant that the rehab floor was currently emptying out and operating losses escalating accordingly. To compound the growing catastrophe, DOH followed the notice of administrative hearing with a June 11 filing in State Court to replace Chambery management with a Caretaker, something Honorable Francis A. Affronti, Supreme Court Justice, refused on June 21.

In the meantime, Beechwood filed its injunction request, which Judge Larimer heard on June 15 and rejected the next day. Later, on June 16, while we were preparing our defense for both of the state actions against Beechwood, we received a new statement of deficiencies (SOD) and a termination notice. Now we had to deal with the sudden business-related demands of termination while needing to have our June survey rebuttal ready for submission within ten days to preserve our right to a federal appeal.

There are simply no words to describe the atmosphere by the time of the hearing. Beechwood was being dismantled while we were swamped by legal activity. Adding to this unbounded nightmare was the terrible fact that while the director of nursing and I were compelled to attend the hearing, our long-term care patients were being relocated, the rehab floor was emptying out, and the staff was quite properly wondering about their own livelihoods. By July 7 the rehab floor was empty. By July 16, all of Beechwood was empty—and closed, never to reopen.

## The timing of the notice was unreasonable

Section 301. 2 of Article 3 of the New York State Administrative Procedures Act (SAP) states that a party to a hearing "shall be given reasonable notice." 10 NYCRR (New York Codes, Rules, and Regulations), Section 51.3(c), defines *reasonable notice* as "at least 15 days prior to the date of the hearing." Nevertheless, it was wildly unreasonable to provide Beechwood with the minimum notice period considering the gravity, unique nature, and lack of forewarning of the sanction being requested. Finding proper legal representation, researching the law, and preparing a defense in fifteen days? Impossible. The action is an example of something (as lawyers sometimes put it) lawful but awful. And it certainly met the goal that the director of the Bureau of Hearings (BAH) within the Division of Legal Affairs (DLA), Russel Altone, set of "expediting" the process.

## The limit on pre-hearing discovery was unreasonable

Section 305 of Article 3, of the NYS Administrative Procedures Act states that "Each agency having power to conduct adjudicatory proceedings may adopt rules providing for discovery and depositions to the extent and in the manner appropriate to its proceedings." Title 10 NYCRR, Section 51.8, which governs DOH hearings, states that (a) except as otherwise agreed to by all parties, there shall be no disclosure, including …exchanges of documents, summary of witness testimony to be given, depositions, interrogatories, discovery and requests for documents." The rules of the game blindfolded and handcuffed one of the players, namely the defendant trying to assemble a defense. If the goal was to create a fair contest, the regulation was a terrible failure. If, however, it was intended to produce a desired outcome, it was spot on.

## The inability to probe retaliation was unreasonable

On the second day of the hearing, Beechwood learned that the ALJ was "not inclined" to allow questioning of DOH witnesses to uncover potential bias. In fact, he did not permit the defendants to be questioned about any bias, either before or after Beechwood received the subpoenaed materials during the hearing.

## THE HEARING OBJECTIVE

"Let's kick their asses," Deputy Director of the Division of Legal Affairs Jerry Jasinski emailed prosecutors David Abel, John Darling, and Marie Shea on August 6, 1999. In the tightest little nutshell possible, *this* was the object of the hearing. Otherwise, it was totally unnecessary.

As mentioned, federal Medicare/Medicaid certification was required to maintain an operating certificate. Beechwood could have requested an expedited federal hearing, had the State not interfered. If certification was not regained, the license would automatically be in jeopardy. That is why a hearing of this nature had never been carried out before.

No, this was different. This was personal.

The New York State Department of Health used the hearing to maintain control over the administrative legal process, button it up against a judicial appeal, and ensure Beechwood's operating license was revoked before we could have any opportunity to get a federal appeal or get recertified.

The DOH also did not want the facility to remain in existence on private, non-Medicare, non-Medicaid business. As Leeds stated to Rubin on April 29, 1999, "The issue is this: how much of his resident population is public pay. He may not be concerned because he has a strong private pay contingent in his home. So that being the case ... we have to be prepared to also revoke his operating certificate."

Shea, the lead prosecuting attorney, demonstrated on July 8 just how useless the hearing was when she asked Mary Jane Proschel, a Quality Assurance Coordinator in the Rochester DOH office who was testifying, "hasn't this situation gone on so long that restoring [Beechwood] to the point that it can truly function is at this point pretty doubtful?" When Proschel responded in the affirmative, the ALJ demanded of Shea, "so what is the point of the hearing?"

Shea answered: "For revocation of the operating certificate." "What if my recommendation is not to revoke the license? Then you are saying it doesn't matter?" the ALJ asked.

"At this point, it has gone very far, Judge," Shea concluded.

It was kabuki—for everyone, that is, but us, our employees, and our residents.

## The Division of Legal Affairs (DLA) was serving at the pleasure of the program staff

Hank Greenberg, who served as chief legal counsel for the Commissioner, oversaw the operations of the Division of Legal Affairs (DLA) and provided legal advice to DOH staff. He testified that the DLA was the in-house law firm of DOH, and when a referral was made for an enforcement action, it was prosecuted—without independent analysis for legal sufficiency. Altone affirmed this when he stated that the Bureau of Hearings (BAH) represents the Department of Health (DOH) in adjudicatory proceedings "initiated by the Department." Likewise, Steve Steinhardt, Senior Attorney, Bureau of House Counsel testified that he felt the role of house counsel was simply to carry out directives from program.

## The Department of Legal Affairs was heavily invested in what Altone called the Beechwood "offensive"

Dennis Whalen, Acting Commissioner of Health, called the Beechwood case "very important" for the DOH. Greenberg stated that he "oversaw BAH and Litigation in connection with the proceedings to revoke Beechwood's operating certificate." And when Whalen admitted that he was "worried about the Beechwood case," Greenberg immediately directed Altone not only to attend some of the hearing but to make "monitoring this case his highest priority." Altone testified that he was never a decision maker in the Beechwood case. He said that case development was reviewed and approved by those in the DOH higher than he. Who could this be? The only possible inference was that it involved Greenberg and Whalen.

In an interrogatory response, Greenberg wrote that "a number of attorneys working for the DLA or the Department [of Health] were involved in the investigation, discussions, advisement and prosecution of Beechwood." The ALJ remarked at the end of the state hearing that, out of the 105 attorneys in the DLA, "There must be [a DLA attorney] out there" somewhere who "has not been involved in the Beechwood case."

## The ALJ, as part of the DLA, was not impartial

The Introduction to New York State Executive Order #13, states that the ALJ must be impartial and free from inappropriate influence. Title 10 NYCRR 51.17 states that an ALJ can be disqualified for bias, which includes "prior acquaintance with the parties" or "other predisposition with regard to the case." However, the ALJs work within the Bureau of Adjudication, a department within DLA, and the DOH adjudication plan stated that the General Counsel (Henry Greenberg) was to review and approve ALJ performance evaluations done by the supervising ALJ and meet with the ALJs once a month to discuss issues. In addition, the ALJs receive formal designation from the Commissioner of Health. They are essentially beyond the reach of any remotely objective, disinterested authority. Many of the mornings during the hearing, I encountered ALJ Zylberberg looking for a space in the parking garage at the same time that I was. His vanity license plate provided all the information you needed to know not only about his self-perceived power but about his actual power: "ALJ 1." Judging from his employment history report, which revealed numerous significant raises in pay, the DOH appreciated his performance. From all appearances, he was on the DOH fast track. As you will learn shortly, one of the DOH witnesses in the hearing was Dr. Roger Oskvig, Associate Professor of Medicine, University of Rochester Medical Center. After initially resisting allowing Oskvig's testimony, Zylberberg relented and allowed him to appear but complained that it was "unfortunate that *the Department* saw to *put* both *me* and Dr. Oskvig *in this position.* It should not happen. It should never happen again.... I am controlling my anger" (italics added).

No ALJ should have contact with one of the parties in the case before him outside the presence of the opposing party. But, one morning before the day's session started, I saw Zylberberg give Joe Rohm, the PR person DOH assigned to the hearing, $7.00 for the bottle of Dinosaur Barbeque hot sauce Rohm purchased for him the night before, when the pair had dinner with the DOH prosecutors.

Zylberberg's decision also demonstrated the bias that comes from working for the DOH. He declared that all DOH witnesses were credible, but all of Beechwood's were not. He made findings about me that clearly had no support in the record. He changed the legal authority for the hearing and the sanctions sought from those claimed by Shea, Finally, he made clear that he intended his decision to send a "message" to the industry on behalf of the Department.

### THERE WAS NO SPECIFIED JURISDICTION FOR THE HEARING
On June 23, day one of the hearing, Beechwood requested that the hearing

notice—and, therefore, the hearing itself—be dismissed for failing to precisely specify the section of the law DOH was using to establish its jurisdiction. Section 51.3(a) of Title 10 in the New York State Laws, titled "Notice of hearing and statement of charges," states that a "notice of hearing shall contain a statement of the legal authority and jurisdiction under which the proceeding is to be held." Shea stated that the DOH was not claiming its authority under 2806-b, but under 2806-1. She further explained that 2806-b applies to mandatory actions, whereas this hearing was voluntary under 2806-1 authority. As an aside, Shea's reliance on 2806-1 was already demonstrating inconsistencies in presentation of her case. She had just finished her opening statement in which she represented that the multiple problems cited by the surveyors and the resistance offered by the facility left DOH "no choice" other than seeking revocation. This would imply a mandatory action.

ALJ Zylberberg responded that he needed to review the statutes, but he nevertheless allowed the hearing to go forward. On July 12, he issued a letter stating that he would not dismiss the case on the basis of failure to identify legal foundation—an issue, he quite remarkably said, he did not consider important. Nothing further was forthcoming on this matter until the hearing decision, where he blithely referenced 2806-b as the authority.

One other authority was introduced at the hearing, which had not been referenced in the Statement of Charges (SOC), namely Article 139 of the Education Law (8 NYCRR Part 29). Clearly, DOH had been planning to refer to it in the hearing for quite some time. On May 18, Rich called Milene Sower of the New York State Education Department, asking if she would testify at the hearing regarding nursing "scope of practice." In her opening statement, Shea had stated that she would proffer witnesses who would testify that Beechwood nurses were functioning beyond their scope of practice. As she went through every finding with her witnesses, she always ended with the question, "Was this consistent with accepted nursing practice?" The answer would always be "no, because of the deficient practices cited."

### THE ULTIMATE BIAS—THE HEARING WAS BROUGHT BY THE COMMISSIONER, FOR THE COMMISSIONER

Greenberg verified that Whalen, as the Acting Commissioner, was the petitioning party for the hearing. However, Whalen was also to be the ultimate decision maker. After the ALJ requested that the commissioner let him, the ALJ, be the final arbiter, and after the attorneys had discussions with Whalen about this, the ALJ reported that his role was limited to reporting and recommending to the Commissioner. This ran contrary to a decision by the NY Court of Appeals in *Beer Garden Inc. v. NYS Liq. Authority* (79 NY 2nd 266, 279), which held that the common law rule of disqualification embodied in judicial law section 14 also applies to administrative tribunals. Judicial Law #14 states that "One who participates in a case on behalf of any party ... [shall] take no part in the decision of that case ..." Whalen's role as prosecutor was inherently incompatible with his subsequent participation as its judge.

## The ALJ had no authority to dismiss sanctions sought by the DOH

After being told that his authority extended only to reporting and recommending to the commissioner, ALJ Zylberberg discussed the fact that he had no authority to dismiss the revocation sanction sought by the DOH. He knew that, according to 10 NYCRR 51.9(d)(2), such an action could be overridden by the Commissioner and that he could be replaced as the ALJ for attempting it.

### The totally inappropriate commissioner's signature

By the time the ALJ report went to the Commissioner's Office for signature, Dr. Antonia Novello was the Commissioner of the Department of Health. Nevertheless, Dr. Novello stated that Dennis Whalen, the acting commissioner, stayed involved with enforcement proceedings and would verbally brief her on them. Thus, she relied on Whalen for knowledge of precisely what her signature pertained to. When the ALJ report regarding Beechwood reached her desk, she "just signed it in the process of all the things that came in that day," paying so little attention to the matter that she did not know or recall whether she was aware that this order caused the revocation of Beechwood's license. Has any warden ever claimed inability to understand the significance of signing a death warrant?

Having Novello sign the order violated Executive Order #131, Section III B.1, which dictates that an administrative adjudication plan shall, at a minimum, "adhere" to the principle of insuring that proceedings are "expert," as outlined in Section II A. Novello was a physician, had been in her position less than six months, and did not have experience at being a signatory in this type of legal matter.

Commissioner Novello adopted the Report and Recommendation of the ALJ on December 23, 1999 and ordered that Beechwood's operating certificate be revoked. However, she could not get her story straight as to what she personally did to review the matter before signing the order. In an affidavit she stated that she "reviewed and considered the hearing record" during the time she had it, and then signed the order. Later, in her deposition, she testified that she did not recall getting the material, didn't understand legal material, and didn't spend time on the matter between 12/13 and 12/23 before signing the order. In fact, "being new to the job," she found it "completely adequate" to sign since it was the ALJ's recommendation. She must have also been heavily influenced by Greenberg's memorandum requesting her signature after he personally "forwarded the Report and the entire hearing record" for her "consideration."

Greenberg stated that either the ALJ, Altone, or house counsel could have drafted the proposed order. He also stated that the "in-house counsel" was to "proactively contact the decision maker," and that Novello would have been "independently" consulted (but not by formal memo) about her need for advice. The Bureau of House Counsel would typically function as this "resource" to Novello after reviewing the ALJ reports, and then make a recommendation to the Commissioner. The acting head of the house counsel at the time was Steve Steinhardt, who had worked on drafting the regulatory changes required by the Department's 1997 court stipulation in this case, and whose "understanding" was that "a [program] decision had been made ... to replace the operator by whatever means."

On March 7, 2005, in a FOIL request (#05-03-054), Beechwood requested the "identity of the DLA attorney who received and reviewed Marc Zylberberg's October 8, 1999 recommendation to the Commissioner ... instructions given this attorney by his supervisor concerning his responsibility ... the date this individual again forwarded the recommendation, and to whom, and indicate whether there were any other comments." Fifty-six pages of material and a few e-mails were identified but withheld under the "intra-agency exemption" to protect the deliberative process of the government, a claim upheld by the Court.

## THE ALJ LACKED KNOWLEDGE OF NURSING HOME MATTERS

The introduction to Executive Order #131 (9 NYCRR 4.131) states that the ALJ must be knowledgeable. Chapter 2 of the State Hearing Officer Manual explains that "knowledgeable" means that the ALJ "must" know the governing rules and regulations of the agency, so as to have sufficient knowledge to allow the hearing to proceed *independently*. Indeed, the very premise on which the Administrative Procedures Act of 1946 was founded is the need for a class of regulators and administrative adjudicators who possess specialized knowledge in areas about which elected legislators would almost certainly lack adequate subject area expertise. Since the Beechwood hearing was the very first of its kind, with no policies, procedures, or regulations for dealing with such a matter, ALJ Zylberberg could have acted neither independently nor knowledgably. He had no history of in-service education regarding nursing home issues and had never run any hearing regarding nursing home issues. He thus lacked subject area expertise, the single element that provides arguable grounds for the concept of administrative law.

Zylberberg's questions and comments repeatedly demonstrated his lack of knowledge. He did not know that "SNF" is an acronym for skilled nursing facility. He needed to ask Shea how substandard quality of care (SQC) was identified on the federal scope and severity grid. He demonstrated unfamiliarity with the term "DPOC," and confusion over the answers he was getting from DOH. Finally, he did not know what a "340" neglect issue was. On August 5, after 19 days of hearing, he had to ask Baker whether she was applying different standards to Beechwood because of its unique focus on rehabilitation. More importantly, he was not at all familiar with the typical survey appeal process a provider might use and whether it would result in a federal or state hearing. He even felt compelled to ask, "so what was the point of this hearing?"

## "ABUSE AND NEGLECT" WAS NOT AN ISSUE FOR THE ALJ

Rich testified that hearing results were to help determine whether two of the cases cited would be "converted" to "Chapter 340 [abuse and neglect]" cases before closing the case files. Thus, they were using the hearing and the ALJ to make a case that they could not justify earlier with their own charges. As will be explained shortly, Zylberberg had no legal authority to hear an abuse case, let alone rule on one. This did not prevent him from declaring that Beechwood was "facing charges which were in essence counterparts or equal to abuse and neglect."

Both DOH (PHL 2803-d) and the Medicaid Fraud Control Unit (MFCU) (SSA 1903(q)) have the responsibility to investigate abuse and neglect.

Nevertheless, the two agencies created a Memorandum of Understanding (MOU) to better coordinate their activities in this regard. The MOU was structured such that an MFCU investigation represented the first and the last word on any criminal or civil determinations regarding neglect, abuse, short-staffing, or other potentially fraudulent offenses alleged from whatever source. Under New York State Executive Law 63(12), the Attorney General may apply to the State Supreme Court for an order enjoining the continuance of such business activity and directing restitution and damages. Standard DOH procedure was that any observation or determination of abuse or neglect was referred to the AG for a final decision on whether legal action was warranted. If not, the matter could be returned to DOH for administrative-level actions. Without first referring any allegation of abuse or neglect to the MFCU, DOH was in violation of the MOU.

### THERE WAS NO SEPARATE STATE-LEVEL DEFINITION OF WHAT CONSTITUTES A VIOLATION OF NEW YORK STATE CODE

In the federal survey process, facts are cited within patient findings, findings are cited under deficiencies, and deficiencies are then graded as to scope and severity. A "deficiency" is what constitutes a violation of federal or state code and is cited as such on the SOD. In the Beechwood case, findings were lifted from the SOD, but reworked and reassembled without proper "deficiency" structuring to provide clarity or specificity as to the alleged violation of state law or its severity. Let me put it more bluntly: the charging document failed to fully define the charges. The Sixth Amendment to the Constitution guarantees, among other things, that the accused "be informed of the nature and cause of the accusation."

On the first day of the hearing, Shea demonstrated that she was moving away from the federal regulatory framework. What had originally been a finding on the SOD was now portrayed as a deficiency—a violation of law—in and of itself and without any mention of scope and severity. After discussing each finding, she would ask the surveyor, "What deficiencies in care did you cite?" In each instance, the surveyor (in this case, Elizabeth Rich) answered that the "deficiencies" were the factual allegations or issues cited within the body of the finding. Shea would then go on to ask whether these "deficiencies in care" for each resident were "deviations from accepted practice," and thus, in and of themselves, violations of code. By proceeding this way, Shea violated the federal code and survey process DOH was contractually bound to uphold.

Not only were survey findings on the SOD falsely constructed by intentionally leaving out or misrepresenting facts so as to support the conclusions the DOH desired, but the director of the Bureau of Hearings, Russel Altone, explicitly instructed Shea to "charge failed to do something," in order to make "direct connections between …[a] pattern of deficiencies [and] neglect." Shea worked with the surveyors and their supervisors to construct the findings and deficiencies on the SODs so that at the hearing she could present a case for failure to monitor, assess, provide intervention, notify the physicians, or obtain proper medical authorization. If the SOD cited a deficiency that by itself was not strong enough to prove neglect—for instance, the mere absence of policies and procedures to prevent abuse (F224)— Shea simply added a state code requirement to the SOC to arrive at the "neglect" dimension that Altone demanded. In this way, the absence of policies and procedures, was framed as a failure to provide necessary services under 10 NYCRR 415.12. Shea twisted the pretzel to magnify each cited deficiency into an instance of abuse and neglect.

## SOWER'S UNAUTHORIZED TESTIMONY

To support the surveyors' testimony that deficiencies in care were actually deviations from accepted practice, Shea produced Milene Sower as a witness. Sower was on the witness list, but we had no idea who she was or what she was going to testify about. Acting under color of 10 NYCRR, Section 51.8, the statute governing DOH hearings, which does not require "summary of witness testimony," Shea did not reveal the subject of Sower's testimony. She was, it turned out, a registered nurse with a Master's degree, and a PhD in "administrative education." After a stint in academia as dean of a nursing program, she joined the New York State Department of Education as the Board of Nursing Executive Secretary. It was a position that made her "responsible for setting up all the disciplinary hearings in the State for the nurses that are brought up on charges." She also worked "with a board of 26 members, the Board for Nursing, which decides issues on scope of practice, conduct and discipline." In this work, she might provide the Board with information to "portray what the State Education Department legal counsel has opined in previous years, and give [her] personal opinion on nursing problems."

Shea had Sower testify that a number of things done at Beechwood constituted "practicing beyond the scope" of typical nursing practice. The testimony was sown with problems, beginning with her statement that neither the nursing board nor the State Board of Education publishes legal opinions—because their "legal counsel does not allow" it. She continued to explain that "Many times the [issues] are setting specific—if the setting changes it's quite possible that there's a nuance that's different." Shea had failed to cite any specific acts by specific Beechwood nurses, and nothing had been sent to the Board of Nursing for investigation. Nevertheless, Sower publicly offered legal opinions in the absence of context (which she herself said was necessary), without any specificity, and which her own Board does not allow. Moreover, Sower's opinions were delivered without having "review[ed] any" of the medical records to determine specific situations and facts, or whether a physician had approved or disapproved the treatment in any of the cases. She simply responded to Shea's general questions, giving the DOH attorney what the DOH attorney asked for.

It gets even worse.

The Federal code (42 CFR 483.20(k)(3)(i)) states that any standards of clinical practice cited are to be "published" by professional associations, licensing boards, or other regulatory bodies. Not only was the Beechwood survey done under precisely these Medicare / Medicaid guidelines, but the New York State Medicaid Plan stated that the Bureau of Standards Development within DOH was the "primary resource to OHSM [New York State Office of Health Systems Management]" on qualifications and scope of practice for particular professions. Did Shea accordingly call a witness from this bureau? Of course not.

Finally, Sower testified that the Nurse Practice Act "is very specific about what the nurse may and may not do," and "the professional misconduct rules are extremely specific about what cannot be done." Yet Sower admitted that neither of these sources states that a nurse cannot do the things she had testified that Beechwood nurses could not do. Moreover, while the NYS Education Law regarding professional misconduct defines as a violation a physician's practicing beyond the authorized scope of his or her practice (Article 131-A), it does not do so for nurses (Article 130, Section 6509). And, even in the case of physicians, practicing beyond the scope of his or her practice is not a violation unless it is done "with gross incompetence, with gross negligence on a particular occasion, or negligence or incompetence on more than one occasion."

The DOH attorneys were not prosecuting a case. They were conducting a

scorched-earth offensive. *Nine months* after the hearing, Russel Altone personally drafted a letter to the Department of Education enclosing a copy of the ALJ
report and pointing to nursing issues in the hearing record that he urged the
Department of Education to consider for disciplinary measures. Forty-five days
later, he received a response stating that, after completing a review, the Department concluded that the information provided was not "specific enough to initiate case openings." It was a bureaucratic version of a stinging rebuke. Yet Altone
refused to let the matter rest. On March 21, 2000, he directed Marie Shea to find
out what further information the Department of Education needed to facilitate
DOH actions leading to licensing proceedings against Beechwood nurses.

Clearly, Altone felt that it was not enough to put Beechwood out of business.
Professional careers needed to be attacked and, if possible, destroyed. Accordingly, on March 16, 2001, two DOH investigative nurses signed allegations of
neglect against Beechwood's director of nursing (DON) and a supervisor on the
evening shift. On June 24, 2004, three years after these allegations and five years
after the DOH hearing, the Department of Health again sent a referral to the
Department of Education. There, however, sanity prevailed, and no action was
taken.

Yet that raises three questions: who, at the Department of Education, authorized Sower's testimony and its specifics and in response to whose request? These
have never been answered. In any event, if the Beechwood nurses had truly been
practicing "beyond the scope," such acts would most likely amount to neglect or
abuse and would therefore have to be reported to the MFCU of the attorney general's office for investigation and prosecution.

Why were no such reports filed with the attorney general? The answer is
starkly simple and obvious. There was no neglect or abuse.

## OSKVIG WAS A CONFLICTED NON-REBUTTAL REBUTTAL WITNESS

At about two on Friday afternoon, July 30, after our lawyers had concluded presenting our case, ALJ Zylberberg was addressing a list of "character witnesses"
DOH put forth as part of their Rebuttal. On it was Roger M. Oskvig, MD. The
ALJ stated that he "had served on committees with him" and was therefore "not
comfortable having him testify." "Can you get anybody else?" he asked. Prosecutor David Abel responded: "Well, he was available."

Subsequently, Oskvig testified that the first time he had been contacted about being a witness was the afternoon of Thursday, July 29, the day before the DOH presented its rebuttal witness list. The DOH attorney who reached out to him told him what "they were looking for in an expert" and discussed the "generalities of the issues." Oskvig responded to that attorney with "concern that there was a conflict because of [his] activity on the Board of Professional Medical Conduct [PMC]," pointing out that "board members are not permitted to be experts." On July 30 *"over the course of the day,* [Oskvig] consulted with the attorneys at the university to see if there was a conflict in the corporate level" (italics added). Because no answer was forthcoming from either corporate or DOH counsel, Oskvig had not, in fact, committed to testifying when Abel told Zylberberg that Oskvig was available. Oskvig stated that his next contact with the DOH was Friday evening at "approximately 6:30, 7 p.m." Thus, Abel's statement on Friday afternoon, that Oskvig was available, was false.

Dr. Oskvig faced additional obstacles to his availability. As part of his salaried duties at the University of Rochester, he was "on call" as a physician that weekend. This allowed him very little time "sprinkled through the weekend" to prepare, and he had either to arrange coverage or rearrange his schedule for Monday and Tuesday, including his medical director responsibilities at a local nursing home.

Not only was the issue of Oskvig's availability in question, not to mention the integrity of the DOH attorney concerning this issue, the physician stated that he had had only six to eight hours to review the records brought to him, and had been given no way to determine if the documents he received represented the entire chart or certain sections or views of the data from the electronic record, with which he was unfamiliar. He also testified that none of the material provided included what the patients' physicians had written in rebuttal to the survey findings or their testimony transcripts from the hearing.

This raised an obvious question: Just what was it that Dr. Oskvig was rebutting as a rebuttal witness? During his testimony, Shea handed him pages that were tabbed and highlighted. Using these, he simply parroted the DOH themes Shea had prepped him with.

Dr. Oskvig came to the hearing shrouded in doubt as to his availability and to his ability to act as genuine rebuttal witness. Abel also claimed that this physician "was recommended as being the best source we had for the information we wanted to put in."

But was he, in fact, the best source for testimony? He testified that he had never testified in a medical malpractice case or as an expert witness in any case. He further testified that there were approximately 450 board certified internists in Rochester, among whom were more than a dozen who had experience in nursing homes and could testify in this case. Indeed, there was also no reason why Dr. Coughlin, the Rochester area Medical Director for DOH, who was involved with the Beechwood case and in prepping Dr. Oskvig for his testimony, could not have testified. Shea had no comeback when Beechwood's attorney objected to Oskvig's testimony because of Coughlin's involvement in the case and yet his not having offered testimony in the DOH affirmative case.

On Tuesday, August 3, Abel stated that his *"understanding* was that *the Department* asked for a witness and they went to PMC [Professional Medical Conduct, a division within DOH] to ask for an expert in the field, not necessarily a board member, we had no knowledge that this individual was a board member." Abel continued, stating that DOH "asked for a list of who were the experts ... and this doctor came up on the top of the list as the expert." Here again, Abel's statements were subsequently proved to be false. Deputy Director of the Office of Continuing Care Laura Leeds later testified that there was a list of "about two hundred and seventy physicians," Board members that are "appointed to serve" on panels as adjudicators in hearings, and that there is a separate list of those consulted for expert opinions. Oskvig himself explained the reason for the separate lists: "In Professional Misconduct, the board members are not permitted to be experts. We can't be in conflict. So the physicians who are board members don't testify as experts in Professional Misconduct proceedings ... Since this was a Department of Health action, I was concerned about, that this was getting very close to that, that barrier that we erect in order to keep Professional Misconduct objective on behalf of the Respondents and the State." Oskvig told DOH officials on Thursday afternoon that he was on the Board and thus set forth his concerns.

Indeed, Oskvig had also been on the PMC Board since 1990, and served on the Executive Committee, as well as various hearing committees and investigation committees. He was well known in these roles. Dr. Coughlin knew him, and so did Leeds, who later testified that she probably worked with Oskvig at PMC, where she was the assistant director and oversaw investigations. These connections could easily bring other conflicts of interest, not the least of which was being informed on Friday evening that the ALJ knew him, and a ruling would be needed as to whether he could then testify.

What was going on? Why did DOH see a need for *this* particular witness?

As mentioned earlier, on July 21, just three days into the presentation of Beechwood's case, ALJ Zylberberg declared that he did not understand what was going on and noted that Beechwood was refuting everything. Director of the Rochester DOH Office Sandy Rubin described it as a "very crucial part of the hearing" and on September 7 wrote that "The facility was countering our nurses' testimony with their DOCTORS' testimony. The administrative law judge was being persuaded by their doctors. It became *painfully obvious* that we needed a physician expert to testify on the state's behalf" (italics added). DOH needed someone who could be trusted to do what the Department wanted and that the ALJ could not discredit. Moreover, it needed that person fast. After noting the phone numbers of the PMC Director and the Rochester regional office, Altone wrote "Roger Oskvig, M.D. Laura Leeds knows. Great!" Rubin wrote "Dr. Oskvig, literally on a moment's notice prepared himself over an entire weekend, came in the following Monday to be prepped by our attorneys, and then testified the following day."

So, DOH had identified a witness but had no time to prep him. That's when a miracle happened—a bolt from the blue, a message from on high.

On Friday, July 30, 1999, at the start of that day's hearing and just after Oskvig had been contacted the night before, Zylberberg stated, "I am thinking of cancelling Monday (8/2/99), ... I got a notice I need to stop in my office, and it's kind of difficult for me to do that." At the end of the day's testimony, he announced, "We won't do Monday." Behold, the New York State Department of Health now had the time they needed to prepare their witness—and the ALJ had the time he needed to seek instruction from his superiors in Albany. On Tuesday, Zylberberg confirmed that he had a discussion with his supervisor on Monday.

That Monday, August 2, at 8:43 in the morning, the local DOH attorney John Darling (AC01249) notified Director of the Division of Legal Affairs Henry Greenberg that "To bolster our case, and rebut the physicians, we are attempting to secure a medical expert ... unfortunately, the ALJ has indicated he is uncomfortable with the chosen peer, Roger Oskvig, as he frequently sits with him on OPMC Boards. The ALJ does not want to have to rule on the doctor's credibility. Our position is, TOO BAD." The Commissioner's office was going to get its way.

Period. Although an ALJ is barred from discussing matters outside of the presence of both parties, Darling continued: "We will know today whether the ALJ will attempt to block the doctor."

In the meantime, preparations for testimony went forward. Oskvig stated that, on Monday afternoon, Abel, Shea, another attorney (probably Darling), surveyors Cynthia Francis and Elizabeth Rich, and Dr. Coughlin were at his house. Shea stated that this meeting lasted about four hours.

On Tuesday, August 3, before Zylberberg formally decided to allow Oskvig to testify, Shea argued: "Judge, we feel that the Commissioner has a right to a full and fair rebuttal in this situation. And while you will be making a decision regarding this matter, it will not be the final decision and *the Commissioner has a right to this*" (italics added).

Before finally yielding and allowing Oskvig to testify, Zylberberg stated that he had a concern about whether the testimony by Oskvig was "proper rebuttal," but an even "bigger concern" was about "the bias issue," and "in [his] gut whether [he, the ALJ] could be impartial or not impartial." After this spasm of soul searching—at least for the record—the ALJ concluded, "I think I can be."

ALJ Zylberberg allowed Oskvig to testify, but he also made it known that "Dr. Oskvig came in to say hello to me before, and he's got some problems with testifying as well." He "[indicated to me] that he doesn't feel that great today ... and he would be more than happy for me not to let him testify." Oskvig stated that his role as a PMC Board Member is to "determine credibility of the witnesses that appear before us. ... In this case, one of the questions that I had was whether my knowledge and work with the Judge would affect his determination of my credibility and affect the ruling either on behalf of the State or on behalf of Beechwood."

Yet the testimony proceeded, and, following it, Zylberberg stated, *"I think it's unfortunate that the Department saw to put both me and Dr. Oskvig in this position. It should not happen. It should never happen again. Dr. Oskvig indicated that he doesn't testify in OPMC proceedings for good reasons, and he should not testify in any DOH proceedings.... I am controlling my anger"* (italics added). Darling had no difficulty dismissing this "vent on the record" as a "minor problem."

The question lingers: Why did Oskvig testify, and why did he provide the testimony he gave? The facts are that he never stated that he would testify, he was not a willing witness, and he was self-consciously conflicted in at least four ways:

1. By his position as a PMC Board member
2. By his connections to DOH in general, and to the ALJ specifically
3. By the lack of proper preparation to testify as a rebuttal witness
4. By his employment by a nursing home in competition with Beechwood

These personal conflicts were never resolved, a fact that apparently made him physically ill prior to his testimony.

But we will never know why Oskvig did what he did. We do know that DOH did not wait for any personal commitment from him before announcing that he would be testifying—and then delivering the materials to him on Friday evening. We do know that both Oskvig and Zylberberg were very uncomfortable with this testimony but went along with it nevertheless. Most revealing, we do know that Shea argued that the Commissioner "had a right" to this testimony, and Zylberberg angrily declared that the DOH "put" Oskvig in the position of testifying. One can only wonder what control DOH was exercising over Dr. Oskvig or his employer.

Not that Oskvig was an innocent victim. His lack of clarity and candor concerning his employment was very disturbing. He identified himself as a faculty member at the University of Rochester but did not explain that he was the medical director of the alternate level of care unit at Strong Memorial Hospital, and director of the credentialing office for Strong Memorial and Highland hospitals, both of which are in the University of Rochester system.

Even more troubling, Oskvig never mentioned that he was currently the medical director at Shore Winds Nursing Home, a facility operated by ROHM Services Corporation, which operated many Rochester-area facilities. Oskvig used the name "Lakeside" instead of Shore Winds, simply stating that he had attended residents there. The tense was past perfect. His misnaming the facility and his failure to identify his role as medical director of a competing nursing home do not appear to have been accidental. He not only knew the owners of Shore Winds, but the role of its medical director involved a very substantial portion of his work week and carried commensurately substantial responsibilities.

Oskvig further failed to explain that his work at Shore Winds was on a contract basis for the University of Rochester, which, as of the date of his deposition, had contracts with 30 facilities in the area and also operated facilities itself. Years after the hearing, in his deposition for our lawsuit, he admitted that these relationships had business advantages beyond the contracts, namely keeping patients within the University of Rochester system, and that all of these facilities were Beechwood's competitors.

Had Oskvig revealed this information, it would have led to further exploration of his conflicts of interest in testifying against Beechwood. He worked for major competitors, who were also huge political forces in the Rochester community, and Beechwood offered very tough, successful, and innovative competition. These organizations had compelling reasons to try to stop Beechwood's advance and to grab a piece of its pie. Indeed, after Beechwood closed, and under Oskvig's ongoing watch as medical director, Shore Winds/ROHM Services hired Beechwood's medical director (who had no knowledge of Oskvig's testimony as a rebuttal witness) along with two therapists, three nurses, and probably others who had worked at Beechwood.

## INADEQUATE DOCUMENT PRODUCTION

On day two of the hearing, Thursday, June 24, Zylberberg signed the subpoena for survey documents Beechwood requested. Darling, who was put in charge of this document production, turned over a couple boxes on Monday morning, June 28. He declared, "The Department undertook a review of all the materials it had available ... We identified all of them and we have produced copies of everything, including personal notes of the various investigators and survey team personnel." This turned out to be far from the truth.

Regarding the notes of Sharon Carlo, Continuing Care Director for the Western Region of New York, Darling stated that the documents included "certain notes of communications with counsel in preparation for the hearing, and we will be exercising or stating our privilege regarding those."

"Okay," Zylberberg responded. "On those, you are going to redact what you think should be privileged?"

"Yes. ... Other than that, they will be complete," Darling assured the ALJ.

Thus, Zylberberg allowed the DOH to decide what was privileged without so much as requesting a log of documents and explanations of what privilege was claimed and why. Carlo's notes would become the focus of document chases for years to come.

On July 22, well into presentation of its case, Beechwood's attorney told Zyl-berberg that we still had "lots of questions" about the lack of email messages received pursuant to the subpoena. He asked the ALJ to remind DOH of its obligation to disclose. Darling admitted that, in response to the subpoena, they had not checked for deleted emails. Beechwood therefore requested that a "thorough search" of emails be done by a system administrator to recover the total emails sent and identify what was relevant to the subpoena. Darling answered, "we still are ongoing, reviewing what we have, and we'll produce it as it comes our way."

On July 23, Altone, checking his own archive of documents, forwarded some 90 emails addressed to himself. He never revealed that he had this archive until years later, when Beechwood discovered one page from the document transfer made during the hearing. The page had been inadvertently included in documents he took with him to his deposition, and he had to explain where it came from.

On July 28, Zylberberg asked whether the issue of deleted e-mails had been resolved yet, stating that if such documents still exist, they should be produced. He was primarily concerned about whether any such record could have influenced witness testimony, and he was anxious to preserve evidence for future legal use. He was aware that within a "couple of years," the "system will have been completely erased, so there will be no way to enforce that." Thus, he stated that "even if it's not relevant for this hearing … you should try to produce them. And if they are not relevant for this hearing, at least it's retained."

On July 30, Laura Iwan from the Healthcom Services Bureau of DOH stated that the Department kept daily system backups for seven days and then weekly backups as of each Sunday, but only going back twelve weeks. This being the case, by the time the backup information was ordered, Healthcom could only go back to May 9, 1999. Digital evidence was evaporating fast.

On August 3, after Beechwood had finished presenting its case, Darling handed us emails gleaned from the backup tapes. He explained, "The only thing I have removed were items which related specifically to preparation of the defense of the 1983 [Beechwood's Civil Rights] action. Also stuff relating to or anything that was after I believe July 4th of this year … And anything that did not relate specifically to Beechwood. Other than that, it's all in there." Yet again, the ALJ did not require a log of the items removed and under what specific exemption claim. And again, these documents would be the source of legal battles for years to come.

Although the documents received were far from complete, they did reveal a mass deletion of emails and some perverse motives. The deleted emails obtained were marked as exhibits M5416-M5456 and entered into evidence the next day. Putting these documents into evidence without the opportunity to call and examine witnesses about them was a very tough decision to make because we did not want to give the ALJ the opportunity to make a ruling, as he ultimately did, that there was "not a shred of evidence" of any retribution in this material. But we did not know if there would ever be another opportunity to get them into the record. The legal complexities were simply too great to sort out at this point. We had to enter them into evidence and hope for the best. The delays and withholds in the production of documents worked very much to the advantage of DOH. Beechwood was rendered incapable of adequately mounting a proper defense. Documents retrieved through subsequent legal proceedings demonstrate that the document production during the hearing—or, more accurately, lack thereof—was calculated to mold the narrative as the DOH wanted it revealed, in a way that hurt us and limited the Department's liability. By doing this, Altone failed to follow DLA policy, which mandates that, to preserve the integrity, credibility, and fairness of the hearing process, there is to be full and timely disclosure of evidence the DLA has knowledge of that contradicts material facts alleged by the DOH and that tends to prove the innocence of the accused party. Curiously, Greenberg sent a memorandum to Altone and Steinhardt on September 1, 1999, after the hearing, explaining that it was "intended to memorialize and endorse [this] policy and practice ... that is currently in place ... although not required by statute, regulation, or case law."

On August 4, our attorney Kevin Cooman stated for the record: "We have had a chance to go through the deleted emails. ... I guess I have perhaps naively had a higher view of what a State government process should be about and it is extremely disturbing to me to see when government takes a turn, that it decides essentially that it has an enemies list, and when it gets to that point, simply misjudgments are made, clear violations of constitutional rights and prejudgment of outcomes. And the record will soon show that sorry tale based on about 10 or 20 E-mails." He continued:

> "I would like to have the record show at this point that Beechwood makes a demand on the Department of Health that they immediately cease and desist, and dismiss this proceeding, and make every effort immediately to intervene

with HCFA and have the federal funding reinstituted to this facility, so that as of today, August 4, we can begin to stop and mitigate the damages that have been caused, not only to this facility financially, but to the 90 people who are out looking for jobs around this community, and the 60 or so residents that have been needlessly displaced. I think they should take that very seriously. I think they should take it to the highest levels of this Department which would be at least at a level of Mr. Greenberg and the Commissioner, because it's very clear to me the E-mails of Ms. Leeds and Mr. Rubin are in grave jeopardy."

"I can't respond," Zylberberg responded.

# CHAPTER 5

# A Grandiose Sense of Entitlement, Arrogance, and Power

C hapters 3 and 4 include significant portions of the external drama in the Department of Health's quasi-judicial hearing. DOH officials interminably delayed producing documents we requested during the hearing and then produced them selectively. We had to demand that they find and recover emails that DOH officials had deleted. This chapter relates what Cooman aptly characterized as a "sorry tale." Its plot included monumental foot-dragging on evidence production and the revelation of a departmental "enemies list," as well as a free-wheeling willingness to violate constitutional rights and act in accordance with "prejudgment of outcomes."

A "sorry tale"? The digital documents are not so much "sorry" as tragic. They paint a lurid picture of the actions of a government of men and women, not of laws. They outline the systematic execution of a retaliatory motive aimed against me—who, as one DOH email put it, was considered "notorious." Notorious for what? For having challenged departmental authority.

Events that unfolded in a Rochester hearing room during nineteen days in the summer of 1999 were and remain either unknown or obscure beyond Western New York, and the memory of Beechwood Restorative Care Center has faded considerably. Yet what happened during those nineteen days has national significance that endures to the present day. These events demonstrated how a few determined administrators, unelected and accountable to no one, can with impunity deny any one of us at any time, and for whatever reason, what we all have been assured are "absolute" rights under the Constitution.

On August 4, 1999, Beechwood's attorneys submitted forty DOH emails for the hearing record. At least ten bring into razor focus high-level personal retribution. They are powerful evidence of an offensive led from the top, its outcome predetermined, with management from both the state and regional levels involved in assembling the false claims that were made on the statements of deficiency (SODs). The officials involved in these emails included the following at state and regional level:

**Dennis Whalen:** The Acting Commissioner of the New York State Department of Health (DOH)

**Laura Leeds:** The New York State Deputy Director, Office of Continuing Care (OCC), who reported directly to Whalen

**Anna Colello:** The Director of the Bureau of Long-Term Care and Quality Assurance, who reported directly to Leeds

**Henry Greenberg:** Director of the Division of Legal Affairs and General Counsel to Whalen

**Russel Altone:** Director of the Bureau of Administrative Hearings

**Sanford Rubin:** Acting Director of the Seventeen-county Western Region, including Buffalo and Rochester

**Sharon Carlo:** Continuing Care Director for the Western Region

**Susan Baker:** Provisional Director for Long-Term Care for the Western Region

In the spring of 1998—one year before the offensive:

1. April 8: Rubin asked Leeds what "remedy" could be employed to get the "notorious" Brook Chambery to "cease and desist" from "consistently challeng[ing] the authority of DOH."

2. April 13: Rubin told Leeds that Chambery's complaints to Health Care Financing Administration (HCFA) were "becoming an extremely serious matter ... [and that] it all stems from his lack of acceptance of DOH authority."

3. April 14: A staffer emailed Leeds that Chambery's activities "scream" problems ahead, and if they "can nip this in the bud somehow, it may be well worth the effort."

4. June 25: Leeds replied, "I too am concerned that we handle this differently" than strategies used in the past.

In April 1999, while the surveyors were only discussing potential deficiencies:

5. April 21: Altone asked Colello about an April 16, 1999 meeting in which potential termination and a "bigger picture" were discussed. He wondered how a termination could be based on an unsubstantiated finding. The same day, Carlo wrote in her notebook that the Office of Special Prosecutor (OSP), Feds, and Altone are all involved and that they need to "do [the] global picture."

Before the April Statement of Deficiencies (SOD) was even delivered:

6. April 26, 1999: Leeds wrote that "We have been working with HCFA on this one and HCFA has been cooperative as Mr. Chambery has tried to go around the state to HCFA. ... the closure is going to be tough."

7. April 27, 1999: Rubin revealed that, in a move contrary to federal requirements and standard practice, Carlo and Baker, working closely with the central office staff and HCFA Region II, "developed" the Statement of Deficiency (SOD).

Before the May 11 revisit:

8. April 29: Leeds ruminated that Chambery "changed the entire way we do discharge appeal" and concluded by declaring, "we must be prepared to revoke."

9. April 29: Rubin (with copy to Carlo and Baker) told Leeds that he agreed with the need to revoke Beechwood's license, stating, "Another advantage on our side is that Region II [HCFA] claims it will back us all the way ... They too have been harassed by Chambery. The chickens are coming home to roost."

During the May 11, 1999, survey revisit, ostensibly to assess compliance, a critical conference call took place among Altone, Leeds, Colello, Carlo, Baker, and Kelly (the regional federal administrator). After the conference, Altone wrote to Greenberg (with copy to Rubin and Colello) that "we are preparing for revocation" and a caretaker application, and that the "the Feds would be responsible for doing the termination of provider hearing."

As Leeds stated, it was an important case to them. Except for Altone, all these officials had assumed their positions within the last couple of years and were now attempting to exercise their newfound authority to send a message to the industry that they did not want this authority challenged.

The thing I could not understand is why they should have embarked on such a novel, bizarre, and destructive action against us. How could it have been worth it to them? What did they have to gain? And couldn't they see how easily this could all blow back on them?

The only answer to *why?* was *because they could.*

Leeds was in charge of three divisions and nine bureaus controlling all aspects of post-acute care delivery in the state. For all intents and purposes, she was "The Program." Rubin was "responsible for regulation of (all) health care facilities in the 17 county western region." All the other program-level supervisors reported to Rubin and Leeds. Whalen was the DOH Commissioner and could authorize anything, including the participation of the legal division in the offensive. Leeds stated that management was involved in every aspect of the decision making, and they had the necessary "clearance at all levels of DOH and HCFA." As Rubin put it, they were resolved, did not underestimate their "opponent," and strongly believed that their "ducks [were] in line." In short, they had power, it was effectively unchecked, and they used it.

As incredible as it may seem, the briefest summary of the regulatory environment, Beechwood's interaction with it, and some other brush strokes of background on the regulators are enough to show how easily power can be seized and abused.

Beechwood was licensed by the State of New York Department of Health (DOH). New York is a "Certificate of Need" (CON) state, which means that DOH "experts" determine the types of care that can be delivered, the current need for such services and for what populations, and who may obtain licenses to provide these services. Potential operators apply to fill the declared need in what is called the "establishment process." Establishment entails DOH review of the background and financial capability of the proposed operators, a review of the proposed physical plant and whether it meets state health building and fire code requirements and obtaining agreements regarding any operating constraints demanded as a condition of gaining establishment, such as the percentage of

Medicaid admissions.

Once licensed, a provider is subject to a myriad of state operating requirements, one of which is that the facility maintain its certification status for participation in the Medicaid (MD) and Medicare (MR) programs. This is where federal regulation enters the picture. State certification, for the most part, depends on compliance with the federal standards of care. Although the states can establish certain standards that might be higher, this is rarely done, and New York chose not to do so. Certification status is determined through surveys in which DOH acts, through contract, as the agent for the federal government—in particular, for the Centers for Medicare and Medicaid Services (CMS), which is a division of the Department of Health and Human Services (HHS). In 1999, CMS was called the Health Care Financing Administration (HCFA).

CMS, the federal agency, is responsible for training and certifying the state DOH employees that are to be sent out on survey. Surveyor training consists of a two-week course, and certification comes after passing a test. After the survey is completed, DOH supervisors are to certify the results to CMS, and CMS must formally concur with the survey results and sanctions that may be desired by the state survey team. Thus, the feds have the final word on certification issues.

As is clear from this brief overview, the proper functioning of the healthcare delivery system and the regulatory process, including dealing with technological and service innovations such as Beechwood's, depends on the discretion, reasonableness, and industry knowledge of the particular regulators involved. In the case of the regulators who targeted Beechwood, these officials cared more about themselves and their own agendas than they did about the professional, objective, and just discharge of their official duties, which carried a high degree of public trust.

———————————

The DOH fought vigorously to keep us from obtaining emails at the hearing. In many cases, the emails had been deleted by DOH officials, but we were able to obtain them after demanding that backup tapes be searched by the systems administrator. Even then, production was very selectively forthcoming. It took many years and legal battles to obtain the documents needed to fill in the blanks. Many will never be recovered. "Spoliation of evidence" is a legal term used to describe the withholding, hiding, altering, or destroying of evidence, whether by intention, recklessness, or negligence, and, as we will see, it was a topic that was front and center years later at trial.

The emails that were submitted were far from complete, but they nevertheless provide a chilling glimpse at why state officials would either fight to withhold evidence or attempt to destroy it. The subject matter in the recovered emails is rich with insight into how Beechwood made it onto the radar screens of these DOH officials.

I was never a passive healthcare provider in New York State. I made my concerns heard, sometimes writing to the DOH commissioner about the status of the health care delivery system in our state. For instance, I responded to a 1996 State Task Force Report regarding "Reform of the Long-Term Care Financing System." I also sent a detailed "Report Card on the New York State Long-Term Care Industry" and a dissertation on roadblocks to the implementation of electronic medical record systems, something we at Beechwood were pioneering. Doubtless, such engagement from individual providers was relatively rare. My work did not move the DOH to any response other than pro forma thank you letters which assured me that my suggestions would be taken under consideration. Of course, they were filed away without further thought.

The state's attitude of benign neglect changed radically when I began corresponding about the lack of DOH compliance with state and federal regulations that directly impacted the success of Beechwood's programs or reputation. When the prescribed overtures, discussions, and negotiations failed to resolve the issues, I did not hesitate to take appropriate legal action. Such aggressive advocacy by a single entity is far from typical in a highly regulated industry. Why? The war launched against Beechwood and me demonstrates why.

I knew that I was poking the beast with a stick. But I believed it was absolutely necessary. Beechwood had begun operating on a new healthcare frontier, and many of the contested issues were crucial to its existing and emerging business and its competitive position. Innovation is rarely compatible with passivity. Besides, we had every legal right to pursue these matters. As the Second Circuit U.S. Court of Appeals stated in its January 2006 decision in the action we took against the DOH officials (p. 11), "It is undisputed that Brook Chambery's complaints, protests, and lawsuits are protected speech"—protected by the First Amendment to the Constitution. The Second Circuit (pp. 4-7) summarized the various interactions between Beechwood and the regulators:

"In 1994, Brook Chambery and DOH began clashing over regulatory matters. When DOH denied Beechwood's application to add two short-term beds in 1994, Chambery challenged the denial in an Article 78 petition; DOH backed down and requested that the proceedings be dismissed. When DOH identified two D-level deficiencies in the course of federally-mandated surveys of the Beechwood premises in 1995, Chambery challenged the deficiencies in an informal dispute resolution process afforded by federal regulation; DOH backed down and the deficiencies were withdrawn. *Beechwood Restorative Care Center v. Leeds*, 317 F. Supp. 2d 248, 256 (W.D.N.Y. 2004). In November 1996, three more D level deficiencies were alleged by DOH, one of which was withdrawn after Chambery lodged a challenge. Id. In 1996, Chambery commenced an Article 78 proceeding challenging DOH's procedures for the transfer and discharge of residents from nursing homes; the proceeding was ultimately resolved by a consent order in March 1997. Id. at 256. According to the Chamberys, this pattern of challenged deficiencies continued through 1999, escalating in frequency and seriousness. Id. at 257.

"Beginning in 1996, Chambery opened a new front. As the district court characterized it, Chambery "began sending . . . a 'voluminous' series of letters and other papers to DOH and other state officials protesting various aspects of DOH's policies and practices, and advocating a number of changes." Id. at 256. Thus, from 1997 through 1999, Chambery engaged in a "campaign with DOH to either enforce or eliminate" a requirement that nursing home operators sign Medicaid Access Agreements in order to make major changes to their facilities. Id. at 257 (internal quotation omitted). Chambery contended that this requirement was onerous and unnecessary, and that it conferred competitive advantage on operators who signed the Agreements without intending to comply. Id. at 256."

Jerry Solomon, the U.S. Assistant Attorney General for Medicaid Fraud, also presented a summary of these interactions in an investigative closing memorandum, which was written in April 2003:

"Brook Chambery's relationship with the NYSDOH can be described as rocky at best. Prior to 1995, Beechwood rarely received deficiencies as a result of DOH surveys. From 1995 through 1998, Beechwood received a handful of deficiencies during DOH surveys, not out of line with the results of other homes in the region. However, unlike other homes, Chambery almost always disputed the survey's findings. From 1995 through 1998, he challenged almost every deficiency by exercising his right under the applicable regulations to oppose the findings in Informal Dispute Resolution (IDR). The relationship between Chambery and DOH's Regional Director became so strained on Chambery's part that he regularly complained to upper level DOH management about the Western Region Office and its Regional Director, claiming there was a vendetta against him. As early as 1996, Chambery filed an Article 78 proceeding against the Commissioner and protested to HCFA regarding DOH's alleged "failure to conduct the survey process with respect to the facility in accordance with federal law and regulations." In 1998, Chambery sent a letter to HCFA requesting a formal investigation into the practices and procedures employed by DOH's Western Regional Office."

All of these issues remained unresolved and outstanding as of April 1999, the month in which the survey and general assault on Beechwood began.

1.  On January 7, 1999, Daniel Walsky, who was a member on Sue Kelly's staff at HCFA, acknowledged that the pattern of problem survey procedures was sufficiently troubling to justify an investigation by HCFA. As of April 1999, this investigation had not been conducted.

2.  In the March 1997 consent order, DOH stipulated that it would change its regulations to comply with federal regulations, as Beechwood had demanded. This was not implemented until September 23, 2015.

3.  The DOH commissioner assigned Leeds to answer my continuing correspondence regarding inadequate DOH policies and practices and conflicting DOH regulations. On July 3, 1997, she responded to me: "There is no easy or quick fix to what you identified as conflicting regulations. Regulatory reform is a lengthy process at best. The changes ordered by the Court … have begun that process. …" Yet it took the department eighteen years to implement the changes ordered by the court. If that was the beginning of the process, how long would the implementation phase actually take?

4.  When Leeds failed to make adequate answers regarding the regulatory issues I had raised, I appealed to HCFA—the federal agency—in an effort to compel DOH—the state agency—to change its policies to align with federal requirements. There followed a series of letters and intense discussions with various officials at HCFA's central office in Baltimore, which resulted in a six-month silence before Nancy Archer, a Health Insurance Specialist with the Clinical Standards Group, wrote on February 25, 1999 to apologize for the long delay. She explained that "many of the issues you raised were outside the purview of our center and we needed to consult with the experts." Yet the only answer they could come up with is that "while HCFA has broad guidelines … the actual procedures are left up to the individual states … [This review of state regulations for consistency and compliance] is something that HCFA does not do. States are sovereign entities …" In other words, *although you have brought up valid issues, we are not going to enforce our own regulations because of the politics and national implications involved.*

5. On April 6, 1999, nine days before DOH unleashed its surveyors against Beechwood, Leeds acknowledged to Pat Whitman, of the Governor's Office on Regulatory Reform, that the Medicaid Access requirement to obtain establishment approvals had outlived its usefulness—if it ever needed to be there in the first place. Yet on April 15, the day the surveyors descended, Charles Murphy, the Director of the Division of Health Facility Planning, who had just met with Leeds on April 2 about this matter, told Whitman, "We clearly intend to apply the Medicaid admission requirements ..."

What neither Assistant Attorney General Jerry Solomon's 2003 memorandum nor the court noted was that I had also requested a homecare license. Beechwood's rehab clients continually requested homecare service, and I had corresponded with the DOH for several years regarding this expressed need and our desire to meet the need. Our clients were so thoroughly satisfied with the care we provided that, if further care was needed at home, they wanted us to furnish it rather than their having to seek care from a source unfamiliar to them. On August 16, 1996, I sent a letter to DOH commissioner (1995-1998) Dr. Barbara A. DeBuono stating:

> In the midst of tremendous need for home care services, and the tremendous need to try better and more efficient methods of delivering service, the State is not approving any more agencies to deliver certified home care services, and allowing the currently approved agencies to grow virtually unchecked and without competition.... Beechwood, as a certified skilled nursing facility, and because of its rehab program, is already directly providing a more extensive and comprehensive range of certified medical services than the code demands of the typical certified home health agency.... Why should we be prohibited from providing certified home care services and the continuum of care that the patient desires?

On February 14, 1997, Robert Dougherty, the Assistant Director of the Bureau of Home Health Care Services in Leeds's office, responded that "The SHRPC [State Hospital Review and Planning Council] has continued its review of the certified home health agency CON [certificate of need] issues, and I will advise you of their final recommendation once these discussions have been concluded."

The emails Beechwood discovered, recovered, and wrested from the grasp of the DOH revealed that, by 1997, Leeds, Rubin, and others in DOH were now painfully aware that we at Beechwood had run out of patience. Moreover, because the issues raised were of great significance, a loss in court would put their newly obtained leadership positions in jeopardy. They knew that HCFA had now acknowledged a pattern of valid survey issues and that these federal authorities were now indicating the need for investigation. They were also acutely aware of my past history of successfully taking legal action and of their own lack of an adequate defense on the issues. Moreover, they correctly feared that legal action was imminent. For, on July 14, 1997, I had "put [the] Department on notice that serious irreconcilable regulatory conflicts exist which need to be resolved" and all administrative appeals had been exhausted. Finally, they knew I was correct in writing that the "State of New York is risking its own Federal Financial Participation if it does not get the policies and procedures in place."

---

The key officials at the New York State Department of Health knew all of these things. They must also have known that the morally, ethically, and legally correct response was simply to remedy the problems I had identified. Instead, they focused their great administrative powers, unchecked by the constitutionally constituted political and legal system, in a despotic effort to eliminate the source of the agitation.

The DOH emails reveal that, in April 1998, Rubin and Leeds were discussing legal options to get me to "cease and desist." By April of the following year, 1999, they had made a plan to eliminate not just me as an operator, but Beechwood Restorative Care Center. To protect themselves from liability, they were determined to create a financial and legal nightmare for me and everyone associated with Beechwood—staff and patients alike.

At the same time, Whalen, Leeds, Murphy, and others in the central office were secretly and corruptly providing favors to others, actions that would eventually be the subjects of separate investigations by the offices of the New York State Attorney General and the DOH Inspector General:

> February 7, 2000: *The New York Times* reported that the Medicaid Fraud Unit of the Attorney General's Office (DAG) was actively investigating allegations that DOH officials had improperly expedited CON (certificate of need) applications. The Times reported that DOH admitted some blame for excesses exposed on December 30, 1999 by the DAG indictment of Lawrence Friedman, MD, owner-operator of Parkshore Adult Health Care Center in Brooklyn, in a scheme to defraud the Medicaid program of $62 million. The DOH had allowed Friedman's day care program to expand exponentially even while the DAG was

investigating him for fraud and during a period in which DOH had formally issued a moratorium on any further day care expansion in the area. The Times also questioned how DOH could give Friedman's programs outstanding performance reviews in surveys when the DAG was investigating and indicting Parkshore for falsifying medical records regarding services that were billed but never furnished.

March 26, 2000: *The New York Times* reported that the DAG investigation was now turning to "senior" DOH officials and that the Office of Inspector General (OIG) was "poring over DOH records" in pursuit of "senior" officials who had expedited projects.

September 23, 2000: Laura Leeds, who was the Director of Continuing Care services for the state and a defendant in the Beechwood case, resigned her position as a direct result of the OIG investigation in the Parkshore case.

October 16, 2000: *The New York Times* reported that both the DAG and OIG investigations were zeroing in on two lobbyists, Joseph Goldberger and Joseph Menczer, who were doing healthcare lobbying, including lobbying on behalf of Dr. Lawrence Friedman. The "Joseph brothers," as they were known, had raised a half-million dollars for Governor George Pataki and were members of his transition team. They had been referred by Pataki's aide, Jeff Wiesenfield, and had regular contacts with DOH Deputy Commissioners Joseph Chiseri and Dennis Whalen.

April 6, 2001: Lawrence Friedman, MD, pleaded guilty to tens of millions of dollars in fraudulent Medicaid billing.

July 16, 2001: The New York State Ethics Commission served Charles Murphy, Director of the Division of Health Facility Planning, with a Notice of Reasonable Cause regarding violations of the Public Officer's Law for three violations: inducing a lobbying firm, "which had matters before [his] division" (CON applications and property reimbursement matters), to hire his wife and assign her work on CON applications; misrepresenting the scope of employment to DOH counsel; and giving favorable status to CON applications that came through this channel. Commissioner Antonia Novello subsequently demoted Murphy, who later retired.

July 23, 2001: The State Ethics Commission served Dennis Whalen, Deputy Commissioner of Health, with a Notice of Reasonable Cause regarding violations of the Public Officer's Law for holding at least 23 meetings from 1996 to 1999 with the "Joseph brothers" and accepting gifts from them, as uncovered during an IG investigation into "alleged irregularities in the nursing home industry." This notice was referred to Commissioner Novello for whatever action she felt appropriate. That action ended up being a fine of one week's salary. Although the Ethics Commission had the authority to fine Whalen, it did not.

July 25, 2001: *The New York Times* reported that Whalen admitted the Ethics Commission allegations that he met with the "Joseph brothers" at least 24 times between 1996 and 1999, accepted gifts from them, and "facilitated" meetings with other officials for them.

July 27, 2001: The New York Times reported that Roger Benson, President of the Public Employees Union, 3,500 members of which belong to DOH (more than half its 6,000 employees), publicly called for Whalen's resignation. He stated that "inspectors must be of the highest character and beyond reproach given their critical duties." He said that he was "appalled that a regulator had his hand in the nursing home industry cookie jar," observing that such behavior undermines public confidence and trust and destroys employee morale.

February 20, 2002: The State Ethics Commission served Laura Leeds with Notice of Reasonable Cause regarding four instances of violating the Public Officer's Law by using her influence with DOH after leaving its employment to the benefit of members of the Healthcare Association of New York State (HANYS), for which she worked. On April 23, Leeds signed a disposition agreement with the Ethics Commission and agreed to pay a fine of $2,500 for these alleged violations of the Public Officers Law.

December 8, 2003: The IG's office, after a three-year investigation, issued a report that found serious problems relating to favoritism at the highest levels of DOH and involving the same officials instrumental in the Beechwood matters. The report found:

1. "Evidence that Lawrence Friedman, when seeking DOH action on a project ... was afforded unusual access to then Deputy Commissioner Chiseri and to then Director of the Division of Health Facility Planning Charles Murphy. The evidence indicates that these two officials thereafter gave Friedman's project priority, if not preferential, treatment, and accorded Friedman and his staff a level of attention that other CON applicants did not routinely receive."

   "That Chiseri did not inform his superiors at DOH that Friedman had offered him a $20,000 cash payment, nor did he inform them that Reiter, Friedman's employee, had offered him tickets to a Broadway show and had purchased dinners for him."

   *Laura Leeds,* Director of the Office of Continuing Care, stated, "her office reviewed CON applications to evaluate the need for the project and the character and competence of the proposed operator," and that "Murphy's approval was the crucial last step for CON applications, prior to their submission to the DOH Commissioner for approval (in case of administrative reviews) or to the Public Health Council (in case of 'full reviews')."

2. "That DOH Executive Deputy Commissioner Dennis Whalen accepted

gratuities from individuals with whom he met to discuss DOH business including, in some instances, the status of CON applications."

3. "There was a "perception among some DOH employees that the CON process and the DOH staff responsible for that process were susceptible to pressure from outside influences."

"Evidence that CON applications submitted by the firm of CSVC received priority, if not preferential handling. CSVC was afforded such treatment through its practice of hiring former DOH officials. The understanding on the part of DOH employees that the firm's business was to be given priority attention impaired and compromised a review and approval process that was intended to be immune from pressure by outside sources."

5. "Evidence that the CON process, as implemented, was subject to outside pressures and influences."

Unfortunately, the investigations did not go far enough and review the retribution these same officials levied on those, such as Beechwood, who declined to play their game.

The report stated that as a result of the investigation, one person (Robert Shapiro, a former DOH employee now working for the firm of Cicero, Shapiro, Velazquez, and Cicero [CSVC] was arrested, tried, and convicted, that two others were referred for Ethics Violations, and two others for disciplinary action.

1. Leeds "resigned her position."

2. Murphy was "demoted from his position" during the investigation. Whalen wrote the demotion letter on April 6, 2000 and Murphy retired on April 1, 2002.

3. Whalen was fined one week's salary ($2,652) by the Commissioner of DOH and directed to reimburse the persons from whom he received gifts.

4. Chiseri was terminated.

In consequence of the investigation's recommendation that a study be conducted by an outside agency to help set up a better system, the Rockefeller Institute was hired. Unsurprisingly, the resulting report did nothing to get at the internal problem. On May 25, 2005, Whalen was speaking at the public policy forum of the Rockefeller Institute. Richard Nathan, who introduced Whalen, stated that "Dennis has especially worked with the Rockefeller Institute on ... studies we've done for the Department, like on the Certificate of Need process." In his address, Whalen stated that "To me, no other job has such a mix of power, authority, resources, and responsibilities critical to the mission."

---

On June 26, 2009, former DOH Commissioner Antonia Novello pleaded guilty to a felony for filing false documents with the state concerning use of her state-furnished limousine for private business. Judge Stephen Herrick (State of New York County Court, Albany County Judicial Center Transcript) addressed the commissioner (p.9): "It would appear that during the time you served as a NYS Health Commissioner, you had a sense—this is my opinion—that you were somehow above the law and the rules and regulations … You had a grandiose sense of entitlement, and arrogance. … Power, Dr. Novello, is a narcotic. It can be abused. It can be addictive."

CHAPTER 6

# "Now It Was a Vendetta ..."

L aura Leeds was not a Beechwood employee and not a Beechwood lawyer. She was deputy director of the Office of Continuing Care, New York State Department of Health. On September 21, 1999, a few months after her agency forced us to close, she was speaking at a seminar for area administrators and confessed to her audience:

> We had to close [Beechwood] this year. The staff at that facility was excellent. It was a horrible situation that I hope to never go through again. We had to close that facility for all the wrong reasons. And do you know that the staff there cared unbelievably for those residents. Our surveyors were there monitoring the whole time. ... Many of these nurses and aides continued to care for the residents right until the transfer of these residents was completed. Although these nurses and aides were obviously faced with loss of their jobs at Beechwood, they nonetheless continued to assist in packing resident belongings and otherwise cooperating in the transfers. [Laura Leeds, per Paul Kesselring, September 22, 1999; confirmed by Leeds affidavit, at least to the "essence of what was said."]

Laura Leeds was not the subject of a criminal investigation, of course, but her belated honesty conveyed what any prosecutor would call consciousness of guilt—in this case, collective guilt. She knew that she had participated in something very wrong, not that this helped our former patients, our staff, or me. By the time of this seminar, the pain, the emotional carnage, the damage to the community, and the risk to life posed by the closure of Beechwood had already been inflicted. In their blind haste to destroy me, the administrators at the New

York State Department of Health DOH, including Ms. Leeds, gave no thought to avoiding harm to the community, staff, and residents. I was their target. To our self-proclaimed opponents, everything and everyone else were collateral damage. I still treasure a newspaper photograph from June 22, 1999 showing members of our staff protesting outside the State Courthouse on the day the DOH was asking Judge Francis A. Affronti to place a caretaker in the facility. The signs they carried said, "We Love our Residents" and "Beechwood has Love." I never saw anyone, anywhere with a sign expressing similar sentiments about the Department of Health.

———————————

I think back to January of 1999, which began on a high note for Beechwood, its residents—and its staff. Its innovative rehabilitation program, which moved us to call ourselves a "Restorative Center" rather than a nursing home, was doing phenomenally well. Our quality stats were in the stratosphere and our staff, accordingly, were being recognized with good pay and substantial performance bonuses. In a December 30, 1998 letter to the staff, notifying them of a 7.5% Performance Bonus in addition to their customary Christmas Bonus of 3%, I wrote: "We thank you for the many efforts put forth to help achieve the outcomes and reputation which Beechwood enjoys today. We are simply the best." And we were.

Within four months, a small group of New York State regulators launched an administrative blitzkrieg with the single purpose of destroying not only Beechwood as it existed but as what it promised to become. June 25, 1999, well into this act of vandalism, was a day ALJ Marc Zylberberg had scheduled for a break from hearing activity. I used it to call a meeting of residents and staff so that I could tell them, in person, that I was powerless to stop or change the course of events then unfolding.

We had exhausted every possibility, and we were out of moves.

We had submitted proposals of correction (POC)—our proposed remedies for ills that did not even exist—but they were duly ignored. We sought an injunction to slow, if not halt, the juggernaut, but the U.S. District Judge, David G. Larimer, blithely denied it. Judge Affronti refused to appoint a temporary receiver for the facility and at the same time refused to hear patient care issues addressed in his court room when, in fact, issues of patient care were the very reasons for requesting a receiver.

Now that the hearing was barreling ahead in the DOH's own forum, Beechwood was present as a kind of dead man walking. The facility had been terminated for Medicare and Medicaid reimbursement, which meant that these residents had to leave immediately, but since private insurance providers required facilities like ours to be certified as Medicare and Medicaid eligible, those patients covered by insurance would also have to go. Beechwood could not afford to remain open with the remaining uninsured patients and, given the damaging publicity and decertification, it could not attract others.

So, it was the end, and that was the incredibly painful message I chose to deliver in person on June 25, 1999. Staff, patients, and families were stunned. Tears flowed and anger erupted, directed against the surveyors who attended that meeting. Sorrow and outrage had no effect on the state. We had lost this round, and it was a momentous loss. Forty-five years of serving the community were ended. Yet, even at that very moment, I saw the loss as less than final. Out of business, yes. But I was determined to fight on.

In the meantime, Beechwood had been under siege for more than sixty days. "Siege" was a literal term in our case, not a figure of speech. Surveyors took over our computer systems, seated themselves at nurses' stations, watched every move, and questioned everything that we did to care for our residents. It was beyond disruptive. Important work was delayed, overtime was extensive, nerves were shredded, and everyone was exhausted. As for the staff, there was bewilderment and disbelief. What was bothering the surveyors? Facility policies and procedures, staff and staffing ratios, supervisory personnel—none of these things, which had been so highly rated by the state itself for so long, had changed. Why were the surveyors acting so oddly? Why didn't they ever discuss any of the presumed wrongdoing with staff before writing up deficiencies that made it appear that absolutely everything at Beechwood was being done wrong? Some staff members heard that surveyor Cynthia Francis had let slip comments concerning "a problem" between Brook Chambery and Sandy Rubin, the acting director of the DOH Western Region office. They had heard that Francis had said that it was time to leave Beechwood if a nurse valued her license. The rumors multiplied the confusion and darkened the prevailing mood.

Well, Leeds's remarks at the September 21 seminar inadvertently answered the questions and addressed the doubts. As it turned out, the surveyors daily stalking the facility found nothing wrong. In fact, Leeds could see that the staff "cared unbelievably" for Beechwood's residents, which meant, of course, that they were not about to put lives in danger. Even after the executioner's blade descended on the facility, Leeds herself pointed out, many of Beechwood's nurses and aides, well aware that they were about to be unemployed, "continued to care for the residents right until the transfer of these residents was completed. Although these nurses and aides were obviously faced with loss of their jobs at Beechwood, they nonetheless continued to assist in packing resident belongings and otherwise cooperating in the transfers."

It was true that patients were being endangered—not by Beechwood policies, practices, or staff, but by a Department of Health that was needlessly, indeed fraudulently, forcing transfer of vulnerable patients when there was no need. There is a name for the harm caused even by necessary transfer. It is *transfer trauma,* and it is an amply documented risk, one that the professional staff of the DOH understood as well as anyone but deliberately chose to ignore. As Leeds herself highlighted, the Beechwood staff not only knew the dangers of transfer trauma, they cared deeply enough about it to put the interests of their patients above their own. Their aggregate selflessness, which Leeds characterized as an attitude of unbelievable caring, speaks volumes.

I was not surprised, and neither should anyone in the Rochester community have been. It was general knowledge Beechwood had assembled one of the most caring and competent staffs in the area. Its programs were widely known and respected, and the staff was directly responsible for these outcomes. Staff members testified in court and represented to the attorney general's office that, despite their concerns that survey events at Beechwood would impact their future job prospects, they actually discovered that quite the opposite was the case. Thanks to the reputation of Beechwood, they found themselves in high demand. The fact was that no one in the industry believed the Department of Health's reports. Indeed, some staff members were given glowing recommendations by the very same DOH personnel who had been involved in leveling accusations against Beechwood!

After closing, Beechwood paid the discharged staff for their unused sick and vacation time, 401(k) contributions, and so on, but it could not afford to provide any other lay-off benefits. These would have to wait for the settlement that came thirteen years after the closing. Moreover, while most of the staff readily found new jobs, the transition was rarely rapid. Not a few discharged employees were forced to raid their 401(k) funds to make ends meet. And while most did find new employment in the profession, it was very often at lower pay and, almost always, without the bonus opportunities Beechwood had offered. We invested in our staff because we wanted to build and retain the very best staff possible. Indeed, initially, many former Beechwood staffers resisted looking for nursing positions elsewhere. They believed they would be unable to find positions as personally fulfilling as what they had experienced at Beechwood. In the end, however, most bowed to financial necessity or their love of the work, and eventually found themselves back in their chosen field.

Still, the fate of our staff and our residents was for me the most gut-wrenching dimension of what happened to Beechwood. Our staff was in the trenches, on the front lines, dealing with the surveyors. Going home at the end of the day provided little or no relief as each of them worried about what it could possibly be that they were doing wrong. For some, it provoked soul searching as to whether to remain in the profession. Their sacrifice and perseverance kept the operation going as the director of nursing and I were stuck in the hearing room all day, day after day. They had to endure the emotional pain of seeing their patients moved. They absorbed the slings and arrows of DOH-crafted news releases blaming them, collectively, for alleged horrors in a nursing home portrayed as a snake pit. And hardest of all, it was the staff who had to see to the orderly shutdown of operations, closing both a chapter of their professional lives and a source of livelihood.

I still marvel at the significance of Laura Leeds's spontaneous act of witness before a large audience of industry professionals in the context of a seminar on a totally unrelated subject. Paul Kesselring, Beechwood's assistant administrator, was there and described her emotion and manner as she declared, "It was a horrible situation that I hope to never go through again." Clearly, guilt and shame were buried deep within her. If the facility had truly been so poorly operated that the staff was causing harm to residents, she should have referred them to the Medicaid Fraud Control Unit (MFCU) not praised them, unbidden and in glowing terms. If her original accusations had been true and she reported this truth to the enforcing authorities, the memory of her role in the destruction of Beechwood would have been one of glory and satisfaction, not something "horrible."

The fact was that the DOH compounded the harm they did. In their single-minded haste to destroy me, they failed to plan for avoiding harm to the facility, its staff, and its residents. I doubt any such consideration entered their minds. Had it, they would never have pushed the Healthcare Financing Administration (HCFA) to terminate us as a Medicare/Medicaid provider, nor would they have pressed on with their plans after Judge Affronti refused to grant the request for a caretaker.

———————

Reputedly, the infamous Soviet dictator Joseph Stalin once quipped, "A single death is a tragedy; a million deaths, a statistic." The true extent of an injustice cannot be fully understood in its legal dimensions alone. Injustice creates injuries and leaves scars. The detailed and moving testimony by several of our staff at the DOH hearing, and later in the federal civil rights suit, presents a vivid picture of the harm inflicted.

**Assistant Administrator Paul Kesselring (deposition):** "This situation …was incredibly difficult to go through, to see patients have to be discharged when they didn't want to, to see a phenomenal staff literally be thrown out on the street, and then to be the 401(k) plan administrator that is giving them access to their 401(k) funds, so they don't lose their houses, or because they have huge drops in their income, or because they are having trouble finding jobs was very difficult. Quite frankly, I've tried very hard over the years to put this whole debacle out of my mind.

"[It was stressful] to the point of not sleeping, diarrhea for days on end, worried what is going to happen to the patients, what is going to happen to the facility. You have to understand my ownership mentality of the facility. … That building today, which I still think of as my building, sits empty. … That tremendous building that we maintained right up through 2000 just sits there decaying. The whole thing is difficult. Now factor in the fact that this is an organization, a family facility, that I had every intent of working my whole life for, as did a lot of other employees there, as evidenced by nurse aides with 20 years, nurses with 25 years, and so forth. That was taken away.

"How many people out there have a job that they actually look forward to going to every day because of their interaction with families, the patients, the staff; feeling that they are doing something to make a difference in peoples' lives, and you're on the leading edge. You've got satisfaction levels that go up and beyond –whether staff, families, patients, compliments after the fact, because they were able to go home and function here and there. All that was gone.

"Yes, it is safe to say I was angry with the DOH, and I still am." (pp. 59-61)

**Personnel Director Mary Wenderlich (deposition):** "It was incredibly emotional for four months. ... It was a very difficult four months for everybody involved in the situation. ... I realized after, I could no longer work in health care. ... because we had an amazing place with amazing employees. I got a job offer at St. Ann's shortly after—a couple months after—and I couldn't take it. ... I was on unemployment. I had no job for six months. To supplement, it took a lot of savings." (p. 12)

"I remember that we were in the second-floor dining room with the patients and the families, telling them ... that they would have to leave, and the Health Department came up after Brook had the chance to talk to the families. ... And Cindy Francis was standing to my right ... and the families were expressing their outrage—was a good word for it—of what was happening, and Cindy Francis's upper lip was quivering. She was trying not to cry. ... I said something to the effect of, you did this and you're going to have to live with this for the rest of your life." (p. 17)

**Long-Term Care Unit Supervisor Charlene O'Connor (deposition):** "The night they had that meeting ... with the families and all the staff there. ... There was a lot of anger that night.

"I've been in long-term care my whole life. I love the elderly. It was my job to make sure that they were safe and well cared for. They had loving families. I have letters from people –thank you for the wonderful care, thank you for this. People would come in all the time.

"I know what kind of facility that was. I lived there. It was my life. I know what kind of care I gave my residents. ... I think it was terrible for the residents. I think it was terrible, not as much for the staff. Everyone can find a job elsewhere, but what they did to those 80 people was terrible—terrible, and several died right after that." (pp. 93-95)

**Long-Term Care Unit Supervisor Charlene O'Connor (hearing testimony):** "What am I doing right now? Nothing. Chopping down trees. I don't think I could go back to this. I have a very supportive husband, and I have three grandsons, and I am spending some time with them and I am really going to heal ... it has been pretty stressful."

"I started at Beechwood in 1972. 29 years! ... My extended family. Katrina had worked with me since 1975. Bonnie has worked with me since 1975. Dee [Pardner] ... has worked for me for eight years. ... we have a couple that have come and gone within a year, but most of us have worked together for a long time."

"The residents on the floor are 'my family.' They have been my family. Some have been there 10 years, 11 years. I got to know them very well and the families very well and I love them.... At Christmastime, [for] the ones that don't have family, [the staff] chipped in and bought them presents. It is unheard of. We have a collection, a charity jar, that every month we would collect change out of our pockets and sent it to different charities. Everyone would get a chance to pick one. $60, $65 a month. These are caring people."

**Director of Nursing Donna Richardson (deposition):** "I was out of work a few months—maybe four or five months. I decided I wasn't going to be a nurse anymore. ... Because the Health Department was absolutely brutal, and I did not want to encounter them ever again.

"Then I decided I loved being a nurse. I am a good nurse, and I'm not going to let the Health Department intimidate me." (pp. 49-50)

––––––––––

Depositions and testimony in legal proceedings are often quite dry, but Beechwood staff painted vivid verbal pictures of what it was like "working" with the surveyors and other Department of Health personnel.

**Long-Term Care Unit Supervisor Charlene O'Connor (Deposition):** "[Cindy (Surveyor Cynthia Francis)] was on the unit practically every day. ... It seemed they were there every single day. I know she came to that unit every day with a clipboard in her hand and she'd write absolutely everything that happened. ... She would talk to the other surveyor, which was Liz. ... They would get together and they would be in the doorway and they would be constantly writing. And I know the staff members came and they'd say, what do we do, what do we do, they are making me nervous, what do I do. ... The staff was still pretty nervous having somebody there all the time." (p. 84)

"One resident, I remember in particular, that they came in and ... they said that he had a decube [decubitus, bed sore]— a baseball decube. ... They said, you need to come in and look at this. ... he had probably a one-fourth centimeter area on his heel that looked like a mole or a small scab. And they would go to the extreme of—you need to treat him for this, has the doctor seen this [?]. And it was something that was insignificant at the time. I did have the doctor look at it the next time when he came ... but he said there is no treatment." (p. 86)

"[Liz (Surveyor Elisabeth Rich)] told me a lot about her life, and I told her about mine. We had conversations every day. We talked about different nursing aspects, a lot of different things. And then one day she would just say to me, be careful what you say to me, we may be looking at each other in a courtroom some day. And other times, it was just a surreal feeling because I really liked her. And then she would say—One day she said to me, be careful, because we are just players in the greater scheme of things. And she would say things like that, and I would not understand what she was talking about. And one day, I went down, and I said to Brook, why is she saying this to me? ... He said that he didn't know. ... just carry on like we normally do. ... print up what they want, give them any access to the computer, print up any care plans they want. They did not—In my observation, they did not like our computer system. They didn't want to deal with it. They wanted everything printed up for them. They didn't like the fact that the [Certified Nursing Assistants] could go into the computer and print up their own care plans or look at it or make suggestions. They just didn't like progress notes written in the computer. They just didn't like our system at all." (p. 89)

"I personally felt that they were out to get us as a facility. I didn't want to think that until the very end. ... The little tiny things that they would find and make them into mountains." (p. 95)

"There were 'no' major problems at Beechwood in the spring of 1999; there were 'no' minor problems, either, at least not 'on the third floor.'" (p. 98)

**Long-Term Care Unit Supervisor Charlene O'Connor (hearing testimony):**
"No, the surveyors never once asked me why I had implemented a certain plan of care. They would—to be honest, [Liz (Surveyor Elisabeth Rich)] would always fill me with self-doubt. She would look at this, and in my mind she was saying

to me, 'Why are you doing this? This isn't proper, you shouldn't be doing this.' I always would question [myself], 'Oh, my God, I must be doing this wrong. I must have to do something different.' I don't think I slept four hours a night during this whole time frame. I would lay awake thinking, 'How should I do this and how should I do that? Maybe this really is a decubitus.' For 29 years, I haven't had a problem deciding what is a serious decubitus .... Our history, we have had very few decubitus[es] in the facility, and there are a lot of long-term residents there."

"We were a pretty aggressive facility. We didn't believe [in patients being walked a little, and then slumped in their wheelchairs the rest of the day]. We believed in activities ... We had exercise classes. We didn't just get somebody out of the chair and walk them, we made them want to walk. ... We could do any activity we wanted to. We had strawberry socials. If somebody said, 'Let's make an apple pie,' the activity director had carte blanche. She could go to the store, buy apples, buy crust and in the afternoon they would sit around and make apple pies."

"This was their home, this was how I was initiated to the building. These people, this is their home ... we treat them with respect and dignity. We don't want to tie them in the chair all the time. We will keep them as safe as we can, [like using bed and chair alarms if we don't want them to walk]."

"The aides? They were terrified, they were disgusted. They just said, 'I wish they could go away and leave me alone.' It made them extremely nervous to have somebody in there. They worked there 20 years. They give excellent care, they do their [the patients'] nails, they bring in sweaters from home, they bring in ribbons, they bring in makeup, they brought in jewelry, perfumes. These people don't make an awful lot of money, but they really gave to their residents."

"It has probably been the most difficult time of my life. ... I had to justify everything I did, which is ok ... but this was total harassment, no one was there to help us, no one was there to give guidelines, no one was there to give anything but to make me feel insecure. I had my heart ripped out, and I doubt very much if I will ever work in nursing again because I could never ever go through this again, never."

"[Liz (Surveyor Elisabeth Rich)] was very buddy-buddy, she was informative. She told me this was a very nice facility. She told me to be careful of what I say to her because we could end up on opposite sides of the courtroom. ... She said,

'Cookie [Charlene's nickname], remember you and I are just players in the greater scheme of things.' And I thought, 'What is this all about?' Boy, was I in for a surprise."

**Third-Floor Nurse Rose Tillman (hearing testimony):** "No, [the surveyors never discussed the issue with me]."

**Personnel Director Mary Wenderlich (deposition):** "They came in like they owned the place. ... It felt like a raid. They just came in unannounced and went wherever they wanted.

"They were abrupt, they were unprofessional." (pp. 19-20)

**Second-Floor Nurse Qwen Westbrook (deposition):** "[What happened back in April of 1999 is still remembered] because it was very shocking. It was very intimidating. I've never been through something like that before."

"[Cindy (Surveyor Cynthia Francis) would stand around the med cart or something of that nature, but never spoke to me. ... My med cart would be right here in front of the desk, and she would always linger here on the side, looking at books, because we kept our treatment books on top of the eave of the desk." (p. 63)

"Correct," [until the conversation we are about to talk about, the only interaction you had with Ms. Francis is you would see her on the floor looking at books?] (pp. 63-64)

"I was there when they [first] came. ... And I was out for about a week, and when I came back, it seemed like they were all over me. I was trying to do my work on my books and stuff like that. She [Surveyor Cynthia Francis] would be right here looking at my book. I got to the point when I asked her, can I turn the page, because she was looking at them so much. ... it was like, what was going on?

"Everything was happening around me, and I was like, 'What is this going on? Something is wrong here.' ... I said that part to myself, but then I spoke out loud. I was like, 'Lord, do I need to get another job or what?'

"What did I walk into? Because I was feeling really intimidated. Did I walk into something or what is going on here? And that is when Cindy [Cynthia Francis] told me the situation. ... She said, 'You know there are other places to work at besides this place, and if you value your license, you wouldn't work here.' And I looked at her, and I'm like, value my license; I just got these and I worked hard for these. So, I went to Janice [Okafor, a charge nurse]. I said, 'Janice, what is going on here.' (p. 65)

"[Cindy (Surveyor Cynthia Francis)] just planted herself on my cart, and we would have little conversations—like one thing I kind of maybe initiated this one. I was like, 'I don't know what is going on' ... And that's when she was telling me there was 'a problem between your boss and my boss. ... a lawsuit.' I said [to myself,] 'What did I get myself into now, dear Lord?' So then that is when I went to Janice again. ... She didn't answer me." (p. 66)

"I worked over[time], because being out so long I needed a paycheck. I picked up a little overtime. So, I stayed over, and I talked to one of [my] co-workers ... Dee Pardner. ... Dee was the one telling me that they said that they were going to shut us down. I'm like, 'Shut us down. What do you mean, shut us down? What are we doing wrong?' That is when all this started. ... So I kept going to Donna [Richardson, Director of Nursing]." (p. 67)

"Another time "we were in the back room where our computer—That's where we put our books and stuff away and look at our logs and things like this. If the doctor is coming in, we look and see so we can have our patients' files ready and all that. And [Cindy (Surveyor Cynthia Francis)] was looking through it, and I asked her, 'Can I just get in here and get my stuff and then you can do whatever you want to do.' That's when she said, ... 'Yeah, I got them.' I said, 'Woah, wait a minute, wait a minute. I do all I'm supposed to do in here. What they have taught me, I do. What they showed me, I do.' And she put her hand on my shoulder, and she said, 'No, not you—the physicians.' And that was it—another interaction. She was all over me. I started just dodging."

"I felt very intimidated. I've never been in a situation like that, and even though I had eight years as ... a nurse, I had surveyors come in and we do what we are supposed to do—give them the information. Like I told her, 'If I don't know something, I'll be glad to find it out for you.' And I'd recommended her to my supervisor, because me being new in the facility, I didn't know everything. I felt really nervous, very intimidated, because I think it was even more because I had just become a nurse, eight years under my belt. But nobody knows how hard I worked for the LPN license." (p. 70)

"She never spoke to me or anything anymore. She said something about somebody had changed a date on the physicians' logbook, and she didn't think the people were going to be seen or something of that nature." (p. 72)

"[The patients were being moved way before the employees left. I left when] there were no patients left. … I went to Lakeshore … the administrator called me back and asked would I come back and work for him." (p. 78)

"It was just so—It made me nervous; it made me scared, and the word is scared, to be honest. I was frightened. … I've never been in anything like that. … We were scared to take a break. I didn't even eat lunch." (p. 82)

**Director of Nursing Donna Richardson (deposition):** "Cindy's [Surveyor Cynthia Francis's] attitude changed one year before 1999.

"We had an electronic medical record, and they did not like it, and they made me print out papers and papers and papers. … That's right, [they wanted the hard copy]. … [Cindy] said that the electronic copies were not legal. We had to have a hard copy available at all times. … [Thus,] there was tension between me and her. I don't know about the rest of the staff.

"I really thought she was being absolutely ridiculous to not use the computer. We trained them how to use the computer. … They came to the facility for a whole day, and we worked with them. … We answered all their questions. I stayed with them all day. And they just sort of ignored it. … The next time they came in, it was as if we hadn't showed them anything at all. They still insisted that they still had to have a paper copy." (pp. 26-29)

"In 1998, something happened, and they were very—It's like it was—Now it was a vendetta. You come in and find everything you can that is wrong, and there is no way that—It was already determined that we couldn't correct it." (p. 45)

# CHAPTER 7

# Report to the Commissioner

Whe he died in 2009, John W. Hardwicke had recently retired as Executive Director of the National Association of ALJs (NAALJ). Four years earlier, on March 15, 2005, he presented a paper for a NAALJ panel discussion in which he observed: "Agency expertise is a derivative from agency culture; the agency head or the in-house hearing officer may be embedded in that culture which few members of the affected public can understand. It is only by taking the hearing responsibility away from the agency, and away from agency culture, that we can be assured of fair play." Thus, an administrative law judge who had served as a mentor and guide to a generation of ALJs urged that the responsibility for hearing a case should not rest with the agency that brought the case. What was done to the Beechwood Restorative Care Center is proof of the wisdom and justice of what Judge Hardwicke had recommended.

---

I believe that ALJ Marc Zylberberg, a DOH attorney who worked for the Bureau of Adjudication within the New York Department of Health's Division of Legal Affairs (DLA), was determined to do what he had to do to keep his job within the DLA.

By the time the hearing started, DOH had put itself into a very precarious position entailing potentially staggering liabilities. The ALJ cherished his position sufficiently to affix a vanity license plate that proclaimed him "ALJ 1." The pressure on him now to uphold the reputation of the DOH was intense. He never pushed back against that pressure. On his watch:

> DOH served the Statement of Charges (SOC) and filed for a court appointed caretaker before the final certification visit and while the facility was still complying with the mandated directed plan of correction (DPOC).

> DOH gained the commitment of the Healthcare Financing Administration (HCFA) to terminate Beechwood as a Medicare/Medicaid provider *before* the first deficiency statements were even written. Moreover, HCFA executed the termination without having received proper certification materials and without any immediate jeopardy (IJ) present in the facility.

> DOH falsely represented to the public that there was imminent danger and an urgent need to force patients to move. DOH had no legal authority to move the residents in the absence of such a situation.

> Judge Francis A. Affronti ruled that it was not in the public's interest to appoint a caretaker to replace Beechwood's management, and yet DOH continued with the termination and license revocation processes.

> DOH failed to calculate the degree of hostility that its actions elicited from patients, families, and the public. DOH had created a crisis situation—for DOH.

> The attorney general, who represented DOH in court, warned the agency that it could be sued for a billion dollars if it had failed to act properly.

> ALJ Zylberberg stated that Beechwood was "facing charges which are in essence counterparts or equal to abuse and neglect," but DOH had never referred its charges to the Medicaid Fraud Control Unit (MFCU), which was responsible for investigating and deciding such matters under NYS PHL 2803-d, SSA 1903(q) and the national Nursing Home Initiative.

By the time the hearing ended, the facility had already been closed. DOH had ruined a very valuable business; 120 people had lost their jobs and suffered a blow to their reputations and careers; and worst of all, vulnerable patients had been forcibly transferred to other facilities. What ALJ was going to rule against the department that employed him, especially now that the damage had been done? An ALJ need only formally recommend taking away Beechwood's operating certificate to supply the necessary legal cover for the DOH.

DOH had such confidence in its own hearing process that it persisted in its fraudulent endeavors. After losing the caretaker case in State Court, Director of the Rochester DOH Office Sandy Rubin simply underscored the importance that DOH prevail in the revocation hearing. Dennis Whalen, Acting Commissioner of Health, was worried about the case, but instead of stopping it, directed that Hank Greenberg, chief legal counsel for the commissioner, put his best and strongest legal talent on the case. As Greenberg said, it was "very important to the department." Indeed, the ALJ himself remarked that so much legal talent had been assigned to the case that it was just about impossible to find an attorney in the DLA who had not been involved—even though the DLA was the size of some of the largest legal firms in the country. At the time, it had 105 attorneys and 41 staff. Two thirds of the DLA attorneys worked as prosecutors within the Bureaus of Administrative Hearings and Professional Medical Conduct doing administrative hearings.

---

DLA's Russel Altone, who supervised the development of the Statement of Charges (SOC), tried to make Zylberberg's task super easy. Altone later wrote in an interrogatory response that "It was really a matter of whether ... we could ... meet our burden of proof ... within the context of a ... [DOH administrative] hearing." He knew that this burden would be very light indeed. There was no state operations manual to provide guidance like the one published at the federal level, and Altone stated that he tried "to stay away from federal criteria in evaluating the appropriateness of state actions." Baker, Francis, and Rich each testified that there was no separate state surveyor certification process, and surveyor in-service records contain no evidence of any training or certification in the interpretation and application of New York State code. The fact was that there had never been a hearing like this before. Unsurprisingly, therefore, the ALJ had no knowledge whatsoever in this area, and he didn't even know why a hearing was being held.

Prosecutor Marie Shea stated that the burden of proof was on the Department of Health to show by substantial evidence the existence of problems so egregious as to warrant license revocation. She went on to say that the revocation action was being taken voluntarily under NYS PHL 2806-1(a), which simply stated that "a hospital operating certificate may be revoked ... on proof that the hospital has failed to comply with the provisions of this article or rules and regulations promulgated there under." This is a ridiculously low standard of proof for an action of such magnitude, and it is a staggeringly vague law on which to rely without any interpretive regulations or policies.

By forcing termination, patient transfers and the closure of the facility before the end of the hearing, the ALJ no longer had the burden of deciding whether the IJ actually existed or posed such a risk that the residents had to be transferred, as PHL 2806-b required. As Shea got Mary Jane Proschel, a Quality Assurance Coordinator in Rochester DOH office, to testify on July 8, near the start of the hearing, the situation had already reached the point that restoring Beechwood to anything like adequate functioning was pretty doubtful. Deciding to go along and rubberstamp the revocation sanction therefore did not appear to carry with it any further negative impact. The damage was done.

---

ALJ Zylberberg took breathtaking liberties in (1) changing the jurisdiction under which DOH had stated it was bringing the revocation action, in (2) citing and interpreting the NYS Public Health Law and regulations, and in (3) justifying the actions taken by DOH.

First, after Shea repeatedly stated that the DOH was bringing the hearing as a voluntary action under 2806-1, Zylberberg simply decided to change it to a mandatory action under 2806-b. To justify his reasons for recommending revocation, the ALJ wrote in his decision (p. 95) that in accordance with 2806-b (a) & (b), "there is no doubt" that the DOH proved that a number of conditions "existed" at Beechwood that were in substantial violation of the standards. However, the use of the past tense conflicts with the language in 2806-b, which explicitly states that the condition must currently exist—in the present—to revoke or take other licensing action. To overcome the problem of the law's present tense, Zylberberg switched to the present tense to meet the legal obligation under 2806-b(c) stating "there exist operational deficiencies at Beechwood which form a pattern of violation of the standard." Obviously, he was trying to make up for the fact that no declared immediate jeopardy (IJ) or substandard quality of care (SQC) existed according to the final survey report, and that he relied on a "pattern of violations" as a reason for recommending revocation. In this, he was aided by the fact that there is no separate definition of what constitutes a "deficiency," a "pattern of violation," and a "substantial violation of the standards" under state law or regulations.

Next, changing the focus from the deficiencies, which the he stated (p. 94) were correctable, the ALJ decided to (p.59) insert Article 139 of the NYS

Education Law (8 NYCCR Part 29) into the authorization for the revocation. This section of the law deals with standards of nursing practice. Shea had made violation of scope of practice a major theme during the hearing without any mention of it on the statement of charges (SOC), and since no nurse had been cited for any violation of nursing standards, she tried to provide cover by insinuating that all the nurses at Beechwood were violating standards of practice. However, DOH could not explain why all the nurses could be violating standards, except to say that they thought it might be due to direction from the administrator or director of nursing. To help the DOH make the case, the ALJ (p. 63) stated that the hearing was similar to a physician licensing revocation proceeding. Pulling in 10 NYCRR 415.1 (b)(1) & (2), he decided to put the blame on "the facility," or Brook Chambery, for (p. 59) "empowering" or "authorizing" nurses to do tasks "outside the scope of nursing practice," and (p. 60) not "ensuring" that "employees, medical directors, and consultants follow generally accepted standards of practice and not act negligently."

The ALJ did not stop here. He used another organization and administration regulation, 10 NYCRR 415.26, and chose to place the blame squarely on Mr. Chambery's "unwillingness" to work with the DOH as the basis for closure (p. 91) and recommending revocation (p. 94). He stated (p. 94) that "There is no question … The sole responsibility for the closure rests with its administrator, Mr. Brook Chambery, … and since I believe that Mr. Chambery will continue to place the needs of the facility over and above the needs of its residents, I have no choice other than recommending revocation." In stating that he had "no choice," he was again varying from Shea's original stance that the DOH was taking the revocation as a voluntary action under PHL 2806-1. He was also ignoring the fact that the SOC was issued before the final survey to assess compliance and that in the final survey, DOH did not cite any IJ or SQC as in the previous surveys. Nor did he take note that he himself (p. 91) had chastised DOH for "indifferently" refusing to provide information as to why the POCs were being rejected.

---

The ALJ's switch in positions between the time of the hearing and the decision, and the breadth of the topics incorporated in the decision—by a person who just a few weeks earlier had shown such little understanding of the skilled nursing facility environment—were stunning. The natural question to ask was, who wrote the decision? The most likely answer is that the ALJ did, albeit closely following the outline given to him by DOH attorneys in their proposed findings and conclusions.

On July 21, 1999, during a morning break in the hearing, I heard the ALJ tell Shea that they should consider compromise. Absent an amazing cross examination by DOH, he said, he did not understand what was going on. Later, Cooman reported that during the lunch break, the ALJ told the attorneys he had not prejudged the case and hadn't seen all the evidence or heard the rebuttal, but documents (and, of course, the accompanying testimony) submitted by Beechwood "significantly refute" a large number of the charges. Once again, he said that he didn't understand what was going on. In fact, he suggested that Altone and Shea discuss the case with Greenberg, since, in a recent seminar, Greenberg had warned the attorneys to keep straight who DLA represented, the Department or its employees.

Beechwood had entered the complete medical record of each cited resident into evidence at the hearing. This allowed Beechwood to demonstrate to the ALJ how DOH did not accurately report facts from the record. As Beechwood complained in its survey rebuttal, surveyors had requested certain time-limited progress notes, care plans, and federal assessments (MDS) that had been submitted, but specifically told nurses they did not want the full assessment data or the change in condition reports from our system. A note made by Susan Baker confirms that she was only reading progress notes. Without our complete assessment data, the surveyors were presenting a skewed picture of the documentation and what care was being rendered. They also had never bothered to question staff about any documentation or care rendered. We will never know what "pieces" of the medical records the surveyors were told to get, but if Beechwood figured the copying would take two full days, and Baker testified that she and Carlo did it in three hours, obviously something was missing.

It only got worse for DOH. The bulk of Beechwood's physician testimony came over the next two-and-a-half days, leading Rubin to write that "The administrative law judge was being persuaded by [Beechwood's] doctors. It became painfully obvious that we needed a physician expert to testify on the state's behalf." The problem was, their case had already been presented. All they had left was the opportunity to present a rebuttal witness.

As the ALJ discussed the non-rebuttal nature of Dr. Roger M. Oskvig's testimony in his decision, he (p. 65) stated that "Dr. Oskvig mostly reinforced the testimony of previous Department witnesses." The ALJ stated that he "found that the overwhelming majority of charges and observations were justified and entirely proper" and that the testimony of the Department witnesses, including Dr. Oskvig, was knowledgeable, honest, forthright, trustworthy, reliable, credible, and without bias (pp. 55-56). The issue then becomes how it was that the ALJ came to see the testimony of *Beechwood's* witnesses (pp. 57-58) as unsupported by the medical records, or that such records were not documented properly, or that Beechwood's physicians and their testimony now somehow appears not credible and biased by financial interests? Even the MFCU staff, after reading the hearing testimony, stated that "testimony during the hearing ... refuted the contention that poor care was given."

The answer to the question of why the ALJ changed his interpretation may be found in the DOH's proposed findings and conclusions. We will never know who might have helped the ALJ do the actual writing of his opinion. Greenberg's interrogatory response acknowledged that attorneys involved with the prosecution of the case did receive copies of the ALJ report, but he stated that he had no specific recollection as to whether they made any written comments. We also know that prosecutor John Darling wrote to the survey team that he would "keep everyone informed on any developments as the decision process proceeds." Beechwood tried through FOIL and interrogatory requests to discover just who was involved in writing the decision or in discussing it with the ALJ, but the DLA claimed that no such documentation existed. However, the ALJ decision closely tracks the verbiage given to him in the proposed findings and conclusion, a submission that the deputy director of the Division of Legal Affairs stated was intended to "kick [Beechwood's] asses," again.

---

The fact is the ALJ's decision was purposely structured to fill in the blanks left after the hearing, to drive further investigations, and to gain judicial support. Let's break it down.

### REGARDING NEGLECT

On August 4, the second-to-last day of the hearing, surveyor Elizabeth Rich testified—or, more accurately, announced—that DOH was waiting on the outcome of the hearing to see whether to pursue any "individuals" for neglect. This was followed the same day by a statement from the ALJ that Beechwood was "facing charges which are in essence counterparts or equal to abuse and neglect," even though, early in the hearing, he had demonstrated his lack of knowledge when he stated that he did not know what a "340" neglect referral was.

In his decision (p. 59), the ALJ stated, "Proof that a nurse failed to exercise the care that a reasonably prudent nurse would exercise under the circumstances is sufficient to sustain a finding of negligence in a licensing misconduct proceeding." He went on (pp. 58, 59, 76, 77, 78) to cite many so-called facts from the falsely structured survey findings as evidence of nurses practicing outside the scope of practice. Then (pp. 66-67), discussing various issues dealing with residents assessed as being in immediate jeopardy (IJ) in April, he stated that Beechwood "residents were neglected by Beechwood in several significant aspects of care."

By itself, "neglect" is a vague and subjective term, so it is important to refer to its definition under applicable law, which is found at 42 CFR 488.301. There it is defined as failure to provide goods and services necessary to avoid physical harm, mental anguish, or mental illness. State regulations (PHL 2803-d; 10 NYCRR 415.12) add that *an individual must be identified* who failed to provide the services and the specifics. In a deposition, Surveyor Cynthia Francis stated that an abuse, neglect, or mistreatment case is labeled as a "340," and always involved someone accused of a specific abuse, neglect, or mistreatment. Thus, "you had to focus on that person and investigate that incident."

The Social Security Act, Section 1903 (q)(4), requires the New York State Medicaid Fraud Unit in the Attorney General's Office—which Jerry M. Solomon, it's regional director, labeled as "a white collar law enforcement agency established under federal legislation"—to review complaints of abuse and neglect at facilities receiving Medicare or Medicaid funds. The MFCU must then either act upon those complaints or refer them to other state agencies for action. NYS Public Health Law, Section 2803-d, also requires the NYS Department of Health to investigate any allegations of patient abuse. Thus, a Memorandum of Understanding (MOU) was drawn up between the MFCU and DOH, which dictated how abuse, mistreatment, or neglect investigations were to be coordinated between the two agencies.

Under the MOU, DOH was responsible to immediately notify MFCU of any complaint or discovery of alleged physical abuse, mistreatment, or neglect. This was called a "340" referral. Solomon testified that when there are allegations of abuse or neglect, the protocol is that DOH is "obligated" to report that "immediately" to his office. Likewise, Rubin testified, "By virtue of that memorandum of understanding we called Solomon's office immediately to share the information we had" regarding any "complaint received that had to do with the abuse or neglect of a nursing home resident." Solomon stated that there is an obligation to report even a "possibility of allegation of patient neglect" because, although the DOH has primary investigative responsibilities, the "mission" of the MFCU is to investigate and prosecute patient abuse. If the case is not considered "egregious enough" to handle criminally, MFCU will refer it back to DOH for "administrative action."

According to the MOU, DOH was to forbear any investigation of its own until the MFCU advised it in writing when such a forbearance could cease. If the matter was referred back to DOH, DOH was to send any resulting statement of charges (SOC), ALJ report, and final order to the MFCU. Solomon stated that "in the normal course of events" there is one investigation at a time, with the MFCU proceeding first." If immediate jeopardy (IJ) is involved, DOH might be in the facility at the same time, "doing whatever they do to ensure the patient's safety."

In the case of Beechwood, no citation of neglect accompanied the survey results. While there was some internal discussion at DOH about trying to build a case for neglect, such as Gray writing on April 15 that "A patient neglect complaint was investigated by the WRO regarding neglect at Beechwood," or Rich writing on April 16 a notation to "consider neglect" of care against our director of nursing (DON), or Shea asking in a note on May 11, "Can we make a direct connection on neglect?" the MFCU never received a referral regarding neglect at Beechwood, a step required by regulations and protocol in any allegation of neglect.

On May 26, Altone wondered whether any nurse had been referred to the MFCU for a 340 (neglect) investigation. None was. Likewise, the statements of deficiency (SODs) did not identify or make the case for any neglect. The term "neglect" appears nowhere in the SODs. On April 29, Daniel (at HCFA) told Baker that if there was an intention to allege neglect on the SOD, no such allegation was clear. What had been cited was F224, a lack of policies or procedures to prevent neglect or abuse. (F223 was the neglect and abuse deficiency tag.)

By introducing neglect into the picture, even without evidence, the ALJ made it a basis for future investigations or actions. In his decision (p.59), he stated, "Proof that a nurse failed to exercise the care that a reasonably prudent nurse would exercise under the circumstances is sufficient to sustain a finding of negligence in a licensing misconduct proceeding" and then concluded (p. 66) that the "residents were neglected by Beechwood in several significant aspects of care." Yet nowhere in the SOD, SOC, hearing transcript, or *even in his own decision* is a *specific* nurse or aide cited for any *specific* act that would constitute neglect. In fact, the ALJ (p. 91) jaw-droppingly contradicted himself in stating, "I believe that the care given by many of the nurses who testified was generally good care, and that they themselves were concerned, caring individuals with the best of intentions." He then went on (p. 92) to imply that these "caring individuals" might not have documented their actions properly, so that others somehow were disabled from providing adequate care or may have tolerated negligent acts by others—who, of course, remain unnamed. The whole thing is wildly hypothetical and, at that, highly improbable.

Another issue is "egregious neglect," on which the ALJ does not have legal authority to rule. Egregious levels of neglect constitute crimes that must be prosecuted by the MFCU against specific individuals. Reaching a verdict of guilt in a case of egregious neglect requires meeting a standard of proof that is beyond a reasonable doubt. Raising egregious neglect in an administrative procedure was an improper attempt by DOH to influence other proceedings while avoiding its own legal duty.

## REGARDING MEDICARE FRAUD

First, some background. The MFCU is responsible for fraud investigations in the Medicaid and Medicare programs. Solomon testified that in April 1999, his office had decided to "look at nursing homes in general for possible fraud cases for not supplying services. Every region was looking to find someone to look at it." There is plenty of evidence that DOH was pursuing this interest with MFCU, specifically in regard to Beechwood as the IJ situation was being concocted. In his deposition, Solomon stated, however, that "When [Beechwood] was put in immediate jeopardy [in April 1999], I thought that would be a good home to take a look at, but I wanted to wait for the DOH proceeding to play out. ..."

[because I] was looking at this solely as a Medicaid fraud case, not as a patient abuse case."

On April 14, 1998, a year before the surveyors raided Beechwood, Francis recorded "Meet[ing] with S.R. and Jerry Solomon re: Beechwood. 3 hrs." In response to our statement of facts in the 1983 case, DOH admitted that Rubin, Carlo, and Baker were involved in seeking advice from Solomon on using their investigations as a basis for civil and criminal fraud prosecutions, and Carlo admits her involvement in her interrogatory. Carlo notes on April 17, 1999, "Sandy called re: Gerry Solomon—fraud for failure to deliver care." Two days later, on April 19. Baker noted a discussion with Carlo: "Sandy/Jerry Solomon— re: DAG getting involved for Medicaid reimbursement when services were not provided. ie. - SQC – IJ [substandard quality of care—immediate jeopardy]. On April 21, Carlo wrote, "Solomon's staff will be there? OSP part of the process." The next day, Carlo, Baker, and Rubin had a morning meeting in Solomon's office. Carlo noted, "Directive from NY (&) Md fraud unit across country, make case with substandard facilities and take back $."

In deposition testimony, Solomon stated that he recalled one meeting in "early April" where he was told that Beechwood "[was] going to be placed in immediate jeopardy. I asked to receive a call when it happened, and I believe someone called me to let me know." In response to our statement of facts in the 1983 case, DOH admitted that Baker was to keep Solomon informed, and Solomon testified that he did get a call from DOH staff inquiring about "escorting" them to the exit conference. As Baker recorded in a memo on June 3, 1999, "Jerry Solomon would like to meet again, possibly on Monday," regarding their project and facilities that might qualify for investigation related to Medicaid fraud. "Beechwood comes to mind immediately." On June 14, Solomon and Neil Davis (of the MFCU) attended the final survey exit conference. Solomon stated that besides being kept informed of what was happening with the DOH investigation, he asked to be kept informed of the hearing, and he did attend. Clearly the DOH wanted to ensure that this fraud investigation took place, and—yet again—it was the ALJ who became the vehicle that made this happen. Solomon testified that he "got the transcript and read the transcript before opening the investigation," but he also had the ALJ decision in his Beechwood file.

The ALJ had no authority or knowledge in this area—Medicare fraud and egregious neglect—and had no evidence in the record to support pronouncements about unreimbursed care or insufficient staffing. But he made the pronouncements just the same.

With regard to unreimbursed care: I made statements in the course of my testimony about trying to get nurses to understand how busy patient physicians are and not to annoy them with trivial matters. The ALJ (p. 63) pounced on my brief statements in my recorded testimony and, without any other evidence in the record, turned them into proof of my refusal to supply unreimbursed medical care. "In my opinion," he stated (p. 64), "Beechwood actions ... are intertwined with reimbursement policies of Medicare. Beechwood nurses are prevented from calling physicians because there will be no Medicare reimbursements. The focus from Beechwood's administrator ... is to maximize Medicare and insurance reimbursements and not the necessary care and treatment of its residents."

A refusal to supply care because of reimbursement concerns could amount to Medicaid/Medicare fraud, and the ALJ intended his statements to lead to such an investigation. And it did.

With regard to Insufficient Staffing: The ALJ (p. 63) twisted my testimony about efficient use of staff to mean that "Beechwood does not have sufficient nursing staff ... because they are not getting sufficient reimbursements and/or want to maximize revenues." This pronouncement was made without a shred of evidence in the record. In fact, Rich testified that staffing was not an issue at Beechwood, and Baker testified that nursing or aide shortages were not cited.

But short staffing would also amount to Medicaid/Medicare fraud, and the ALJ intended his statements to lead to such an investigation. They did.

## ALJ COMMENTS ABOUT THE PLAN OF CORRECTION (POC)

Toward the end of the hearing, the ALJ, who had earlier demonstrated a complete absence of knowledge about what a POC or DPOC was, stated that POC compliance was an important element to consider regarding the remedy being sought, and requested testimony from DOH regarding the issue. DOH obliged by producing Mary Jane Proschel, the Rochester DOH Quality Assurance Coordinator who had earlier testified that she and others had used the typical POC review process. She now went on to describe why the POCs were rejected. In his report, the ALJ determined Proschel to be a credible witness with "exact and reliable" testimony and relied on her testimony to find against Beechwood, even though he (p. 91) questioned why Proschel and others did not communicate perceived POC problems to Beechwood when it requested such information.

As will be shown later, there is no evidence supporting Proschel's testimony about her review of the POCs and the reasons for their rejection, but even her testimony did not give the ALJ (Decision, p. 90) the basis for making such statements as "the POCs were a denial of events, attacks on the messengers, and a barrage of irrelevant or inconsequential information." In making such statements, he ignored or deliberately disregarded Proschel's testimony that the DPOC response was "considered to be within reason." It is beyond all logic to claim that the DPOC response was within reason, and yet the POC itself is completely unacceptable. The ALJ also ignored or disregarded Proschel's testimony that if a problem cited is corrected, the POC does not matter. In this case, the April survey cited (incorrectly) IJ but no IJ was found in May. SQC was cited (incorrectly) in May but none in June. The POC did not matter, a fact to which Proschel herself had testified.

The ALJ decision also cited lack of correction, stating (decision p. 90) that "Perhaps more serious than the inadequate POCs was the fact that monitoring visits revealed that needed changes had not been made to correct deficiencies cited." Yet again, he ignored or disregarded the testimony of Baker, Rich, and Francis, all of which revealed that the IJ should not even have been cited in April. He ignored or disregarded Baker's testimony that Beechwood had put systems in place, including systems to monitor, and that we were submitting the reports requested. He ignored or disregarded Proschel's testimony that the DPOC response was "considered to be within reason." And he ignored or disregarded the fact that, according to DOH's own claims on the statements of deficiency (SODs), the IJ alleged in April was no longer present in May, and the substandard quality of care (SQC) alleged in May was no longer there in June.

## DOH WITNESSES WERE CREDIBLE; BEECHWOOD'S WERE NOT

In his June 16, 1999 decision denying Beechwood's injunction request seeking to avert closure, Judge David Larimer stated, "Surely, the bias and animus of those bringing the charges would always be a matter of defense and could be raised appropriately in these state proceedings." He saw "no basis why these factual matters [i.e., retaliation] [could] not be raise[d] in the state proceedings."

Yet, on June 24, 1999, the second day of the hearing, when Beechwood did raise the bias issue, Bureau of Administrative Hearings director Russel Altone objected, stating that the defendants could not be questioned about these matters since the AG represented them in the other case. The ALJ looked at Judge Larimer's decision but then stated that he was "not inclined" to go there. Nevertheless, despite his limiting Beechwood's ability to explore bias on the part of those making the accusations, the ALJ decided to rule on credibility of the witnesses.

A minor triumph for justice? Please ...

As was to be expected from a DOH employee employed to judge his employer, the ALJ (p. 55) found that all the DOH witnesses were credible—and, conversely, all of Beechwood's were not. He generally pronounced DOH witnesses confident, knowledgeable, forthright, reliable, unshakeable, sure of the process and team concept, exact, and reliable. I would have to agree that they were well-prepared and confident. Who couldn't be, given the protections they enjoyed, including the rule against discovery and the inability to question as to bias? Yet, to crown the DOH witnesses with haloes of credibility, the ALJ had to ignore or disregard glaring problems in their testimony. I have already cited many. Add to them the following:

1. Baker testified that "In April, the IJ determination/situation was based on closed records (discharged patients)" yet had earlier testified that "we have to have the evidence of jeopardy at that moment ... one of the residents to whom this IJ applied must be present in the facility at that time." Rich also testified that IJ cannot exist when the resident has been discharged. Furthermore, Baker and Francis both testified that the IJ was lifted in May because they did not find any *current* residents in IJ.

2. Four of the six patients about whom Dr. Oskvig testified—testimony the ALJ (p. 65) found mostly to reinforce the testimony of DOH witnesses— were those Baker had inappropriately labeled as being in IJ (Residents #1, #3, #6, and #7).

3. On May 10, Baker wrote, "After consultation with Sharon Carlo [about the results of monitoring visits] ... we could not extend the [POC] due date because the residents were still in immediate jeopardy." Nevertheless, she admitted at the hearing that "No, we did not" find any residents experiencing IJ as a result of the monitoring visits."

4. Baker testified that she was not aware that revocation was an objective as of May 12, even though, on April 29, Rubin had copied her on his note to Laura Leeds, which read, "Laura, I think we may well be in a situation where

we need to revoke. On May 10 Baker wrote, "We will begin to copy all materials related to this termination to send to Albany for a statement of charges," and on May 11, 1999 there was a major telephone conference between program and legal officials at DOH and HCFA, which Baker attended. The substance of this conference included discussion of beginning revocation proceedings after May 14. Arlene Gray, in Laura Leeds's Albany Office of Continuing Care, also testified "yes, it is true" that, as of May 11, plans were in place for revocation.

5. Baker testified that it was "absolutely not" their plan to terminate Beechwood as of May 12, even though on May 10 she had written "After speaking with Arlene Gray, the immediate plan [is for a] termination date of May 15, 1999," and in the May 11 meeting, which Baker attended, the discussion focused on the expectation of termination.

But what of Beechwood's witnesses?

The ALJ (p. 56) stated that they all were biased by employment, licensure, and financial "personal interests." In this, not only did the ALJ reveal his own bias based on his employment and personal financial interest, but failed to take into account that all of the testimony by Beechwood witnesses came on or after July 16, 1999, the date the facility was closed. Except for Donna Richardson, our Director of Nursing (DON), the witnesses had no ties with the business any longer, and no one expected Beechwood to be back in business any time soon. There were also no perceived licensing concerns, since none of the witnesses believed they had done anything wrong and none of them was personally named by DOH in any of the charges. Finally, in stark contrast to the DOH witnesses, Beechwood's witnesses had much to fear. Unshielded by the provisions of administrative law, they could be prosecuted for perjury. If anything, it was the DOH witnesses who had employment and financial interests at stake, motivating them to toe the company line. In fact, many of them later received recognition awards and promotions for their efforts in destroying Beechwood Restorative Care Center.

## ATTACKS ON ME

And then there was me, the epicenter of the Department of Health's use of the nuclear option. At the core of the entire proceeding was the motive of personal retribution. I was the primary target. Everything and everyone else—staff, patients, patients' families, an innovative health care business, and the Rochester community—were just so much collateral damage.

The statements about me simply continued the personal attack the ALJ had commenced in discussing Charge #13, regarding Beechwood administration, the alleged unwillingness to produce acceptable plans of correction (POCs), and so on. ALJ Marc Zylberberg stated conclusively that I was not a health care professional, as demonstrated by how I ran the facility, that my primary focus was monetary and not resident care.

## OVERKILL: NOTHING WAS RIGHT AT BEECHWOOD

In any grade-B horror movie, the monster cannot simply be killed. It must be killed dead: overkilled. The motive of overkill is blatant in the ALJ decision. Its purpose was not only to present a case but to button it up against appeal. Beechwood was portrayed as a facility that could do nothing right (pp. 58-66).

To read—even to skim—the findings, anyone would wonder how on earth Beechwood ever functioned all these years, even holding the national spotlight for excellence and innovation in restorative care. The ALJ painted a picture of nurses empowered by administration to practice beyond their legal scope of practice, no communications with physicians, physicians improperly writing standing orders, inadequate assessments, care plans that lacked individualization, nurses not documenting the care given, short staffing, lack of preparedness for the rehab population being served, and on and on. The result of these atrocities? Falls, pressure sores, improper administration of medications and oxygen, physicians unaware of changes in the condition of their patients, and on and on and on.

The ALJ stated (pg. 62) that whether there was actual harm involved or not does not matter. Perceived danger is just as important. Perhaps. Yet the total absence of actual harm surely indicates that the perceived danger has been grossly overestimated, especially given the scope and severity of the problems alleged at Beechwood.

The fact is that the DOH officials could—and did—paint the picture any way they wanted to. They could—and did—shut down a facility without a hearing and with such authority that the judicial courts established by the Constitution would be extremely hesitant to intervene.

Let's look at the ALJ's conclusions, topic by topic.

### Regarding the patient care issues:

"The Department has proven by a preponderance of the evidence that

Beechwood has committed multiple and serious violations … forming a pattern of inadequate care to its residents" (p. 92).

*Regarding Leeds's public statement that Beechwood was closed "for all the wrong reasons":*

"I find nothing contained therein to have any effect on my report and recommendations. Ironically, some of the comments of Ms. Leeds are consistent with my observations, findings and conclusions. As I indicate in my discussion below, Beechwood's permanent longtime employees, who testified at this proceeding, seemed to be very caring. Unfortunately, the administration chose not to cooperate … refused to remedy the deficiencies … submit appropriate plans of correction … [and] exacerbate and escalate the situation" (p. 4).

*Regarding the 40 emails submitted at the end of the hearing:*

"I found no evidence of a conspiracy between the State and the Federal governments against Beechwood or Mr. Chambery. Similarly, there was no conspiracy between the supervisors or any other Health Department employees against Beechwood or Mr. Chambery. Whatever hostility existed appeared to me to be coming more from Mr. Chambery rather than from Department employees" (p. 92).

"Beechwood's claims of a conspiracy against it and/or Mr. Chambery [were a] total, complete, and ridiculous fabrication without a shred of evidence or support" (p. 55).

## WITHOUT A SHRED OF EVIDENCE?

In its 2006 decision in our federal civil rights suit, a three judge panel at the Second Circuit U.S. Court of Appeals unanimously disagreed with ALJ Marc Zylberberg's finding that our claims of a conspiracy were without a shred of evidence. More important than this, I believe that any unbiased reader would question the deleted emails that we submitted for the record at the end of the DOH hearing. Indeed, Zylberberg himself had stated, off-the-record, that he felt Beechwood was significantly refuting allegations being made by DOH. Rubin himself confirmed that it was "painfully obvious" that the ALJ was being "persuaded" by Beechwood's defense.

The truth? ALJ Zylberberg was doing just what Altone had wanted him to do if we put forth a claim of retaliation. Well aware of the deference the judicial courts give the agencies under administrative law principles, Zylberberg simply went about buttoning up DOH's position in anticipation of an appeal.

ALJ Zylberberg made a blatantly political statement on behalf of his employer, the New York State Department of Health: "I conclude that the sanction of revocation is warranted to protect the public, to ensure the health and well-being of the community's nursing home population, and to deter future misconduct. *This sanction will send a clear message to Respondent and the medical community* that there can be no tolerance for such resident treatment and failure to address and correct deficiencies" (p. 96; emphasis added). He knew where his loyalties lay. He knew that the role he played had been written for him by the Department that he served. Justice had no part in this drama.

# PART II

# Heart of Darkness: 2000-2004

# CHAPTER 8

# The Strategy: Live to Fight another Day

Nursing homes receive negative survey results from time to time. When that happens, it is up to the individual facility to make it right. Termination of a facility at the command of the state, however, is vanishingly rare, especially when the termination takes place at lightning speed and in the absence of any IJ, SQC, or history of poor surveys. In fact, a termination preceded by a state hearing of the kind to which Beechwood was subjected was literally unheard of. It had never happened before. Such a demonstration of arbitrary power focused on the revocation of an operating license and the ruin of a business should have rallied the healthcare industry in general and the nursing home sector in particular. We were shuttered while the hearing was ongoing and before we even had a chance to refute a single charge. Trashed along with Beechwood was the Constitution and the civil liberties it protected.

Truly, the ground of law and justice had shifted. If Beechwood could be targeted and destroyed, any regulated healthcare enterprise was at risk. Yet the silence from the industry was deafening.

The display of boundless DOH authority terrified the other operators. Instead of banding together to condemn the actions being taken, they climbed all over one another in an effort to "cooperate" with the Department of Health. In part, they acted from fear, hoping that their abject display of obedience would appease the regulators. In part, they were eager to exploit the situation. Beechwood Restorative Center was a formidable competitor in western New York.

Our competition, frankly, would not miss us.

Indeed, DOH had been covertly approaching Beechwood's competitors about their possible interest in being a receiver before we had any idea that revocation of our operating certificate was being contemplated. Department personnel made overtures after the April 15, 1999 survey but before the first revisit to assess compliance—and, of course, without approaching us about voluntarily agreeing to a receiver.

I guess I should not have been surprised, let alone shocked. Operators generally try to stay on the good side of regulators so that surveys go easier or they are in line for other favors—such as lucrative receiverships. With bed allocations limited by the certificate-of-need (CON) process, operators often try to expand operations by getting appointed as temporary receivers for troubled facilities in the hope of turning those operations around with limited financial exposure, thereby positioning themselves to eventually take over as permanent operator. As early as May 13, 1999, as deputy director of the DOH Office of Continuing Care Laura Leeds was still trying to "make the case," Sandy Rubin, acting director of the DOH Western Region, was already recommending two possible receiver candidates. On June 3, 1999, just before serving the notice of hearing, Sharon Carlo, Regional Director of Continuing Care, noted others who could be contacted about interest in being receivers. Later, after it had been announced that patients would have to move, the daughter of a Beechwood resident told one of our social workers that, while she was inquiring about a possible transfer to another facility, the administrator there bragged about being at the top of the receivership list for Beechwood. The candidate actually chosen was from Buffalo, and according to Carlo, personally approached and chosen by Leeds.

## OPPORTUNITY VERSUS PRINCIPLE

During the hearing, and after failing to get a court order for a caretaker, DOH attorney David Abel was actively engaged in discussions with competitors interested in acquiring Beechwood's beds. On July 15, 1999, a physician who was a witness for Beechwood sat in the lobby waiting to testify. He later made an affidavit concerning statements he overheard Abel making during a phone conversation. Abel stated that someone in Rochester desired 30 beds, but all 80 beds had to go as a package. Another party wanted 80 beds but wanted to transfer them to Buffalo. Abel did not think that was feasible because it would leave an empty building without a CON, which would make the building very difficult to sell.

Eager to please DOH and fill empty beds, competitors accommodated DOH and accepted the transfer of Beechwood's residents even though they knew that it would lead to significant transfer trauma. I was able to learn what happened to thirty of our transferred residents from former Beechwood staff members who had taken it upon themselves to visit these patients and from family members who would call me. Within the first few weeks after transfer, 23% had died; 13% suffered marked deterioration in activities of daily living (ADLs); 44% exhibited noticeable deterioration in behaviors, including confusion and diminishment of ADLs; 17% were doing okay; and 3% actually seemed to be doing better.

On August 27, 1999, Rubin wrote to Bureau of Administrative Hearings director Russel Altone that he had "received a copy of a letter addressed to Sue Kelly from the niece of a Beechwood NH resident," who stated that "Today, Aug. 9, my uncle died in a nursing home that was not his home. Thanks to the Dept of Health & Human Services, my uncle died because he was *forced by you* to leave his caring home to live with strangers. At 97 he was not able to adjust ...." Transfer trauma is real, significant, and devastating to the health of frail elderly people. DOH, not Beechwood, was creating immediate jeopardy to the lives of these individuals.

Even before the ALJ's decision was signed, other competitors requested that DOH not allow Beechwood's CON to be transferred, thereby willfully advocating for the destruction of our assets, which would better their own market position. On August 2, 1999, for example, Linda Underhill from the Senior Health Alliance (Jewish Home, Friendly Home, St. Ann's Home, St. John's Home, and the Episcopal Church Home) wrote a letter to Robert Barnett, director of the DOH Office of Continuing Care (with copies to Rubin, Leeds, Whalen, Novello, Carl Young, and Garth Brokaw, and a blind copy to Carlo): "We recommend the NYS DOH take no action to redeploy these beds ... [given] our situation locally with excess bed capacity.... The pain of closure has already occurred ... why create the pain of closure, unnecessarily again in the future." On September 3, 1999, Garth Brokaw of the Fairport Baptist Home and representing the Rochester Area Association of Homes and Services for the Aging (RAHSA), wrote DOH a letter recommending "no action to redeploy [Beechwood's] beds ... Our situation locally is one of excess bed capacity ... We recommend that New York State take these beds offline permanently ... since the residents were able to be placed into the existing community capacity with minimal problems. Leeds responded to Brokaw on November 3, 1999: "I understand the concerns of your organization in regard to this situation and *want to assure you* that the Department of Health will make every effort to take the needs of the community into consideration" (emphasis added).

## STATE ASSOCIATION OFFICIALS KNEW THAT DOH ACTIONS WERE RETALIATORY

On March 30, 1998, during a phone conversation about a novel short-term admission agreement that I was developing, attorney Sara Birn at the Albany law firm of O'Connell and Aronowitz, which did work for the New York State Health Facilities Association (NYSHFA), stated that she knew DOH officials were upset with me, and that a meeting must be arranged and a truce negotiated. I shrugged it off at the time, and went back to the business at hand. But her statement stayed with me. Later, in a conversation on September 17, 1999, Ed Stafford, the Executive Director of NYSHFA, verified with me that (as he told others) Laura Leeds called him in advance of actions that were to be taken against Beechwood and requested that the association not intervene. On October 18 of that year, after the ALJ hearing decision, Stafford wrote a letter to New York Health Commissioner Novello stating that Beechwood "has been a member of NYSHFA for several decades. We have always known it to be a provider of excellent care with a long-standing reputation for quality and dedication to its patients / residents. We are, therefore, both shocked and extremely concerned about the drastic action recommended. ... we would appreciate it if the Department could defer taking any final action until after we have had an opportunity to review Judge Zylberberg's Report. There are several matters of concern that have been raised."

On November 18, attorney Neil Murray of O'Connell and Aronowitz and Stafford persuaded DOH to propose suspension of our operating certificate instead of revocation. According to DOH, this would allow transfer and sale of the empty facility for use as a nursing home and at least allow Beechwood to recover a few million dollars from the destroyed assets. DOH was also to provide an "expedited (CON) review" for this process. However, in exchange for allowing this residual value to be realized from the physical assets, DOH demanded my agreement never to operate or have any connection with any healthcare facility in New York State, surrender my administrator license, discontinue any federal civil rights actions, release DOH officials from any liability for actions taken, pay a fine, stipulate never to challenge the agreement, and acknowledge DOH's right to pursue any and all sanctions or remedies against any individual employed by or practicing in association with the facility. On November 26, Murray called to tell me that "Russ Altone is pushing for decision by Monday." Neil's position was that he didn't like the terms but advocated taking the offer. He then decided to add a little pressure of his own, stating that if Beechwood didn't accept the agreement, he didn't know what other support NYSHFA could provide. On that same day, Altone wrote Greenberg to update him on the "general status of discussions regarding the settlement, … Murray has described the DOH offer to the Chamberys as a 'tough sell' but has been careful not to appear to be 'negotiating' and has said nothing which implies that our offer is anything but fair and reasonable."

On January 24, 2000, the NYSHFA Legal Action Committee Members voted unanimously to allocate $25,000 to help fund an Article 78, which is a state court appeal of administrative actions. The committee members voiced "outrage," stating that the e-mails obtained in the last couple days of the hearing were very clear evidence of targeting. They also wanted to support the federal civil rights case that Beechwood was contemplating (Chapter 10). But Murray warned them against putting NYSHFA's imprimatur on any case that named DOH officials, especially with a civil rights action, because it would damage the association's relations with DOH.

## Politics trumped principle

On January 31, 2000, attorney Murray wrote a member of NYSHFA to explain why the Legal Action Committee chose not to support a civil rights action. He stated that, legally, more than circumstantial evidence is needed to overcome the qualified immunity that accompanies state actors. He fumbled along, noting that "it is true here Beechwood has something more than circumstantial evidence … which arguably would establish some animus … But even malice, by itself, is insufficient … facing the rulings on the patient care issues … For all the foregoing reasons, I do not think that a so-called 1983 action is the best way to proceed." But then he came to the main point: "I also question the wisdom of

NYSHFA's involvement, direct or indirect, in any 1983 action. *No matter how you slice it, once our association becomes involved in any lawsuit supporting the recovery of monetary damages against specified state officials, that compromises the Association in a wide range of other matters"* (emphasis added).

Murray followed this message with a fax to Beechwood on February 28, 2000, in which he got even more specific: "NYSHFA cannot support the (1983) petition in its present form with personal references to Laura Leeds. While we understand the Petitioner's concerns, NYSHFA must serve its entire membership. Ms. Leeds is an important official with whom we deal with on virtually a daily basis. We do not think it is essential to the Petition to specifically name her in the pleadings or to characterize certain of her actions in the manner contained in the Petition. See e.g., Paragraph 34. We believe the Petition can be amended, without leave of the Court to delete specific references to her without compromising its integrity." In an earlier telephone call, he also reminded our attorney, Kevin Cooman, that the lack of NYSHFA's support would jeopardize any support from the American Health Care Association (AHCA), the national association.

Beechwood replied the next day, February 29: "We cannot accept your suggestion. In our judgment, the specificity of Beechwood's allegations involving Ms. Leeds are a necessary part of our claim … firmly anchored in objective facts … Her improper motives and directives (along with Sandy Rubin's) were the reason for the precipitous actions taken … While we understand that you and other Association representatives may work with Ms. Leeds frequently on other matters, this does not justify her conduct toward Beechwood, or lessen the imperative for the Association to support Beechwood's petition … It would be most unfortunate if the Association and its membership chose to ignore Beechwood's plight (which could just as easily be their own), in the interest of 'accommodating' the relationship with Ms. Leeds. We believe NYSHFA best 'serves its entire membership' by insisting that DOH officials act with propriety and in accordance with the rule of law."

On March 2, Beechwood received a letter from the NYSHFA Executive Committee: "On Wednesday, March 1, 2000, NYSHFA's Executive Committee held a telephone conference to review its commitment to the Article 78 proceeding … NYSHFA has previously committed to provide … $25,000, and to request comparable support from the American Health Care Association … Mr. Murray has also been authorized to file an amicus curiae brief … The telephone conference was called because of some concerns that the language in the draft ... might cause NYSHFA problems in terms of its relationship to officials in the central office of the Department of Health. ... Despite these concerns, the Executive Committee has decided to continue financial support of the (Article 78) litigation in an amount up to $25,000, and to seek support from AHCA. It has also instructed Neil to seek amicus status."

Murray sent a letter to Beechwood on May 16, outlining the issues NYSHFA would be addressing in an amicus brief for the Article 78 appeal. "First, NYSHFA is extremely concerned about the fairness of the administrative process. We do not believe that the Administrative Law Judge ought to be able to rule on questions of retaliation and retribution ... Second, NYSHFA is particularly concerned about the revocation of the operating certificate given the facts of this case and the ALJ's own findings that the deficiencies were 'correctable' and that 'the sole responsibility for the closure of the facility rests with its administrator' ... [W]e do not believe that that justifies shutting down the entire operation and transferring patients. There were a wide array of other remedies available ... Third, the Association is extremely concerned about the usurpation of the Public Health Council's authority with respect to establishment applications." The last issue regarded Greenberg's letter of February 2, in which he took the position that, absent a ruling by the Public Health Council, the CON had evaporated with the loss of the operating certificate and closure of the facility.

As we will discuss shortly, we ultimately dropped the Article 78 appeal over concerns that it would interfere with the civil rights case. The association was paying lip service regarding their concerns but, to preserve the association's own shortsighted self-interest, was unwilling to directly confront those responsible at DOH.

## PRESSING ON

Maybe you've seen some of those World War II newsreels of London neighborhoods leveled by the Nazi blitz. If you look past the debris and devastation, you see people going about their daily business. Why? Because they have to.

So it was with us, amid the destruction and legal maneuverings, we had to press onward. Beechwood had been closed, but business had not stopped. We had many obligations, much to deal with. We could not walk away as we might have if the business had been sold. Payrolls still had to be processed, employee benefits settled, and bills paid. The heat had to stay on, the building had to be maintained, and the mortgage paid. Equipment and supplies had to be inventoried and medical records carefully sorted out and properly stored. Running a healthcare facility involves complex financials and cost reports. These had to be done, audits had to be endured, and final settlements had to be made. Some of this work would require years, but we had a legal, moral, and ethical obligation to do it. Besides, my philosophy has always been to deal from a position of strength, especially when the other side thinks your position is weak. I was determined that we would remain financially viable, handle whatever was thrown our way, and then go on the offensive ourselves. The initial battles had been lost, and that was terrible. Nevertheless, I was determined that the ultimate battle would be on my terms and would end in vindication.

Thankfully, Beechwood had an extraordinarily dedicated staff, and those who were needed volunteered to stay. Gradually, as the number of tasks diminished and people found other suitable employment, some left, but whatever work remained unfinished, others picked up. By January 2000, only a couple of maintenance men, a bookkeeper, and the assistant administrator were left. My wife, my mother, and my sister augmented this skeleton crew in sorting and inventorying records and equipment. The last to go was my assistant administrator and all-around righthand guy, Paul Kesselring, who had been with Beechwood since 1974. He stayed on until September 2000. There was still a mountain of maintenance, , accounting, and administrative chores left to do, along with the endless legal matters. Legal battles as well as the exercise of outright tyranny, are first and last, wars of attrition. One side counts on the other wearing down until it can no longer offer battle. The DOH officials were counting on my being worked into submission. Fortunately, my brother Dale came to help out in April 2000. He could not have known it at the time, but he would be helping to keep me afloat for another twelve years. He did not falter or fail.

If I had any hope of coming out victorious at the other end of this ordeal, I had to uncover the story, the truth, behind what happened. I began this task as soon as the hearing concluded, beginning with a meticulous review of every scribble on every shred of paper in the boxes of subpoenaed documents we had received during the hearing, including printouts of the emails DOH had deleted.

These documents, the hearing testimony about involvement by Western Region DOH acting director Sanford Rubin and Office of Continuing Care deputy director Laura Leeds, and some affidavits filed by the defendants in response to our request for an injunction provided the starting point. But an initial three-week run-through of this material led me to realize that I needed much more documentation. Since we did not have any legal standing in court to allow us access to court-ordered discovery, I decided to make maximum use of the Freedom of Information statutes and file FOI requests. The 1966 Freedom of Information Act is the basis for various other federal (FOIA) and state (FOIL) statutes requiring full or partial disclosure of previously unreleased documents controlled by the federal government and, under various state laws, state-controlled documents. It is impossible to overstate the crucial role that FOI statutes played in obtaining the information necessary to build our case, eventually allowing us to create a very efficient and finely tuned discovery process.

Even before the hearing decision in October 1999, I had sent two FOI letters with eleven different requests for documents. I did not know it at the time, but Russel Altone was just as surprised as our own counsel, Kevin Cooman, that I decided to use the FOI forum to obtain information. Altone responded by doing all in his power to control and delay response to my requests. No matter. I continued to do the hard work of determining what information I needed and issuing FOI requests accordingly. When documents were forthcoming, I had the daunting task of sorting through, deciphering, and cataloging them, all the while building spreadsheets and other documents needed to maintain control of the information I had acquired.

In 2000, the primary instrument for transmitting legal documents was the fax machine, and mine became a very busy piece of equipment. It was not unusual for legal documents to be coming in and going out pretty much back-to-back. I was out of business, but I had never been busier than I was during the first few months of 2000. In January of 2000, we were still dealing with the ramifications of the order to revoke our operating license, including the legalities of what this meant for our certificate of need (CON), which was all-important to selling a building that had been purpose-built as a healthcare facility. By the end of February, we had received the letter from the director of the DOH Division of Legal Affairs, Henry Greenberg, stating that there was effectively no CON to transfer and had filed the Article 78 appeal regarding the DOH revocation of its operating certificate and the CON. We had also started the administrative level appeal regarding the Medicare/Medicaid program termination.

By early March I had drafted the original version of "The Story," a narrative laying out what I had pieced together about the DOH offensive as of this early date, and we were beginning the enormous job of sorting Beechwood medical, financial, and other business records for storage (or shredding), and were inventorying all moveable equipment and supplies. Later in the month, we received word from our former director of nursing, two other RN supervisors, and the medical director that DOH was pursuing licensing actions against them. This was followed on April 3 by the bombshell I had expected: our first of five grand jury subpoenas from the Medicaid Fraud Control Unit (MFCU), a division of the New York Attorney General's Office, and the beginning of a three-year criminal investigation into Beechwood and myself. Having destroyed a business, the DOH had escalated its attack into the criminal realm.

This frenetic existence lasted right up to the civil rights trial of 2012. My life was driven by legal meetings, motions, and court dates. The research, document review, and problem solving was extensive, and the tools needed to control it all were very sophisticated. Dealing with audits, cost reports, and issues with the physical plant only added to the burden. Working in a building with the heat turned down—in Western New York winters—added to the misery.

## MORTGAGE DEFAULT, EQUIPMENT AUCTION, AND PROPERTY ABANDONMENT

Finding a buyer for a building designed and built according to state mandated specifications but without the CON allowing it to be used for the purpose it had been built was a very tall order. By September 1, 2000, after trying unsuccessfully to find a buyer, we stopped paying on the mortgage, which soon went into default. The mortgage did not cover moveable equipment, so, on November 16, 2000, we auctioned it all off. The tedious, torturous effort to get everything ready for the auction fell mainly to my brother, sister, and mother, who also suffered with me the emotional devastation of seeing the pennies on the dollar we got for it all. The grand total received for the complete equipment and furnishings of a state-of-the-art care facility amounted to some $40,000.

After packing our financial and medical records into storage containers, we abandoned the building on November 22, 2000, and moved our remaining office functions to the headquarters of our former software company in Webster, New York. Although we had abandoned the nursing home property, we soon learned that we either had to assume responsibility for winterizing and maintain it or find ourselves in another legal battle. We opted to maintain it, a responsibility that landed mostly on my brother's shoulders. Even with his help, however, I was the one on call at night and would often field automated calls from the fire alarm system, having to respond without the benefit of electricity or tools. Usually, it was a spider tripping a detector. No big deal in and of itself, but yet another of the myriad annoyances that haunted my life. These events were punctuated by major physical plant crises, such as broken water pipes or flush valves failing due to inactivity. I had to call everyone available—all hands on deck—to address the problems of a building, once the source of a proud livelihood that benefitted an entire community, that now had become an unquiet corpse. It was not until April 22, 2002, that the building was finally legally transferred to the bank, freeing us at last of responsibility for its care.

### THE CONTINUING REGULATORY ONSLAUGHT

*Staff licensing actions.* On March 27, 2000, eleven months after the survey that started it all, a DOH letter went out to two Beechwood nurses, informing them that DOH was conducting an investigation into reports of neglect to a resident, and requesting that they provide their account of the alleged incidents. Sixteen months later, on July 24, 2001, DOH attorney Marie Shea sent a letter to both nurses, informing them that, based on her review of a recent investigative report concerning one patient and involving a six-day period in February 1999, "there is sufficient credible evidence that you have violated PHL 2803-d (patient abuse laws)." After another thirteen months, on September 9, 2002, another DOH attorney, David Abel, who had been involved with the agency hearing, followed up with Statements of Charges against the two nurses. Naturally, this whole affair and the long span of time through which it dragged caused extraordinary stress to these nurses. Neither of them—or their spouses—wanted to settle, but, on the sound advice of counsel and without admitting to the charges, the nurses each paid a $300 fine to put the matter to rest.

*Medicaid Fraud Control Unit (MFCU) criminal investigation.* On April 3, 2000, the MFCU issued a Grand Jury Subpoena for timecards, PRIs (patient assessment forms), staff schedules, payroll records, census, therapy records, and billing records from January 1995 to July 1999. The criminal investigation I had anticipated since Attorney General Solomon's appearance at the DOH hearing—and made all the more likely by the ALJ decision—had commenced. My business was gone. At stake now was my freedom and good name.

As the subpoena was directed at me as well as Beechwood, Kevin Cooman and Paul Barden would continue to represent Beechwood, and we found a criminal attorney, David Rothenberg, to represent me personally. On April 13, Rothenberg and Barden met with Solomon, who was heading up the investigation. He told them that the push was on from the U.S. Attorney in Philadelphia who was looking for a subject against whom to bring a case of Medicaid fraud. The New York DOH, he said, had handed it to him on a platter. But then, inexplicably, Solomon added that "nothing will come of it," and told the attorneys that I did not need a criminal attorney. Rothenberg commented that these remarks from Solomon were "amazing." Barden noted that Solomon seemed to be reluctant even to take the case, but warned that "the audit will be tough."

We were not aware of it at the time, but Solomon's peculiar remarks may have been the result of his organization's distrust of DOH, for as we discussed earlier, the Office of the Inspector General (OIG) and the MFCU were both currently investigating corruption at the highest levels of DOH, including Acting Commissioner of Health Dennis Whalen, Laura Leeds, and Director of the Division of Health Facility Planning Robert Murphy. If these DOH officials could abuse their authority by accepting gratuities and granting preferential treatment in return, they could just as easily abuse their authority to revoke a license. AG Solomon was well aware of Beechwood's reputation for exceptional quality. In a climate that warranted a corruption investigation, the DOH action against us must have seemed suspicious to him.

Whatever Solomon's doubts, on May 3, 2000, Beechwood received a second Subpoena, this one for 124 Medicaid charts and billing records going back to 1995. We were obliged to gather electronic records from a couple of different databases and merge them to create a separate database for the investigators. Fortunately, we had my brother, a master programmer, to do the needed work. For about five months, while the nursing home computer system was still operating, the investigators periodically descended upon the facility, spread themselves out in the physical therapy room with its two computers, and did their work. After we moved out of the facility, we gave them a disk they could use in their own offices.

Early in September 2000, Solomon requested a list of all employees, whom he began interviewing. One nurse reported to me that an investigator named Hinchey told her that he had to ask his boss "what happened here" because "everyone I talk to thinks the place was great." Hinchey told another nurse that it sounded like Beechwood was a "good place to work." He told both of them that he was getting tremendously hostile reactions from staff interviews over what DOH had already done and for continuing to investigate Brook Chambery.

On October 18, 2000, just after Leeds resigned from DOH as a result of the OIG investigation, Beechwood received a third subpoena for incident/accident reports, nurse manager and QA meetings, complaint logs, and nursing policies, and from February through March 2001, investigators interviewed former staff, mostly licensed practical nurses, regarding their documentation.

Solomon, on March 19, 2001, issued a subpoena to DOH for "all records and reports" relating to the activities at Beechwood Nursing Home from January 1, 1998 to July 31, 1999, and on April 20 of that year, he informed my attorney, David Rothenberg, that he had nothing on me and was issuing instructions to begin wrapping up the investigation. Still, in July 2001, numerous aides and temp staff were interviewed. Four temp staffing agencies were interviewed on July 18 and reported that they were "shocked" that DOH took the action that it did, that Beechwood was one of the finest homes in Rochester, and that some of their staff quit healthcare because of what happened to Beechwood. On August 1, lead investigator Neal Davis interviewed Paul Kesselring, volunteering to him that he was perplexed as to why the facility had been closed. Indeed, this ended up being the major theme of his interview questions. Beechwood attorney Paul Barden was also present, and his notes corroborate Kesselring's report that Davis was saying he was "perplexed" by the closure.

On August 3, 2001, Paul Barden spoke to Solomon, who told him that the New York City MFCU office was driving the investigation forward despite his efforts over the past eighteen months to wrap it up. New York City insisted that there *must* be something criminal in the matter. He reiterated to Barden that he had nothing on me except unsubstantiated allegations concerning the director of nursing's interference with getting physician orders.

Solomon met with Carlo and Francis on August 6, 2001 and on the same day issued a fourth subpoena to Beechwood, this time for the "Complete Medical Record" of 30 patients reviewed at the DOH hearing. It is significant that the MFCU asked for the complete record. They had already collected from DOH

Beechwood's plans of corrections (POCs) and rebuttal material, including physician statements. MFCU also had the hearing transcript and could therefore study Beechwood's defense. They could verify documents and facts from the hearing and study the whole medical record. They could read the testimony by staff and physicians, which they were continuing to verify with their own interviews. By looking at the "bigger picture," MFCU could easily determine that the DOH view of the care given at Beechwood was incredibly skewed and terribly wrong. They knew that this is what Beechwood was complaining about. They were seeing even more disturbing evidence than the ALJ originally had when he warned the DOH prosecutors about what they were doing.

In August, September, and October 2001, numerous families, patients and physicians were interviewed, and on October 16, 2001, Director of Nursing Donna Richardson was interviewed. She reported that, toward the end of the interview, an MFCU investigator asked "Didn't Brook realize that it was suicide to continue to fight the DOH?"

On October 25, Davis interviewed Kesselring again, with Barden present. Barden's notes show that Davis was still investigating the "closing." MFCU notes confirm the interest in how the "situation between DOH and Beechwood deteriorated to the point of closure," and the fact that the attorney general's office was "perplexed" by it. In November, the wife of Beechwood's medical director called to notify me that the attorney general would like to hear the story from "key players" regarding what happened at Beechwood. They had a "need to know." A fifth subpoena was issued to Beechwood on November 21 for admission and discharge records.

It was nearly a year later when, on October 11, 2002, Solomon once again told Beechwood defense attorneys that he wanted to drop the investigation into Chambery, but was having difficulty getting sign-off from the New York City office and might have to write a report justifying why he was recommending a case closure without any action being taken. Six days later, on October 17, Solomon announced that he was dropping the investigation. On December 5, Paul Barden called Solomon to check on progress of case closure. Solomon vented his frustration, explaining that despite his position and years of experience, his boss in the New York City office, Tom Staffa, would not take his word that there was nothing to this case and had asked for a very detailed and time consuming report as to the reasons for dropping it. On the hopeful side (as far as he was concerned), with Staffa set to retire shortly, he thought he could wait and deal with Staffa's boss, who was familiar with the case and might be more sympathetic to taking him at his word. Presumably, that was the case; for, on September 19, 2003, AG Solomon returned Beechwood's records.

*Administrator licensing actions.* On December 28, 1999 I formally requested that my administrator license be put on Inactive Status, and on August 12 of the following year, I sent a letter to DOH notifying them that I no longer desired to maintain the license in any manner and was relinquishing it. Nevertheless, three days later, DOH served notice of a hearing to revoke the license I had already surrendered. The notice also referred to my mother's license, which she had already relinquished by not keeping up with mandatory continuing education credits. She was now seventy-five, and her knees were still shaking uncontrollably as a result of the events of the past eighteen months.

The hearing was convened on September 19, 2000. Our initial defense was that the status of both licenses left no reason for a hearing or any formal action to revoke. The ALJ was persuaded by that argument, requested submission of papers on the subject, and adjourned the hearing. On January 31, 2001, the ALJ ruled that "Brook Chambery has validly surrendered his nursing home administrator license. Therefore, there is no jurisdictional basis … As a matter of law … action against Brook Chambery should be discontinued while this matter may go forward against Olive Chambery." Yet on February 21, 2002, the Board of Examiners, "in exercise of its discretionary powers … to decide that charges should be heard," overrode the ALJ's decision and put the hearing back in motion for both me and my mother. We requested, on November 24, 2003, an indefinite adjournment of the proceedings while other federal proceedings were going forward. The license hearing was never rescheduled.

## THE ABORTED ARTICLE 78

As provided for in Article 78 of the New York State Civil Practice Laws and Rules, an appeal of the outcome of an administrative hearing is made by filing what is known as an Article 78 proceeding at the appellate level of the state courts. In our case, the related issue of the taking of the Certificate of Need (CON) without any hearing was also of concern. So, both the ALJ hearing and the CON issue were bundled together and filed at the trial court level. The case was assigned to

Judge Francis A. Affronti, who had earlier handled the caretaker case. He, however, decided to have the entire case transferred to the appellate division.

As Judge David Larimer summarized in his Summary Judgment (SJ) Decision #1:

> On February 28, 2000 [Beechwood] filed an Article 78 petition in New York State Supreme Court, Monroe County, seeking, *inter alia,* a declaration that the DOH administrative proceeding, the ALJ's report, and the DOH's December 23 order were null and void, for a number of reasons, and requesting a stay of enforcement pending a determination of the Appellate Division. The petition alleged in part that "DOH's misconduct was in retaliation against and to penalize Petitioners for their exercise of constitutional rights in vigorously advocating for improvements in the nursing home industry and regulatory system over the last three years. ... On May 15, 2000, Justice Francis A. Affronti issued a decision finding that plaintiffs' petition "raise[d] a question relative to the sufficiency of the evidence at the [DOH] hearing ...," which required that the Article 78 proceeding be transferred to the appellate division. Following that ruling, however, the proceeding stalled, for through some unknown reason the proceeding never actually got transferred to the appellate division, and Beechwood had decided to abandon it. ... Plaintiffs candidly admit, however, that they had "no incentive to press the Article 78" proceeding (Plaintiff's Memorandum of Law at 71), so they simply ceased prosecuting it. That lack of incentive, plaintiffs state, arose partly from the fact that:
>
> 1. Beechwood had already been closed,
>
> 2. Damages are not available in an Article 78 proceeding,
>
> 3. There was concern that if the Article 78 proceeding was prosecuted to its conclusion, the state court's rulings on the issues presented in the Article 78 petition might be given collateral estoppel effect in any later actions initiated by plaintiffs, such the 1983.
>
> 4. The plaintiffs would not have had the same opportunities for discovery in the Article 78 proceeding as in the 1983 civil rights case.
>
> 5. An Article 78 proceeding would also not allow Beechwood to pursue the full range of constitutional claims that would be possible in a suit under Section 1983." (p. 9)

Larimer summarized Beechwood's complicated situation. Besides the typical appeal on the facts, we were also claiming misconduct due to retribution, which is a constitutional issue. Although constitutional issues could be addressed by the state court and we wanted to have the patient care issues addressed, we decided to abandon the case for the reasons Judge Larimer outlined. We understood that the chances of winning the patient care issues were very slim, given that, under the rules of administrative law, the record reviewed would be the ALJ decision and not the hearing record. In addition, the standard of review would be to uphold the ALJ decision unless found to be totally arbitrary or capricious, or unsupported by any evidence. Since the ALJ had also addressed the retribution issue, Beechwood could not take any chance on case law being established that would hinder its federal civil rights case, in which individuals could be sued, the record and evidence fully reviewed, and damages collected. So, we abandoned the Article 78, knowing that the ALJ's determinations on the patient care would stand unchallenged, and forged ahead with the federal administrative appeal on the patient care issues and a "1983" civil rights suit.

# CHAPTER 9

# Beechwood's Offensive Begins

FREEDOM OF INFORMATION

A s mentioned in Chapter 8, we lacked the legal standing to access court-ordered discovery, but I was familiar with another window into the facts surrounding the actions, behavior, mindset, and motives of the DOH and its officials. That window was the Freedom of Information (FOI) statutes at the federal and state level. My FOI strategy was to gain as much knowledge as possible, as quickly as possible. I needed to know everything I could about DOH, its organization, its staff, and policies and procedures on everything from survey and enforcement, to document handling and retention, to contractual arrangements with other state and federal agencies. I needed to know the players involved with our case, their roles, their job descriptions, employment history with DOH, and so on. I needed to be able to reconstruct where they were, what they were doing, and what reports they were writing during relevant time periods. I also needed to retrieve as many of the Beechwood specific records as possible, and before they were lost or destroyed. This included enforcement files containing decisions regarding sanctions, and authorizations, as well as survey reports, emails, worksheets, and timesheets. I intended to do the same with HCFA, to the extent necessary.

I also knew that after the DOH hearing, it might be quite a while before any court case alleging retribution and violation of civil rights could be filed. To survive any attempt by DOH to dismiss the case as frivolous, especially given the propensity of the courts to grant extravagant deference to the agencies, I needed to have substantial evidence just to get as far as discovery. So, I needed to move on FOI preemptively.

FOI is no magic bullet. The problems with using Freedom of Information requests are many. To begin with, requests must be very specifically targeted and carefully constructed to avoid early rejection and to hold up against appeal. Second, public information officers within the various agencies typically route the requests to the individuals responsible for whatever is being investigated. Thus, there is an inherent vested interest in limiting the level of response and the exemptions claimed. Information officers may also route requests through agency staff attorneys, who might then take the lead in coordinating responses, including bogus privilege claims on "sensitive matters." Third, there is a high probability that success in securing requested documents will require a court order. To succeed in such a court application, the plaintiff often needs previously acquired documentation, which helps demonstrate why current requests are well-grounded and thereby avoid agency requests for in-camera reviews by a judge who has limited knowledge of the matter, or its context. The requirement for existing documentation can introduce a chicken-and-egg dilemma. More-over, things may get very expensive very quickly. The alternative is surrendering to injustice and tyranny. That leaves little choice. You must make use of every opportunity to build your case for presentation to the court, or you may not survive a summary judgment, which will block you from a court-ordered dis-covery process.

My earliest FOI requests were to DOH and requested organization charts and policies and procedures on a huge array of subjects, job descriptions, and who filled these jobs over the relevant periods. Later, I requested employment and salary histories, civil service exams passed, certifications, on-the-job train-ing, work schedules, timecards, and notes on and reports of activities. I also took the emails we had received and leveraged them to get additional communica-tions and information about topics the emails touched on. When FOI responses weren't answered, I did not hesitate to turn to the courts to get orders for the requested items, or affidavits concerning why items might not exist, or to further provide explanation and clarification.

While mining for FOI documents, I became an ardent student of relevant state and federal laws, prior court decisions, and agency actions. This led to even more FOI requests for executive orders, adjudication plans, memorandums of understanding, and contracts controlling joint agency activities, Medicaid State

Plans, and information on other enforcement activities undertaken over the years. For instance:

State and Federal enforcement actions—fines, terminations, license suspensions, caretakers, and so on—taken against providers in the last thirty years

Investigations of DOH and reports regarding the conduct of DOH officials

Medicare law, preambles, rules and regulations, public comments on proposed regulations as well as agency answers and interpretations; State operations manuals (management and oversight of operations at the state level), federal surveyor training courses and content

The New York State Medicaid Plan, addendums, and federal approvals granted

MFCU underlying legislation, regulations, policies and procedures, joint initiatives, past activities, the memorandum of understanding (MOU) with DOH, and so on

State policies and procedures regarding retention of both electronic and physical business documents, including archiving policies

The "Beechwood file" contents from the Rochester, Buffalo, and Albany offices of DOH, the New York and Washington offices of HCFA, and Rochester office of the MFCU

Worksheets of surveyors and supervisors concerning findings, team decision making regarding deficiencies, documentation sent to central office and HCFA, and higher-level involvement and decision making regarding deficiencies and enforcement directions to be taken

Worksheets and decision making concerning HCFA concurrence with DOH recommendations on deficiencies, timetables, enforcement actions to be taken, and so on

Documentation made by state and federal employees concerning the transfer of patients to other facilities

Survey and quality stats (OSCAR) and federal cost report data from HCFA on all New York facilities to prove Beechwood's high standing from a statewide perspective

To my advantage was the fact that I already knew the FOI laws very well because I had made numerous FOI requests in the past. I also had plenty of experience with writing successful requests and appeals. As I mentioned earlier, I saw FOI requests as a way to get information quickly, before documents were destroyed. But I also wanted to put the agencies on notice that litigation was coming, and their documents had better be handled with care. We made extensive use of FOI requests until the Second Circuit Court of Appeals reversed Judge Larimer's District Court ruling in January of 2006, which finally allowed Beechwood to proceed with court-directed and court-supervised discovery. The bulk of the requests were to DOH. There were eighteen letters containing 108 specific requests before Beechwood filed its Civil Rights Complaint in April 2002. The information gleaned was indispensable to putting the case together and, later, in framing interrogatories and using depositions to maximum potential. There is nothing like being able to put documents in front of a deponent to elicit more definitive responses than "I don't recall." The idea was to cement positions for testimony in court. The defendants would be trapped by their own policies and testimony regarding how things should work, documents showing what they did regarding Beechwood, and their utter inability to justify their own actions.

The FOI actions also succeeded in putting DOH and HCFA on notice that documents must be preserved. Russel Altone stated that at some point after the hearing, when FOI requests "began coming to the division of legal affairs," and with the litigation pursued, "an effort was made to centralize" documents "either sent to the various attorneys involved in the case or generated by those attorneys" and that had "existed in other places in the state." These documents were retained in a multi-drawer locked file at the central office of BAH in Albany, but there was also another file cabinet in Rochester. Carmel Camp, a DOH secretary in Rochester, stated that, besides the formal survey material, much of the material in the Rochester DOH office file, including surveyor notes, came as a result of the FOI requests.

The information was obtained at significant cost. DOH virtually ignored our FOI requests. After eighteen months of stonewalling, Beechwood initiated court proceedings. A series of proceedings and three State Court orders (June 2001, September 2001, and June 2002) from Judge Evelyn Frazee produced the first 850 pages of documents and 26 affidavits from DOH officials. After demonstrating our willingness to use the courts to enforce our requests—and even sue to recoup legal fees—DOH became more responsive to future requests, which were contained in twenty-one letters containing seventy-seven items.

In October 2002, Beechwood filed suit against DOH for the legal fees necessary to enforce its FOI requests. This ended up being a three-year legal battle through all levels of the New York State courts and cost more than the damages we were trying to collect. In the end, the effort was not successful, even though it had the backing of major news organizations and their association. The case, *Beechwood Restorative Care Center v. Signor,* hung on the interpretation of the courts as to what the law meant by allowing fees to be collected for obtaining documents of "public interest." It was Beechwood's interpretation that its case had been highly publicized by DOH when it happened, and the public had a right to know what was in DOH files about the case.

Unfortunately, Judge Frazee (Supreme Court, Monroe County, March 17, 2003), five judges at the Appellate Division, (11 A.D.3d 987 (2004)), and seven judges at the Court of Appeals (5 N.Y.3d 435 (2005)) saw our FOI efforts mainly as a private effort to get documents for further private legal actions. But our actions were not in vain. A few months after New York's highest court, the Court of Appeals, rendered its decision on October 25, 2005, heavy lobbying by the news organizations resulted in the state legislature changing the law to eliminate the provision that the documents had to be of "public interest" before damages could be sought when an agency failed to provide them. On August 23, 2006, I received a letter from Robert Freeman, of the New York State Committee on Open Government: "I recognize that this may be too little and too late, but your efforts paved the way for positive change, and many should be grateful to you. I am."

## Relitigating patient care:
## The Federal administrative appeal

As we discussed earlier, Beechwood was licensed by the State of New York, but the whole survey and certification process upon which state licensure and Medicaid/Medicare participation depended was federalized. Before Beechwood knew anything of the DOH hearing plans, we had been formally notified by Susan Baker, provisional program director for Long-Term Care, that we had a right to a federal hearing, the procedures for which are governed by the federal Administrative Procedures Act (APA). Beechwood filed the paperwork to get the process started, which normally would have resulted in an expedited hearing, but we had to request that the hearing be delayed because of the unprecedented DOH hearing. Now there was to be an unprecedented second administrative hearing based on the same survey, but at the federal level.

On October 19, 1999, after receiving the DOH hearing decision, we notified HCFA that we were ready to move forward with the federal hearing. ALJ Steven

T. Kessel was assigned to the case and requested that the readiness report regarding issues and evidence was to be submitted by December 3, 1999. The pre-hearing process of determining issues for the federal administrative-level appeal began in February 2000. The hearing itself did not begin until April 2001 and ended up consisting of a couple of hours by phone and just one day in person in Rochester. The ALJ heard three witnesses for Beechwood on topics not covered in the DOH hearing, but he did not get to hear or evaluate any of the witnesses from the DOH hearing. The Centers for Medicare and Medicaid Services (CMS) produced no additional witnesses. Everything was basically built around written submissions using excerpts and documents from the DOH hearing. Beechwood agreed to this process because it could not afford another extended hearing to put the same medical record evidence on another hearing record just so another biased ALJ could rule on it. In any event, the chances of success for any appellant in a HCFA/CMS administrative appeal process are dismal. According to the Department of Appeal Board (DAB) website in 2003, the "vast majority of cases" before the ALJs are settled, withdrawn, or dismissed by the Civil Remedies Division. Those that survive for hearing are typically very long and complex cases. Very few cases, if any, involve termination.

The federal administrative process differs from the state process in three ways. First, the ALJ determinations are final, as opposed to being recommendations to the commissioner. Second, appeals of ALJ determinations go to the internal Department Appeal Board (DAB) before ever being presented to a court. Essentially, this provides the agency with another layer of safety and an opportunity to cement its position, while making it appear to the court that the agency has provided as many opportunities for fair review as possible. Finally, a court appeal begins at the federal district court level, whereas appeals of state hearings move directly to the appellate court level. Each of these differences has its own legal ramifications. The DAB website trumpets the fact that the DAB panel is made up of "career civil servants," who are appointed by the secretary so that they can bring impartiality to the process. Their authority is outlined at 45 CFR Part 16. However, their impartiality is brought into question by the statistics regarding the outcomes in these appeals. From the published data, it appears that 2.5% of the approximately 17,000 full surveys done in a year were being appealed. Only about 10% of those end up at some sort of hearing at the ALJ level. Of those, 30% were dismissed on technical grounds, including those in which CMS took off the sanctions (such as fines), leaving the matter no longer eligible for appeal. Thus, just 7% of appeals are heard. Of this, 82% are ruled in favor of the agency; 6% end up in some sort of split decision; and 12% are successful, at least to some extent. Thus, when the appeal is written, there is approximately a 1% chance of success. This equates to a .02% chance of a surveyor having findings challenged and overturned.

In addition, to have any chance of success, a plaintiff or his attorneys must learn everything about previous case decisions regarding the issues to be adjudicated, whether the decisions were from the ALJ assigned to the case, other ALJs, or at the DAB. The litigant must also know the law, regulations, and state operations manual. There is very limited legal expertise in this area and, if found, typically involves a large legal firm based in Washington, D.C. Unless the plaintiff has the time or inclination to do this research—or is a large corporation—the legal fees are overwhelming. If the provider has not been terminated, it must also weigh the risk of annoying the regulators with any appeal. The costs continue to mount with board-level appeals and become astronomical when proceeding to federal court.

Given this environment, you may well wonder why anyone would decide to embark on such a project. The answer lies in the importance of the case, and this one, we believed, was crucially important. True, it was incredibly complex, and we had no idea how it would turn out, but we felt no alternative to pursuing every available opportunity. We hoped that the highly structured federal regulatory environment would force an outcome different from what the state delivered, but we had grave doubts because, even at the federal level, it was yet another administrative process, outside of the constitutionally established judiciary, and staffed with hearing officers inherently biased toward the regulatory agencies. Imagine the controversy that would be created for the state if the federal process overturned the MD/MR program decertification, when the state process had already revoked a license based on the same survey.

Since we were already spending substantial legal fees on other cases, I decided to act per se, that is, as my own attorney, at least through the ALJ and board-level administrative appeals. I did the research and drafted the briefs, while my attorney, Kevin Cooman, edited and helped to provide the proper legal structure. DOH had created a monstrous case by citing 26 tags, 42 residents, and 68 findings over the three surveys. The effort needed to tackle the federal appeal was nothing short of astounding and, even representing myself, the legal costs remained very significant. In the four years that it took to get this appeal through the administrative process there were two ALJ decisions (one on remand), two DAB decisions, and a DAB order for HCFA to release the Beechwood file. Just about every submission involved multiple three-inch binders, with each binder capable of holding 1500 pages. By the last submission to the DAB, the case record was over 6,000 pages.

The year 2003 was consumed in obtaining the Beechwood file from HCFA officials. The result was not surprising. Regional HCFA administrator Sue Kelly did not have any required documentation regarding certifications from DOH, reviews by her staff, or of her own "initial determinations" on the matter. Kelly had been sending alerts regarding a "Critical program development that the Administrator and/or CO Central/Office Head needs to be aware of," on an "Issue that has received or is expected to receive interest from major media," as well as "significant congressional interest." Kelly was flying to Rochester to support DOH while also claiming that it was her "intended purpose ... [to ensure] that the provider had been given every opportunity to bring itself into compliance." Yet, she had no documentation to prove that she did her own job properly. The whole federal administrative proceeding, which was incredible in every possible sense of the word, is the subject of the next chapter.

# CHAPTER 10

# Federal Accountability Denied

T he DOH administrative law judge (ALJ) operated without precedent, let alone regulations or policy manual, to interpret what was and was not a violation of state law or how serious an alleged violation was. In contrast, the federal Health Care Finance Administration promulgated an exhaustive set of patient care regulations under 42 CFR 483, "Requirements for States and Long-Term Care Facilities," with a zero level of tolerance for non-compliance. To be certified under Medicare and Medicaid, the provider *must* meet every requirement. In the spring of 1999, there were 371 comprehensively defined deficiency tags, comprising more than 530 requirement categories and sub-categories, with the word must used approximately 160 times. The regulations also designate a scope and severity grading system that is to be applied to every deficiency, as well as a system for deciding what remedy or sanction should be applied proportionate to the scope and severity of the problems found.

As specific as the federal regulations and surveyor guidelines are, there is always a subjective element in surveying activity. Terms like "potential for" and "harm" are used extensively and are very subjective, as is the grading system built around it. The state Operations Manual and other surveyor guidelines published by HCFA are comprehensive, but common sense and reasonableness are also needed, since the reputation and livelihood of providers and their staff are at stake. This is made even more crucial because survey results are posted on the internet.

With the subjective element so prevalent and the results so crucial, it is extremely important that the survey agency at least follows established policy and procedures in arriving at its conclusions. The structure imposed greatly affects the outcome derived. Thus, 42 CFR 488 Subparts C & E contain mandated forms, methods, and procedures to assist surveyors in maintaining consistency and obtaining valid conclusions. HCFA uses the term *must* 29 times in specifying what the survey agency is to do. HCFA maintains final review of the survey results and is to make the final determination as to any sanctions to be applied. This responsibility is so great that 42 CFR 442.30 dictates that a state's Medicaid agreement can be terminated if HCFA determines that the survey agency failed to follow proper procedure.

## HISTORICAL PERSPECTIVE

Following federal regulations, Susan Baker, DOH provisional program director for Long-Term Care, offered the right to a federal appeal in her covering letter to the April statement of deficiencies (SOD): "If you disagree with this determination, you and your legal representative may request a hearing before an administrative law judge of the Department of Health and Human Services, Department Appeals Board. Procedures governing this process are set out in 42 CRF 498.40 et. Seq."

When Baker failed to add a statement about the right to appeal the May findings, I initially wrote it off as an oversight. It was no oversight. Susan Baker had direct knowledge of—indeed, participated in—plans to use the state hearing to pre-empt the federal hearing, and to keep those plans secret. Recall that, in April, Deputy Director of the Office of Continuing Care (OCC) Laura Leeds was already telling DOH Western Region acting director Sanford Rubin (with copies to Baker and Carlo), "I don't think [Chambery] gets an appeal." Rubin at this time was stating that "Region II [HCFA] claims it will back us all the way," and Bureau of Administrative Hearings (BAH) director Russel Altone was telling Division of Legal Affairs director Henry Greenberg that "The Feds would be responsible for doing the termination of provider hearing."

The federal officials were thus colluding with their state partners to destroy a right that a provider has under federal law. How was this extraordinary level of HCFA commitment reached by early April? Altone's interrogatory provides a glimpse. At #14, Altone stated that, at "various points" before, during, and after the DOH hearing, there were "several communications," primarily by phone, between HCFA and BAH attorneys, including himself. Altone described their purpose as "cooperative information sharing" as well as "coordination with HCFA." At #15, Altone stated that he recalled one or more phone discussions with HCFA attorney John Gura, who would later handle the Beechwood appeal and make pre-hearing motions to exclude from the hearing challenges regarding survey protocols, scope and severity, remedies applied, notice of deficiencies, time frames used, and constitutional claims. How could Gura take on the responsibility for "doing the termination of provider hearing," and be so very confident of the outcome? HCFA not only writes and interprets the regulations that determine what will be heard on appeal, it controls the outcome by using its own hearing and appeal board officers. Gura also knew the federal courts would be very deferential to the administrative determinations.

### PRE-HEARING ISSUE DEFINITION: "NO ACCOUNTABILITY"

Gura seized on every opportunity to deliver what he promised Altone. In the pre-hearing posturing regarding the issues for hearing—

March 3, 2000: Gura wrote (1) that the legal issue to be determined was whether Beechwood had a deficiency during each relevant survey which put the facility into non-compliance, and (2) that HCFA believes the present case can be decided without the need for in-person testimony.

June 29: Gura submitted HCFA's brief in support of its motion for partial summary disposition regarding its claim that the "Petitioner has raised issues that cannot be decided by this Court." The issues were (1) the DAB's (Department of Appeal Board) authority to review the Petitioner's challenges to "HCFA determinations," (2) "Petitioner's challenge to the State's survey procedures," (3) Petitioner's contest of "HCFA's selection of remedies," (4) Petitioner's challenge to remedies that HCFA claims were imposed by the State, (5) Petitioner's challenge to the justification for termination, (6) Petitioner's challenge to the improper notices from HCFA, and (7) Petitioner's objections on constitutional issues.

August 15: Gura submitted another brief in support of its motion for partial summary disposition. He reiterated that (1) HCFA believed survey protocols and procedures used by the state agency are not subject to review in an administrative hearing; (2) nothing in the regulations precluded a state from acting under its own authority to administer the licensing and operation of facilities within its borders; and (3) that late notice of remedy, while "technically in error, did not prejudice the Petitioner in any way."

October 27: Gura briefed the ALJ on the concept that holding a federal hearing would be a waste of resources because the facility had already lost its operating license.

## KESSEL'S PRE-HEARING DETERMINATIONS:
### FOLLOWING SUIT

On September 5, 2000, ALJ Steven T. Kessel issued a pre-hearing ruling regarding HCFA's motion for partial summary judgment. Consistent with Gura's suggestion, he ruled:

(1) "I do not have authority to hear and decide Petitioner's challenges of actions [i.e., gross violations of survey protocol] taken by the NYS survey agency."

(2) "I do not have authority to hear and decide Petitioner's constitutional arguments."

(3) "I lack the authority to decide that HCFA's choice of a remedy is improper, even if they contravened its regulation."

(4) "HCFA's determinations are not invalidated by any irregularities in the notices that it issued to Petitioner or gave the public."

Kessel ruled against Gura on November 20, stating that Beechwood would get a hearing; however, because both parties agreed to include the DOH hearing transcript as part of the record, the hearing would be limited to new issues. Additionally, after almost a year of motions and rulings regarding Beechwood's request for a subpoena to HCFA for its certification file, Kessel denied the subpoena, instead directing HCFA to provide notes and work papers. On February 16, 2001, after HCFA failed to produce any information pertaining to a "certification file," Beechwood renewed its subpoena request, to which Kessel responded on November 20, "I deny Petitioner's request for a subpoena. Petitioner's request for a subpoena essentially is a demand for broad discovery of HCFA's records concerning Petitioner's certification status. I do not have the authority under the regulations which govern hearings involving HCFA at 42 C.F.R. Part 498 to order the broad discovery that Petitioner seeks."

## KESSEL'S HEARING DETERMINATION.
### *BEECHWOOD SANITARIUM V. CENTERS FOR MEDICARE & MEDICAID SERVICES*, CR821.

The hearing lasted a mere ten hours, a couple of hours by telephone on April 3, 2001 and a day in Rochester on April 17. The decision was handed down on October 3, 28 months after the facility was terminated. Kessel focused on the June survey, reviewing only two of the ten deficiencies and sustaining them without determining whether there was any harm, as originally alleged by DOH. He used this as his basis to support termination, ruling, "I must decide whether or not Petitioner failed to comply substantially with any one of the 10 participation requirements ... in order to decide whether CMS was authorized to terminate Petitioner's participation in Medicare. Failure by Petitioner to comply substantially with even one of those requirements provides CMS with authority to terminate Petitioner's participation." (p. 6)

Next, Kessel went on to the May survey, reviewing just two of the ten deficiencies, and again sustaining them without determining whether there was any harm or substandard quality of care (SQC), as DOH had originally alleged. This he used as his basis to support the denial of payment remedy, ruling: "CMS is authorized to impose against Petitioner the remedy of denial of payment for new Medicare admissions ... because Petitioner failed to prove that it was complying substantially ... as of the May 1999 survey.... I discuss Petitioner's failure to comply substantially with two of the requirements that are cited in the May 1999 survey report.... I do not address Petitioner's compliance or noncompliance with the other eight requirements that are cited in the report because it is unnecessary that I do so." (p. 20) Instead of supporting the SQC originally claimed, Kessel simply ruled that "the evidence established a pattern of deficient care presenting a potential for more than minimal harm."

He failed to review the April deficiencies at all, stating, "I dismiss Petitioner's hearing request insofar as it addresses findings that were made at the April 1999 survey because there is no issue arising from that survey that I have the authority to hear and decide.... Petitioner has no right to a hearing concerning the April 1999 survey findings because they are not the basis for any remedy determination made by CMS. 42 C.F.R. § 498.3, 498.5." (p. 4) He added: "CMS imposed no remedies against Petitioner based on the findings of noncompliance that were made at the April 1999 survey." (p. 6)

## FIRST DEPARTMENT OF APPEAL BOARD DECISION.
## *BEECHWOOD SANITARIUM V. CENTERS FOR MEDICARE*
## *& MEDICAID SERVICES,* DAB NO. 1824.

In a process required before filing any court action, Beechwood appealed Kessel's pre-hearing and hearing decisions to the Department of Appeal Board (DAB). On April 11, 2002, the DAB directed ALJ Kessel to reconsider his decision to review only certain deficiencies issued for May and June, and to review April. DAB's reason for remanding the matter to the ALJ for review of April was that, as Beechwood appealed, April was the basis for the directed plan of correction (DPOC) remedy application. The DAB did not dispute the ALJ's position that the April 1999 survey was "irrelevant" to the issue of whether HCFA could impose the remedy of termination of participation in Medicare in June 1999, because it agreed that HCFA was authorized to impose that remedy based solely on the compliance findings made at the June 1999 survey.

## KESSEL'S DECISION UPON REMAND.
## *BEECHWOOD SANITARIUM V. CENTERS FOR MEDICARE*
## *& MEDICAID SERVICES,* CR966

Upon remand, on October 28, 2002, Kessel decided to maintain his novel position that, in the interest of efficiency, he only had to review deficiencies until he found one deficiency that he supported, which would mean the facility was non-compliant. This was the very concept Gura had put forth on March 7, 2000; however, by not ruling on the alleged scope and severity, which by definition is an element required to cite a deficiency, Kessel was violating the federal regulatory structure.

Even though Kessel maintained that he was permitted to limit his review, he yielded to the DAB direction to review the April deficiencies. In a review of all six deficiencies, Kessel sustained two (F224, F324), but consistent with the position he had taken, he did so without supporting the scope and severity levels that had been alleged in the statement of deficiency (SOD). In fact, regarding the F224 findings, which were each cited at the immediate jeopardy (IJ) level, he stated that, "viewed individually … [the findings] do not depict necessarily a failure" and added that "no real consequence attached to whether or no Immediate Jeopardy existed." Kessel also sustained an administration tag (F490), which the DOH ALJ, Marc Zylberberg, had used to castigate me personally, but he did so, he explained, only because it was "essentially" a derivative of the other findings. Kessel found that the other three tags (F314, F514, F493) did not even present a prima facie case for a violation, even though they each had been graded at the "harm" level and had been such a major issue in the DOH hearing.

The bottom line? As a result of Kessel's decisions, Gura got his way. The termination, along with other remedies preceding it, were sustained—without finding any support for the IJ, SQC, or even harm, which DOH and HCFA had heralded to the public as the reason for the termination and license revocation. Termination was sustained because of at least one deficiency "from the June survey," which had the "potential" for more that minimal harm, which would be classified a "D" level, the lowest scope and severity level that counts as a deficiency. HCFA had succeeded in corrupting the system, and ALJ decisions have been plagued by this precedent ever since.

## SECOND APPEAL BOARD DECISION.
### *BEECHWOOD SANITARIUM V. CENTERS FOR MEDICARE & MEDICAID SERVICES*, DAB 1906

Beechwood again appealed to the DAB. The new appeal included a renewed request for a subpoena to HCFA for documents, which prompted the DAB to issue an order for documents on May 19, 2003. The resulting production demonstrated the non-existence of a Beechwood certification file. On July 14, 2003, Beechwood then filed an auxiliary brief pertaining to the fact that there was no official document prepared by any CMS official with respect to the May or June surveys, including the required—per 42 CRF 498.3(b)(7)—"initial determination" before issuing any notice of noncompliance or remedies to be applied. Incredibly, yet unsurprisingly, it was to no avail, and, on January 23, 2004, the DAB issued its final decision, supporting the ALJ and sustaining the remedies imposed by HCFA.

### THE RESULT: NOTHING IS AS IT APPEARS
A few regulatory provisions and DAB rulings in the Beechwood case have effectively peeled back layers of HCFA responsibility that would appear to have been established under the law and within the broader regulatory scheme. To wit: The provider is held accountable for every requirement, no matter how subjective that requirement may be, while HCFA/CMS and its state level survey agents have

no accountability. The following are three of most significant issues:

*Survey protocol.* According to the law (USC), regulation (CFR), and guidelines (State Operations Manual)—

> 42 USC 1395i-3(g)(2)(c) mandates that surveys *"shall* be conducted based upon protocol which the Secretary has developed, tested, and validated."

> 42 CFR 488.26(d) mandates that the "State survey agency *must* use the survey methods, procedures, and forms that are prescribed by HCFA" for it (e) *"must ensure* that a facility's actual provision of care and services .... are assessed in a systematic manner." This is reiterated at § § 431.610(f)(1) & (2), 442.30 (a) (4), and 488.318(a)(1)(iii) & (iv).

> 42 CFR 388.110 and 42 CFR 305(a) *specify* the survey tasks and *requirements* for a recertification survey.

There are extensive guidelines published in the State Operations Manual (SOM) regarding survey team composition, note taking, decision making, how to determine the scope and severity of the problem, and whether it amounts to a deficiency. The CMS Brief in support of dismissal in Beechwood's "1983" civil rights case (pp. 4-5) states that the "statute also sets forth detailed procedures for the inspection of nursing home and the enforcement of health standards.... The survey *must* ... [use] survey protocols [that] do not impose any independent requirements on providers; instead they specify procedures to be used by surveyors to ascertain a facility's compliance."

All of this is valuable; however, the integrity of the system is undermined by the following regulations and administrative hearing decisions—

> 42 CFR 488.305 (b): The agency's failure to follow proper procedure will not invalidate *otherwise legitimate* deficiency determinations.

> 42 CFR 488.318 (b)(2): Inadequate survey performance does not invalidate *adequately documented* deficiencies.

> In its April 21, 2006 Memorandum of Law in opposition to the Beechwood motion for summary judgment (p. 48), CMS wrote that "This (488.318(b)(2)) regulation is consistent with the overarching statutory goal of protecting Medicare and Medicaid beneficiaries."

HCFA stated in the Federal Register that the two regulations listed above were the agency's interpretation of what Congress desired under 42 USC 1395i-3 (g)(2)(C), which states: "The failure of the Secretary to develop, test, or validate such protocols or to establish such minimum qualifications shall not relieve any State of its responsibility (or the Secretary of the Secretary's responsibility) to conduct surveys under this subsection." Clearly, this interpretation is wrong because the law discusses the responsibilities *in spite of* the establishment of valid protocols. Once the protocols have been developed, tested, and validated, they should be followed. Yet the 488.305 and 488.318 negate this responsibility. How does one know whether the deficiencies are adequately documented and legitimate unless the protocols are followed?

The DAB took full advantage of these regulatory escape clauses—

DAB Decision, April 11, 2002: "The Board stated that the ALJ understood his role clearly, and sustained his analysis that it was outside the scope of authority delegated to him to judge the "lawfulness of processes or procedures that were used by a State survey agency." (p. 13)

"We agree with the ALJ that alleged defects in survey procedures or in CMS' procedure in reaching its remedy decision are not grounds for dismissal of the remedies against a facility ... How those deficiencies were discovered is irrelevant so long as Beechwood had notice of and a fair opportunity to contest them." (p. 14).

CMS Reply Brief, February 10, 2003: "It is obvious from the context of the language quoted from the regulations that it imposes an obligation on the Petitioner to base its care on such an assessment, and it is not a directive to surveyors or to CMS on how to evaluate compliance." (p. 22)

DAB Decision, Jan. 23, 2004: "Beechwood misconstrued the thrust of the cited regulation which speaks to the obligations of the facility in caring for patients, not the surveyor's procedures in evaluating care." (p. 81)

The DAB Decision reached a high level of absurdity in passages such as these:

DAB Decision, January 23, 2004: "Another example of the irrelevance of details of survey procedures is Beechwood's argument ... that "not one resident review sheet was properly completed by the surveyors. (Beechwood Brief at 40) Such paperwork peccadillos, even if proven, would do nothing to dilute the significance of cited deficiencies unless Beechwood demonstrated that it was in fact in compliance with the requirements cited." (p. 44, footnote 14)

DAB Decision, January 23: "This issue is one of many in which Beechwood referred to the content or the absence of notes in the surveyor's worksheets as proving that allegations in the SOD were not based on true contemporaneous

observations by the surveyors. These worksheets are generally scribbled nota-
tions, highly abbreviated and personal in style, that appear to be memory aids
rather than attempts to record narrative or verbatim quotations.... We do
not believe the ALJ erred in not viewing an absent or ambiguous notation as
somehow rendering the SOD or testimony of the surveyor inherently suspect."
(p. 51, footnote 18)

DAB Decision, January 23: "We also agree with the ALJ that no significance
attaches to the fact that the surveyor who observed ... was not yet federally certified.... Beechwood goes too far when it describes the surveyor as unqualified."
(p. 41)

DAB Decision, January 23: "Beechwood ... argued that a deficiency may be
determined only during a survey and a monitoring visit is not a kind of survey.... It is true, but irrelevant that monitoring visits are not listed as a form of
special surveys at 488.30. (p. 40)

**Remedy selection.** According to the Law (USC) and Regulation (CFR):

42 USC 1395-i3 (h) specifies certain remedies, and (2)(B) *expects* enforcement
criteria with "incrementally more severe fines for repeated or uncorrected
deficiencies."

42 CFR 488.404: The seriousness of deficiencies *"must"* be determined in order
to select the appropriate remedy.

42 CFR 488.408: If remedies are to be chosen, they *"must"* follow the criteria
set forth in 42 CFR 488.406, and thus calibrated to the severity of the noncompliance.

However, there is this vague caveat within the law: 42 USC 1395i-3(h)(2)(A)
adds: "Nothing in this subparagraph shall be construed as restricting the remedies available to the Secretary to remedy deficiencies." And the CMS interpretation of this law is that the remedies chosen by CMS cannot be challenged: 42
CFR 488.402(g)(2): "A facility may not appeal the choice of remedy." As for
HCFA, it took it upon itself to limit the permissible challenges to its following
"initial determinations":

1. 498.3(b)(7) - Termination Remedy

2. 498.3(b)(12) - Findings of non-compliance leading to a Remedy

3. 498.3(b)(13) - Level of non-compliance leading to a CMP (Monetary
   Penalty)

In short, the scope and severity ("level of non-compliance"), which is included in the definition of a deficiency, can be challenged if it leads to a Monetary Penalty (3), but not for something as severe as program termination (1). Although, under HFCA rules, the finding of non-compliance can be challenged if it led to a remedy (2), this was not applied in the case of Beechwood because the agency took the position that it does not have to decide how serious the issue is, as long as it determines there was at least the "potential for harm" (a "D" level deficiency). Thus, a termination decision can stand with an ALJ supporting one deficiency and citing the potential for harm, even when the agency may have originally used widespread immediate jeopardy (IJ) as a reason for applying the termination.

This amounts to both pure insanity and the absence of due process. In *Shalala v. Illinois Council* 529 U.S. 1, 22 (February 29, 2000), the Court stated: "CMS has also declared, and the Supreme Court of the United States has reiterated, that termination of a certified nursing facility from the Programs—which will necessarily mean the involuntary transfer of elderly and infirm residents, unemployment for health professionals, the demise of a community resource, and economic loss to its owners—is "rare and generally reserved for the most egregious and recidivist institutions" that violate Program requirements and are unable to correct them."

A reasonable application of this Court guidance should lead to a determination that limiting provider challenges to an agency termination decision does not imply the absence of ALJ or DAB responsibility to rule on the severity of the findings and reassess the remedy accordingly. Unfortunately, however, the DAB did not act reasonably as it tried to protect the agency in its own proceeding. In its decision on April 11, 2002, the DAB (p. 20) endorsed the ALJ position from his October 3, 2001 decision (p. 6) that "Failure by Petitioner to comply substantially with even [one requirement] provides CMS with authority to terminate Petitioner's participation." And, in its decision of January 23, 2004 (p. 32): "Nothing in the regulations suggests a facility determined [to be out of compliance] can preclude CMS from terminating its provider agreement on Beechwood's theory that some further "justification" is called for. The argument amounts to a back-door objection to CMS's discretion to select what remedy to impose." That decision went on to reinforce the DAB's resolve to uphold termination at all costs:

"It would hardly be meaningful for the regulations to insulate the determination of scope and severity from challenge by a facility if the result was to impose an obligation on CMS to prove the level found in every case without such challenge. We uphold the ALJ's conclusion that, in the posture of this case, he need not decide what level of scope and severity was shown for a given deficiency, so long as the proof supports a scope and severity level that exceeds the minimum required." (p. 37)

A reasonable application of the court guidance should lead to a determination that the ALJ or DAB must not be able to limit review of the deficiencies issued, since the scope of the problem is just as important as the severity in choosing a sanction; however, DAB decisions persisted in rationalizing the ALJ's actions:

DAB Decision, April 11, 2002: "We are not persuaded that the ALJ's approach (of only choosing to review certain deficiencies supporting the remedy) is reversible error.... this exercise of judicial economy is within the ALJ's discretion.... it likely provided Beechwood with a more timely decision" (p. 21)

DAB Decision, January 26, 2004: The "Board concluded that the ALJ was within his discretion in choosing to 'discuss several deficiencies that he determined to be persuasively established,' minimizing the risk that the case would have to be remanded if one of his findings was overturned, and at the same time exercising judicial economy. (p. 3)

**CMS initial determinations.** The Social Security Act "Requirements for, and Assuring Quality of Care In, Skilled Nursing Facilities" reveals an agreement among law, regulation, and Operations Manual:

SSA 1819 (h)(1): IN GENERAL. -- If a State finds ... that a skilled nursing facility no longer meets a requirement ... (A) ... the State shall recommend to the Secretary ....

42 CFR 498.3(b) states that HCFA is required to make "initial determinations" including findings of noncompliance resulting in remedies, the level of such noncompliance, and whether to terminate a provider. 42 C.F.R. § 498.3(b)(7), (12), (13).

The Operations Manual (SOM 2772) requires that the certification package (Forms 1539, 462L, as well as the 2567 and POC) must be sent to the RO [CMS Regional Office] by the SA [survey agency], and by the state agency representative (SOM 2762, 2764(D)), and that the RO is to review that documentation before making its initial determination.

Astoundingly, the DAB simply refused to be bound by the consistency of law, regulation, and manual. HFCA document productions in response to the order of the DAB and Beechwood's Freedom of Information requests (FOIL #03-08-91) proved that there was no file containing the required DOH certification of survey results to HCFA and no record of initial determinations by HCFA regarding the Beechwood survey results and sanctions to be applied. Yet, in its decision of January 23, 2004, the DAB ruled:

"The regulation [498.3(b)] does not restrict appealable items to only such determinations issued by CMS after a specific documentation process." (p. 30)

"Beechwood cannot prevail by simply denying the existence of "official CMS action....It would defeat the existence of jurisdiction for any appeal under Part 498, since such jurisdiction arises only over an official CMS action in the form of a listed initial determination." (p. 30)

"The existence of any prior "decision-making process" by CMS is as irrelevant as its content or quality. The relevant decision-maker on all the contested issues once an appeal was taken was the adjudicator." (p. 30)

"We conclude that the question of whether CMS engaged in any particular decision-making process at all is equally outside the scope of this appeal process." (pg. 30)

Met at every turn by the federal government's abrogation of responsibility in an assault on the constitutional guarantees protecting my business and myself, we pressed on with our parallel strategy of bringing federal suit under the Civil Rights Act of 1871, 42 U.S.C. § 1983. That action is the subject of the next chapter.

# PART III

# From False Dawn to Discovery: 2004-2010

# CHAPTER 11

# Civil Rights (Denied)

A fter long labor invested in Freedom of Information requests, combing through and analyzing documents, building an array of spreadsheets and other reference material, researching the law and case law, and with the statute of limitations at our backs, the time had come to file our federal civil rights case.

The legal planning and resources necessary for making an appeal on the basis of a violation of civil rights are daunting. Claims have to be thought out with infinite care. You get but one chance. There are no do-overs. The complex task before us was made yet more complex because we were naming New York State Department of Health (DOH) officials and federal Health Care Finance Administration (HCFA) officials. Many strategy meetings with our own attorneys, and consultations with other legal minds across the country were required before we finally filed the complaint on April 26, 2002. It was filed in the US Court, Western District of N.Y. under the civil rights statute 42 USC Section 1983, which states that:

> Every person who under color of any statute, ordinance, regulation, custom, or usage, of any State or Territory or the District of Columbia, subjects, or causes to be subjected, any citizen of the United States or other person within the jurisdiction thereof to the deprivation of any rights, privileges, or immunities secured by the Constitution and laws, shall be liable to the party injured in an action at law, suit in equity, or other proper proceeding for redress …

In the Beechwood case, we sought compensatory and punitive damages from two federal defendants, and seventeen state defendants for deprivation of rights secured in the Constitution by Article VI and the First, Fifth, and Fourteenth Amendments, as well as various provisions of the laws of the United States. Our basic premise was that the defendants conspired together and then individually and jointly committed acts, under color of State law, that deprived plaintiffs of these rights. The suit asserted that this conduct was oppressive and malicious, motivated either by evil intent or undertaken with callous or reckless indifference to the constitutionally protected rights of Beechwood and the Chamberys. It further asserted that the actions of the defendants caused severe damage.

The complaint stated that, with a desire to punish plaintiffs for their aggressive advocacy of health care regulatory reform, etc., these officials misused and manipulated federal survey process, and corrupted the licensure and hearing process provided by state law. In the guise of concern for Beechwood's residents, the defendants shut down the nursing home, causing the loss of a valuable community resource, the loss of employment and dislocation of its staff, and the involuntary transfer of its residents, some of whom died as a direct result of the transfer trauma. Moreover, in their determination to further crush the plaintiffs financially, the defendants took another unprecedented step and unofficially annulled the certificate of need (CON) for the facility, thereby effectively wiping out whatever value might have been left in the physical plant. More specifically, there were seven claims in the Civil Rights Complaint.

1. The first dealt with violation of procedural due process rights under the Fourteenth Amendment, to wit, the refusal of DOH to allow the physical plant to be used as a nursing home by any other entity, without going through the formally established process.

2. The second dealt with retaliation for my exercise of rights guaranteed under the First and Fourteenth amendments, namely freedom of speech. We claimed that the survey process, the refusal to accept our plans of correction (POCs), the unprecedented state hearing, and the ALJ/Commissioner decisions were all part of the retaliatory conduct. Furthermore, Beechwood argued that it had no opportunity to litigate such constitutional issues in the DOH hearing, and that the ALJ did not and could not resolve such issues because he lacked proper jurisdiction.

3. The third claim dealt with equal protection rights under the Fifth and Fourteenth Amendments, specifically that Beechwood was singled out by DOH enforcement actions never taken previously.

4. The fourth addressed Beechwood's protected substantive rights under the Fourteenth Amendment, namely the lack of legitimate governmental interest in the arbitrary and abusive acts taken, which were motivated by bias and improper motive.

5. The fifth claimed that the defendants violated the supremacy of federal law over conflicting state law by commencing a DOH hearing under state law regarding federal survey matters before that survey was completed and while the facility was still a federally certified Medicare and Medicaid provider.

6. The sixth claimed that the improper survey procedures, claims made, and lack of proper reviews by HCFA were all in violation of federal law.

7. The seventh dealt with the federal defendants conspiring with the state defendants under color of federal law.

## THE SUMMARY JUDGMENT MOTION

In August 2002, we began receiving the statements of admission or denial from each defendant and built a spreadsheet to keep track of them. Unsurprisingly in a case like this, on January 31, 2003, the defendants also filed a Motion for Summary Judgment, a motion to dismiss for lack of sufficient evidence. Included with their summary judgment papers were supporting affidavits from each named defendant with claims that they simply followed protocol and held no resentment toward Beechwood or the Chamberys. The core of the defendants' claim was that that Beechwood was simply "rehashing issues it had ample opportunity to litigate" in the state administrative proceedings, that the retribution issue had been properly decided by the ALJ, and that any such action was barred by the doctrine of collateral estoppel or issue preclusion. Essentially, this doctrine holds that "once a court has decided an issue of fact or law necessary to its judgment, that decision ... preclude[s] relitigation of the issue in a suit on a different cause of action involving a party to the first case." But DOH asserted its preclusion claim even though the ALJ had taken the position that he was "not inclined" to let Beechwood discuss or question DOH witnesses about DOH motives for actions taken and sanctions sought. DOH further claimed that the court should abstain from hearing the case because it involved a "state's specialized and comprehensive regulatory scheme," and federal review would be "disruptive of state efforts to establish a coherent policy."

## SUMMARY JUDGMENT GRANTED
## JUDGE LARIMER: BEECHWOOD *RESTORATIVE CARE CENTER V. LEEDS*, 317 F.SUPP.2D 248 (W.D.N.Y. 2004).

In his decision on May 4, 2004, Judge Larimer could not hide his own bias toward government agencies and his distaste for suits against government officials for constitutional violations. He felt that Beechwood had its day in court (p. 26) and was not about to let it get away with what he perceived as an end run around the patient care issues and results of the administrative hearing, as well as Beechwood's "failure" to pursue a direct appeal (Article 78) in state court. The constitutional issues he dismissed as mere window dressing. In their absence, he treated the suit as a substitute for an Article 78 appeal, so gave great weight to the collateral estoppel or issue preclusion defense raised regarding the ALJ's decision. Judge Larimer admitted (p. 38) that, in considering a motion for summary judgment, a court is obligated "to view the record in the light most favorable to the nonmoving parties, and draw all inferences in their favor." In other words, with respect to the motion, he was obligated to give the benefit of the doubt to the plaintiff and not the defendant. He announced his decision to disregard this obligation for the simple reason that nursing homes existed in a "highly regulated industry."

The judge also avoided facing the reality, totality, and context of what Beechwood's suit addressed by examining the issues in isolation, and then claiming that each issue "alone," or "by itself" was "not enough" to "persuade." It was "not enough" that (p. 24) the ALJ was employed by DOH, or that there was a lack of due process, or that (p. 39) the defendants made statements that would indicate improper motives, or that (p. 41) sanctioning of this nature had never been done before, or that (pp. 47 and 48) he had to look beyond the Medicare and Medicaid system to try to find some justification for the actions taken by DOH officials. He refused to add up our assertions and assess their sum. This approach simply defied logic as well as common sense.

### ANATOMY OF INJUSTICE

It is important to break down Judge Larimer's decision to grant a summary judgment against Beechwood's civil rights suit because, in the light of its later reversal by a Circuit Court, it reveals the depth and breadth of the audacity of bias toward regulatory agency authority even among members of the Judicial Branch of the federal government. It is a bias quite capable of blinding the guardians of the Constitution to the motives and machinations not of agencies but of individuals within those agencies. It is a refusal to recognize the very purpose of creating a government of laws and not men. Laws may be corrupted but are not inherently corrupt. The same cannot be said of men—as John Adams and the other architects of our independence and Constitution urgently recognized.

### *Collateral Estoppel / issue preclusion:*

Page 13: "Collateral estoppel, also known as issue preclusion, 'means simply that when an issue of ultimate fact has once been determined by a valid and final judgment, that issue cannot again be litigated between the same parties in any future lawsuit.' (*Leather v. Eyck*, 180 F/3d 420, 424 (2nd Cir. 1999)"

Page 13: "A 'federal court must give to a state-court judgment the same preclusive effect as would be given that judgment under the law of the State in which the judgment was rendered.' ... *Migra v. Warren City Sch. Dist. Bd. of Educ.*, 465 U.S. 75, 81 (1984); accord Leather, 180 F.3d at 424. *The same is true of decisions by state agencies*." (emphasis added)

Pg. 14: "'[W]hen a state agency acting in a judicial capacity resolves disputed issues of fact *properly before it* which the parties have had an *adequate opportunity to litigate* ... federal courts must give the agency's fact finding the same preclusive effect to which it would be entitled in the State's courts.' *University of Tennessee v. Elliott*, 478 U.S. 788, 799 (1986) ... Under New York Law, '[c]ollateral estoppel, or issue preclusion, gives conclusive effect to an administrative agency's quasi-judicial determination when two basic conditions are met: (1) the issue sought to be precluded is identical to a material issue necessarily decided by the administrative agency in a prior proceeding; and (2) there was a *full and fair opportunity to contest* this issue in the administrative tribunal. The proponent of collateral estoppel must show identity of the issue, while the opponent must demonstrate the absence of a full and fair opportunity to litigate.' *Jeffreys v. Griffin*, 1 N.Y.3d 34, 39 (2003)." (emphasis added)

Page 14: "'The New York Court of Appeals has also stated that *in the context of determinations of administrative agencies, "the doctrine [of collateral estoppel] is applied more flexibly,* and additional factors must be considered by the court. These additional requirements are often summed up in *the beguilingly simple prerequisite that the administrative decision be 'quasi-judicial' in character.' (Allied Chemical ... v. Niagara Mohawk Power Corp.,* 72 N.Y.2d 271, 276 (1988))." (emphasis added)

Pages 16-17: "It is ... clear that the standards for application of collateral estoppel have been met here. First of all, the DOH proceedings were quasi-judicial in nature. ... Plaintiffs were given notice of the charges against Beechwood, and had the right to present evidence and examine witnesses."

Page 17: "In addition, the factual issues in the instant case relating to whether the charges did in fact have a solid factual basis, or instead were 'trumped up' were identical to material issues that were necessarily decided by the ALJ. The primary issue before the ALJ was whether DOH had proven its deficiency charges by a preponderance of the evidence."

Page 23: "To say, then that plaintiffs were unable to litigate the factual issues of whether the charges were unfounded or brought for a retaliatory motive, whether Beechwood was unfairly singled out, and whether the various DOH officials involved were acting in concert, is flatly contradicted by the record. They could, and did, litigate those issues, at considerable length."

Page 26: "The plaintiffs 'did have a full and fair opportunity to litigate the issues ... Plaintiffs, then, did have "a day in court."'" Judge Larimer either never read the hearing record, or chose to overlook the ALJ's statements on the record to the effect that he was "not inclined" to allow any cross examination of witnesses regarding motive, or that he had only subpoenaed deleted emails in order to preserve them for future proceedings. Larimer (p. 17) did not even know that the ALJ did not have final decision making authority and was limited to making a recommendation to the Commissioner.

Page 17: "If the charges were [found to be] true, then obviously they could not have been spurious or concocted, as plaintiffs contend." Larimer demonstrated here that he was not going to consider the fact that improper motive could have influenced the charges issued, the scope and severity claimed, the sanctions sought, witness testimony about the charges and the need for sanctions, and the decision itself.

Page 4: "In addition, although the DOH hearing may not have afforded plaintiffs the full panoply of procedures that are available to litigants in a civil action … this fact alone does not make collateral estoppel inapplicable." And page 56: "Although it is technically correct that there has been no formal discovery in this action, in a broader sense to say that plaintiffs have not had any discovery is somewhat disingenuous. … both in the DOH administrative proceedings and in response to plaintiffs' requests under the New York Freedom of Information Law (FOIL), DOH produced well over 1000 pages of documents."

Page 25: "Plaintiffs have also not shown how additional discovery would have altered the outcome of the hearing, or stated exactly what evidence was sought." Larimer not only chose to ignore the limitations faced with document production in a DOH administrative hearing and the limitations of FOI requests as opposed to court-ordered discovery, but in trying to justify his actions, he cast an irrational burden on the plaintiff in expecting Beechwood to show what the discovery process might have discovered.

### Article 78 proceeding:
Page 26: "Even if plaintiffs believed that the result of the DOH hearing had been preordained, they had no reason to think, nor do they now contend, that the same would have been true of the Article 78 proceeding. Although this may not bar them from bringing a § 1983 action in this Court, plaintiffs can hardly be heard to complain that they were not given a full and fair opportunity to contest the issues here when they did not fully avail themselves of the opportunities that *were* open to them. For collateral estoppel to apply, all that is required is a full and fair opportunity to litigate the issues in question. A party cannot deliberately choose not to fully litigate those issues, and then argue that estoppel is inapplicable simply because he failed to take advantage of that opportunity."

Larimer (p. 27) acknowledged that Beechwood did not have the option of collecting damages in an Article 78 proceeding, and he later ruled that Beechwood's appeal of the Medicare/Medicaid termination was moot because he could not award damages, but he nevertheless blasts Beechwood here for not continuing to press its Article 78 action at the state court level when it had the potential of establishing case law that could have negatively impacted the ability to argue civil rights violations and collect damages in a Section 1983 case.

### First Amendment retaliation:

Page 37: *"Plaintiffs' second cause of action, alleging that defendants conspired together to retaliate against plaintiffs in retaliation for plaintiffs' having exercised their rights under the First Amendment, is largely foreclosed by the DOH ALJ's factual findings."* (emphasis added) "The ALJ found 'Beechwood's claims of a conspiracy against it and/or Mr. Chambery to be a total, complete, and ridiculous fabrication without a shred of evidence or support' and that 'there [wa]s nothing in the record which indicate[d] to [the ALJ] that the actions taken and/or conduct of [DOH] was motivated by or taken in retaliation for Brook Chambery's exercise of any of his rights.' For the reasons already given, those findings are given preclusive effect here."

Page 38: *"Defendants' conduct was objectively reasonable* and plaintiffs have not provided sufficient evidence to create an issue of fact about whether defendants acted out of retaliatory motives." (emphasis added)

Page 38: "There is some evidence that some of the defendants made statements … All of these statements though, are entirely consistent with defendants' stated desire to enforce federal and state statutes and regulations … and to ensure that the health and safety of Beechwood's residents was not being jeopardized. If defendants' statements at times seem to express frustration with Chambery, it does not appear to have been because he had exercised his First Amendment rights, but because defendants perceived him as obstructionist and uncooperative in their efforts to determine whether there were deficiencies at Beechwood. See id. at M05417 (email from defendant Rubin complaining that Chambery "consistently harasses[sic] our surveillance staff … tries to intimidate them, humiliate them…)"

Page 38: *"I realize the Court's obligation, on a motion for summary judgment, to view the record in the light most favorable to the nonmoving parties, and to draw all inferences in their favor. As the Second Circuit has observed, however, '[n]ursing homes are a highly regulated industry, and some tension between operators of homes and regulators is to be expected ... '. Blue v. Koren,* 72 F.3d 1075, 1085 (2d Cir. 1995). Given DOH's inspections and investigation of Beechwood, as well as its allegations of deficiencies there (which were ultimately determined in both state and federal administrative proceedings to have merit), it is hardly surprising that there was 'some tension' between plaintiffs and defendants, and that defendants gave voice to that tension on occasion. In my view, *that is not enough to give rise to an issue of fact about defendants' allegedly retaliatory motives."* (emphasis added)

These statements were made by Larimer despite the following facts, which were discussed earlier:

1. Both the Office of Inspector General (OIG) and the Attorney General's Medicaid Fraud Control Unit (MFCU) were investigating senior officials and practices within the DOH.

2. An OIG report of December 8, 2003 detailed the "unusual access" and "preferential treatment' granted by Whalen and Leeds, and the resulting inappropriate project priority and CON approvals granted by Leeds, and those under her, such as Murphy.

3. The OIG report stated that its investigation led to the resignation of Leeds and Murphy, as well as an Ethics Committee ruling regarding Whalen's acceptance of gifts from lobbyists, and a subsequent fine.

4. These events were well publicized by The New York Times and other news media as they occurred and beginning in February 2000.

5. The DOH admitted blame for the preferential treatment and excesses that were exposed with the indictment by the Department of the Attorney General (DAG), and conviction of a provider for massive program fraud.

### Equal protection:

Page 40: "While plaintiffs may be correct in their assertion that Beechwood did not have a lengthy history of above-average numbers of deficiencies, the actions taken against plaintiffs were not on account of deficiencies or other problems from many years earlier, but deficiencies that were found in the 1999 surveys."

Page 41: "Plaintiffs also contend that termination of a facility from the Medicare/

Medicaid program is a harsh, rarely-used sanction, that the DOH hearing was 'unusual and extraordinary,' Plaintiffs' Memorandum of Law at 32, and that the DOH administrative proceedings were carried out on an accelerated time frame. Aside from the fact that these assertions are based largely on Chambery's own conclusory allegations, the fact that a particular action or event is relatively rare, without more, is not enough to satisfy the first prong of a selective enforcement claim. *Certain sanctions may rarely be imposed because there is rarely any reason to impose them. Again, plaintiffs must show that they were treated differently from other similarly situated individuals, and they have not done so.*" (emphasis added)

Page 40: "The plaintiff must ordinarily show (1) the person, compared with others similarly situated, was selectively treated; and (2) that such selective treatment was based on impermissible considerations such as race, religion, intent to inhibit or punish the exercise of constitutional rights, or malicious or bad faith intent to injure a person."

Page 44: "The record demonstrates that defendants had valid, rational reasons for their actions, and there is no evidence of *any* individuals situated similarly to plaintiffs who were treated differently."

### Substantive due process claim:
Page 44: "Plaintiffs allege the various acts of the defendants constituted an 'abuse of governmental power' and denied them the right to substantive due process."

Page 45: "Government conduct may be actionable under section 1983 as a substantive due process violation if it can properly be characterized as arbitrary, or conscience-shocking, in a constitutional sense. ... Defendants are entitled to summary judgment on this claim as well. ... I find no basis for plaintiff's allegations that defendants' conduct was arbitrary, malicious, and had no legitimate purpose, and so on. Rather, defendants' conduct was rationally related to the state's legitimate interest in the regulation of nursing homes, and 'it can hardly be doubted that this interest is of the highest order.'"

### Supremacy clause:
Page 46: "Plaintiffs assert a claim for what they describe as a 'denial of [their]

right to federal law supremacy." Complaint ¶ 76. The basis for this claim is plaintiffs' assertion that DOH should not have conducted a hearing until plaintiffs had first had a hearing before HCFA."

Page 47: *"Plaintiffs also cite various federal regulations, none of which expressly proscribe 'premature' state administrative enforcement proceedings,* in an effort to show the federal government's primary role in the Medicare/Medicaid field, but that simply is not enough to give rise to a right enforceable under § 1983. For that matter, *I am not persuaded that enforcement of nursing home standards is, as plaintiffs contend, "an area reserved for HCFA adjudication by federal law and regulations ..."* (emphasis added)

Page 48: "Although nursing homes must comply with certain federally created standards in order to participate in the Medicare/Medicaid program, *the states also have significant responsibilities with respect to establishing and maintaining standards* to ensure adequate levels of resident care, see 42 U.S.C. § 1396a, and primary responsibility for compliance enforcement, see 42 U.S.C. § 1395i-3(g)(1)(A). Furthermore, *leaving aside Medicare/Medicaid altogether,* the state obviously has a strong interest in seeing to it that nursing homes within its borders provide quality care for their residents. See Blue, 72 F.3d at 1080 (observing that 'it can hardly be doubted' that 'the government interest in the state *and* federal regulation of nursing homes ... is of the highest order." (emphasis added)

Without citing any authority, Judge Larimer simply chose to ignore the whole administrative structure, the contractual obligations of the State under Medicaid, and the fact that a state enforcement action of this nature had never been done before. Earlier in this decision, he acknowledged (p. 2) that Medicare/Medicaid certification was a requirement of the state operating certificate, and (footnote 2) that Medicaid is administered by CMS and state agencies such as DOH. In order to administer Medicaid, the state has to have standards for Medicaid. The state Medicaid contract sets those standards equal to the Medicare standards. Those standards under this system are the quality standards for the State, and the survey process was to enforce those standards.

Larimer cannot simply set aside Medicare/Medicaid. The covering letter of the survey report stated that it was a joint federal/state survey and offered a right to appeal findings to HCFA. Thus, depositions produced the following testimony:

Office of Continuing Care (OCC) director Laura Leeds testified that the federal survey process produces the factual basis for both federal and state enforcement actions like termination and revocation.

OCC director of Bureau of LTC and Quality Assurance Anna Colello testified that she knew of no basis for the Beechwood revocation independent of the basis for termination.

Colello reiterated that in Beechwood's case, the revocation was not independent of the termination.

Bureau of Administrative Hearings director Russel Altone stated, "At 'various points' before, during, and after the DOH hearing there were 'several communications,'" primarily by phone, between HCFA and BAH attorneys, including Gura and himself These were for "cooperative information sharing" as well as "coordination with HCFA." (Altone, #14 & 15 of Interrogatory response)

### Qualified immunity:

Page 51: "Although, given my findings that plaintiffs' claims are meritless and barred by collateral estoppel, it is unnecessary to reach the issue of qualified immunity, I discuss it only to make clear that defendants are entitled to summary judgment on this ground as well."

"Government officials are shielded from civil liability under 42 U.S.C. § 1983 by the doctrine of qualified immunity so long as their conduct 'does not violate clearly established statutory or constitutional rights of which a reasonable person would have known.' *Harlow v. Fitzgerald*, 457 U.S. 800, 818 (1982)."

Page 52: "In its decision (Blue), the Second Circuit held that in order to defeat the defendants' motion, the plaintiff was required to 'offer specific evidence of improper motivation,' and to 'proffer particularized evidence of direct or circumstantial facts ... supporting the claim of an improper motive in order to avoid summary judgment.' 72 F.3d at 1083-84. In so holding, the court observed that '[t]he reasonableness of the [defendants'] conduct is itself substantial evidence in support of the motion and requires in response a particularized proffer of evidence of unconstitutional motive.'"

Page 53: "… plaintiffs in the case at bar have not proffered particularized evidence of improper intent on the part of defendants to defeat defendants' well-founded motions for summary judgment."

### Discovery request:
Page 55: "Plaintiffs have not made a sufficient showing under Rule 56(f), which requires them to submit an affidavit describing: (1) the information sought and how it will be obtained; (2) how it is reasonably expected to raise a genuine issue of material fact; (3) prior efforts to obtain the information; and (4) why those efforts failed."

Page 55: "*Chambery does not state exactly what evidence plaintiffs seek,* what efforts have been made to obtain it, or how that evidence can reasonably be expected to raise a genuine issue of material fact. *While 'Rule 56(f) discovery is specifically designed to enable a plaintiff to fill material evidentiary gaps in its case … it does not permit a plaintiff to engage in a "fishing expedition."'* (Paddington *Partners v. Bouchard,* 34F.3d 1132, 1138 (2nd Cir.1994))" (emphasis added).

Page 56: "Furthermore, although it is technically correct that there has been no formal discovery in this action, in a broader sense to say that plaintiffs have not had any discovery is somewhat disingenuous. Plaintiffs' appendix submitted in connection with the pending motions, consisting of various affidavits and other documents, is some four inches thick, and as stated, the parties here have already been through considerable administrative proceedings. Plaintiffs do not appear to deny defendants' assertion that, both in the DOH administrative proceedings and in response to plaintiffs' requests under the New York Freedom of Information Law (FOIL), DOH produced well over 1000 pages of documents relating to DOH policies and procedures and its surveys of Beechwood. See Reply Affidavit of Harold J. Rosenthal (Docket #83), ¶ 3."

Page 57: "*Clearly, then, plaintiffs are already in possession of a vast number of documents relating to the issues in this case. Chambery's conclusory assertion that 'some facts are still exclusively in the control of the defendants,' Chambery Aff. ¶ 193, is not enough to meet plaintiffs' burden of showing that they need discovery in order to oppose defendants' motions. (See Ying Jing Gan v. City of New York,*

*996 F.2d 522, 532 (wd Cir. 1993)"* (emphasis added).

The foregoing statements are simply unjust. As discussed earlier in this chapter, Judge Larimer clearly knew the superiority of a court supervised discovery process as opposed to use of FOILs, and he was aware that there was a lack of any discovery in a state hearing. He should also have known that Beechwood did not have the right to cross-examine witnesses on motive at the DOH hearing. Finally, he should also have been aware of the lack of compliance with the subpoenas Beechwood issued.

### Taking of the Certificate of Need (CON):
Page 35: *"The simple fact is that plaintiffs did close the facility in July 1999."* (emphasis added)

This is a ridiculous statement. Beechwood might have officially locked the doors on July 16, 1999, but not voluntarily. DOH slammed them shut by terminating the facility's Medicaid/Medicare certification, moving its residents, and creating a media blitz that, as one DOH attorney put it, did "a fine job ... of sullying Beechwood, and the Chamberys' good name." As we saw earlier, at the hearing on July 8, DOH attorneys Marie Shea and Mary Jane Proschel acknowledged that things had already gone too far to restore Beechwood's operations.

Page 35: *"Greenberg, then, was correct in his February 2, 2000 letter* when he stated that *Beechwood was not, at that time, considered 'an existing resource of residential health care facility ('RHCF') beds,'* and that there was, in effect, nothing (other than the property itself) to transfer" (emphasis added).

Larimer adopted Division of Legal Affairs (DLA) director Henry Greenberg's position without citing any supporting law or regulation concerning certificates of need that defines "existing resource" as a facility that is currently open. Certificates of need are routinely granted before owners commit resources to build facilities. In addition, DOH admitted in FOIL #01-01-148, Item #18, that there was no official DOH position stating that closing a facility automatically revokes its certificate of need. Greenberg's letter of February 2, 2000 was drafted by a staff attorney, with Altone providing coordination. The staff attorney took this position even though it was simply his "understanding" of the DOH position after he discussed it with other non-senior attorneys within DLA.

Obviously, Beechwood was an existing resource, even though closed. On July 22, 1999, Altone even noted it was an "82 bed resource" and was discussing—and later proposed to Greenberg—that the DOH require only that any new operator get established. In other words, a new CON would not be necessary because the facility was considered an existing resource. This position was incorporated into a letter sent to Beechwood in November of 1999; however, because Beechwood did not accept other demands in the November letter —which Bureau of Litigation attorney Harold Rosenthal labeled an "overreach"— the resource somehow disappeared by February of 2000, when Greenberg sent a new letter.

Judge Larimer's position also made a mockery of his earlier statement in the injunction decision that he was not sure the business could not have been resurrected if Beechwood eventually succeeded in the hearing or in an appeal. Under his new position, the Chamberys would have been subject to filing for a new CON and also subject to new decisions by DOH about whether such a resource was necessary in the community. This is more of the pure insanity that characterized the hearing, the appeal, and the grant of a summary judgment denying our Civil Rights claim. It is punctuated by this concluding statement by Larimer (page 37): "Plaintiffs received all the process that was due them in the state administrative process that led to the revocation of their operating certificate." The only "due process" that Larimer was concerned about for Beechwood was the "process that was due them" as meted out by the state and federal actors.

# " ... a Retaliatory Motive"

January 29, 2004, brought the final decision from the CMS Department of Appeal Board (DAB) concerning the termination of Beechwood as a Medicare provider. It was very disappointing, of course, but hardly surprising. All along we had assumed that a court case would be necessary to resolve the issues. The infinitely harder blow came in May 2004 when Judge David Larimer dismissed our "1983" civil rights case. Among the most painful aspects of the decision was the hostility directed at me personally and the judge's refusal to consider the evidence we had so carefully and laboriously sorted out and pieced together over the two-and-a- half years prior to filing. Larimer manifested total absence of the conviction he had put in his statement, made almost five years earlier, in his decision refusing to hear our request for an injunction: "These are serious issues, and if, in fact, a state agency or its agent has decided to take action which is arbitrary and without factual basis to cause injury to a bona fide, long-established business, that is most troubling and reprehensible" (p. 24).

I had no doubt about the next moves. We would appeal Judge Larimer's decision to the U.S. Court of Appeals for the Second Circuit in New York City. In the meantime, we had to file our appeal of the CMS administrative outcome at the federal district court level. We chose the DC District Court in an effort to avoid Judge Larimer and filed the case on July 15, 2004. The Second Circuit appeal was filed on September 23 of that year. On Nov. 9, Beechwood filed yet another major case, this time with the New York State Court of Appeals regarding our entitlement to reimbursement for legal fees expended in obtaining three state court orders against DOH for documents. This case and its outcome were discussed in Chapter 9.

By the second half of 2004 and well into 2005, the legal activity orbiting about Beechwood was all driven by Beechwood. In addition to the legal cases, I continued my Freedom of Information (FOI) activity, including using it to begin pursuing the Medicaid Fraud Control Unit (MFCU) for documents concerning the outcome of the criminal investigation. I also communicated with the FBI in an effort to trigger an investigation of DOH officials for program fraud, and with the New York State Ethics Commission about investigating violations of the State Code of Ethics.

The appeal of the CMS administration hearing decision was pursued to counter the legitimacy that Judge Larimer was imputing to the New York ALJ's decision to support a revocation of Beechwood's operating license. It was an immense amount of work, but as we discussed previously, we considered the opportunity to overturn patient care issues to be a very important element in support of the civil rights case.

The appeal of Judge Larimer's decision, however, was crucial and a far different matter. First, legal writing and argument at this level is a very specialized area, as is knowledge of the Second Circuit. Second, there is probably less than a 5 percent chance of getting a decision reversed. Third, another loss—one that was a 95 percent likelihood—would almost certainly mean the end of the road: the inability to collect damages from anyone anywhere. Kevin Cooman, our principal counsel, and I were in agreement that a new attorney or legal team was needed to bring the new perspectives and specialized expertise necessary for this appeal. Quite literally everything was on the line in choosing these attorneys, getting them to fully comprehend the complex issues, narrowing the claims and focus of the appeal, and presenting it to the court. Cooman was instrumental in the search for legal talent, and we soon settled on Mark Grannis to head up the appeal efforts. By May 27, 2004, Grannis was on board, and on June 3, we filed our notice of intent to appeal with the Second Circuit. We decided that the appeal should be limited to just three issues: Retaliation, Equal Protection, and Procedural Due Process. This meant giving up our claims regarding the supremacy of federal law over conflicting state law, as well as violations of federal survey and certification protocol. It also meant giving up any appeal of issues affecting the ALJ findings on patient care, which carried the grave risk that, if the Second Circuit overturned Judge Larimer on the First Amendment retaliation issue and the case went to the jury, the jury could still be left with a mixed-motive case. That is, even if they found that the state officials had an improper motive, legitimate problems might, in their view, still exist at Beechwood. In other words, the jury might conclude that the officials had acted improperly but nevertheless had identified legitimate deficiencies at Beechwood. Such an outcome could significantly lower damages awards; however, we needed to narrow the issues to the most important and make sure we overturned Larimer's decision. We did not expect a circuit court to wade into survey protocol or patient care issues, and we had just initiated the district court-level appeal of the Medicare termination, which addressed these issues.

On September 23, we filed our brief with the Second Circuit. Because CMS and DOH officials were named as defendants, both CMS and DOH had to file reply briefs, which they did in October and November, respectively. We filed our responding brief on December 13, 2004.

On July 7, 2005, oral argument was presented before a panel of three judges. Judge Jacobs asked the state's attorney, Shaifali Puri, whether any discovery had been allowed before the DOH hearing. She answered that there were productions subsequent to subpoenas but did not say when this occurred and avoided directly addressing the question. She then discussed the fact that Beechwood had eighteen witnesses, received emails, and continued to do FOILs after the hearing. Her lack of candor likely raised a bright red flag with the judges.

Later, Judge Jacobs asked Puri if the state had overreached in revoking the license. Even though DOH attorney Marie Shea had stated on the hearing record that it was a voluntary proceeding and as of June 30, 1999 Bureau of Administrative Hearings director Russel Altone had no idea how to answer why DOH was not going for a lesser penalty, Puri responded to Jacobs by stating that the survey and termination were statutorily mandated, adding that the ALJ upheld the survey results, thus implying that the termination was mandatory.

Judge Jacobs then got into the early emails anticipating the termination and shutdown of the facility. He called these "very irregular" and also addressed the documents demonstrating gloating over the "ability to destroy." Puri responded that this was simply "regulatory friction," using the phrase that Judge Larimer had employed in his decision.

When Beechwood's attorney Mark Grannis got his chance for rebuttal, he went straight to the heart of the issue, stating that the ALJ ruled on the bias issue, but that the ruling amounted to "dicta," statements of general principle. He explained that the ALJ was never presented with the contention that in selecting Beechwood for termination and license revocation there was an ulterior agenda that had nothing to do with conditions in the facility. One of the judges responded, "never presented at the hearing?" Mark answered, "no, we had no idea how high this went. Key defendants were not even called as witnesses."

Judge Parker, asked about the argument just made by Puri that the revocation proceeding was mandatory, there was no choice but to proceed, and the ALJ had no choice but to make a decision on it. Grannis responded that the right to perform the inspection was not being questioned, but that DOH cannot prejudge the outcome before going in. Parker asked him whether this sanction, license revocation, would have been applied if Beechwood had been the only facility in the state. Grannis answered that New York does not have an absolute-compliance or zero tolerance standard, as shown by the fact that no hearing such as the one convened over the Beechwood matter had ever been held before—or since. Judge Jacobs responded: "This is the only nursing home that has been shut down on this basis in the memory of man?"

"Yes," Grannis answered

"You're sure about that?" Parker asked. "Yes." Grannis went on to say that he believed it was undisputed in the record, at least since OBRA 87 implementation.

***Second Circuit requests the case record.*** The Second Circuit panel was obviously concerned with what it had seen and heard, sufficiently concerned to ask Judge Larimer to send the "Record on Appeal." Larimer's office did this on September 28, 2005, "as requested," and when we received notice of this event, we knew it was a good sign for us.

## UNANIMOUS SECOND CIRCUIT DECISION TO REVERSE
### *BEECHWOOD RESTORATIVE CARE CENTER V. LEEDS*,
### 436 F. 3D 147 (2D CIR. 2006)
### "BEECHWOOD PRODUCED SUFFICIENT EVIDENCE
### OF RETALIATORY MOTIVE."

On January 31, 2006, the judges of Second Circuit issued their decision.

## Discussion

Page 10: "We review the district court's grant of summary judgment de novo, reviewing the evidence in the light most favorable to Appellants. *See Anthony v. City of New York*, 339 F.3d 129, 134 (2d Cir. 2003). Summary judgment is proper if 'there is no genuine issue as to any material fact' and Appellees are 'entitled to a judgment as a matter of law.' Fed. R. Civ. P. 56(c)." This was in direct contradiction to Judge Larimer, who had stated (p. 38), "I realize the Court's obligation ... to view the record in the light most favorable to the nonmoving parties, and to draw all inference in their favor. ... however ... some tension between operators of homes and regulators is to be expected." The truth was that, instead of a "de novo" review, Larimer (p. 37) relied simply on the ALJ's "without a shred of evidence" statement, and (p. 38) the fact that two ALJs found merit to the deficiencies.

## First Amendment retaliation

Page 11: "To survive summary judgment on a section 1983 First Amendment retaliation claim a plaintiff must demonstrate that he engaged in protected speech, and that the speech was a substantial or motivating factor in an adverse decision taken by the defendant. *See Hynes v. Squillace,* 143 F.3d 653, 658 (2d Cir. 1998)."

"It is undisputed that Brook Chambery's complaints, protests, and lawsuits are protected speech. *Cf. Franco v. Kelly,* 854 F.2d 584, 588-89 (2d Cir. 1988) (describing 'right to petition government for redress of grievances' and 'guaranteed by the First and Fourteenth amendments)."

Page 12: "The district court ruled that the claims were barred by the doctrine of collateral estoppel because in the state administrative hearing concerning DOH's request to revoke the Chamberys' operating certificate, the ALJ considered and rejected the partnership's arguments that DOH was driven by an improper motive. See Beechwood, 317 F. Supp. 2d. at 261-72. In the alternative, the district court ruled that Appellants failed to produce sufficient evidence of any improper motive. Id. at 274-75. We disagree on both grounds."

*Concerning issue preclusion,* the Court agreed with Beechwood's argument, writing:

Page 12: "Under New York law, a prior decision has preclusive effect as to any issue that both was 'necessarily decided' in the first action, *and* is "decisive" in the later action."

Page 13: "Appellants concede that the ALJ 'necessarily decided' the sufficiency of the State's evidence of violations. Sufficiency on that score, however, does not defeat Beechwood's present claim, because a plaintiff can prove First Amendment retaliation even if the measures taken by the state were otherwise justified. *See*, e.g., *Leather v. Eyck*, 180 F.3d 420, 426 (2d Cir. 1999) ... also *Waters v. Churchill*, 511 U.S. 661, 681 (1994) ... also *Gorman-Bakos v. Cornell Coop.* Extension, 252 F.3d 545, 557b (2nd Cir. 2001)."

Beechwood conceded the ALJ's ability to rule on the patient care charges and did not argue the outcome because of the need to remain focused exclusively on the main issue. We took this approach, even though we realized it would leave a "mixed motive" case, such as was present in the Leather and Mt. Healthy cases.

Page 13: "The ALJ's finding that DOH was unbiased was made as part of an evaluation of DOH's credibility. That ruling—if decided necessarily by the ALJ— would be decisive of the present case, which requires a showing of bias."

Page 14: "But the issue was considered in the context of the partnership's challenge to the credibility of DOH personnel. In so doing, did the ALJ decide the issue 'necessarily'? This is a showing that the State, as proponent of collateral estoppel, has the burden to make, *Jeffreys v. Griffin*, 1 N.Y.3d 34, 39 (2003), and most clearly establish, *Colon v. Coughlin*, 58 F.3d 86, 869 (2d Cir. 1995)."

Page 15: "An issue that is 'necessarily decided' must have been both 'actually decided' (as it was here) and 'necessary to support a valid and final judgment on the merits' (which is not so clear at all). See Leather, 180 F.3d at 426; *Wilder v. Thomas*, 854 F.2d 605, 620 (2d Cir. 1988). We are not persuaded that the ALJ's discussion and rejection of the partnership's allegations of improper DOH motives was "necessary" in that sense. ... The ALJ's conscientious discussion of motive concerns the credibility of evidence presented by DOH; and while that may have impacted the ALJ's findings of violations, the State has not shown to us that the ALJ's credibility findings were so influential as to be actually decisive of the ultimate question concerning the quality of resident care: The charges against the partnership might have been sustainable even if they were animated by bias and retaliation. The State, which shoulders the burden on this point, has made no showing as to the scope of the ALJ's jurisdiction, or as to whether a finding of improper motive or adverse credibility would have made a difference— necessarily—in the ALJ's ultimate determination."

Page 16: "Relying on *Scott v. Coughlin*, 344 F.3d 282, 287-88 (2d Cir. 2003)— which held that an agency is entitled to summary judgment on a First Amendment retaliation claim if it can show that 'it would have taken exactly the same action absent the improper motive'—DOH argues that the surveys undertaken, the deficiencies found, and the resulting revocation of the operating certificate, were statutorily required. However, even if the pre-revocation surveys were mandated, and even if the State must commence revocation proceedings once it has determined that certain classes of deficiencies exist, N.Y. Pub. Health Law § 2806-b, the identification, characterization, and classification of the actual deficiencies found are within the State's discretion, and are therefore subject to a claim of improper motive."

The Court then went on to discuss the evidence of retaliatory motive that Beechwood produced:

Page 17: "Beechwood produced sufficient evidence of retaliatory motive to survive summary judgment. Suspect chronology—the close sequence of protest and scrutiny—constitutes circumstantial evidence, along with evidence that the 1999 'Offensive' was pre-planned....

There is direct evidence, however, that the State's hostile pursuit of the partnership was motivated by an intent to punish the partnership for exercising First Amendment rights of speech and petition rather than by—or distinctly in addition to—the antagonism that arises between a regulator and the regulated (a relationship easily inflamed by difficult personalities)."

Page 18: "This is evidence from which a jury could reasonably find that the DOH was campaigning against the partnership as retaliation for the exercise of First Amendment rights. We therefore vacate and remand as to the First Amendment claim."

### The Federal Defendants

Page 19: "Beechwood points to evidence that [HCFA regional administrator Sue] Kelly and Daniel were supportive of DOH's effort to revoke the operating certificate, and were invested more generally in the effort to shut down Beechwood."

Page 20: "Cooperation between state and federal bureaucracies acting in their regulatory spheres supports no inference that the federal actors acted with an improper motive. *See Hafner v. Brown,* 983 F.2d 570, 577 (4th Cir. 1992) (concluding that § 1983 civil conspiracy requires "a meeting of the minds to accomplish the unlawful act" (emphasis added)); cf. *Strickland v. Shalala,* 123 F.3d 863, 868 (6th Cir. 1997)."

I believe the Court should have looked more closely at the evidence they had in front of them concerning the timing of and reasoning for this HCFA involvement. This includes:

> April 21: Western Region DOH Acting Director Sanford Rubin and Western Region Continuing Care Director Sharon Carlo discussed involvement by both federal authorities and Russel Altone in the context of termination and a bigger global picture.

> April 23: Altone writes that Beechwood is currently on a collision course for termination by HCFA.

> April 26: Rubin tells Office of Continuing Care deputy director Laura Leeds that Kelly will back us "all the way. ... The chickens are coming home to roost. (What does "all the way" mean? Terminating the right to a hearing? Rigging the hearing decision?)

> April 29: Leeds tells Acting Commissioner of Health Dennis Whalen that HCFA has been cooperative since Chambery "has tried to go around the State."

> May 11: Altone states that "the Feds would be responsible for doing the termination of provider hearing."

### Due Process (annulling the CON)

Page 24: "On appeal, the parties vigorously contest whether, under New York law, notice and an opportunity for a hearing was necessary—an issue of first impression and some uncertainty. We need not decide the issue because, even assuming that Beechwood was entitled under State law to notice and a hearing, there was no due process violation."

Page 25: "We have previously held that where a due process violation results from a 'random unauthorized act' by state officials—as opposed to an 'established state procedure'—the availability of a 'meaningful post-deprivation remedy' defeats the claim: '[T]here is no constitutional violation (and no available § 1983 action) when there is an adequate state post deprivation procedure to remedy a random, arbitrary deprivation of property or liberty.' *Hellenic Am. Neighborhood Action Comm. v. City of New York,* 101 F.3d 877, 880-82 (2d Cir. 1996)."

Page 26: "An Article 78 proceeding therefore afforded a meaningful post-deprivation remedy for Appellants' claimed violation. See id. at 881-82 (holding Article 78 provided a 'perfectly adequate post deprivation remedy,' and citing cases); see also Gudema v. Nassau County, 163 F.3d 717, 724-25 (2d Cir. 1998) (same)."

Page 27: "'An Article 78 proceeding is adequate for due process purposes even though the petitioner may not be able to recover the same relief that he could in a § 1983 suit.' Hellenic, 101 F.3d at 881."

### Equal Protection Claim

Page 21: "For essentially the same reasons underlying the First Amendment retaliation claim, the partnership alleges a violation of its equal protection rights under the Fifth and Fourteenth Amendments. However, an equal protection claim requires (inter alia) evidence from which a jury could find that the plaintiff was selectively treated as 'compared with others similarly situated.' ... As the district court observed, Appellants have failed to produce evidence of any 'similarly situated' individual or institution treated more favorably than Appellants. Beechwood, 317 F. Supp. 2d at 276-78."

I would point out, however, that proving "similarly situated" is virtually impossible in the context of a very subjective system in which there are more than 300 survey tags; various scope and severity levels, including "the potential for" a problem; different sanctions and time frames for enforcement that can be applied; and an absence of access to the information needed to make these comparisons.

Page 21: "The partnership has adduced some evidence that the revocation of its operating certificate was an unusual measure, but, as the district court soundly observed, some sanctions may be imposed rarely because they are rarely justified. Moreover, as the partnership affirmatively contends and illustrates, it was resistant to DOH recommendations. It is obvious that, given Brook Chambery's confrontational approach to regulation, DOH might well decide that this particular facility presented the highly unusual instance in which harsher sanctions are needed because DOH could not rely on voluntary compliance and willing reforms. Conclusory assertions—that Beechwood was a 'better than average nursing home subjected to worse than-average treatment,' and that Beechwood was subjected to 'harsher-than-usual penalties' and 'shorter-than-usual timetables'—are not enough to show dissimilar treatment among those similarly situated, at least not at this stage of the proceedings. ... '[M]ere conclusory allegations, speculation or conjecture will not avail a party resisting summary judgment.' *Cifarelli v. Village of Babylon,* 93 F.3d 47, 51 (2d Cir. 1996)"

This position by the Court is highly problematic. First, the revocation of Beechwood's operating certificate was not merely "unusual," it was the administrative equivalent of dropping an atomic bomb. DOH had never held its own hearing in order to apply sanctions for patient care survey issues, and doing so is also terribly inconsistent with DOH policy and procedure. Second, the Court stated that there was enough evidence of a retaliatory violation of First Amendment rights and recognized that the "identification, characterization, and classification of the actual deficiencies found are within the State's discretion, and are therefore subject to a claim of improper motive," yet it now refused to use the presence of that same subjective ill will to furnish this second prong of the proof necessary, under case law, to establish a violation of due process. Third, Beechwood did not submit "subjective opinion" or unsupported "conclusory allegations" as to the quality of its care. It referenced official DOH and HCFA data—as of two months prior to the survey and going back five years.

Page 23: "Finally, appellants invite the comparison between their treatment at the hands of regulators before the Chamberys' skirmishes with the DOH began and afterward. In *La Trieste Restaurant and Cabaret, Inc. v. Village of Port Chester,* we held that the plaintiff satisfied the 'similarly situated' requirement by producing evidence that the defendants did not enforce a zoning ordinance against the plaintiff until the plaintiff engaged in protected conduct—that conduct being the only change in plaintiff's circumstances. 40 F.3d 587, 590. Here, the revocation of the operating certificate followed protected conduct; but, as Appellants concede, the revocation also followed substantiated charges of new serious deficiencies. The partnership cannot establish differential treatment through a before-and-after approach."

## "VERY GOOD TO EXCELLENT CARE":
### IN SEARCH OF EXONERATION

The success of our appeal to the Second Circuit, which found that we had "produced sufficient evidence of retaliatory motive" in bringing our "1983" civil rights suit against officials of the both the state and federal governments, was a sweet victory—the first in a seven years of administrative and civil action. It also significantly impacted the directions taken in the following actions.

*Pursuit of the MFCU investigative file.* In September 2003, Assistant Attorney General Jerry Solomon, director of the Rochester office of the MFCU, closed the Beechwood criminal investigation so quietly that he issued no formal notice of any kind, not to Beechwood and not to me. He simply returned all of our business records. Nevertheless, given the politics behind the Beechwood matter, the resources that must have been consumed by the investigation, and my amply justified fear of yet another false prosecution, I welcomed this outcome as if it had been accompanied by Fourth of July fireworks. Not only was it an exoneration of potential charges that could have put me in federal prison, the records from this investigation had the potential of completely offsetting the outcomes obtained from the administrative hearings. Thus, I could not let matters rest. On December 22, 2004, I constructed a new FOI request to begin my pursuit of information from this investigative file. This was followed with a letter of clarification on January 12, 2005.

On May 26, 2005, I received two communications. First was a letter from the Records Appeal Officer, Tom Litsky, claiming exemptions from disclosure under the Criminal Procedure Law. Second, was a call from AG Solomon offering the opportunity to meet at his office to review the investigative file. I accepted and went to his office on June 21.

*The exonerating material is found to exist, but privilege is claimed against its production.* When I arrived for the meeting, Solomon ushered me into a conference room where investigative files were spread out on a conference table. He allowed me to read his closing memorandum, which stated that Beechwood appeared to have provided "very good to excellent care." He also let me read an email from his supervisor in New York City, which included the comment that what happened to Beechwood was a special case and that it looked like we—the owners and operators of the facility—walked away from an enterprise generating a million-dollar profit simply because we had a disagreement with DOH.

Solomon went on to read from the synopsis that accompanied the final "writer's report," which also cited our "very good to excellent care." He then read from a summary of the outcome of the staffing investigation, which concluded that Beechwood staffing levels exceeded the latest Medicare guidelines and that staffing was constantly adjusted according to patient need.

Finally, AG Solomon offered that no wrongdoing was substantiated by anything the MFCU had investigated and that, therefore, no grounds for civil or criminal prosecution existed. Exoneration was total.

After listening to Solomon and reading the material, I asked him whether he had investigated or was anticipating investigating those within the New York State Department of Health who had fabricated a wholly fictitious case and, by so doing, took our operating license. Since I had been intensively studying the criminal statutes relating to healthcare program fraud, I ended by citing the criminal statutes I thought were appropriate in such an investigation. Solomon responded that it was his understanding that the duties of his office did not extend to investigating healthcare program fraud committed by the administrative agencies—in this case the state DOH and the federal Centers for Medicare and Medicaid Services (CMS). He also persisted in his claim to the document exemptions already outlined by the FOIL appeals officer. These barred the release of any documents, including those I had just seen or from which AG Solomon read aloud to me.

In short, Solomon had freely shown me that exonerating materials produced by his investigation existed. He had allowed me to read some of them, and he read aloud from others. The cat, as it were, was out of the bag. And yet he asserted that these documents were exempt from FOI release.

I would have been flabbergasted, but the accumulation of events since 1999 had put me far beyond that state of being. Instead, on June 25, 2005, I sent a letter to the Records Appeal Officer in New York City outlining what I believed were the invalid reasons for withholding release of these documents. Unsurprisingly, the appeal was rejected, and we were forced to wait until we could use legal motions to compel production of these documents under the discovery process. (This is discussed further in Chapter 16.) In the meantime, I wrote to AG Solomon on August 24, 2005, formally requesting either an investigation of the closure of Beechwood by DOH and HCFA or for his department's cooperation with any potential FBI investigation, which I had already requested.

***Pursuit of an FBI investigation.*** As mentioned, I had thoroughly researched the criminal laws relating to the false prosecution that had been attempted against Beechwood and me, and I was convinced that the existing statutes directly addressed the malfeasance of officials involved with administration of the programs as much as they addressed the alleged malfeasance of those who provide and bill for services under the programs. Although our civil rights appeal had been filed with the Second Circuit, the chance of getting the lower court's decision overturned was very slim, so I felt that even if there were no damages in it for us, I wanted these officials brought to justice. I therefore pursued obtaining a criminal investigation of the actions leading to Beechwood's demise.

On May 16, 2005, I met with an investigator from the Rochester FBI office. She questioned me about why facilities that consistently receive very bad surveys manage to stay open. She confessed that her office was fairly new to the area of healthcare fraud and was feeling its way along. She speculated that the statute of limitations was approaching, mentioned that I had my day in court, and concluded that she could see no smoking gun in what I presented. Undaunted, on June 7, 2005, I sent her a letter in which I outlined the specifics of the Medicare/Medicaid program fraud that I had alleged, and the laws violated. I closed the letter by formally requesting an investigation. In response, she called an attorney in the U.S. Attorney's Office about the matter. On September 7, that attorney called me to discuss the matter, but hung up the phone in the middle of the conversation once he heard that I was suing DOH and HCFA officials. I understood. Any conversation with me created a conflict of interest, since his division had the responsibility for defending the HCFA officials being sued.

It was yet another in a long series of catch-22s. But I turned to Beechwood's counsel, Kevin Cooman, to endeavor to find a means of resolution. On October

4, 2005, he contacted the U.S. Attorney, requesting that, due to conflicts of interest involving representation of the HCFA defendants, an outside counsel or special prosecutor be appointed to help with any FBI investigation. And that, it turned out, was the last we ever heard about an investigation. When we sought information from the FBI as to whether it had been started, we were told that they don't release details concerning internal matters.

A couple of months after Cooman's request for a special counsel, the Second Circuit overturned Judge Larimer, putting the civil rights case back in motion. So, we let the pursuit of a criminal investigation rest. We did not want to chance an FBI investigation interfering with our opportunity to place our defendants in front of a federal jury.

***Pursuit of an investigation by the New York State Ethics Commission.*** On July 5, 2005, I sent a letter to the New York State Ethics Commission requesting an investigation of DOH officials for acts committed in violation of the Public Officers Laws. On September 29, legal counsel for the Ethics Commission replied in a letter stating: "For a violation of the State Code of Ethics, there must be a conflict between a state employee's private, personal interests and their official actions. The allegations set forth in your July 5th letter address DOH employees erroneous acts or failure to act in the course of performing their official duties within the agency, and do not include any allegation that the DOH employees' private or personal interests were in substantial conflict with the proper discharge of their official duties. Moreover, the appropriateness of DOH sanctions against your facility is clearly outside the scope and authority of the Commission."

We had two substantial victories, one resurrecting our civil rights suit and the other witnessing the quiet end to the spurious criminal investigation of Beechwood and me. As our attempts were thwarted to hold criminally responsible those who had abused their regulatory authority, we focused on the civil rights suit as well as our court appeal of the agency-level determination to uphold Beechwood's Medicare termination.

# CHAPTER 13

# Bias Unwavering

On July 15, 2004, we filed an appeal of the agency-level determination to uphold the Medicare termination. As mentioned previously, to avoid Judge David Larimer in New York, we made the filing with the federal district court in Washington D.C., delivering a brief whose 90-page length made that term a spectacular misnomer, especially considering that it was attached to a case record now well over 6,000 pages.

## THE BEECHWOOD BRIEF

Beechwood's complaint consisted of twelve claims, or "Causes of Action." From a structural standpoint, the very first was the most important:

> First Claim: The enforcement actions taken against Beechwood were invalid because they were not preceded by any legitimate certifications by the New York States Department of Health (DOH) or initial determinations by Health-care Finance Administration (HCFA). In summary, the "CMS [Centers for Medicare & Medicaid Services] action was arbitrary, capricious, an abuse of discretion, otherwise not in accordance with law, or without observance of procedure required by law, and must therefore be set aside pursuant to 5 U.S.C. 707(2)(A) and (D)."

The next eleven constituted a litany of improper procedure:

> Second Claim: There was a gross failure by DOH to follow mandated protocol, documentation standards, and certification requirements.

> Third Claim: The termination notice was improper.

Fourth Claim: Using termination instead of civil money penalties (CMPs) was a violation of the equal protection clause of the Fourteenth Amendment.

Fifth Claim: The CMPs that were imposed by DOH were illegal.

Sixth Claim: The denial of payment for new [Medicare and Medicaid patient] admissions (DPNA) was issued without proper notice.

Seventh Claim: The CMS administrative hearing was improper in many respects, such as the ALJ failing to rule on the adequacy of CMS's prima facie case, the lack of proper documentation and protocols, and the scope and severity of the deficiencies.

Eighth Claim: The immediate jeopardy (IJ) was improperly alleged on the April survey.

Ninth Claim: The May adjudicated deficiencies were not supported by substantial evidence.

Tenth Claim: The June adjudicated deficiencies were not supported by substantial evidence

Eleventh Claim: The April adjudicated deficiencies were not supported by substantial evidence.

Twelfth Claim: The remedies applied were not justified by the adjudicated deficiencies and findings sustained.

Predictably, the defendants objected to the D.C. filing. At this point, the Second Circuit had not yet overturned Judge Larimer's decision to grant the summary motion to dismiss our "1983" civil rights suit. The DOH, having received a couple of favorable rulings from Judge Larimer and knowing that this related matter would be assigned to his court, was eager to get it into his hands. Although the case could have been heard in D.C., Beechwood had no legal basis to stop the transfer to Western New York. Thus, on June 9, 2005, the Complaint was refiled in the Western New York District. Things moved ahead at their customary glacial pace. After a scheduling conference on October 12, 2005, Beechwood approached Judge Feldman, Larimer's magistrate, about getting the big picture issues out of the way, which might then eliminate the need for having to resolve the fact-intensive patient care issues. On October 13, 2005, Judge Feldman ruled in our favor: "due to the size of the administrative record and the identification of several causes of action which, if decided early in the litigation, may resolve or narrow the need for further proceedings, plaintiff shall be permitted to file a dispositive motion ... with respect to ... [certain identified claims]

… as concern the remedy recommendation, enforcement and certification process followed by defendant and its agents with respect to plaintiff."

On December 30, 2005, we filed a 60-page motion for Partial Summary Judgment. Accompanying the brief was my affidavit citing Attorney General Jerry Solomon's "excellent care" conclusion from his investigative report, along with Beechwood stellar quality (OSCAR) data, the failure of HCFA to supply any documentation to support the Medicare/Medicaid termination decision, and sections of the State Operations Manual (SOM) regarding proper survey and enforcement procedure. The brief stated:

Page 2: Beechwood is "Seek[ing] relief based primarily on CMS actions during its enforcement process, including the failure of CMS and its agent, DOH, to observe the remedy, certification and notice requirements prescribed by federal statute and CMS's own regulations and protocols."

Page 11: "DOH, as survey agent, failed to make the necessary and proper certifications and enforcement recommendations to CMS throughout the entire survey cycle, consisting of the April, May and June 1999 surveys. In turn, CMS did not (indeed, could not) properly and independently determine noncompliance and the proper remedy to be applied. Instead, CMS gave *carte blanche* to DOH, accepted uncertified and even verbal allegations of noncompliance and remedy recommendations, and then simply issued three letters to Beechwood in April, May and June 1999, and erroneous and untimely public notices, which purported to communicate compliance decisions and certifications that CMS in fact never made."

### Regarding the Absence of Any CMS Review Process":
Page 17: Subpoena responses have demonstrated that CMS had "no document prepared by any CMS employee demonstrating analysis, certification or other form of oversight or review of any kind with respect to the May 1999 and June 1999 surveys and SODs which purportedly justified CMS's hasty termination of Beechwood."

Page 18: "Glaringly absent from the CMS records were the required CMS Forms 1539 and 462L for any of the three surveys at Beechwood in April, May and June, containing any formal certification of noncompliance from the DOH survey team. Without that certification, there was no basis on which the CMS regional office could proceed to complete its portion of the CMS Form 1539 ... For whatever reason, no representative of the survey agent or at CMS was able or willing to 'go on the line' to certify any noncompliance, and be accountable for this decision."

Page 18: "The import of the disclosures finally extracted from CMS is profound: because CMS had no documentation showing that it ever actually made any 'initial determination' and certification review concerning the alleged noncompliance by Beechwood, or the remedies to be applied ... no legitimate CMS action ever took place."

Page 19: "This wholesale failure of CMS to actually engage in a deliberative oversight and enforcement process constitutes no less than a willful disregard of its statutory obligations, and its own rules, demonstrates that its enforcement actions were arbitrary, capricious and an abuse of discretion, and not in accordance with the statute or the CMS implementing regulations. CMS's actions and decisions must therefore be overturned.

"Beechwood has been forced to endure years of a CMS administrative appeal process, in order to even get to this judicial forum, which is finally empowered to review the CMS administrative process against Beechwood, and declare it unlawful."

*Regarding the June 1999 survey and CMS remedy imposition:*
Page 21: "On June 29, 1999—two weeks *after* termination occurred—CMS sent to Beechwood a letter retroactively imposing the termination remedy on June 17, 1999. (A.R. 5888 [M6504]). That letter, however, and the earlier CMS letters pre-scheduling the termination (A.R. 3778-9), are the only CMS documents related to the termination. CMS was unable to produce a single scrap of paper demonstrating that it received or scrutinized any of the DOH proposed findings (e.g., the June SOD on CMS Form 2567, or any other materials purporting to certify or document noncompliance or Beechwood's compliance with the DPOC, the facility's own plan of correction and assertion of substantial compliance (A.R. 5916)) before imposing the 'rare' sanction of Program termination, "generally

reserved for the most egregious and recidivist institutions.' *Illinois Council*, 529 U.S. at 22.22 The absence of any DOH and CMS certification (CMS Form1539) for this survey (proving the abject failure of CMS to 'ensure that the SA's [survey agent's] documentation supports the SA certification recommendation' as required by SOM§ 2778) confirms that the final notice of termination given to Beechwood was merely a perfunctory last act of an unsupported charade to which CMS was already committed. (A.R. 5362: 'Region II claims it will back us all the way.')"

*Regarding the May 1999 survey and CMS remedy imposition:*
Page 22: "On Friday, May 21, 1999, CMS sent its two page letter to Beechwood imposing a DPNA effective that day. Again reaching for its ultimate weapon, CMS also "rescheduled" a termination of Beechwood for June 17, 1999. (A.R. 3778-9) The CMS letter did not advise Beechwood of its "[r]ight to appeal the determination leading to the remedy," as required by 42 C.F.R. § 488.402(f)(1)(iv). However, despite the seriousness of the remedies CMS imposed, and the accelerated timetable for termination (just 51 days after delivery of the April SOD on April 27, 1999), CMS failed to undertake any review of the allegations contained in the May SOD. CMS was unable to produce a single piece of paper pertaining to the May survey, DOH's allegations of deficient care, Beechwood's POC, or anything resembling a decision-making process prior to remedy imposition."

Page 23: "Actually, the 'review and certify' dysfunction at the CMS Region II offices in this case reveals agency malfeasance at its worst. Instead of receiving and relying on the required formal certifications of noncompliance (CMS Form1539) and an actual SOD (Form2567) before firing off a remedy at Beechwood, CMS instead chose to rely on falsehoods communicated to it by DOH. In a May 13, 1999 memorandum (the day after the completion of the May survey on May 12), DOH (A.R. 5789 [M6401]) represented to CMS that:

> Immediate Jeopardy did not still exist; however the facility remained Substandard in tag F224 [Abuse and Neglect of Residents] based on minimal progress in affecting correction. None of the deficiencies are corrected from the original visit.

In fact, the actual May SOD *contained no F224 allegations of abuse and neglect at all.*" (A.R. 3814-3843)

The May SOD, devoid of any F224 concerns, was not even sent by DOH to CMS for review until Monday, 5/24/99—three days *after* CMS had already imposed the remedy of an immediate DPNA, and prescheduled termination for June 17." A footnote followed: "On 5/20/99 at 6:22 pm—the evening before CMS imposed the immediate DPNA—DOH Supervisor Carlo wrote to the Albany DOH Central Office: 'The staff here have just finished the latest Beechwood SOD and have given it to me for review.... I noted many, many issues that need clarification and Sue [Baker] and Cindy [Francis] are working on it now. My concern is that it has already passed C[entral]O[ffice] and *it really has a lot of holes in it.'* (A.R. 5377 [M5441]) [emphasis added]

An internal DOH e-mail 5/21/99 3:41 pm [Friday] said: 'Nancy called Lee Pope [HCFA supervisor] ... and he had asked about the SOD from Beechwood and the letter. Just a quick note that *he is looking for it,* I know you are finishing up the final, but as soon as you can, please fax it over." (A.R. 5856 [M6470]) [emphasis added]

"On Monday 5/24/99 DOH finally faxed to CMS the May SOD, which contained no F224 allegations at all. Baker [DOH survey supervisor] fax to Lee Pope [CMS] 'Sorry this is late—we have been unable to make the transmission as we couldn't connect, as a result we're trying this other fax #.'"


Page 24: "Reprehensibly, CMS and its Region II associate administrator have gone to great lengths to cover up the fact that they did not require the proper certification process from their survey agent, nor did they undertake the proper certification process themselves. In addition to the document disclosure gamesmanship by CMS that the DAB finally rebuked, the CMS associate administrator responsible for the termination decision made in May 1999 (Sue Kelly), has already twice misrepresented her actions to this very Court. On January31, 2003, the Associate Administrator filed an affidavit in which she swore that:

> "22. Professional members of *my staff and I reviewed the documentation provided by DOH in support of its May 12th recommendation.* As with the previous materials, we found that the findings were presented in the appropriate form and manner, were quite detailed and specific and were based on the direct observation of care provided residents and medical records reflecting the history of care provided residents. It was our conclusion that the DOH survey team exercised appropriate professional judgment and that their findings and recommendations are amply supported.

"23. By letter dated May 21, 1999, I notified Beechwood that based on the revisit survey conducted on May 12, 1999, the termination action scheduled for May 15, 1999 had been rescinded . . . This conclusion was based upon the recommendations of DOH and staff after reviewing steps taken by Beechwood to correct the noted deficiencies. I also noted that due to the seriousness of the remaining deficiencies, CMS would terminate the provider agreement on June 17, 1999, unless the deficiencies were corrected. (Affidavit of Sue Kelly, sworn to 1/29/03, filed in 02-CV-6235L, attached as Exhibit J to B. Chambery aff.) [emphasis added]" A footnote followed: "In June 1999, CMS Associate Administrator Kelly made this same misrepresentation to this Court concerning CMS's supposed review of DOH's May survey documentation and recommendation, in connection with Beechwood's unsuccessful attempt to enjoin DOH and CMS from proceeding. (See Declaration of Sue Kelly, June 15, 1999, ¶15, filed June 17, 1999 in 99-CV-6241L, attached as Exhibit K to B. Chambery aff.)"

Page 25: "Six months later, the self-serving duplicity of this affidavit to the District Court was unmasked during the CMS proceeding, when the CMS's disclosures ordered by the DAB revealed that *none of the required certification documentation were received and reviewed in advance* of Kelly's May 21 issuance of the DPNA and rescheduled termination remedies. (A.R. 2050-2056) Thus, it was *impossible* for her or her staff to have accomplished what she swore to this Court she had done."

### Regarding the April 1999 survey and CMS remedy imposition:
Page 25: "On May 7, 1999, CMS faxed to Beechwood a letter imposing termination from the Programs on May 15, 1999. The letter recited that DOH had recommended termination to CMS based on the April SOD dated April 27, 1999, which alleged that Beechwood 'was not in substantial compliance with the participation requirements, and that immediate jeopardy to facility residents exists.' (A.R. 5911-5912 [M6527-6528])"

Page 26: "There was absolutely no proper documentation or formal determination by CMS supporting the concurrences CMS blithely gave to DOH to allege Immediate Jeopardy (with respect solely to former residents who were no longer at Beechwood), an onerous DPOC, and a fast track termination scheduled for May 15. At the hearing before the CMS ALJ, CMS abandoned any claim that the April deficiencies rose to the heightened level of Immediate Jeopardy (A.R. 1129)30 - even though this is the unsupported level of hysteria which got the snowball rolling downhill against Beechwood. Had CMS actually undertaken a systematic review of the DOH allegations, it might have recognized that the April SOD alleged only 'past noncompliance' (giving CMS the right only to impose a fine for the days of past noncompliance), that there were no ongoing Immediate Jeopardy level concerns present, and that Beechwood was in substantial compliance on the date of survey. *See* Eighth Claim Argument, *infra.*"

***Regarding the internal Department Appeal Board (DAB) decision:***
Page 29: "The supposed inability, on jurisdictional grounds, of the CMS ALJ to review 'the lawfulness of processes and procedures . . . that CMS used to make its determinations,' because such matters 'are plainly outside the scope of the authority that has been delegated to me' (A.R. 138), even if true, is not a restriction that this Court faces. The DAB also abdicated any authority it may have had to recognize and hold unlawful the defective process by which CMS administrators proceeded against Beechwood. Such utter and repeated disregard of its own rules and protocols provides a hornbook illustration of 'arbitrary and capricious' agency conduct, which is also grounds for setting aside agency action. 5 U.S.C. § 706."

## THE CMS RESPONSE TO THE BEECHWOOD BRIEF

On April 21, 2006, CMS filed its opposition brief, relying on the regulations that it had used previously to limit its liability at the administrative level.

Page 40: "Statute and regulations expressly provide that CMS may impose remedies, including termination, for any instance of noncompliance, and that CMS's choice of remedies cannot be challenged. Citing 42 CFR 488. 408(g)(2), and USC 1395i-3(h)(2)(A), and USC 1395cc(b)(2)"

Page 48: "Inadequate survey performance does not ... relieve a facility of its obligation to meet all requirements for program participation: or 'invalidate adequately documented deficiencies.' Citing 42 CFR 488.318(b)"

CMS also filed a cross-motion to strike evidence outside of the original administrative record, specifically my affidavit as well as the attached exhibits, on the grounds that these documents improperly sought to supplement the official administrative record.

## The Mootness Issue Rises Again:

On May 11, 2006, Judge Larimer held a telephone conference with the attorneys about the case issues, and what he wanted to see in the briefs. He remarked that he was wrestling with the potential intersection with the civil rights case, the parallels, and the complex legal issues involved. (It is important to remember that on January 31, the Second Circuit Court of Appeals had overturned his decision in the civil rights case, finding enough evidence of retaliation to put state defendants in front of a jury and, although the Second Circuit dismissed the federal defendants, it stated its finding of evidence that the federal officials were supporting the state officials.)

Beechwood attorney Kevin Cooman responded that the cases did intersect, but, irrespective of motive, here we were focusing on the objective facts of what CMS did or did not do regarding the sanctions applied. Attempting to change the focus, Christopher Taffe, the CMS attorney, repeatedly "inserted" that he didn't "get" this case, damages could not be awarded, Beechwood was out of business, and the whole thing was therefore moot.

Recall that on October 27, 2000, CMS counsel John Gura had first argued that the appeal of the agency-level determination to uphold the Medicare termination was effectively moot. He did this in response to Beechwood's request for an expedited scheduling of the administrative hearing. He argued that unless the license revocation were overturned, holding any administrative hearing regarding the certification could result in an unnecessary expenditure of judicial and departmental resources. However, CMS had granted a hearing, it was now six years later, and the case record had swelled to over six thousand pages. It did not make sense that Larimer might seriously entertain the idea that the case was now moot, especially when he was so deferential to the findings of the agency, and the agency had granted the administrative hearing. Nevertheless, on May 12, 2006, Judge Larimer sent out a letter asking the parties to address the issue of mootness.

## On June 26, 2006, Beechwood filed its Opposition on the Mootness issue:

Page 40: "This case is not moot because the parties continue to have a concrete interest in the outcome of this litigation. … there are important substantive issues before the Court … If the Court sustains Beechwood's contention that the standards applied and procedure used in the CMS administrative hearing are unlawful because violative of the Act and the regulations, then the CMS remedies employed against Beechwood will be overturned."

Page 40: "At the same time, the way in which CMS proceeds in all future hearings it conducts with respect to sanctioned providers will be overhauled and brought into compliance with law."

Page 40: "Moreover, the "name clearing" impact of any favorable rulings by this Court for Beechwood, and the Chamberys as its owners, is significant."

Page 40: "Thus, there is no danger of this Court issuing a mere advisory opinion for parties that have no real interest in the outcome of this case."

Page 42: "Declarations of unlawful conduct by CMS's survey agents at DOH are sought. These declaratory judgments in Beechwood's favor on one or more of these issues will have important collateral consequences for Beechwood's pending civil rights action."

Page 44: "Defendants seem to suggest that this case is moot because the Court's relief in this case cannot return the parties to the full status quo ante. Beechwood acknowledges that the extraordinary length of time (over five years) that it had to spend in the federal administrative process has made it impossible for this Court to return things to the way they were in 1999. Beechwood employees and residents are gone, and its facility was foreclosed and sold at auction. However, this does not mean that the case is moot. ... For Beechwood, the declaratory relief it seeks, together with the collateral consequences of that relief combine to provide the type of relief that is 'sufficient to prevent this case from being moot.'"

Page 44: "Congress and the Supreme Court have Decreed that Judicial Review of CMS Enforcement Must await Exhaustion of Administrative Adjudication, and hence this Required Delay cannot be used to Render Review Moot."

*On July 17, 2006, CMS filed a reply to Beechwood's Opposition Brief regarding the Defendants' Cross Motion:*

Page 2: "Even assuming the Court were to find that Beechwood's termination was not supported by substantial evidence in the administrative record, Beechwood could not currently participate in the Medicare and Medicaid programs, because it no longer has a state operating license. ... Accordingly, Beechwood's claims that the termination remedy should not have been imposed, or that it was somehow terminated 'early,' should be dismissed for mootness."

Page 2: "Article III of the Constitution requires that the federal courts adjudicate only cases and controversies. U.S. Const. Art. III, § 2, cl.1. When a claim becomes moot, federal courts "lack subject matter jurisdiction" over the claim. ... A claim becomes moot when the plaintiff lacks a "personal stake" or "legally cognizable interest in the outcome." ... Since it is impossible for the Court to redress Beechwood's claimed injuries with respect to its termination, i.e. by restoring Beechwood's provider agreements, Beechwood's claims related to its termination are moot."

## JUDGE LARIMER'S DECISION
### *BEECHWOOD V. THOMPSON*, 494 F.SUPP.2D 181 (W.D.N.Y. 2007)

On August 3, 2006, oral arguments were heard on the mootness issue before Judge Larimer, who did not render his decision until nearly a year later, on July 6, 2007. It was, yet again, flabbergasting. In the face of and despite—

1. A unanimous rebuke from the Second Circuit, who found evidence of retaliation by DOH, and support provided by HCFA
2. The fact that Beechwood was well into the discovery process in his own court
3. The Second Circuit's ruling that the identification, clarification, and classification of deficiencies are subject to a claim of improper motive
4. Evidence from the Medicare Fraud Control Unit (MFCU) file regarding its determination of "very good to excellent care" at Beechwood
5. Lack of evidence from the HCFA file regarding any required DOH certification or HCFA initial determination

Judge Larimer stayed the course. The first sentence of his decision read, "This is another chapter in the contentious relationship between a nursing home and the governmental agencies charged with monitoring its care of patients."

**With regard to the termination sanction,** Larimer avoided having to rule against CMS for an illegal termination by claiming that the issue was indeed "moot." On page 10 of his decision, he wrote: "I find that to a great extent, Beechwood's claims in this action are moot. Beechwood is closed, its state operating license has been revoked by the State DOH, and the building where the nursing facility was operated has been sold."

In this determination, the federal judge allowed a state licensure action to moot a federal appeal right granted under 405(g) of 42 USC 1395ii. He did this after explicitly stating, in his earlier injunction decision, that Beechwood had a right to the federal hearing, acknowledging that Congress made the hearing a post-deprivation right, and earlier refusing to grant an injunction to stop the State from moving independently. Now after four years, five decisions, and a 6,000-page record at the administrative level, he declared, with manifest injustice, that the termination appeal was moot.

In making this declaration, Judge Larimer willfully ignored his responsibility to make certain that the federal agency was acting both responsibly and lawfully. The "effective relief" that Beechwood sought, as outlined in the complaint, was declaratory relief—namely, to get the court's review and declaration that the termination action was improper and void. Beechwood specifically asked that the court "hold unlawful and set aside CMS' action determining to terminate ... as a provider in the MR/MD programs." Under the Administrative Procedure Act (APA), he had a responsibility to "hold unlawful and set aside agency action, findings, and conclusions found to be ... without observance of procedure required by law." What ramifications or reverberations a decision of his could have on licensing actions taken by a state agency was a totally separate matter.

Citing case law, Judge Larimer stated on page 13 of his decision that "Applying ... mootness ... depends in part on whether the business owner has indicated an intention or desire to resume operations if the governmental action at issue is successfully challenged," having observed on page 10 that "there is no indication in the record that the Chamberys intend or desire to reopen Beechwood or a similar facility if they obtain relief in this action." Yet he knew that the case law he cited as well as the intentions of the Chamberys had nothing to do with being able to get established as a health care operation under the Department of Health in the State of New York, especially with the numerous legal actions between the parties that had been drawing on for years. Likewise, he knew that the civil rights litigation, which was now in his court, was so far from being settled that it was ridiculous even to consider the intentions of the Chamberys or what they might do if they ever obtained the declaration they now sought.

Larimer plowed on. On page 15, he stated that "As for the alleged 'name clearing' effect of a favorable ruling ... Beechwood is no longer in business; any name-clearing effect would have no practical impact whatsoever." Here he actually acknowledged the time factor and uncertainty of the civil rights litigation yet completely ignored the fact that reputation is not only key to gaining establishment, or a certificate of need to do business in New York, but in any other business endeavor we, the Chamberys, might want to get into. It was his job to allow the Chamberys to repair a reputation ruined by government actors and allow them to carry on with their lives, not to prejudge that a restoration in reputation would be simply worthless.

He continued, on page.15, by stating that he was "equally unpersuaded by Beechwood's assertion that the case is not moot based on possible 'collateral consequences' of this litigation, specifically Beechwood's stated intention to use any declaratory relief issued by this Court as 'additional circumstantial evidence' in its pending § 1983 [civil rights] action, ... Beechwood has cited no authority, nor has the Court found any, standing for the proposition that a party may pursue an action simply for the purpose of gaining a potential advantage in some other litigation." Yet, in his previous decision granting summary judgment to the defendants in that civil rights action (pp. 38-40), he allowed the fact that deficiencies were "ultimately determined in both state and federal administrative proceedings to have merit" and thus influence his determinations. In particular, he let them influence whether he would review the record in a light most favorable to the plaintiff. Now, all of a sudden, he fails to see the collateral consequences between the cases and refuses to examine how this federal process was carried out! The irony here is that the DOH defendants, who argued that Larimer should dismiss this case, subsequently fought for years to let the unlitigated results of the administrative determinations be allowed to be presented to the jury in the civil rights case.

The clear fact is that Judge David Larimer was fully aware of how intimately interrelated and intertwined these cases were. This is evident in his having wrestled with potential issues during the telephone conference with the attorneys on

May 11, 2006, as discussed above. Thus, the questions arise. Why is he persisting to rule so harshly against Beechwood, especially after the unanimous decision by the 2nd Circuit regarding DOH retribution and HCFA support of it? Is he trying to further protect CMS from reputational damage after the 2nd Circuit dismissed Kelly and Daniel as defendants? What is going on here?

Beyond question, Larimer was continuing to be patently unjust. If three different legal forums were needed against me, then how could complaints against the defendants not be cognizable in any of those forums? If, in a subsequent oral argument regarding document production in the civil rights case, Magistrate Feldman emphasized that a jury would like to see the results of the MFCU investigation, why didn't Judge Larimer attribute the same significance to the revelations cited by Beechwood in this case?

The mootness issue had been raised by Gura before the federal hearing ever got started, and it continued to be raised, but the hearing and the appeals went on for another four arduous years. If Larimer was deferential to the agency on other matters, why was he not deferential to the fact that both the ALJ and the DAB granted the right to a hearing even though the operating license was revoked and the certificate of need (CON) annulled? The circumstances were exactly the same.

**With regard to the monetary penalty,** Judge Larimer stated on page 16 of his decision that "There is one respect, however, in which plaintiff's claims are not moot: plaintiff's claims for monetary relief." How he came to this conclusion defies reasoning since he acknowledged (p. 41) that Beechwood's 1st and 2nd causes of action regarding HCFA's responsibility to make initial determinations cover the monetary penalties as well as the termination, yet he makes no further effort to explain his position. It is quite evident that Judge Larimer simply did not want to address the issues presented in Beechwood's 1st and 2nd causes of action and thereby hold HCFA and Kelly responsible for their lack of proper procedure.

Larimer did, however, choose to address the sufficiency of the evidence used to justify the DPNA (immediate denial of payment for new admissions) sanction. But, under the ever-present guiding principles of the APA, he substitutes the conclusions in the agency record for his own judgment, stating (p. 46) that there is "substantial evidence supporting the factual findings that formed the basis for the DPNA," at least "in light of the deferential standard of review applied by this Court." The case law he cites supports a "highly deferential" standard of review that "presumes the validity of agency action." He also quotes from Northern Montana Care Center (2006 WL 2700729): "Because Defendants had a factual and regulatory basis for their imposition of the DPNA remedy, this Court cannot conclude the Defendants' decision regarding the choice of penalty was arbitrary and capricious, an abuse of discretion, or otherwise not in accordance with the law." He concludes (p. 47) with a quotation from Beverly Health and Rehabilitation Services, Inc (F.Supp.2d 73, 11; D.D.C 2002): "it is not within this Court's province to substitute its judgment for the agency's decision that [the remedy] was appropriate given the scope and severity of the deficiencies found." However, besides the excuses allowed or constraints put on the courts by the APA regarding the inability to use their own judgment about agency actions, the evidence Beechwood presented with Cause 1 and 2 of its complaint was that CMS did not have any factual or regulatory basis for imposing any sanction at the time they did it. Thus, the decision to use the remedy was arbitrary and capricious, and within Larimer's province to decide that it was not in accordance with the law.

The consequences of Larimer's decision were and remain far-reaching. He aided and abetted Kelly's coverup of improper actions, as well as the ability of the agency to continue to disclaim any responsibility for its actions. As a result, the healthcare industry will continue to be plagued by the decisions made in the Beechwood administrative hearing, for many issues were involved, and precedent was set that will continue to become further entrenched.

## OUR DECISION NOT TO APPEAL

As we feared he would, Judge David Larimer had shown his true colors again. He was a government-can-do-no-wrong guy. Even after the Second Circuit unanimously reversed him in the closely related "1983" civil rights case, he dug in and was not going to change. I was furious. My first thoughts went to how to get him off the civil rights case, but our attorneys could not see a way to accomplish that. The next issue was whether or not to appeal.

With everything in me, I wanted to appeal. I had extensive discussions with our lawyers. We discussed the fact that the case law on mootness was very weak, and the Second Circuit probably would remand it back to Larimer, to hear more from him on this issue. The appeal itself would take at least eighteen months and be very expensive, and any remand could take up to another three years.

As mentioned earlier, our hope had been that a positive outcome for Beechwood in appealing the agency decision would provide collateral support in the "1983" civil rights case. However, we had already seen Solomon's closing memo discussing excellent care; and although we had yet to obtain it or figure out how we would get it submitted as evidence in the civil rights case, it could possibly have the same positive effect that overturning the federal termination could have—and even more. In the meantime, that civil rights case was rolling forward. Our attorneys advised us to concentrate our efforts and save our resources for that case.

Outrage is a powerful driver, but despite my strong desire to appeal to the 2nd Circuit in the hope of again overturning Judge Larimer, I became convinced that I had no practical choice but to forgo the appeal. Emotionally, it was one of the hardest decisions I had to make. But it was clear to me that our attorneys were right. Our focus had to be on the civil rights case, and we would have to develop a strategy to use the mootness issue to our advantage in that case, keeping any reference to the federal administrative outcome out of the trial. The 2nd Circuit helped this cause by stating that "it is the revocation of Beechwood's state operating certificate, not Beechwood's termination as a federal Medicare/Medicaid provider, that is the issue in this [1983] case" (Footnote #4 at page 22).

We marched on.

CHAPTER 14

# Motions to Compel

T he Second Circuit decision of January 31, 2006 put Beechwood back in
the game and the defendants facing a jury. However, there were no illu-
sions about the uphill battle that lay before us. As our Attorney Mark
Grannis (who presented our case at the Second Circuit) wrote to me while awaiting the Court's decision:

August 4, 2005:

"I think you face two significant burdens in the trial of this case. The first is
that a nineteen-member conspiracy to punish Brook Chambery for the exercise of his constitutional rights is just hard to swallow. ... to prevail, you will
have to show more than that they didn't like you. You will have to show, for
example, that they wanted to punish you for advocating regulatory reform. ...
For better or worse, I just don't have much confidence that the average jury can
think regulatory conflicts are capable of inspiring the sort of animosity that it
would take to get nineteen people in two agencies united with the common
purpose of putting Brook Chambery out of business.

"The second significant burden is that even if you win [at the Second Cir-
cuit] you will very likely be precluded from relitigating whether the deficiencies actually existed. And even if you weren't precluded, the defendants would
try to re-prove the deficiencies, introducing a great deal of evidence about the
deficiencies that would not be helpful to your case. ... I also believe that you
got screwed by bureaucrats who screwed you bureaucratically, and if you can't
get things like that fixed on direct appeal I'm not sure how well they resonate
with a jury in a civil rights action later.

"By 'screwed bureaucratically,' I mean essentially that DOH used the regulations to screw you ... ... The problem is that in a 1983 action you can't

241

contest the truth of the deficiency allegations; that could only happen under Article 78. So under the best of circumstances, you stand in front of a civil jury as a guy who ran a nursing home where the care was deficient–whether that was true or not."

Nov. 4, 2005:

"I looked over past e-mails, reviewed the factual section of our brief, and picked the brain of one of my partners who has tried lots of cases. Unfortunately, I am unable to be any more bullish about the retrial of your case than I was before. … From my vantage point, I would be stunned if you were to get a verdict of $10 million dollars, and I would think you had done rather well to get anything above $1 million."

On March 28, 2012, as he was trying to push for a pre-trial settlement, Judge David Larimer stated that Beechwood must realize the "heavy burden and thin reed" that exist going into trial with only a single claim left, needing to convince all the jurors, and with two agencies having previously ruled against us. This is exactly why Beechwood had continued to push forward with the appeal of the federal termination, even as it prepared for trial in this civil rights case. We desired a ruling that the termination was illegal and that the ALJ violated every rule in the book in supporting the deficiencies. Even though we already had seen the summary from Solomon demonstrating that the investigators had found "very good to excellent care," we did not yet have the document stating that they felt the testimony given at the hearing refuted the concept of poor care at Beechwood, and we didn't know whether Medicare Fraud Control Unit (MFCU) documents would be ruled admissible at trial. We had to be as thorough as possible in covering all the bases. For all intents and purposes, we needed to be able to prove our case beyond any reasonable doubt, although that was not the formal burden of proof that we would face at trial.

To make matters worse, this was a "nursing home case," and nursing homes don't exactly conger up a warm fuzzy and feeling for the typical juror. To begin with, no one likes the thought of ending up in a nursing home. Unfortunately, the overregulation that accompanied public funding has actually led to protection of the subpar operators and the inability of the good operators to freely innovate and meet consumer desires. This situation only feeds the negative attitude toward the industry.

## THE DISCOVERY PROCESS BEGINS

For twelve years Beechwood used whatever means were legally available to obtain the documentation (notes, e-mails, affidavits, statements of admission, and so on) necessary to prove its case. In the early years, this consisted of FOI requests. After the Second Circuit put the civil rights case back on track, court-directed discovery took the place of FOI activities.

On April 5, 2006, there was an initial conference with Judge Larimer concerning the discovery process. We then began discovery by sending out interrogatories to each of the seventeen defendants. Interrogatories are essentially written questions sent to each defendant, with the expectation of written answers. The basis for the interrogatories was the work done to analyze and catalogue subpoenaed documents, FOI responses, and affidavits. We staggered the release of these interrogatories, beginning on August 15, 2006, and had the responses by March 16, 2007. While we were collecting and analyzing the interrogatory responses, we were also unsuccessfully trying to get documents from DOH, the attorneys within DOH, and the MFCU.

## NOTHING WAS FORTHCOMING WITHOUT A FIGHT

Discovery should have made things infinitely easier for us. It did not. Virtually nothing was forthcoming from the defendants without major legal battles. I would estimate that the cost of this part of the litigation expense was approximately $1 million.

Motions to Compel are not filed with the court until attempts to receive information in the typical discovery process have been frustrated by a continued lack of response or refusal to comply. Each one of the actions enumerated and discussed in what follows was preceded by months or even years of attempts to get information. Letters would be followed by conferences and subpoenas and then motions to compel and court hearings. Thanks to inadequate responses, even under court directions, multiple motions to compel and court hearings were often necessary to extract information. Each motion involved a tremendous amount of work, including wading through inappropriate privilege logs in order to explain to the court what was wrong with them. The following emails illustrate why dealing with DOH took so much time and effort. Gary Levine was the DAG attorney who acted as counsel for the DOH. Harold Rosenthal was an attorney at DOH.

November 29. 2006, DAG Email from Attorney Levine to DOH Attorneys Altone and Rosenthal: "As expected the plaintiffs' counsel does not like my Privilege log. Is it possible (or would it be overly burdensome?) to have someone create an inventory of all the documents in the file?"

November 30, 2006, DOH Email from Bureau of Administrative Hearings director Russel Altone to Levine and Rosenthal: "It would be overly burdensome for me personally to create an inventory of all the documents in the Beechwood 'file' located in BAH office space. The 'file' is voluminous. It fills a 4-drawer file cabinet that is kept locked. There are also two file storage boxes filled with Beechwood related items sitting on top of the file cabinet. Some of the documents are contained in expandable file folders and inside those are manila folders. The folder labels do not always accurately match what is actually inside the folders. Although I originally dedicated the file cabinet to Beechwood related items and placed documents that were in my possession into the file cabinet back in 1999 and 2000, others in DLA have since placed additional items into or on top of the cabinet over the years."

January 10, 2007, DOH Internal Email from Altone to Rosenthal: "I received your hardcopy memo and attachments regarding the need to develop a plan to inventory the Beechwood related documents. ... Before proceeding to do anything, I suggest that we meet ... and you need to actually see the files and the nature of the documents in order to understand that the requested task is enormous. In fact, I do not know how it is even possible to identify what is additional to the hearing records and documents that were provided during the course of the hearing as well as the box of emails that were provided during the extended FOIL litigation."

June 11, 2007, DOH Internal Email from Rosenthal to Altone: "We have received a subpoena ... seeking a voluminous number of documents ... While we have objected ... I need to determine the existence of various records and quantify the difficulty of producing them."

June 26, 2007, DOH Internal Email from Rosenthal to Altone: "I do not see anything that would look like the old OCC file, nor do I see the old collection of Colello emails that I know once existed. Any ideas of what may have happened to them?"

October 15, 2007, DOH Internal Email from Rosenthal to Altone: "Could you please have the attorneys in your bureau check and make sure that no stray boxes of Beechwood documents ended up in their offices. For example, there used to be a box of emails to and from Anna Colello that seems to be missing. We need to do this as part of a last try to locate any documents that need to be produced."

## DOH ATTORNEY-CLIENT PRIVILEGE CLAIMS:
### FOUR YEARS OF INTENSIVE MANEUVERING

I had known that DOH attorneys played a major role in the actions taken against Beechwood, and so we pursued documents they were withholding under claims of attorney-client (AC) privilege. They fought hard against producing these documents, including intentionally creating inadequately constructed and incomprehensible "privilege logs," the supposedly descriptive lists attorneys prepare of documents they claim are immune from disclosure and forcing us through absolutely incredible amounts of frustrating work to clearly explain to the Court how they were inadequate. We ground out multiple "motions to compel"—to force disclosure—over a four-year period. The first phase of this battle consumed about a year and a half, through April 2008.

November 27, 2006: Subpoena to DOH for AC documents

February 14, 2007: Motion to Compel AC documents

April 24, 2007: DOH turned over 1,700 documents previously claimed AC privileged, and two logs of documents for which they were still claiming AC privilege.

April 30, 2007: Oral argument before Magistrate Feldman on the continued AC claim; DOH was directed to produce a proper privilege log.

The transcript of the oral argument on April 30 speaks volumes about an epic campaign of obstruction—

Page 2, Feldman: "Let me get right to what I think the heart of the issue is … Rule 26 provides that when a party withholds information … by claiming that it is privileged or subject to protection … the party shall make the claim expressly and shall describe the nature of the documents, communications, or things not produced or disclosed … [that] will enable other parties to assess the applicability of the privilege or protection. I've been doing this for almost a dozen years and I've seen a lot of privilege logs, but this first one goes into my top three of inadequate privilege logs. … But, the supplemental log is not much better. … The privilege logs that are provided here don't allow anyone to make the kind of informed decision, including the Court that has to be made."

Page 3, Feldman: "You have to demonstrate there was a communication between client and counsel … and that the communication was for the purpose of obtaining legal advice and that is opposed to other kinds of advice such as business advice or administrative advice or any other kind of purpose for the document."

Pages 6-7, Feldman: "Plaintiffs are troubled and I'm obviously troubled too that after your initial log was provided and they made a motion to compel, I guess over 1700 pages of what had previously been asserted as privilege is now being disclosed and that is kind of a disturbing indication according to them that these materials are being improperly withheld. ... I realize that you're asking for things from attorney files, and ordinarily ... the gut reaction here is privilege. But based on the record here, it appears that some things in the attorney files are not privileged. ... I think as to each document being withheld ... that an adequate privilege log has to be provided."

Page 7, Levine: "The last part of your comment hits part of the problem with this case. This is a unique lawsuit. I don't know in your 12 years how many times you've had lawyers sued where the application is for disclosure of the lawyer's files and that is what we have here. It's a file cabinet, as it's described to me, full of materials."

Pages 7-9: Feldman (in response to Levine): "I've had a lot of cases ... where lawyers' advice and lawyers' files and application of the privilege is at issue. But it's also a unique case in that the Second Circuit has said ... the motivations and the communications of the defendants here are at issue. " ... And, when you're dealing with a State agency too which has responsibility for things other than legal advice and that is administering programs, I think that's another unique aspect of it here. One of the defendants here, I guess his title is administrator of the entire program. He happens to be a lawyer and he happens to supervise some lawyers within his office, but he clearly would have other responsibilities other than providing confidential legal advice, and there are lots of cases out there which involve trying to invoke the privilege as to advice which isn't legal advice and that is improper. ... I think you have to be very careful on what you invoke the privilege for. ... I found this to be quite problematic in the email context, there may be portions of emails that offer legal advice but there may also be portions of emails that have nothing to do with confidential legal advice, and those need to be turned over."

As a result of the oral argument, it was decided that, because of the sensitivity of attorney file claims, DOH would have another chance to submit an adequate log but that it would have to be done properly. If not, the entire file would have to be turned over, and the defendants might be assessed for Beechwood's legal fees dealing with this issue. Levine, however, did not leave the matter without returning to the issue of attorneys being sued:

Page 20, Levine: "This matter is going to get more difficult rather than less difficult ... I assume they're going to want to depose all of the lawyers which

I think there are three lawyers. We're going to have to get some, I was going to use the word guidance, but it would have to be stronger than guidance. I think it would have to be an order because there is a big issue as to attorney/client privilege and it's going to have to be addressed."

Page 22, Levine: "There are these big issues."

Page 25, Levine: "I'm just letting the Court know that this isn't just go depose three guys and we're done, this is problematic."

On June 15, 2007, AC Privileged Log #3 was finally produced. It was no better than the others. We followed up on July 13, with Motion #2 to Compel, and—

July 30, 2007: Conference with Magistrate Feldman

August 9, 2007: Three black binders of AC documents submitted to the Court for in-camera review

August 21, 2007: Our response concerning the in-camera submission

September 4, 2007: Oral argument #2

The transcript of the oral argument reveals the usual tactics of attrition:

Page 5: Feldman to Levine: It's virtually impossible for anyone to go through this (log) and figure out what you're talking about.

Page 7, Feldman: "And it seems to me that too many, if not significantly all, these documents, you're just saying they're totally privileged, every single line."

Levine: "Yes, sir, every single line."

Feldman: "I understand some of the defendants are lawyers and you're dealing with litigation files, but you're also dealing with a lawsuit in which the motivations of these officials has been held by the Second Circuit to be very, very relevant."

Levine: "Judge, respectfully, it would be impossible for me to give a dissertation on each document, 51 pages, single space, listing of documents going into details that would disclose the nature of the privilege itself."

Feldman: "If it would be impossible to do that, how is the Court to make a determination as to whether the privilege applies or not?"

Levine: "In camera review."

Feldman: "So it's your proposal that you submit tens of thousands of documents to me to go through line by line and determine whether the document is privileged?"

Page 10, Levine: "I don't think it was 10,000 pages ... The last page is numbered 1,477.... But understanding the nature of the documents is also important. There are strings of emails."

Feldman: "How many of the documents that you're now claiming privilege were turned over in response to FOIL requests or other requests?"

Levine: "I can't give you a definitive answer."

Page 14, Peter Weishaar (Beechwood counsel): "They don't know what they've given us."

Levine: "We have documents, we have boxes somewhere in our office from previous litigation."

Page 19, Feldman: "But if there is something in the materials, pre-litigation materials, that is similar to—we've got a problem here because so and so is really after Beechwood ... deserves everything he is going to get here .. some issue relating to the retaliatory motive ... that may be privileged, but it would also be relevant to what the Second Circuit has said is an issue ..."

Page 20, Levine: "The simple answer is no, when you're talking about anything that shows that they did anything for malice or for retaliatory purposes, there is not one document in there, not one. I can affirmatively assert that."

Feldman: "It's all of the former kind of classification documents, just routine litigation preparation?"

Levine: "We have an investigation, we want your advice, we want your input, we want your involvement."

Page 23, Levine: "If anything, all [the file] shows is that my clients acted properly."

Page 24, Feldman: "It would seem to me that someone is going to have to look at these documents and determine whether they're privileged or not. [Note: Even we conceded that there might be some material that could rightfully be called privileged.]

Page 25, Feldman: "I can tell you that it's virtually impossible for me ... to go through this and determine which documents are being referred to by that privilege log."

Pages 27-28, Feldman to Rosenthal: "I need you to sit down with Mr. Levine and go through ... so you can determine yourself whether the privilege is being correctly asserted or not. ... I want the defendants to be very careful ... there may be a portion of a document that is privileged and the rest of the document is not privileged."

Page 30, Levine: "Judge, ... I might consider if I wasn't waiving privilege by doing this, letting [Beechwood]counsel come to the office and sit down and review the documents and point out what documents he believes he would be entitled to from a point of discovery."

Page 31, Feldman: "That may be the best way to resolve this without them waiving the privilege, identifying the documents which would then be submitted to me in-camera inspection. … That may narrow down this 1,500 page body of documents to something that I would feel comfortable reviewing."

The resolution arrived at on September 4, 2007 was a stipulation that the defendants would make the 1,500 documents available for review without giving up privilege claims. We determined that 200 pages of the 1500 were relevant to our case and not privileged. The parties met on February 25, 2008, but the defendants would not relent on broad claims to privilege. On February 26, we outlined specific claims to every page, but despite formal notice that we needed a response, nothing was forthcoming. Thus, on March 8, 2008, a third motion to compel was made to the court to order release. In his Supplemental Declaration in Support of the Motion, our attorney Kevin Cooman outlined the court's rulings from April 30 and September 4 regarding what constituted inappropriate privilege claims:

(1) Documents previously disclosed to plaintiffs.

(2) Documents involving defendants who have asserted qualified privilege, entitling plaintiffs to see what those defendants were saying and doing.

(3) Documents talking about weaknesses or discretionary choices being made in the DOH case.

(4) Documents related to motivation.

(5) Documents revealing the timing of defendants' actions.

(6) Documents that reflect communication on business or administrative advice, rather than legal advice.

(7) Documents in which the communications are not kept confidential.

(8) Portions of documents not containing legal advice (or work-product communications), but rather facts. (Exhibit B, p. 8-9, and applicable case law)

The Court gave the defendants until March 20, 2008 to specifically identify privilege claims. On March 22, we addressed the court yet again, stating that the time frame had expired without action, amounting to a waiver of privilege, and that we desired the court to order production of the documents. Instead of facing a court order and expenses, the defendants simply agreed to turn over all 1500 documents. The defendants waged a war of attrition only to find themselves the victims of that tactic.

When Levine handed over the black binders on April 23, 2008, he wrote that he "agreed that attorney defendants in this action may be questioned" but this is "not meant to have any precedential significance in any other lawsuit against lawyers representing agencies of New York."

For nearly nine years, the DOH attorneys had hidden the most extremely valuable pieces of the retaliation puzzle beneath the cloak of AC privilege. Slowly, painfully, we continued to gather more of the pieces until, at last, under the rules of judicial civil procedure, the attorney-client claims could not hold up, and the documents had to be turned over. When that happened, the puzzle was fully assembled, solved.

## DOH PROGRAM LEVEL DOCUMENTS:
### 12 MONTHS OF INTENSIVE MANEUVERING

There was far more to obtain, most importantly the Department of Health program-level documents, which were kept in Albany, in a locked four-drawer file with two boxes on top of it and possibly more to the side of it. The DOH attorneys were in charge of maintaining these documents. Here is an abbreviated chronology of the steps involved in retrieving these documents.

March 7, 2007: Beechwood issued a subpoena for DOH documents

March 19, 2007: DOH objected to our March 7 subpoena for further documents, claiming they were attorney-client work product prepared for litigation and adding deliberative-material privileges. They also asserted that the requests were burdensome, overly broad, irrelevant, not reasonably calculated to lead to discovery of admissible evidence, and on and on.

May 23, 2007: We made a Motion to Compel DOH documents

September 4, 2007: Oral argument was made before Magistrate Feldman. He suggested (p. 70) that the parties "meet and confer" about the documents since both DOH and Levine did not want to take responsibility for an official response to the subpoena due to the "astronomical" amount of material and their own demonstrated inability to account for what was there. Levine had been sent eleven boxes containing 6500 documents which he then had Bates-stamped, with each page number prefixed by "OAG-A" so that we could tell the source from which they were derived.

On November 13-14, 2007 Beechwood was allowed to look at the boxes of documents at the DAG offices, determine what was desired, and state the legal justification for having them turned over, based on the guidelines Feldman established.

February 11, 2008: Beechwood requested 209 of these documents, providing justification for the requests.

March 13, 2008: The requested documents were received, including unredacted notes by continuing care director Sharon Carlo.

March 18, 2008: We also went to the AG's office to look through a half box of documents to identify what Beechwood had determined to be "missing documents." The documents were marked, and the defendants released them accordingly.

In June 2008, we were still trying to get such items as Carlo's original notebooks; reports of DLA time and expenses for dealing with the Beechwood hearing; the selection of Marc Zylberberg as the ALJ; what attorneys worked on the ALJ's decision; and how the ALJ decision may have been reviewed, edited, and routed to New York Commissioner of Health Antonia Novello. We were told that these documents did not exist.

## MFCU DOCUMENTS:
### 18 MONTHS OF INTENSIVE MANEUVERING

The previous FOI requests and a subsequent meeting with Medicaid Fraud Control Unit (MFCU) director Jerry Solomon had allowed me to see certain documents and have others read to me. We wanted these documents, and the ability to search through the file to determine what else was there that might be of use to Beechwood. As usual, pursuit of these documents had a story, which is outlined in the following chronology of major events leading up to the release of the entire file:

March 5, 2007: Subpoena for MFCU documents

March 19, 2007: MFCU objects to the subpoena

June 21, 2007: Motion to Compel

August 3, 2007: MFCU continues its objection

August 15, 2007: Beechwood delivers its reply brief to the MFCU objection

September 4, 2007: Oral argument with Judge Feldman

After noting that the MFCU had delivered inappropriate boilerplate privilege claims without any log of specific documents, Judge Feldman (p. 52) said, "So, it's the position of your clients that where a public law enforcement agency investigates something and exonerates a person, that the person exonerated is not entitled to see the results of the investigation?"

Page 57, Feldman: "I assume counsel here would like to use as the report of an official agency, which may be not hearsay under the Federal Rules of Evidence, as the results of an investigation conducted by an agency charged with that investigation, as evidence that the patients received good care, and therefore, the penalties that were imposed were unreasonable. One agency of the state of New York has investigated patient care and has determined there was very good care and another agency of the state has investigated patient care and come up with this finding that there is patient neglect. Why wouldn't that be something that would be helpful to a jury in deciding who's right?"

Page 58: Feldman: "Your agency has expertise in evaluating the raw material and determining whether there is probable cause to believe that a crime was committed and whether to prosecute that crime. ... And you determined there was not cause to prosecute someone for neglect or patient abuse, or substandard conditions, but another agency of your same governmental entity determined to take away somebody's license because of evidence of neglect, abuse, or lack of performance. Why wouldn't that be something that would be relevant to a jury's determination?"

On September 9, 2007, we submitted a supplemental brief regarding the motion to compel, and on March 25, 2008, Magistrate Feldman granted our motion, noting the following:

Page 2: "In its response to the subpoena, MFCU asserted boilerplate objections and generally invoked various privileges, but did not provide a privilege log that met Rule 45(d)(2)(A) requirements."

Page 5: "By voluntarily surrendering documents to the plaintiff (Brook Chambery) to read and review in 2005, MFCU has waived its right to assert that the same documents are now privileged."

Page 6: "The documents shown to Brook Chambery and submitted to the court for in-camera review are to be produced to the plaintiffs."

After this order, the MFCU decided to release the whole file to keep Beechwood from litigating this issue any further and thereby setting precedent. It took the MFCU six months and four document releases (March 28, 2008, April 24, May 16, and August 18) to turn over the complete investigative file. Although some documents were still redacted, supposedly to protect investigative techniques, Beechwood did not challenge the submissions any further.

Just as Solomon had told me personally, out of the thousands of pages of investigative notes and reports, none contained any substantiation of anything stated in the ALJ report, or anything negative about Beechwood at all. The only thing they reflect is that our facility delivered very good care—or even better.

# CHAPTER 15

# Positioning for Trial

After winning access to the documents relating to the outcome of the Medicare Fraud Control Unit (MFCU) criminal investigation and documents for which attorney-client privilege (AC) had been claimed, we now had ample proof of the prominent role the DOH attorneys had played in a massive case of retaliatory prosecution. At this point, then, I decided, much as I had with the appeal to the Second Circuit, that it was time to add fresh perspectives and more varied expertise to our legal team before moving into depositions and preparation for the "1983" civil rights trial.

I approached David Rothenberg about assuming the role of lead counsel for this suit, and I was thrilled when he agreed to join Kevin Cooman for the arduous task ahead. I had gained great respect for David's intellect and expertise in both criminal and civil litigation and was confident that, along with Sheldon Nahmod, a professor at Chicago-Kent College of Law and distinguished author on constitutional torts and civil rights litigation, we now had the best team that could have been assembled.

## THE DOH OFFICIALS THEMSELVES WOULD BE OUR EXPERT WITNESSES

At a team meeting on June 30, 2008, Keven Cooman remarked that we should be thinking about who we would use as expert witnesses. I responded that, as I had been preparing for all along, our defendants would be the experts, and our deposition strategy would be built around the information I had gathered through FOI requests and affidavits over the past nine years. I explained my rationale: our defendants were the people responsible for developing policies and procedures and for supervising operations. They were the decision makers at both the state and regional levels. What better or more qualified experts could there be? We would have them testify about how things should work and their own responsibilities, then put evidence in front of them as to what did or did not happen regarding Beechwood, and leave them unable to explain their own actions. The attorneys thought this was a great strategy, and we prepared for depositions accordingly.

## LEGAL PROOFS AND DEPOSITION PLANS

At this same meeting, David Rothenberg advised that we needed to go beyond the extensive documentation I had already assembled regarding our case and develop the specific legal proofs that were required to prepare for depositions and court. In other words, we had to outline what we would be trying to prove to the jury, and the facts and evidence in support thereof. He suggested that I draw up ten to twelve proofs as a trial run and then get together to review them and see how I did. However, after doing one or two proofs, I figured I understood the task at hand, and without telling the attorneys what I was up to, spent the next four months working sixty-to eighty-hour weeks developing what I believed was a fairly comprehensive set of proofs using a multipage spreadsheet with functionality that my brother, Dale, programmed expressly for this purpose.

As documents were collected over the years, they had been numbered, scanned, and entered into a master spreadsheet called the "Chronology," which Dale had also programmed. Descriptions of events, email texts, dates, time of day, and so on were recorded, along with who wrote, received, might have been blind-copied, or was otherwise involved. I could easily sort or filter the information contained, and by clicking on the document number, it would be retrieved from the archive and brought to the screen. The approach was like the Beechwood approach to medical records, in which we were years ahead of the rest of the industry. Leveraging technology this way had irritated surveyors, managers, and others at the Department of Health. Now we leveraged similar data technology to assist in building our suit against some of these very same people. The Chronology proved a tremendously valuable reference tool for assembling the materials that were in our arsenal and for working with the attorneys on various legal actions. This was the source for building the Proofs spreadsheet. Through all the obstructions that had been erected against us, I had never lost sight of the ultimate task that had been set before me years earlier. I had known the facts needed, and I strove to prove them beyond a reasonable doubt. I now needed to formally assemble them from the Chronology. Aiding in this task were other theme- and event-based documents, which I wrote up and continually updated over the years as more and more information was obtained.

I presented a general overview and a few of the proofs to the attorneys at a meeting on November 5, 2008. They were totally amazed at the extensive nature of what had been assembled, and they were convinced at that point that we were ready to prepare for depositions. I continued to develop and fine-tune the proofs over the next few months as we worked at reviewing and discussing those that were already completed. The attorneys were confronted with so much material to be reviewed and understood that we divided the workload among them, and I worked separately with each attorney in protracted weekly meetings at their offices. This went on through April 2009. At last, on April 30, we convened a discovery scheduling conference with Magistrate Feldman and informed him that we were ready for depositions.

It is hard to estimate the size of those two main documents as of April 2009, but by the time of trial, the Proofs spreadsheet contained 203,321 cells (35 columns x 5,806 rows), and the Chronology contained 175,000 cells (75 columns x 2340 rows). Many of the cells were very large, and more than one computer screen was required to read through the material.

## Depositions get under way

Depositions began on June 19, 2009 and continued through October 13, 2010. In any complex suit, depositions are crucial, and each one involves very intensive preparation and post analysis. Logistics always presents the first formidable hurdle, and it was a herculean task to get our seventeen DOH defendants and four other witnesses deposed during this period. The typical deposition lasted about a day, but three of the defendant depositions extended to two days. In addition, the defense required five days to depose seven individuals.

Again, we made extensive use of digital technology in this endeavor, and again, my brother's skills were indispensable. Information from the Proofs spreadsheet would be filtered in preparation for questioning each deponent and transferred to another multipage Deposition spreadsheet. Each page of the spreadsheet had the material for a specific deponent and was coded according to how the attorney had previously determined to use it. I augmented this with additional material from other sources regarding the deponent's work history, education, and so on. Before each deposition, I reviewed the information with the attorney who would be doing the deposition, and that information became the source for their own deposition worksheets.

After each deposition, a digital version of the transcript was created, and Dale broke out the questions and answers, which he transferred to another multiple-page Deposition Testimony spreadsheet. On this document, we could make annotations and do further coding, analysis, and processing of the information, including updating our Proof, Chronology, and Deposition spreadsheets as necessary for further use in depositions and later at trial. The twenty-four days of depositions Beechwood conducted amounted to 21,500 sets of questions and answers and 4,060 pages of transcript. This translated into 235,500 cells of information in the Deposition Testimony spreadsheet by the time coding and comments were added.

## CMS REFUSED TO ALLOW KELLY TO BE DEPOSED

Although the Second Circuit had dismissed HCFA regional administrator Sue Kelly and acting branch chief Daniel Walsky as defendants, and HCFA counsel John Gura had previously refused to allow them to testify in the federal administrative hearing, Beechwood believed that Kelly's deposition testimony was now necessary, and on September 1, 2009, wrote to CMS requesting permission to depose her. On November 17, 2009, Jackie Garner, the Consortium Administrator, rejected our request, stating that "granting your request would pose an undue burden on CMS." Here is the essence of the reasoning Garner offered:

> Page 3: "Your request for testimony ... relates to claims that are barred by the doctrines of mootness and collateral estoppel. ... It is not in the Department's interest, and would be an undue burden on the agency, to provide testimony with respect to issues for which a court cannot provide any meaningful relief, and that are irrelevant to the claims in the present litigation."

> Page 6: "In light of the fact that the federal defendants, including Ms. Kelly, were dismissed from the Leeds lawsuit, I find no federal interest in having Ms. Kelly testify regarding communications with the State that were found to be part of the normal "[c]ooperation between state and federal bureaucracies acting in their regulatory spheres.

"I also note that, to the extent that you seek to depose Ms. Kelly regarding internal communications with her staff and with NYSDOH employees, as well as her thought process regarding whether CMS should adopt the state's recommendation and why CMS chose to terminate the Beechwood provider agreement, such testimony would fall within the deliberative process privilege."

## MOTION TO COMPEL
### PRODUCTION OF ALTONE'S ARCHIVE

In the previous motions to compel attorney-client (AC) privileged documents, which were also labeled "Altone Documents" in court papers, DOH Bureau of Administrative Hearings director Russel Altone never revealed that he maintained his own archive of emails. However, in his two days of deposition (November 19, 2009 and December 22, 2009), Altone did admit that he periodically forwarded emails to himself from what he termed an "archive" of emails he maintained in electronic format "in cyberspace" in an "archived portion of lotus notes" that "still exists." He would do this so that it would come out in his "current folder" where he could then print the emails.

Beechwood included a request for this "Altone Archive" in its Notices to Produce, but to no avail. Not only did the DOH fail to respond to our Requests to Admit, the department did not produce the archive. In its answer to the Third Notice to Produce, on August 23, 2010, DOH objected to the relevance and scope of the request. On November 11, 2010, Beechwood filed a Motion to Compel. On December 6, 2009, in oral argument before Magistrate Feldman, this was one of the issues left unresolved. Feldman requested a meeting between the parties to resolve them, so that he would not have to issue an order. The meeting was held on December 7, 2010, and resulted in a DOH agreement to produce the file in its native digital format. The file was received on December 18.

### ROCHESTER FILE REVIEW AND DOCUMENT PRODUCTION

Deposition testimony made it necessary to visit the Rochester office of DOH to examine its file of Beechwood materials. An office employee there had testified that, to the best of her recollection, the file had been assembled in response to my FOI requests. We began a review of the file on April 19, 2010. The material was contained in a five-drawer file cabinet and in a box on top of it. The box contained Carlo's unredacted notebook pages produced in redacted version at the DOH hearing. The rest of the material in the box consisted of notes between

Carlo and central office attorneys (Sherwell and Rosenthal) regarding FOIL production and litigation.

The top drawer contained a black duffel bag, which appeared to belong to Carlo; a tote bag containing colored file folders labeled "S. Baker personal files 1,2,3,4"; and a white canvas bag containing two manila folders, one of which said "CTF [Cindy Francis] personal file" and contained 98 emails from Sanford Rubin, acting director of the Western Region of the DOH. The other folder contained three Francis calendars.

The second drawer contained many folders labeled "Beechwood post-hearing." There were press articles, notes on moving patients, information shared with the Office of Professional Medical Conduct (OPMC), subpoenas for documents from the MFCU, and proposed findings and conclusions for the ALJ. The drawer also contained letters from area provider organizations requesting that the Beechwood certificate of need (CON) not be transferred to another party, and a folder including many of Proschel's notes demonstrating what she was doing and when.

The third drawer held various documents regarding the Beechwood "1983" civil rights case. The fourth drawer contained survey documents from 1990 to 1997. The fifth drawer contained survey documents for 1998 and 1999. What stood out is that the survey documents for 1998 and 1999 took up just as much storage as the documents from the previous eight years.

After reviewing the file, we requested certain documents that we should have gotten with the subpoena at the start of the DOH hearing. We received these documents on June 2, 2010. Careful examination allowed us to document Proschel's time by day and hour and prove at trial that she could not have done the POC review she testified about at the DOH hearing. Furthermore, if we had needed it at trial, these documents would have also allowed us to demonstrate the role played by Carlo, Baker, Proschel, and central office officials in drafting and redrafting the deficiency statements (SODs), leaving out major facts, confusing the issues, and drawing improper conclusions.

## Motion to Compel
## Statements of Admission

We had now gone through depositions and 11 years of intensive document requests via FOI, subpoenas, production demands, court proceedings, and court orders to produce. Obtaining Statements of Admission was essentially the final step in discovery. After the production of documents and the completion of depositions, Beechwood requested that the defendants either produce certain documents or admit that they did not exist. As with other attempts to obtain documents, or information, this proved an arduous task. There were three requests (October 30, 2009, February 22, 2010, and June 25, 2010), all of which were met with inadequate responses. So, on October 27, 2010, Beechwood filed a Motion to Compel Answers. DOH filed its objection on the same day, and we filed our reply on November 5, 2010. An oral argument followed before Magistrate Feldman on December 6.

The magistrate once again requested a meeting of the parties to resolve the issues before he was forced to make an order. That meeting was held, and, on December 9, Beechwood sent its Fourth Request for Admission. On January 6, 2011 we finally received a satisfactory response. The sobering results were read into the record in front of the jury after Beechwood's closing arguments in the liability trial:

### Survey Decision Making Notes

Admits 1 – 5: "No survey notes were made by the survey team members, which reflect or document the deficiency decisions for Beechwood that are embodied in the April, May and June Statements of Deficiency."

Admit 18: "Defendants are unable to produce any contemporaneously made notes regarding review of the SODs for April – June."

### Participants in decision making

On the Third Request for Admission at #41, the defendants admit that all survey team members must be identified on the HCFA 670 per 42 CFR 488.314 and the State Operations Manual, Appendix P, and Survey Task #6 under that appendix. Yet, in direct conflict with this admission, at #42, they deny that all those participating in the survey decision making process should be identified in decision making notes. At #43, they deny that all decision making notes must be memorialized on the HCFA Form 807, that the notes (#44) must contain the date and substance of the group decision making discussion, and that (#45) Form 807 should collate and reflect what was observed with the concerns noted by the surveyors during the survey. At #46, they deny that only federally certified surveyors were to be designated as members of a survey team and participants in the survey outcome decision making process.

Rubin's email to Office of Continuing Care director Robert Barnett on April 27, 1999 is a good reason for these denials: "Carlo and Baker, working closely with Gray and others in the CO [central office] developed an IJ SOD [Immediate Jeopardy Statement of Deficiency] and DPOC [Directed Plan of Correction] "in conjunction with Region II." The outcome had been fully predetermined.

### Surveyor certifications

Admit #14: Carlo was not a HCFA certified surveyor.

Carlo testified falsely that she was certified.

Admit #15: Carlo and Leeds were not even HCFA certified as surveyors.

Yet both were heavily involved as decision makers as to survey outcomes and remedies to be applied.

Admit # 16: Rubin was not a HCFA certified surveyor.

Admit #17: Altone was not a HCFA certified surveyor.

Admit #61, on Third Request for Admission: Director of Bureau of LTC and Quality Assurance Anna Colello was not a certified surveyor.

Yet she was also heavily involved as a decision maker as to survey outcomes and remedies to be applied.

### Survey certification to HCFA by DOH

Admit #7: No HCFA Form 1539 was ever completed, signed or submitted by any DOH official with respect to the surveys of Beechwood in April, May or June 1999.

This is major, since according to SOM 2762, the HCFA 1539 form is the certification that accompanies the survey materials to be submitted to HCFA, certifying that all was done according to survey requirements.

### Plan of Correction (POC) reviews

Admit #19-20: No signed or dated reviews were made, or produced, by any defendant or other DOH official with respect to POCs submitted by Beechwood in response to the April, May, or June surveys.

Admit #21: Defendants are unable to produce *any* April POC review documents.

Admit #22: Defendants can't produce *any* April POC review documents because they are lost or destroyed.

Admit #23: Defendants are unable to produce *any* May POC review documents.

Admit #24: Defendants can't produce *any* May POC review documents because they are either lost or destroyed.

These admits exposed the following hearing testimony as falsehoods:

Mary Jane Proschel, the DOH quality assurance coordinator, stated that she was involved with and used the customary POC review process when Beechwood's POC was received.

Proschel stated that the surveyors were requested to review the POC before May 18, 1999.

Baker stated that she reviewed the POCs along with Proschel and the surveyors.

Baker and Proschel testified that DOH is to judge a POC for reasonableness and whether it appears that it will work, or likely to succeed.

In addition: Baker and Carlo wrote to their attorneys that DOH does not critique the detail in the POCs.

The POC is a federal remedy, and SOM Sections 7400.3 and 7500.E are very specific as to the four elements needed for an acceptable POC. This does not include having surveyors evaluate a POC according to what they believe is reasonable or likely to work.

### Directed Plan of Correction (DPOC) review

Admit #6: No communication was written by any defendant concerning Beechwood's compliance or non-compliance with the Directed Plan of Correction imposed by Baker's letters of April 27, 1999 and May 21, 1999, and the statements contained in the June statement of deficiencies.

### Carlo's notes

Admit #10: Defendants are unable to produce Carlo's original spiral notebooks from which various pages were produced at the hearing.

Admit #11: Defendants are unable to produce Carlo's notebooks for they were either lost or destroyed.

### Gray's file

Admit #12: Defendants are unable to produce Gray's original Beechwood file, as maintained and previously produced for inspection at the DOH administrative hearing.

Admit #13: Defendants are unable to produce Gray's file for it was either lost or destroyed.

## Unique hearing

Admit #8: DOH has never commenced any DOH administrative enforcement proceeding against an SNF [skilled nursing facility] seeking revocation of its operating certificate based on allegations of inadequate patient care resulting from a Title 18/19 (MR/MD) survey, other than that against Beechwood in 1999.

Admit #9: Since the implementation of OBRA 87, DOH has never commenced such a proceeding while the facility was still federally certified as a Title 18/19 (MR/MD) provider, other than the 1999 proceeding against Beechwood.

## Statements of admission not read into the trial record

The following Statements of Admission pertaining to the lack of DOH decision making regarding enforcements were, for some reason, never read into the record at trial.

## Enforcement

From the First Request for Admission:

Admit #1: There was no known "formal referral memo" pertaining to enforcement action taken against Beechwood.

> This should have been prepared by the DOH Bureau of Surveillance and Quality Assurance within the Office of Continuing Care and sent to the DOH Bureau of Administrative Hearings. It was not.

Admit #5: There was no known "enforcement file."

From the Third Request for Admission:

Admit #17: The defendants are unable to produce any enforcement decision making notes.

From the Third Notice to Produce:

Item #50: No litigation hold was ever instituted

In summary, there are no decision making documents of any sort, from survey to enforcement. Clearly, the decision makers did not want their signature on anything. Kelly and Baker were forced into signing a few documents that were sent to the provider; Henry Greenberg, director of the Division of Legal Affairs, signed the caretaker and revocation papers; and Leeds was forced to sign an affidavit for the caretaker case. Otherwise, the claim is that everything was decided by the "team" and group "consensus," without note keeping, and that memories have faded as to who the participants were. A business was destroyed, patients put at risk, and a community deprived of a valuable healthcare facility without anyone having taken responsibility for their actions.

<h2 align="center">MOTION TO COMPEL EMAILS<br>FROM DOH SYSTEM BACKUP FILES</h2>

The major question of whether DOH maintains departmental level backup files that extend back further than ninety days from the date an email was written remains a mystery. The DOH maintains that the file does not go back further than ninety days. Until Altone made his deposition comments regarding his own archive, DOH had declared only the existence of certain backup tapes as a way of retrieving non-current or deleted email.

On July 30, 1999, during the DOH hearing, and in response to Beechwood's subpoena for deleted email, Laura Iwan, the DOH information security officer, wrote Altone regarding our request to restore deleted email that had been referred to her office. In this memorandum, to which repeated reference had been made over the years in response to further requests for email retrieval, she only addressed the backup system. She stated that weekly backups were made every Sunday, but only kept for twelve weeks, before they were reused for new backups. Deleted emails pertaining to Beechwood were produced from this backup system, but by the time Altone made the request to her office, nothing could be retrieved if it was created before May 10, 1999, or if it had been created and deleted within the same week. This obviously left Beechwood at a huge disadvantage in being able to reconstruct a complete picture of DOH activities. However, it also had major implications from an overall perspective as to compliance with state laws on document retention and retrieval abilities.

In an internal memorandum dated August 18, 2000 concerning a FOIL request, Anthony Sherwell, of the program staff, told Gene Therriault, the DOH records officer, that "email in question from 1999 is no longer available from this office. It has long ago been deleted. The only way to retrieve this email would be from tape backup. It is suggested that you contact computer security to obtain the email from backup copy from their archives."

In a December 26, 2001 affidavit created during FOIL litigation, Rosenthal, acting after review of DLA files, and stating that he was only addressing items with some relevance to the DLA, wrote: "The Department has previously advised the Court in the Affidavit of James H. O'Meara, dated June 13, 2001, that the Department can retrieve deleted e-mail notes for up to 90 days after they have been deleted by the computer. Therefore, in some cases there may have been relevant email notes, but such notes were deleted and are no longer retrievable."

In a February 6, 2004 response to a FOIL request for documentation of the data processing structure for DOH as it existed in 1999—including data files back-up and retrieval policies and procedures, what can be down loaded to staff PCs, and instructions for file maintenance—Beechwood was told that the Department had no responsive documents.

In a November 21, 2007 response to a Beechwood Motion to Compel that asked for email that may exist on electronic backup systems, including archives, Rosenthal wrote that "As described in the (attached) affidavit of Barry Krawchuk, the email/calendar backup system is for disaster recovery, not archiving, and any deleted entry is not retrievable after ninety days."

Because virtually everyone involved in the Beechwood case communicated via email about virtually everything that happened in in the actions taken against the facility, the issue of obtaining full email records was obviously critical. We persisted in our attempts to get to the bottom of the email retention issue. It seemed to us inconceivable that the New York State Department of Health, a state agency and key regulatory body for which nothing should have been more important than record keeping and documentation, would fail to retain email for more than ninety days. In some ways, proceeding to trial without the full email record was like attempting to stage Hamlet without Hamlet. But there was only so much we could do, and the most pressing priority was, at long last, to go to trial.

# PART IV

# Reckonings:
# 2004-2012

# CHAPTER 16

# Anatomy of a Fraud

### THE MFCU INVESTIGATION

Not content with putting Beechwood out of business, leaders of the New York State Department of Health wanted to see me convicted criminally. The Medicaid Fraud Control Unit (MFCU) investigation that was opened up against me was based, according to the MFCU Auditor's Report of August 18, 2003, on a NYSDOH decision to terminate the Beechwood, to shutter it, and to move all its residents to other facilities, all because of numerous state-alleged instances of serious deficiencies that placed residents in immediate jeopardy. The MFCU audit was begun to determine if my actions, which moved DOH to close the facility, were not merely civil in nature but also criminal.

Deputy Attorney General Jerry Solomon, who directed the Rochester MFCU office, stated that because failure to furnish services in accordance with regulations constitutes Medicare/Medicaid fraud he waited for the administrative hearing to "play out" and for the opportunity to review the ALJ decision and resulting transcript before opening a criminal case. And then, for three long years and through five subpoenas for documents, the MFCU pursued me for criminal activity. Investigators examined 154 medical records, including those of at least 30 residents involved in the DOH surveys, conducted over a hundred interviews, and reviewed the 4,000-page transcript. They gathered and analyzed carloads of business records including payroll records, staffing schedules, census reports, patient assessment data, billing records, minutes of quality assurance committee meetings, facility policies, and on and on. The MFCU auditor, Neil Davis, stated:

"The audit focused upon staffing levels, PRI [Patient Review Instrument, the New York State patient assessment form used to determine level of care] data, medical records content and extensive interviews.... Staffing levels ... were examined and compared to both peers and proposed federal guidelines (and) ... traced to PRI data ... The required change in staffing needs due to the emphasis on rehabilitative residents was also confirmed.... DOH Surveys, QI Reports, and the transcript from the ALJ hearing were reviewed and used to identify the specific patients to be audited.... Additionally, all available records from [facilities that residents were admitted from or discharged to were retrieved.] Interviews of residents, family members and/or responsible parties for all residents were conducted. Extensive interviews of both former employees and staff employed until the facility closed ... were also conducted."

The results were hardly what the DOH leadership wanted. The MFCU audit emerged as an astounding indictment of the ALJs decision, including his assessment of the credibility of the witnesses for Beechwood.

### Regarding fraud

The ALJ (p. 56) stated that Mr. Chambery's testimony makes "it obvious that his primary and foremost concern is monetary and not resident care" and that (p. 91) he "placed the institution and its needs far above the needs of the residents." He asserted that Beechwood accepted higher-acuity patients to receive higher reimbursement, but "did not change their methods of operations ... to reflect the needs of those residents" (p. 94).

AG Solomon stated that in "deciding whether there was sufficient evidence of criminal conduct, a determination had to be made as to whether or not the evidence that served as a foundation for the charges sustained by the ALJ ... would be sufficient to satisfy our burden of proof beyond a reasonable doubt. It is my opinion that it would not." George Quinlin, an upstate New York supervisor, concurred but went even further: "Any civil or criminal prosecution would have been pointless."

### Regarding "poor care"

The MFCU auditor's report stated that "testimony during the hearing and interviews conducted by their office refuted [the] contention" that poor care was given. Both the auditor and Solomon stated that "the vast majority of those interviewed (over 100 interviews were conducted) indicated that the patient care at the facility was very good to excellent." Even employees who were terminated or had resigned as a result of disputes with the Beechwood director of nursing (DON) praised the facility. Solomon noted that several residents' families also staged protests against DOH sanctions of Beechwood, especially while the DOH was trying to get a receiver appointed by the Court. The auditor stated that, during interviews, "several former employees in addition to family members criticized DOH for their handling of the situation." Auditor Davis wrote a Memorandum to the File noting that three of four staffing agency managers were "shocked" by the actions DOH took, and one of the three stated that Beechwood was one of the "finest homes in Rochester and their staff loved working there." The fourth manager called Beechwood "one of the top five nursing homes in the Rochester area" and noted that some of his staff "quit health care because of the Beechwood closing."

Solomon specifically refuted three charges sustained by the ALJ and stated that it was "unnecessary to go through each." After seeing the results of the extensive review, Patrick Lupinetti, the head of the special projects unit, who had just convicted a provider for Medicaid fraud, remarked, "It doesn't look like there is much to work with here."

### Regarding insufficient staffing

The ALJ (p. 63) stated that "Beechwood does not have sufficient nursing staff ... because they are not getting sufficient reimbursements and/or want to maximize revenues." The MFCU investigation found precisely the opposite. Solomon wrote that "the vast majority of former employees believed staffing levels to be adequate" and that "cost reports and staffing sheets [were used] to independently determine the adequacy of staffing levels. The home met or exceeded the proposed federal guidelines ... DOH personnel also indicated that staffing levels were not an issue at Beechwood."

The MFCU auditor's report added that staffing levels for all employee categories were examined and compared to peers and proposed federal guidelines. Staffing levels were also traced to PRI (patient assessment) data to confirm that the necessary staffing was available. The required change in staffing needs due to the emphasis on rehabilitation was also confirmed.

1

### Regarding the credibility of Beechwood's witnesses

The ALJ (p. 55) found that all of the DOH witnesses were credible and all of Beechwood's were not—because (p. 56) they were all biased, either by employment, licensure, or financial interests. AG Solomon noted this assessment but did not agree with it. His investigators analyzed the medical records and interviewed staff about their documentation and the care given. "I believe it's unnecessary to go through each charge and the testimony of the nurse or doctor claiming that proper treatment was rendered," Solomon remarked, concluding that "while the ALJ sustained Beechwood's violations by a preponderance of the evidence, testimony of [Beechwood's] witnesses ... would make it difficult indeed to prove, beyond a reasonable doubt."

### Regarding abuse and neglect

The ALJ (p. 66) stated that Beechwood "residents were neglected by Beechwood in several significant aspects of care."

Even though he considered this issue to be going "beyond the survey claims," on March 19, 2001, Solomon issued a subpoena to DOH for "all records and reports relating to the chapter 340 investigation" of Beechwood nurses, an investigation that DOH was not even authorized to undertake without reporting it to Solomon's office first. On April 20, 2001 and August 3, 2001, Solomon told Beechwood attorney Paul Barden that he was looking into several instances of as yet unsubstantiated allegations of neglect against the nurses.

On August 9, 2001, MFCU investigators wrote, "The Health Department has brought administrative charges against two of the nurses ... DOH is preparing the records for our review subject to [redacted] ... We will be reviewing DOH's records regarding the administrative charges and have requested their assistance in examining their records in an attempt to confirm as yet unsubstantiated allegations that [redacted] vetoed doctors' order for certain tests."

On October 16, 2001, MFCU investigators interviewed Beechwood's DON about these matters but ended the interview inquiring about why Beechwood was closed. The MFCU never charged any Beechwood staff with neglect.

### MY OWN INVESTIGATION
### Regarding the Plan of Correction (POC)

At the ALJ hearing, DOH had produced Quality Assurance Coordinator Mary

Jane Proschel to testify about the Beechwood plans of correction (POC) the DOH rejected. Proschel testified that she and others had used the typical POC review process and went on to describe why the POCs were rejected. In his report, the ALJ determined Proschel to be a credible witness with "exact and reliable" testimony. Relying on this testimony, he wrote in his decision (p. 90) that "The Plans of Correction were not acceptable" characterizing them as "denials of events" and "attacks on the messengers," which "failed to address the concerns of the Department."

Now, years later, it was proved that Proschel was not a credible witness at all. At the hearing, she testified that she was involved with the POC review and used the customary process to review the POC materials Beechwood submitted for the April 22 survey. She stated that she found the POC to be unacceptable and expounded on the reasons for its rejection, often stating that a Beechwood policy was not acceptable because she expected it to say something else. Not only was this hearsay testimony—since she admitted that she did not have expertise in the nursing areas involved—but she later testified at deposition that it was not the role of DOH to make suggestions or to tell the facility how to correct. The department has a checklist that is used to indicate whether components are in the POC or not. That is the extent of their responsibility.

Proschel stated that her review of the POC would have been done on May 12 or later, but before Baker sent out the rejection notice on May 18. However, she clearly had had no time to review the April POC from May 12 to May 18. At deposition, she testified that her review of a POC would take her, on average, about half a day. She had 2.5 hours on her May 12 time sheet devoted to Beechwood but acknowledged that this was for attendance at the conference with the survey team about whether immediate jeopardy (IJ) continued to exist. The next noted occurrences of time dedicated to Beechwood was 2.5 hours on Saturday, May 15 and an hour on the May 17. There is no documentation and she reported no recollection of what she was doing on either of these days, but Proschel did testify at the hearing that she lacked the proper qualifications to judge several of the Beechwood POC elements, and thus asked "for input from the individuals who are involved in writing the deficiency," especially with an IJ situation, where she asked for "quite a bit of input." However, neither surveyors Cynthia Francis nor Elizabeth Rich noted any time dedicated to review of Beechwood's POC during these periods. Proschel noted another 3.5 hours spent on Beechwood on May 18, but other documents demonstrate this was consumed in entering "practice statements" of May survey findings into the computer for the surveyors.

Proschel testified that no one else did any POC coordination or review in May 1999. Baker identified Proschel as "the point person to review the POC" and the one "responsible for the final review."

Normally, when Proschel reviewed a POC, she noted the outcome and signed and dated her work. She did this with many other reviews of Beechwood POCs prior to April 1999, as found in MFCU files and DOH files. However, as discussed in the last chapter, DOH admitted there are no such documents relating to the April, May, and June POCs.

At trial, Proschel was confronted with timecards and her own documentation of what she had worked on during the dates when POC reviews could have been done. Review of Beechwood POCs was not present on the cards, and Proschel was left with no defense for her testimony at the DOH hearing. A clearly disgusted Judge Larimer admonished Proschel to be careful with the one step down getting off the witness stand; he did not want her to feel that she was in immediate jeopardy.

## THE DOH OFFENSIVE

The decision to prosecute Beechwood was a decision waiting for a case. As Altone testified, "There was never a point in time that it appeared doubtful that some form of administrative enforcement action would be appropriate." And as DOH Bureau of House Counsel attorney Steve Steinhardt admitted, "It was my understanding that a [program] decision had been made ... to replace the operator by whatever means was legally sufficient."

**As you read the following documents and testimony, take note of those marked with an asterisk.** These are what the ALJ had before him when he stated that he found the DOH witnesses extremely credible and declared that there was "not a shred of evidence" of a DOH conspiracy against Chambery or Beechwood.

### The target coming into focus

On April 8, 1998, one year beforehand, DOH acting director for the Western Region Sanford Rubin emailed to Laura Leeds, deputy director of the Office of Continuing Care:

*"You will recall the notorious Brook Chambery and his Beechwood NH rel-ative to a battle we had with him on discharge appeal a couple years ago. This has been an ongoing saga. At any rate, the purpose of my sharing this with you, and requesting your advice and assistance is that there is a common theme with all of what Chambery does: consistently challenges the authority of DOH, and what we may and may not do in and to his NH re: regulations.... the coun-sel I am seeking with you is some type of remedy. For instance, a letter from us in the WRO, perhaps co-signed by you/Bob, and someone in our office of counsel, ... asserting our authority under article 28 to carry out our duties, and warning him that he must cease and desist his unacceptable behavior. Please advise."

*April 13, 1998, Rubin emailed Leeds and a few central office people under her supervision (including Karen Cornwell and Arlene Gray). A copy was also sent to Francis and Proschel:

"I saw the note relative to Brook Chambery complaining to Lee Pope (HCFA) ... This is becoming an extremely serious matter... so bad that I have convened a meetg with the DAG in Rochester ... I am not at all surprised that he con-tacted Lee Pope ... this is his m.o.... when he doesn't get his way with us ... immediately contact those up the line, and/or bring legal action ... it all stems from his lack of acceptance of DOH authority.... Lee must know that this is a very bad provider who is attempting to reverse the applecart, and go on the offensive."

April 13, 1998 (later in the day), Rubin emailed the survey staff in his office:

Subject: Beechwood "As you are all aware, Mr. Chambery is doing all he can to discredit the work of this office as it pertains to our regulatory responsibilities with Beechwood NH. Most recently, Sherry Emrich and I sat in with Mr. C. and his DNS in an IDR ... The IDR ended abruptly with Mr. Chambery storm-ing out of my office, dissatisfied with our response to his appeal. "Subsequent to this meeting I learned that Mr. Chambery contacted HCFA Region II to lodge a complaint against our LTC staff and our process. This is to advise you that I contacted the individual at Region II and explained our side of the story, and also conveyed our concern about care at Beechwood NH."

April 14, 1998, Francis noted: "Meet with S.R[ubin]. and Jerry Solomon [DAG] re: Beechwood. 3 hrs."

*April 14, 1998, Cornwell responded to Leeds, with a copy to Gray:

"This 'screams' New Paltz. A provider who always perceived staff to be out to get them, and an operator who was hostile, and angry. From the perspective of someone who spent almost one and a half years of my work life on the coordination within the Department/AO/DLA/DAG for the [New Paltz appeal], if we can nip this in the bud somehow it may be well worth the effort."

*Gray testified at the DOH hearing that Brook Chambery was *"infamous"* in Albany, because he was so confrontational.

June 25, 1998, Leeds emailed Central Office staff:

"I know this seems like a long time ago, but I would like to know if anything has happened with the investigations at Beechwood or with Chambery's request to [Central Office staff member] Lee Pope about the facility IDR [Informal Dispute Resolution].... I too am concerned that we handle this differently than the New Paltz, please send me any suggestions."

## A changing of the guard: an opportunity to create the perfect storm

During the eighteen months preceding the DOH offensive, a group of administrators sympathetic to the cause of destroying Brook Chambery, a thorn in the department's side, had risen to positions of authority at the regional, state, and federal levels, allowing them full power to move against Beechwood and me. This changing of the guard created the elements of a perfect storm:

Sue Kelly became the HCFA Region II administrator in March 1998

Dennis Whalen became Acting Commissioner of Health in November 1998

Laura Leeds became Deputy Director of the Division of Continuing Care in December 1997

Anna Colello became Director of the Bureau of Long-Term Care and Quality Assurance in November 1998

Sanford Rubin became Acting Director of the Western Region in January 1999

Sharon Carlo became Continuing Care Director for the Western Region in January 1998

Susan Baker became Provisional Director of Long-Term Care for the Western Region of New York in July 1998

*Perspective.* Francis and Rich had been at Beechwood on April 15, 1999 for an abbreviated survey. At the exit conference that day the two had discussed only "potential" deficiencies. Rich admitted, as of the exit conference, that she did not have any idea of what the citations were going to be. She noted that no findings had been written and that direction had to come from supervisors. Baker further clarified that "on the 15th everything was still very tentative."

After the exit conference on April 15 Francis and Rich went home. The next morning, there was a professional seminar in Batavia, N.Y., which, together with travel time and lunch, took Rich and Francis until about 2 p.m. We know this from Francis's calendar; the attendance and activity reports of Francis, Rich, and Baker; the survey worksheets of Francis and Rich; and the survey teamwork schedule. There was a subsequent two-and-a-half-hour discussion in the office about Beechwood matters, but Baker testified that she and the surveyors had "absolutely" not concluded anything as of April 16, and further surveying was necessary. There are no notes of any call to Albany during this meeting, and it is highly unlikely that any conversation took place, for Altone and Colello were in charge of a 3 p.m. meeting in Albany regarding "Protection of Residents in Adult Homes," which was scheduled to last an hour. Bureau of Administrative Hearings senior attorney John Stefani was not at this meeting. At 4:30 p.m. on April 16, the survey team left the office.

*The plan.* *Yet on April 16, 1999, probably in the morning, there was a meeting in Albany involving Anna Colello and Laura Leeds as well as attorneys John Stefani and Russel Altone, to discuss potentially terminating Beechwood's provider agreement and also to consider a "bigger picture," including "legal options for state purposes." Carlo also documented a discussion with Leeds and noted that she needed to "put note to Dennis [Whalen]."

Colello testified that it was "obvious" that Altone and staff were preparing for termination and revocation, and Whalen stated that he had a "general rule" that he wanted his staff to alert him about issues that would be raised to a significant level of public attention."

The obvious problem raised by the occurrence of the April 16 meeting was that no "basis" existed for any discussion of potential termination or a license revocation.

Leeds testified at her deposition that she had no idea how Altone and Colello were discussing Beechwood's termination on April 16, noting that, without survey findings, there was nothing to refer to DLA. In addition, the discussion regarding DOH's enforcement "options" would not start until the last two or three months of the 180-day timeframe. Colello testified at deposition that Altone would not be involved until her office made a referral for enforcement and that there could not be talk of enforcement until after a Statement of Deficiency (SOD).

Altone testified at his deposition that he didn't know now, and "doubt[ed] that [he] knew then," the basis for the April 16 discussions or what he meant by the "bigger picture," but it was fair to assume he had a bigger picture in mind.

Altone explained that the typical procedure was that "as prosecutors, the staff of the bureau primarily become involved in enforcement matters only when departmental program staff refer a matter to the bureau for prosecution." "No matter what, program makes some sort of enforcement referral to start the process." DLA has "always over many years requested approximately thirty different programs to supply us with [necessary documentation and evidentiary materials] to allow a decision to be made by bureau staff whether the prosecution should be pursued] at the outset. ...There are always facts to support a referral to the division of legal affairs ... and usually those take the form of survey statements of deficiencies that exist prior to the referral."

Altone described the referral packet as a manila folder containing an "endorsed cover memo," the SOD, a write-up of the SOD, program staff contacts, and settlement instructions. The cover memo would bear an "original signature" of a high-level program manager, and possibly another signature of someone even higher as an endorsement indicating that the case was worthy of referral and had withstood a programmatic chain of review. Yet, in response to Beechwood's First Request for Admission (October 20, 2009), the defendants responded (Admission #5) that there was no known "formal referral memo." At trial (Admission #5), they admitted that there was no "enforcement file."

Altone testified that "This referral did not come as a neatly packaged file from the program, from the nursing home program. It started out as meetings, "Meetings rather than a referral packet."

Colello stated in an interrogatory response that there were several meetings in Delmar, a suburb of Albany, with attorneys to discuss options, involving herself, Leeds, and Altone. Altone added that at several points the meetings included HCFA attorneys.

Leeds stated: "I know the process takes time and we have to prepare on multiple level at the same time. ... All levels of the Department and HCFA" were involved, "everybody, ... including the attorneys." Altone added that, in Beechwood's case, things happened in a "different manner"; there was a "preliminary determination" by program that they wanted legal folks involved; program officials "needed legal advice and attention as far as options," and his "advice was sought with respect to what would be needed to prepare for [revocation] and how that might be coordinated" with termination and a caretaker application. In fact, there never was a decision as to whether the prosecution of Beechwood should be pursued. Yet: "There was never a point in time that it appeared doubtful that some form of administrative enforcement action would be appropriate."

We do not know when these meetings got under way, how often they were held, the full slate of individuals involved, and how plans unfolded. Emails were deleted, and due to an incomplete response to a subpoena issued by the ALJ, we were only able to recover emails back to May 9, 1999. Furthermore, Altone's file begins with a telephone conference on May 11, 1999. Bureau of Litigation attorney Harold Rosenthal stated that "In some cases there may have been relevant e-mail notes, but such notes were deleted and are no longer retrievable."

Carlo's notebooks, which were a good source of information, disappeared. There was, as mentioned previously, no enforcement file, and Whalen, Office of Continuing Care director Robert Barnett, Leeds, Colello, Rubin, Greenberg, and Steinhardt all stated that they kept no Beechwood file. In addition, both Rosenthal and Altone stated that they had no documentation regarding the determination or authorization to involve DLA. Although there may have been documents hidden under beds at home—as was rumored with Rubin! —we were never able to obtain them.

Conveniently, no one had any memory of the relevant events. Leeds recalled "very little," Colello and Rubin did not recall the "details," Altone had no answer, and Whalen, Greenberg, and Barnett had no memory of the events whatsoever. Nevertheless, as the principals' statements indicate, this was a major undertaking, and it could easily have been in the planning since Leeds signaled her interest to Rubin in June of 1998. It was not only a bold initiative to take down a high-performing facility, a license revocation had never been done. The defendants admitted this at trial. On July 3, 1999, the Rochester D&C reported that Kelly stated, "This is the first (termination) in this region in 10 years or so." Baker testified in her deposition that, in her thirteen years with DOH, "We have not done this before, a termination." Solomon testified in his deposition that in his 23 years with MFCU, he had not seen another administrative proceeding to revoke an operating certificate. Altone, Barnett, Leeds, Gray, and Baker all had worked at DOH since the 1970s, and all testified that Beechwood was the only revocation action that they could recall.

Furthermore, the operation required close coordination between the state and federal agencies. Attempting to initiate a state-level license revocation while the provider was still federally certified was especially tricky since it conflicted with the State Plan, a federal contract governing joint state and federal Medicare/Medicaid responsibilities. The defendants admitted they had never done a revocation hearing while a provider was still federally certified. Indeed, it is doubtful that such a thing ever happened in any other state.

There had also never been any other application for an involuntary receiver in New York State. Barnett testified at his deposition that he did not recall dealing with another caretaker action, and Judge Affronti stated, "There are limited, if any, cases directly on point as regards this particular issue."

The number of people who would have to be involved, and the number of buy-ins that would have to be obtained would also complicate matters. Leeds testified that if she were involved, it would be "as high up as it would go for the referral to be made," for she *was* "The Program." However, she also stated that the decision to seek a revocation would involve a variety of people, "a whole lot of other people," including "at all levels of DOH and HCFA coming together," and once plans were in gear, she would have to "answer to a whole lot of other people" also. For instance, Whalen testified that Leeds would need his concurrence, since he was the signatory.

Leeds stated that she met with Whalen over every single statement of charges issued. This was part of her responsibilities in the Office of Continuing Care. But since Beechwood was such a significant case, the approvals could and did involve the governor's office. Whalen stated that the commissioner or acting commissioner is a direct report to what typically is titled the Deputy Secretary of Health in the governor's office, and that it is the responsibility of the deputy secretaries in the governor's office to know what is going on in the agencies, especially about things that were bound to draw public interest.

Greenberg stated that assistant counsel and program persons within the governor's office "supervised" the operations of DOH "very carefully," thus it would not be "inherently unusual" that since a revocation proceeding, closure of a facility, and removal of an operator is a significant matter, that it be *"run"* by the governor's office. Since the governor's office had no documentation, Beechwood could not verify the extent of its involvement, but the level of officials involved in the early planning would indicate that the operation had at least the approval, if not the direct participation, of the governor's office. As Greenberg put it, "heaven forbid" if things did not go right, "it would reflect poorly on the governor's office."

Gray testified that she recalled "numbers of discussions" with Colello regarding how the revocation (and all connected with it) was going to happen. It was so "unusual ... it took a lot of planning and organization." Colello testified that a revocation is a "very big thing," a "long process." Leeds testified that it "takes time and we have to prepare on multiple levels at the same time." So many DOH attorneys were involved that the ALJ stated "There must be [a DLA attorney] out there" somewhere who "has not been involved" in the Beechwood case.

*The "bigger picture."* By the morning of April 21, 1999, departmental documentation begins to reveal what was meant by the "bigger picture," or the "global picture." Not only is DLA "on board" and providing advice, other agencies are getting into it as well. Rosenthal stated that, according to "Mr. Altone's recollection," there was an undocumented meeting (by April 21) in which a determination, or authorization, was made by the DOH to "involve DLA members," and in which DLA got "on board" and was "prepared to assist."

Steinhardt testified that it was his understanding that a program decision had been made to replace the operator by whatever means was legally sufficient. On April 11, 1999, Carlo noted that *"OSP [is] part of the process; Feds [are] involved: Termination? Do global picture, ... Altone involved."

By April 23, 1999, Altone, in a document hidden for years under attorney-client privilege, revealed a four-pronged offensive aimed at achieving four separate enforcement actions: termination, revocation, fines, and receivership. Writing to Associate Attorney David Abel, he stated: "Please see me to discuss this anticipated referral for enforcement. I expect to assign it to Shea (Buffalo office attorney) when it comes in. She has already had some involvement in what is regarded as a serious matter. It is currently on a collision course with HCFA for termination of the provider agreement. OCC [Office of Continuing Care] may refer it for revocation/fines/receivership. It could get real sticky for Brook Chambery is very litigious."

The offensive anticipated that a case would be made.

*Altone's strategy.* Russel Altone laid out for attorney Marie Shea a strategy to prepare for an "administrative hearing seeking revocation." On May 11, 1999, in a document also hidden for years under attorney-client privilege, Shea documented Altone's five needs:

1. Needed: "IJ (imminent danger) to get revocation." Revocation was the DOH "offensive."

2. Needed: HCFA termination, coordination with HCFA to hold off on right to hearing regarding the termination, and mandated transfers of Medicare/Medicaid residents.

3. Needed: Serious, widespread, and persistent "violation of service regulations."

4. Needed: Argue "in face of IJ, no steps to correct—total disregard" ... "demonstrated depraved indifference."

5. Needed: "Conditions so bad, can't allow operator to stay without moving the residents."

In short, Altone's strategy was to paint the situation at Beechwood as one in which "lives [were] in jeopardy and [there was a] complete failure to take steps to correct."

Again, Altone had to admit that it was "not the norm" for his bureau to become involved like this before there is any referral for prosecution. Furthermore, because an SOD hadn't even been drafted yet, there were no specific facts as of April 23 to justify *any* enforcement. The offensive was considered so important that it involved "all levels of the [DOH] and HCFA," and the governor's office. As executed, the offensive was so massive that the ALJ questioned whether there was an attorney "out there" in the DLA who had not been involved. As Altone testified at trial, his staff was told not to plan any vacations. The offensive was so all-encompassing and labor-intensive that Carlo had to enlist "the entire WRO LTC staff" and needed managers to keep other Continuing Care programs "on track" and "focused." Yet the offensive was so sensitive that alerts were being issued at both the state and federal levels regarding the degree of public attention that was coming. Moreover, the DOH public relations department was engaged to handle the "crisis management." Indeed, this was an offensive so unique, unethical, and illegal that one is still amazed it was ever attempted. But Altone and the others placed great reliance on sheer force and the depth of the public trust to succeed.

## MAKING THE CASE

*Leading up to April 15.* The labor of making the case began before the survey of April 15, 1999. On March 26, Francis, the complaint supervisor and experienced surveyor, received a patient care complaint (labeled DM), and coded it as a routine "general care complaint." Baker testified that "routine surveys and complaints did not require her direct intervention," at least not until after staff had been out to investigate and came to conclusions about problems. *Proschel added that Baker would not really be involved in such matters until the surveyors had investigated and determined that a deficiency existed at the level of immediate jeopardy (IJ). *Baker confirmed that it was a general care complaint, yet acknowledged that she took direct charge in assigning Rich to "review the record, get copies of pieces of it, and bring it back so that we could decide if there was an issue." *Baker then left for vacation on March 27, 1999.

On March 31, Elisabeth Rich went to Beechwood to investigate the concerns that Francis had written on the complaint intake form. Since DM had been discharged to the hospital, Rich also went to the hospital on April 6, spending four hours to investigate the hospital record and write her report. Her conclusion was that none of the concerns outlined by Francis were confirmed. *In other words, the complaint was unsubstantiated, an outcome confirmed by Colello's note to Altone, and Altone's follow-up. *On April 12, Francis spent a half hour doing the paperwork to close out the DM complaint investigation and complete the appropriate forms. This outcome was also entered into the federal electronic database that HCFA maintains.

On April 7, Baker came back from vacation and was having frequent discussions with Gray, at the DOH Central Office in Albany, about a "Beechwood situation." However, she had not had time to discuss any Beechwood matter with Rich, who was busy working on "special projects" all day, before leaving for her own vacation on April 8.

*On April 8, Carlo's note reveals that they were already trying to make the case for an immediate jeopardy situation. She noted "Beechwood … Possible IJ … Arlene [Gray] will come." Colello verified that she did request Gray to "assist," and Carlo subsequently acknowledged that Gray did come from the Albany office. *Gray testified that she was in Rochester for three days in April/May but claimed her activities were "kind of a blur." Gray's Beechwood file disappeared, and DOH failed to produce her travel vouchers in response to FOIL requests.

*On April 13, Baker was in Rochester and had a DOH physician, Dr. LaMonaco, spend a couple of hours reviewing the DM complaint file even though neither Francis nor Rich were available to discuss the case with him. Francis and Proschel testified that physicians would normally not be involved even if there were an IJ determination. Dr. LaMonaco made some notes, but they were inconclusive.

On April 14, Rich came back from vacation but was at an out-of-town facility all day. Francis noted on her calendar that she spent four hours in preparation for a visit to Beechwood. One hour was allocated to another complaint (EO) regarding a lost ring, and three hours on an unidentified "2803" neglect matter. Thus, it appears they were discussing reopening the DM complaint and turning it into a case of abuse or neglect. They were tired of waiting for an opportunity before pouncing. They intended to make the case.

**Back to where we left off.** On April 15, Francis and Rich went to Beechwood. *Baker stated, "it was my decision in concurrence with Ms. Carlo ... We felt in talking with the surveyors there were absolutely still concerns regarding care, so we absolutely needed to continue the investigation." Yet, Rich testified at deposition that she had no memory of discussing the DM complaint with Baker before the April 15, and there was no reason for Baker or Carlo to be involved.

*Baker testified that the surveyors were told to expand the survey, and get copies of patient records and to bring them back to the office for review and decision making about problems that may exist. Francis testified in her deposition—and Baker confirmed in her deposition—that she did not recall any other occasion when Baker served in such an integral role as a member of the survey team, even going on site. *However, Baker revealed that the Central Office was part of the supervisory control being exercised.

Baker's instructions are the reason why the surveyors were very vague at the entrance conference about the problem and information desired, and *left, stating at the exit conference, only that there were potential deficiencies. Baker, Rich, and Leeds all testified in their depositions that the survey team was to give the specifics of each finding at the exit conference.

*The lack of understanding as to how the case was to be made is the reason that, on April 21, Altone was still wondering how an unsubstantiated complaint was to relate to the basis for termination. It is the reason that, on April 19 and 20, Baker and Carlo violated survey protocol by *focusing on copying the closed records of discharged patients to take back to the office, where they could try to create problems that might not be found on survey observations by very experienced and senior surveyors. It is the reason why, after Baker and Carlo could not figure out how to make any case for IJ, Baker faxed scribbled notes to Albany at 9:49 a.m. on April 21 to solicit some direction from the Central Office. In her deposition, Baker admitted that it was not their usual process to send notes like that to Albany and that her notes did not have any mention of IJ.

*The fact is that, in this case, as Francis, Baker stated, and Colello admitted, Albany was involved in the IJ decision, even though Leeds testified at deposition that the scope and severity decisions are to be made at the regional level by those who were at the facility, and Baker testified that Albany cannot make its review until the SOD is written up by the Regional Office. *Baker testified that there was a conference call with Albany, in the course of which it was decided that there was an "IJ situation." This must have been before 3:59 p.m. on April 21 when Baker sent Gray (Colello's office) another fax, the covering letter of which says: "Following are 3 'J's. A fourth is still being written." This was the beginning of a lot of "back and forth" with Albany concerning deficiency construction.

On April 22 at 2:10 p.m., and in a rare show of force, Baker, Carlo, and Rubin accompanied the surveyors Francis and Rich on the official exit conference. *The survey team verbally relayed what it tentatively expected the written report to contain, but stressed that they were still working on the findings. Whatever was relayed concerning patients, tags, scope and severity levels, and so on was quite vague. *However, one thing was made very clear: they were discussing widespread IJ involving six or seven patients, just as Altone had advised, and Carlo had noted they needed to claim "poor care," which would lead to a Medicare/Medicaid fraud investigation for "failure to deliver care."

After the exit conference, an extensive amount of drafting and editing of deficiency statements and findings took place. In violation of the subpoena by the ALJ in the DOH hearing, only a few scattered pages of this documentation were produced at the time. It took another twelve years before a much larger picture of this activity was uncovered during the discovery process. The many drafts and edits, often handwritten, included the deletion of pertinent facts from the medical records that were included in original drafts, changes in conclusions drawn and deficiency tags utilized, and wild swings in the scope and severity assessed on the individual findings. This activity was in high gear on April 23, when Altone laid out his four-pronged legal offensive. On April 24, Carlo was still personally making "revisions," and on April 26, Francis's calendar has 7.5 hours to "finish Beechwood finding."

This period, between the exit conference on April 22 and the delivery of the SOD on the 27th, also reveals more evidence of HCFA involvement, which Altone and Carlo had discussed on April 23. In an interrogatory response, Kelly stated, "sometime after April 22, 1999 she participated in a conference call with Laura Leeds ... [and recalled] being advised that Beechwood was being considered for placement in immediate jeopardy. ... This conversation was initiated by Ms. Leeds ... regarding ... assistance or guidance from CMS." On April 26 Leeds wrote, "We have been working with HCFA on this one and HCFA has been cooperative as Mr. Chambery has tried to go around the state to HCFA." *And on April 27, Rubin wrote that "Sharon Carlo and Sue Baker of our staff, working closely with Arlene Gray and others in OCC developed an immediate jeopardy SOD and directed POC in conjunction with Region II (HCFA)." Kelly had been a deputy commissioner at the New York DOH and was now in charge in Region II at HCFA. So, DOH not only had HCFA's support but also their outright assistance in the state's fraudulent operation against Beechwood and me.

The defendants (3rd Request to Admit, #4) admitted that there are no notes documenting any survey decision-making about these findings or about who was involved in them. The absence of documentation was not only a violation of survey protocol but another example of the intentional absence of an audit trail that would reveal who was responsible. When the statement of deficiency (SOD) was hand-delivered on April 27, it differed significantly from what had been represented at the exit conference on April 22.

At four in the afternoon on April 27, in a rare show of force, Rubin, Carlo, Baker, Rich, and Francis personally delivered a 32-page Statement of Deficiency. It alleged widespread IJ, yet, in flagrant violation of survey protocol, not one deficiency was supported with any observation made while a surveyor was in the facility. *Baker testified that "In April, the IJ determination/situation was based on closed records (discharged patients) ... We did expand and look at some current residents ... but none of them were in IJ."

*At the DOH hearing, Rich testified that IJ cannot exist when the resident has been discharged. *Baker testified that "we have to have the evidence of jeopardy at that moment ... one of the residents to whom this IJ applied must be present in the facility at that time." *And both Baker and Francis testified that the IJ was lifted in May because they did not find any current residents in IJ. But Altone had prevailed.

Not only did the SOD fail to mention that the findings came from closed record reviews—discharged patients—but Finding #1 answered Altone's question on his April 21 email cited above. How could a complaint, previously investigated and filed as unsubstantiated, be connected to a basis for termination? Simple: Just turn it into an IJ!

Altone had gotten his widespread IJ—albeit only through fraudulent presentation of the facts and violation of survey protocol. He knew, however, that the ALJ would either ignore these issues or determine that they were outside the scope of his authority. Altone figured he was home free.

He also got the accelerated termination track he wanted. Any deficiency puts a facility on a termination track because of the zero-tolerance federal system, but HCFA protocol mandated a 23-day "fast track" termination if IJ is alleged. Typically, this meant that the IJ situation had to be fixed within 23 days, but in Beechwood's case, DOH stated that it expected all alleged deficiencies to be corrected in this period. DOH also took the opportunity to mandate a Plan of Correction that they directed (DPOC), and instituted monitoring visits to theoretically assess the corrective measures being instituted.

DOH officials fully expected to continue to claim IJ and stick to their termination schedule. As early as April 15, Francis had told a Beechwood nurse that surveyors would be in the facility for 30 days. *On May 7, before any revisit to assess correction, Baker wrote that, "after speaking with Arlene Gray, the immediate plan [is for a] termination date of May 15, 1999.

DOH knew that basing enforcement actions on these fraudulent claims would be shaky and that there would be appeals and other legal actions. Accordingly, they began lining up their forces. On April 26, Leeds wrote to Whalen, "We do have the evidence to sustain our position, but the closure is going to be tough." *On April 27, Rubin wrote Barnett: "The main purpose of this note is to alert you ... that we now expect that the current survey outcome will be contested in some type of hearing ... None of this has changed our resolve at all. ...

we do not underestimate him as an opponent in court. We strongly believe our ducks are in line." *And Baker wrote that Daniel Walsky (HCFA) told her that they were "Doing a great job ... Agree a monster of a case... don't weaken the case ... work together with HCFA." However, he also warned Baker about a potential weakness with the April SOD, commenting that it was "Hard to get a sense of aspect or a sense of neglect. The condition of care gets lost. The SOD needs to be absolutely care exhaustive and ... clearly identify the foundation for the deficiency. However, it is not good to re-issue an SOD."

The warning did not discourage DOH officials, who were confident of the power residing in their arsenal. *On April 28th, Leeds told Rubin: "I don't think he gets an appeal. ... The issue is this: how much of his resident population is public pay. He may not be concerned [with Medicare/Medicaid termination] because has a strong private pay contingent in his home. So that being the case... we have to be prepared to also revoke his operating certificate." *On April 29, Rubin answered: "Laura, I think we may well be in a situation where we need to revoke ... I have no doubt we would prevail ... Another advantage on our side is that Region II [HCFA] claims it will back us all the way ... They too have been harassed by Chambery. The chickens are coming home to roost." The facility could be terminated and closed before any appeal could be heard or be of any value.

*The gang at DOH knew that the ALJ would ignore Baker's testimony that, as of May 12, it was "absolutely not" their plan to terminate Beechwood, even though on May 10 she had written, "After speaking with Arlene Gray, the immediate plan [is for a] termination date of May 15, 1999." *They knew he would ignore the fact that Baker also testified, "No, we did not" find any residents experiencing IJ as a result of the monitoring visits, when, on May 7, she wrote, "Can't take off IJ," and *on May 10, wrote, "After consultation with Sharon Carlo ... we could not extend the [POC] due date because the residents were still in immediate jeopardy."

*In fact, the DOH conspirators knew that the ALJ would ignore Baker's testimony that, as of May 12, she was unaware that revocation was an objective, even though on May 10 she wrote, "We will begin to copy all materials related to this termination to send to Albany for a statement of charges." *They knew that the ALJ would ignore the fact that on May 10, Rubin forwarded the note Baker wrote that day to to Greenberg, which commented, "this looks like the real deal for termination."

Thus, Baker was not worried as she testified that she didn't believe the surveyors were aware that their activities would be used for a statement of charges until "probably late May," even though she sent Francis a blind copy of her May 10 email, and a Beechwood nurse (Qwen Westbrook) stated in an affidavit and testified that on May 10 that a co-worker told her that surveyor Cynthia Francis told her the facility would be shut down by Friday, which was May 14, 1999.

*Reaffirmation of plans.* On May 11, 1999, a major telephone conference took place between program and legal officials at DOH and HCFA to coordinate their activities. The topics: "S. Kelly- putting notice in paper - expecting termination … terminate – move res. 5/15 … begin revocation proceedings after Fri. (14th)." Altone testified that the discussion was "primarily between the federal HCFA folks … and the senior program people in the office of continuing care."

After this conference call, *Altone wrote Greenberg that "we are preparing for revocation and application in court for a caretaker. Marie Shea will prepare to handle the administrative hearing seeking revocation. The Feds would be responsible for doing the termination of (the) provider hearing. Steve Steinhardt is preparing to make an application for a caretaker. The strategy is still in flux and partly depends on what is found the next couple of days." *He then told Rubin that "DLA is on board and prepared to assist."

In her deposition, Leeds had to admit that not only did she not recall what evidence she had on May 11 to justify the revocation plans, but that the decision to revoke was probably made sooner than this.

In his interrogatory responses, Altone stated that, to his "best recollection," it was on or about this date when he received "direction" from program staff to "commence" or "to move forward with revocation, a caretaker and program termination." This meant that they had "moved into full gear," even though, as he again had to admit, he was "not at that point familiar with the details, the specifics of patient care." In fact, Altone stated that he doubted that the outcome from the revisit that was scheduled for the next day had any effect whatsoever on the work his office was to do regarding the revocation or caretaker actions.

Altone again violated his own protocol. He testified at his deposition that, typically in making a decision whether to prosecute, he "would want to see … what is in the statement of deficiencies … There's much, much more," we "have to intensively review and evaluate the evidence." However, in this case, the evidence and the charges were "being developed simultaneously," and Shea played a pivotal role. Her notes from May 11 demonstrate that Altone directed her to arrange to be in Rochester on May 14. She was to coordinate with Carlo, become familiar with the April SOD issues, and "find more bad things" for the May SOD. As Leeds had reflected on May 13, after the May 12 survey revisit, "the attorneys may not think we have sufficient report." Altone wanted them to "show [serious violations of services regs] more widespread than currently have" and was wondering whether "[they had] immediate jeopardy to get revocation." On Friday, May 14, Carlo wrote to Leeds, "We're all on the same page ... the staff are working on the new deficiencies even as we speak."

Altone further told Shea, that they were "mounting a revocation action ... [and] going to court for a caretaker." For the caretaker, they would be arguing to the judge that conditions are so bad, that they can't allow the operator, who shows total disregard, to stay in control. He expected HCFA to terminate the Medicare/Medicaid agreement as of May 15 because of a "complete failure to take steps to correct ... [and] demonstrated depraved indifference." He told Shea that Beechwood did "have a right to appeal, but after the fact." In her deposition, Leeds admitted that it was "handy" for them that the federal post-remedy appeal process might take ten years, and she could not hold back a burst of laughter.

Shea's notes of May 11 and before the revisit planned for the 12th, show that Altone expected HCFA to start moving residents after the 15th. He also anticipated that a DOH notice of hearing (NOH) and statement of charges (SOC) would be issued on May 21. However, as Altone knew, the strategy entirely depended on what they could claim from the revisit on the May 12, and that a another fraudulent IJ claim would become the focal point of a federal appeal. In fact, as Baker was at the facility on the May 12 revisit, Walsky from HCFA asked her: "are resid[ents] in immed[iate] and serious danger?" Baker responded, "not sure yet ... trying to look at actual resid[ents] ... no one jumping out as IJ."

***Strategy adjustment, but plan remains.*** *At seven on the next morning, May 13, Leeds wrote to Whalen that, in a long meeting after the survey, a decision was made that "immediate and serious jeopardy did not exist," so they were going to instead claim "substandard quality of care" (SQC), which would "still" allow them to recommend to HCFA that instead of termination, an "immediate denial of payment for new admissions (DPNA)" be applied. She also stated that they would be recommending a newly rescheduled "early termination" date of June 17, even though in her deposition, she later testified, there was no reason to shorten the timeframe from the typical 180 days if there was no IJ. She ended her May 13 note by stating that "We will continue to see if we can make the case for a caretaker next week. (John, this is the only piece we do not want public.) [She was addressing John Signor, DOH Public Affairs Group director.]"

Leeds testified that every one of these decisions reflected plans made earlier, because the process took time and they had to prepare at multiple levels; however, no documentation of these earlier decisions exists.

At 11:23 a.m. on May 13, Whalen responded: "Laura, if immediate jeopardy is removed, what is the basis for moving to an involuntary receiver?" Leeds replied: "they still have deficiencies in the level of SQC [substandard quality of care]. These are a pattern involving harm. These are serious deficiencies and warrant strong response from us. The attorney's [sic] may not think we have sufficient report." It was crucial to maintain such claims as SQC for pursuit of the caretaker and revocation, and to continue with an accelerated termination date, but Leeds knew that, in the end, it would not take much to justify the termination. *As Barnett told Rubin, "Implementation of a caregiver is still under consideration since termination from Medicare and Medicaid is still a possibility if they do not correct ALL substandard quality of care issues by some future date certain."

*At the exit conference that day, May 13, Baker relayed to Beechwood that they were "recomm[ending] [an] early term[ination] [date of] 6/17/99" to HCFA unless "substantial compliance" was obtained, and an "acceptable POC" was submitted. All these elements were completely within the discretion of DOH officials.

On the same day, Baker wrote to Walsky at HCFA, falsely claiming that they did a follow-up survey on May 12 to determine whether IJ was still in existence; *she later testified that no IJ was ever identified on any monitoring visit. Baker also falsely claimed that "the facility remained Substandard in F224," but the SOD delivered on May 21 did not have any F224 tag. And there was a third false claim, that "all aspects of the Plan of Correction were reviewed to determine progress." The truth was that Altone did not want any corrective actions recognized, Colello had told Baker not to accept the POC, and, before trial, the defendants admitted they have no notes of any POC review.

As all this took place on May 13, Kelly was arranging for the program termination notice to be placed in the newspaper, as they had planned on May 11, before the revisit. On May 20, Kelly left Cahill a message: "They (DOH) cannot prove credible evidence (to support termination) before revisit, so we (HCFA) should have maybe waited (before placing the public notice in the paper) – it's a judgment."

Also on May 13, Altone put a note in his file that he had spoken with Cahill about the lack of any IJ, and that she boldly proclaimed "the facility will be terminated nonetheless because of the severity of the findings" which hadn't even been written or submitted to HCFA. He then notes: "still enough for caretaker."

On May 18, Rich, who was supposed to be writing up deficiencies from the May 12 revisit, and who had Shea assigned to her office to help find "more bad things" while working up the statement of charges, called Sower, the Executive Secretary at the Board of Nursing within the Department of Education, to see if someone from her office would testify at a hearing.

On that same day, May 18, Baker issued a formal notice rejecting Beechwood's POC. *At the ALJ hearing, Baker falsely testified that she, along with Proschel and the surveyors, reviewed the POCs. *As we saw earlier, Proschel also falsely testified that she was involved with and used the customary POC review process and that she found the POC unacceptable; she also gave her reasons. Likewise, Francis and Rich falsely signed an affidavit for the Statement of Charges in which they affirmed that "Plans of Correction (POC) submitted to date have not adequately addressed the many and severe problems identified."

***Kelly's illegal concurrence and testimony concerning that concurrence.*** On Friday, May 21, at 3:30 p.m., Kelly faxed a letter to Beechwood: "please be advised that due to the seriousness of the deficiencies still remaining, the termination of your Medicare provider agreement has been rescheduled for June 17, 1999, unless the deficiencies are corrected by that date." In her January 31, 2003 affidavit, made in response to our "1983" civil rights action, in which she was named as a defendant, Kelly stated (#22) that "professional members of my staff and I reviewed the documentation provided by DOH in support of its May 12th recommendation. … We found that the findings were presented in the appropriate form and manner, were quite detailed and specific. … It was our conclusion … that their findings and recommendations are amply supported." In #23, she stated, "By letter dated May 21, 1999, I notified Beechwood … CMS would terminate the provider agreement on June 17, 1999, unless the deficiencies were corrected."

The problem with Kelly's affidavit statements is that they are intentionally misleading and intended to cover her improper procedures.

1. There was no "May 12th recommendation" by DOH. The survey was done on May 12, and the exit conference with the facility was not held until the following day.

2. The only document Kelly and her staff reviewed before her May 21 letter to Beechwood was the letter Baker sent to Daniel on May 13.

3. If Kelly and her staff reviewed any "detailed and specific" documentation of findings, and presented in the "proper form and manner," it was not until after her May 21 concurrence letter.

   *On May 20, Lee Pope, in the HCFA office, told Cahill, in Colello's office, that, after a week of hounding Kelly for concurrence with Baker's letter, she finally concurred and drafted a letter to me (Brook Chambery); however, he requested the SOD and any correspondence concerning it. Ten minutes after faxing the letter of concurrence to me at Beechwood on May 21, Pope repeated the request for the SOD. On May 24, Cahill stated that Proschel told her that HCFA's fax machine would not accept her transmission of the SOD, and she was still attempting to send it. On May 26, during a call with Beechwood's attorneys, Pope stated that he had just received the SOD that morning.

4. Kelly (Trial Admit #7) never received the required HCFA 1539 or proper certification for the statement of deficiencies that was sent on the May 26.

5. Kelly had no intention of allowing Beechwood to come into compliance by June 17. In its brief to the Second Circuit (p. 38), HCFA stated that her May 21 notice represented Kelly's "ultimate decision," a decision "finally concluded" with the SQC in May.

Cahill was quite excited when Kelly issued her concurrence letter. *Cahill told Baker to "Have a good weekend and have a couple drinks on all of us here in Delmar!" Only a couple of hours later, Gray told Altone that they need to conference next week to "discuss the next step." Altone testified that it was around May 25 that he received "direction" from program officials to "commence" the enforcement action.

*Secure in HCFA's commitment to terminate, DOH officials pressed on with their offensive.* On May 21, the second 30-page SOD was hand-delivered to Beechwood, claiming substandard quality of care (SQC). On May 11, Altone had counseled Shea to "charge failed to do something," to make "direct connections between care or level of it" and a pattern of deficiencies and neglect. He also directed that they portray widespread and serious violation. She took this direction to heart. For instance, Baker's survey notes had the F281 (Resident Assessment) and F309 (Quality of Care) tags at a D level. The subsequent SOD put F281 at an H level and F309 at a G level.

Baker's covering letter accompanying the SOD stated that "this office has decided to" continue state monitoring and the DPOC requirement, with, however, the added requirement that a consultant be obtained to develop and implement an "acceptable" POC. At trial, Carlo admitted that DOH had no authority to mandate such a consultant. The covering letter also stated that there would be an opportunity to correct until June 16; however, while Beechwood was busy responding to the findings and following the mandated directives in an attempt to get its POC accepted, DOH was, of course, still secretly moving in the opposite direction. The department had no intention of allowing Beechwood to continue in operation. The overall plan, or "offensive," continued as Altone laid out in his email of April 23—something hidden for years under attorney-client privilege.

On May 26, the official date in the DOH computer system for the commencement of the revocation action, and with Shea having already spent 90% of her time on the planned Beechwood enforcement actions since May 11, Carlo (with Shea and Baker on the telephone) falsely told Beechwood attorneys (Kevin Cooman and Paul Barden) that there was no other agenda than to get Beechwood up and running and back in compliance. That same day, there was a DOH conference Carlo attended along with Leeds, Colello, Baker, Altone, Shea, and Steinhardt. Carlo's notes record the themes to be used for the revocation action: "Re: Revocation: Habitual practice of violation of standards; Cont to neglect residents; failed to implement accept POC; ... Cont risk to residents ... flagrantly kept himself out of compliance ... need to present 'horrible' condition to judge."

At the same time, HCFA was being deliberately evasive. On May 26 Pope stated that a shutdown was not in anyone's interest and that he did not think it was on the DOH agenda to shut the facility down, something they could not, in any case, do without HCFA. On May 27, Pope again stated that it was not in any-one's interest to close the facility, and that he was going to call Kelly and Rubin and, he hoped, work this out soon. Pope was to return the call but it never happened. Instead, the Civil Remedies Division of HCFA sent Beechwood's request for a hearing to John Gura, the HFCA "regional attorney," *the same person whose role Altone had stated was to do "the termination of [the] provider hearing."

On May 27, Shea faxed Altone a partial SOC, which he forwarded to Stein-hardt, stating "Here is a partial draft ... Marie [Shea] should continue writing throughout the day and not concentrate much on verification by witnesses ... Our aim right now is to produce a draft statement of charges (SOC) by noon Friday [May 28] that can be shown to Whalen. I think Marie is doing an excellent job of extracting the essence of violations from the overwritten and somewhat confusing SODs. ... whatever is shown to Dennis [Whalen] will need to be presented with caveats regarding the need to fully confirm with witnesses before serving or going to court ..." Steinhardt responded that "as soon as we know Dennis' position, I can get on the affidavits, and Joe can alert the AG."

On June 1, Beechwood, still unaware of the real agenda and the fact that its POC would never be accepted, submitted its rebuttal to the May SOD, along with a revised POC. Again, the labor involved was horrendous. Altone's description of the SODs as "overwritten and somewhat confusing" was a vast understate-ment. They were grossly overwritten, deliberately confusing, and intentionally left out many important facts from the medical records.

In her deposition, Leeds stated that once the SOC was drafted, she would have to meet with Whalen to discuss it because Whalen had the ultimate author-ity to charge a facility. But Whalen's office wasn't even as high as the conspiracy went. Altone stated that Whalen wanted the proposed caretaker fully approved by the governor's office before serving the notice of hearing in the revocation action. However, even though Greenberg stated that "if per chance, heaven for-bid the person appointed by the department was not of the appropriate charac-ter, competence and experience and something were to happen,...it would reflect poorly on the governor's office," politics won over expertise. On June 4, Leeds emailed Carlo that she was waiting for approval of her proposed caretaker but still needed Carlo to get his "past experience ... and [the] facilities he runs/owns."

On June 7, Greenberg, who testified that he was relying on the quality of the work done under him, stated that he signed the SOC, assuming that the necessary approvals had been done, even though he had not seen the typical "buck slip" regarding the approvals. Later that day, Beechwood was served with a Statement of Charges (SOC) and Notice of Hearing (NOH) seeking revocation of the operating license and a $94,000 fine. The hearing was to begin on only a 15-day notice.

This was an incredibly shocking event. Beechwood was still under a DPOC and subject to a revisit to assess correction. Beechwood had been told there was no other agenda than to get it back into compliance. As Leeds had stated, there was no reason to revoke unless terminated. But of far greater concern was that this type of state hearing had never been conducted before, and it was in direct conflict with the federal Medicare/Medicaid structure, as well as the Medicaid state plan, which stated that DOH would adhere to the federal appeal process. Baker's covering letter to the April SOD acknowledged this right of appeal, and Beechwood had applied for a federal hearing. Baker had never mentioned anything about the possibility of a state hearing. The legal complexities were mind-boggling. DOH was relying on some old provision in the state law that had never been used and had become totally obsolete under newer federalized Omnibus Reconciliation Act (OBRA) requirements. As Altone stated in his interrogatory response, "awaiting either the completion of a federal survey cycle or a federal HCFA administrative hearing concerning Beechwood did not factor into any decision making by me in connection with the commencement of the State administrative hearing."

DOH had now come out from under the shadows and was to make everything public. Besides trying to comply with the DPOC and somehow stave off the HCFA termination, and while dealing with monitoring visits and preparing for the next survey revisit, Beechwood was now forced to defend itself on 15 days' notice in a state proceeding with no precedent and with significant legal questions as to authority and due process. Altone intended to move very quickly and maintain the element of surprise and legal confusion. His whole strategy was to put Beechwood's business in jeopardy.

Two days later, on June 9, Beechwood filed a 1983 (Civil Rights) Complaint in Federal Court and sought an injunction or temporary restraining order. This was denied by Judge Larimer on June 16. *In response to the news, Carlo responded:

"HOT DIGGITY DAWG!!!!!!!!!!!!!!!!!!!!!!!!!!!!!!!!!!!!!!!"

In the meantime, DOH delivered into the midst of the June survey revisit two bombshells. *One was a letter from Carlo, dated June 11, totally rejecting the May POC. The other was a petition filed with the New York State Court on June 11 seeking to remove me as operator of Beechwood and appoint a caretaker. Also on that day, since things were getting very intense legally and about to spill out into the public's view, Kelly sent an "ALERT" to the Office of Communications and Operations Support within HCFA. She considered the Beechwood matter a "significant facility issue" with expected "interest from major media" as well as "significant congressional interest."

On June 14, there was another exit conference and, again, accompanied by a major show of force. Present were not only Rubin, Carlo, Baker, Francis, and Rich, but also Solomon and Davis from the MFCU. Carlo and Baker stressed repeatedly that all citations being mentioned were tentative. Baker stated that she "stress[ed] tentatively, for we do review everything through our QA process, meaning both locally and through the CO [Central Office] before final determinations are made regarding the contents of the deficiencies."

Carlo concluded the June 14 exit conference by stating that "termination, as you know, is an issue," and that DOH "recognize[s] the seriousness of the issue for [Beechwood], the Department, residents and everybody," and thus the Department will look at this "very very very closely." However, during discovery years later, the defendants admitted that no notes were made by members of the survey team documenting any further discussion about the noncompliance alleged at the June exit conference.

It is important to note that termination was only an issue because DOH had demanded total compliance by this "early termination" date, and compliance was at their discretion. As Leeds later testified, absent IJ, the ordinary thing would be to allow 180 days to correct. There were no longer any allegations of IJ or SQC being relayed in the DOH tentative findings; they knew quite well that they would have to defend them on appeal of the termination action. But on June 4, Baker noted that Gray told her they could still terminate with only a D-level deficiency. The bar couldn't go any lower as a reason to terminate and move patients.

The next day, June 15, and without any allegations of IJ or SQC, DOH issued a Press Release claiming that "Serious Harm" at Beechwood was behind their petition for a caretaker, the termination by HCFA, and the revocation action.

The release stated the caretaker petition was to "ensure" the health, safety and well-being of residents, due to significant quality of care deficiencies, including serious resident harm and an unwillingness to address these serious problems, which include a pattern and practice of habitual violations of state regulations. This information was faxed to all the media and posted on the internet.

On June 16, Baker had the June SOD hand delivered. It had a covering letter stating simply that the facility was not in compliance (as opposed to any IJ or SQC) and that it would be terminated effective June 17, 1999 "as recommended by HCFA." However:

1. Baker's termination notice was without any formal final concurrence of the SOD from Albany, which was obtained a day later.

2. Baker did not receive any final HCFA concurrence from Kelly until June 29.

    > On June 18, Baker told Carlo that she told me that "we had not been given a final determination from HCFA [Kelly], and that we had been in contact with HCFA and central office about this matter."

3. Baker did not send the June SOD to HCFA until June 30, which was after she received the HCFA concurrence letter.

4. The defendants admitted at trial that Baker never provided HCFA with any proper certification of the June SOD.

On June 21, 1999, Judge Affronti denied the caretaker application brought by DOH. At 10:30 a.m., Carlo and Rubin were discussing this outcome with Charles Steinman, the attorney from the AG's office who handled it. Carlo noted that Steinman stated "I'm not a medical person ...Sure as hell hope that all our i's are dotted and t's crossed. ... BNH [Beechwood Nursing Home] is saying nothing is true. Doesn't want to see DOH tangled up in more litigation. ... * *Sole Concern= If our reports are weak, and if we've made all the mistakes they allege, then they'll sue NYS for a billion $.*"

Steinman's reservations notwithstanding, at 3:25 p.m. Carlo documented a conference call with Altone, Rubin, Colello, Steinhardt, Rosenthal, Abel, and Kristine Smith (DOH Public Affairs Group). Altone billed this as a major telephone conference to "get everyone on the same page." They rolled forward with what Altone described as the "offensive" as if nothing had happened. After the conference, Rubin told the Public Affairs Group, "We believe the caretaker request dismissal was merely a technical determination. The real substantive issues will be aired at the revocation hearing."

In the meantime, however, Carlo's notes reveal that Altone was asking about the "authority to relocate" patients without IJ. Colello responded that there was none, so they were going to "need to interview residents gently." Whalen was separately discussing the same topic with Colello and noted specific federal laws and regulations prohibiting movement of residents without immediate jeopardy and dealing with patient rights. Whalen followed with a note to Greenberg, saying he was "worried about the Beechwood case." However, instead of suggesting that that they suspend the actions planned, he stated that the case "is important for us," and requested that Greenberg put "our best and strongest" attorneys on it. *Greenberg responded to Whalen at 5:53 p.m. on June 22, stating that Dave Abel would be added to the case full-time and that Altone would make monitoring this case his highest priority. Along with Shea, they "should make a formidable prosecution team."

No one had the conviction to stop what they all knew was wrong. In sum, the patients were sacrificed to protect certain DOH officials and their fraudulent mission. The official mission of DOH had just been sacrificed as well. DOH materials state that "Patient protection represents a major area of BAH enforcement activity," and Colello testified that, in the 1990s, this protection mission was her main function, both as a staff and a supervising attorney. On November 15, Barnett recorded Greenberg as stating that "should have been IJ when termination occurs," and he was concerned about the legal vulnerability on that point.

*On June 22, at 2:30 p.m., Carlo noted another conversation with Colello, Leeds, Baker, Cornwell, and others on the subject of relocation of residents, and the notification letters that needed to get sent. Carlo wrote that "counsel's office (is) not interested" in this aspect, for there are "fed regs" and "SOM sections on relocation."

The same day, Cornwell sent a fax to Colello, Carlo, and Altone regarding federal regulatory provisions on resident transfer issues in preparation for what was supposed to be a 3 p.m. conference call. These directives addressed (SOM 3008.3B) the need to have a transfer policy that considers the nature and severity of the noncompliance, and (SOM 3110A) the fact that you need to have immediate and serious threat to health and safety when onsite in order to cite an IJ condition. Gray had this fax in her Beechwood folder, which she brought with her to her deposition. The contents of the folder were recorded by Beechwood's attorney, but they have never been seen again. Defendants admitted that they were unable to produce the file again because it was either lost or stolen.

*On June 23, as the DOH hearing began, Carlo, Baker, and others were still working on a relocation plan. As completed, it violated federal policy in that it did not address the reasons that might create a need to relocate. It addressed only the mechanism for handling the relocation of residents, thereby avoiding a legal dilemma.

*On June 23 as well, Beechwood residents were sent notices that they would have to relocate due to the termination of Beechwood's Medicare/Medicaid provider agreement. The notices stated that the termination was the result of "failure to correct serious deficiencies." This lie was further perpetuated by Kelly on July 16, when she wrote family members: "In the most recent complaint investigation, the NYS DOH found that resident health and safety were in immediate jeopardy and that the facility was providing substandard quality of care. Opportunities to correct these situations were available to the facility's operators. However, the facility failed to do so." As mentioned earlier, when Beechwood finally received its notice of termination from HCFA on June 29, the document simply stated that the termination was due to the fact that Beechwood "had not achieved substantial compliance" as of June 14, as opposed to the immediate jeopardy and substandard quality of care that had been alleged on the previous two surveys respectively.

On June 25th, after Beechwood held a meeting for residents and their families, Barnett told Leeds that "Assemblywoman Susan John did attend the 10:00 a.m. meeting at Beechwood. She said the meeting was a 'nightmare' to the extent families were learning of the imminent closure and need to transfer visibly distraught family members etc." The anger and negative press led Kelly to come to Rochester on July 1st.

On July 1, Kelly flew to Rochester, meeting with Rubin and staff to discuss termination proceedings, to show support for the relocation team, and to meet with the various media. The same day, DOH issued a press release about additional charges being levied against Beechwood. The news media reported that one of the new jobs of Antonia Novello, the new public health commissioner, would be to decide on the revocation of Beechwood's license. Solomon also made an appearance at the DOH hearing on July 1.

On July 8, Carlo told Baker, "The discharge of residents at Beechwood continues ... We are beginning to press a little, due to the fact that some of their families are difficult to please...." By July 16, Carlo was able to write: "As of 1 PM today all residents of Beechwood Nursing Home have been discharged. ... We sincerely appreciated the help and direction on crisis management and media relations that Kris [Smith] and Joe Rohm provided. ... Keep the faith!!" On July 12, Bureau of Administrative Hearings senior attorney John Darling wrote to Kristine Smith that "Joe has done a fine job through the press of sullying Beechwood, and the Chamberys' good name."

On July 16, Beechwood Restorative Care Center closed its doors, even as the hearing continued. Beechwood had just begun presentation of its defense the day before.

On August 5, the hearing ended.

Shortly thereafter, a group of eighteen Western Region staff including Shea, Rohm, Proschel, Rich, Francis, and Baker (M20312), received the Commissioner's Recognition Award for "extraordinary efforts" as part of the "core" group that "assured" that the rights of 82 [Beechwood] residents to "safe, appropriate care were respected," and Francis and Shea were given promotions.

On October 8 the hearing officer's recommendation to revoke the license was issued for the DOH commissioner's consideration.

On November 15, 1999, Barnett noted that Greenberg stated they "need to protect the Department, as well as DOH employees, from venomous attacks by Brook Chambery." Thus, in a proposed stipulation to allow the transfer and sale of the facility, Greenberg demanded that I agree to discontinue any federal civil rights actions, release DOH officials from liability for actions taken, acknowledge the right of DOH to pursue licensing actions against Beechwood staff and physicians, and agree to never operate or have connection to another healthcare facility in New York. I refused.

On January 4, 2000, Beechwood received notice that on December 31, Commissioner Novello had signed the order to revoke Beechwood's operating certificate. As we covered earlier, Novello stated in her deposition that she recalled a document signed by the ALJ, and assuming that he knew what he was talking about, she simply signed it in the process of all the other things that came in that day. She considered her action to be "completely adequate" for she was new to the job, and had nothing to doubt. She verified that she had no legal training and never had any adjudicatory functions in previous jobs, so this was something entirely new.

On December 31, 1999, Altone wrote to Greenberg and 29 other Department of Legal Affairs Attorneys that "This was truly a team effort of outstanding quality and effectiveness. The Beechwood case stands as a great victory for the Department in protecting the public."

On January 6, Beechwood approached DOH (M08221-2) about the ability to transfer the Certificate of Need (CON), which would allow the physical plant and equipment to be sold for use as a nursing home. On February 2, this request was denied. Altone could not resist gloating: "Chambery has nothing but bricks and mortar to sell."

# CHAPTER 17

# Coverup and Conflict

I t should be clear by now that the state-employed DOH attorneys within the Division of Legal Affairs (DLA) were not simply involved in the vindictive, retributive, and fraudulent offensive against Beechwood, they were instrumental in it. Like all lawyers, they were officers of the court who had taken a constitutional oath of office, yet they were part of a fraud that would not have happened without them. Russel Altone, director of the Bureau of Administrative Hearings, was key to the advance planning of the campaign of retribution and to both gaining and coordinating the support and full cooperation of a federal agency, the Health Care Finance Administration (HCFA) in executing it. He provided counsel to DOH program staff throughout the offensive and was central to obtaining the legal outcomes the DOH desired.

The campaign Altone coordinated did not stop with termination and revocation of the operating certificate. It was relentlessly scorched earth. After achieving victory—terminating Beechwood and revoking its operating certificate—Altone called the shots and crafted the strongarm tactics in an attempt to compel me and my family to sign away our constitutional rights on pain of losing all assets. Altone piled on legal action after legal action to support determinations reflected in the ALJ report and to coordinate and control FOIL and discovery responses to cover up and protect the state and in particular the DOH leadership from liability.

**APPLYING THE STRONGARM AGAINST CONSTITUTIONAL RIGHTS**
We heard rumors that the DOH was contemplating taking the position that the

certificate of need (CON), the state approval required to build and open a health-care facility in New York, evaporated with the revocation of the operating certificate. This was a position that the New York State Health Facilities Association (NYSHFA)—among other things, a politically powerful lobby—did not want to become a legal precedent. Before the DOH commissioner issued a revocation order, NYSHFA officials approached Division of Legal Affairs director Henry Greenberg and Deputy Commissioner of Health Dennis Whalen on Beechwood's behalf in early November of 2000 seeking some sort of settlement to allow the transfer of the Beechwood building and CON.

On November 15, 1999, Office of Continuing Care director Robert Barnett noted that Greenberg was intent on using the DLA to protect the DOH and its employees from Brook Chambery's "venomous attacks." Altone accordingly drafted language for Greenberg to send to me, dictating terms that would permit transfer of our building and CON. The language mirrored the proposal Bureau of Litigation attorney Harold Rosenthal had prepared for Altone on July 21 of that year in a document meant to be used in settlement of the DOH hearing. Beechwood refused this language then. On November 18, Greenberg sent us the new proposal, which would permit transfer of the physical plant and CON, with expedited review by DOH, but which included my agreeing never to operate or have any connection with any healthcare facility in New York State and that I would discontinue any federal civil rights actions, release DOH officials from all liability, pay a fine, stipulate to never challenge the agreement, and acknowledge the absolute right of DOH to pursue any and all sanctions or remedies against any individual employed by or practicing in association with Beechwood. I again refused this regulatory blackmail.

When Rosenthal had first proposed such stipulations in July, he told Altone that "seeking a release may be an overreach, ... I do not know if we have ever sought such a release." The law (PBH 2810.2) dictated that when the department revokes an operating certificate, "no security interest in any real or personal property ... shall be impaired," nor shall the department "engage in any activity that constitutes a confiscation of property without the payment of fair compensation."

On January 6, 2000, after the DOH commissioner signed the order revoking our operating certificate, Beechwood again approached Greenberg regarding the department's official position on allowing the physical plant to be sold as a nursing home. Ignoring the law, and the fact that the facility had been closed on July 23, 1999, when Altone had taken the position that settling the hearing would "allow an 82 bed facility to remain in the community," on February 2, 2000, Greenberg sent a letter to Beechwood stating that, because the facility was closed, there were no longer any more beds to be transferred, and DOH was not reviewing any new CON applications for additional beds. Altone knew what the official department position would be, when on January 7, 1999, he wrote Greenberg that "Chambery has nothing but bricks and mortar to sell."

## PILING ON WITH HARASSMENT AND INTIMIDATION

On January 7, 2000, Altone wrote, "Chambery is not a 'sleeping dog.' He will continue to attack the Department. ... The Department will likely be bringing several actions against employees of Beechwood for alleged patient neglect. The Board of Examiners will be receiving a petition and charges alleging "unethical conduct" [against Chambery] ... There may be actions by OPMC [Office of Professional Medical Malpractice] against physicians who practiced at Beechwood."

As Altone had done in his email of April 23, 1999, the January 7, 2000 communication accurately outlined the legal actions to be taken—in advance:

*The owners' administrator licenses.* As Altone indicated, the action against the nursing home administrator's licenses was already under way. In July 1999 Altone and Bureau of LTC and Quality Assurance director Anna Colello communicated about "Beechwood Nursing Home and Board Action," not wanting to forgo the chance to charge "unethical conduct," and betting that they would "at least obtain a censure or reprimand." Altone and Colello felt so strongly about pursuing this that they did not want to give it up in the settlement negotiations.

On January 20, 2000, Office of Continuing Care deputy director Laura Leeds signed the petition to revoke the administrator licenses of Brook and Olive Chambery, even though Altone and his associate attorney, David Abel, were aware that neither my mother nor I had renewed our registration and were thus currently "unregistered." On May 17, 2000, the administrative licensing petitions and charges were sent to the Board of Examiners of Nursing Home Administrators, basing the proposed actions on the ALJ's operating license recommendation and the need to "deter future misconduct." Next, on June 7, 2000, Altone received a referral to issue charges and hold a hearing. Senior Attorney John

Darling was to be the attorney for the hearing.

On August 16, 2000, having served the required papers on the Chamberys the day before, Darling wrote Abel and Altone: "It seems Olive let her license lapse earlier this year, and Brook sent his in as a voluntary surrender last week. They really don't want to go through the expense of fighting this one at this time. Therefore, the question is, does the board still insist on a revocation for each?"

Obviously, the Board did. On September 19, 2000, the revocation hearing began. Since the Chamberys had no current licenses, the ALJ leaned toward a dismissal for lack of jurisdiction. Darling responded by preparing a letter on the issue, taking the position that DOH should "vigorously" argue against dismissal. Altone agreed with Darling's position, stating that "an ALJ cannot deprive the Board of its statutory jurisdiction and responsibility to prove that the respondents are guilty of unethical conduct ... To hold otherwise would allow a wrongdoer to escape a determination of guilt by the licensing board."

In fact, the matter eventually faded away—perhaps because of Leeds's resignation—and the hearing was never rescheduled. Nevertheless, Altone's comments to Darling demonstrate exactly what he thought about how the administrative hearing could be used to the benefit of the DOH position.

*Staff nursing licenses.* At the DOH hearing on August 4, 1999, surveyor Elisabeth Rich testified—or announced—that DOH was waiting on the outcome of the hearing to see whether to pursue any "individuals" for neglect regarding the patient DM matter, which she had originally investigated and found to be an unsubstantiated complaint. This was followed the same day by a statement from the ALJ that Beechwood was "facing charges which are in essence counterparts or equal to abuse and neglect." Months later, on January 18, 2000, DOH was "converting" the DM complaint to a "340," or "PHL 2803-d," abuse and neglect complaint, and labelling the record as "confidential," conveniently allowing DOH to claim that the records could not be provided to Beechwood with FOIL requests. This 340 classification without any subsequent formal referral to the MFCU was a violation of the memorandum of understanding (MOU) between the departments and thus a violation of internal policy. On March 1, 2000, Rich made a memorandum "To the Record of EO [patient's initials]," also modifying the original outcome, and adding that there was "neglect" for "failure to provide appropriate care."

In the meantime, on February 3, 2000, Altone personally drafted a letter to the Office of Professional Responsibility with a copy of the ALJ report and references to the nursing issues he felt the office should consider. On March 15, the Office of Professional Responsibility responded to Altone's referral, stating it had "completed [the] review of the Findings of Fact relative to the closing ... And potential cases of professional misconduct by licensees. The information provided is not specific enough to initiate case openings." Instead of letting the issue go, however, on March 21, 2000, Altone directed Shea (with copies to Colello and Abel) to follow up with the Office of Professional Responsibility, to find out what further information was necessary, and to facilitate the appropriate actions.

Thus, on March 27, 2000, eight months after Beechwood had been closed, a DOH letter went out to two Beechwood nurses stating that "This office is conducting an investigation into reports of neglect to a resident ... we request that you provide your account of the alleged incidents." On May 3, 9, & 11, 2000, [DOH nurses Patricia] Culligan and L. Lopian were doing interviews of various Beechwood staff members, and concluded that there was sufficient credible evidence of neglect against both the DON and a supervisor. On October 31, 2000, Shea told Altone that Culligan was completing the case against the nurses and that she told Culligan he might want this expedited. Shea also stated that, "after a year, they [Culligan and Lopian] may have lost some of their immediacy" to finish this work. On March 16, 2001, Culligan and Lopian signed detailed allegations of neglect against the nurses which they considered to be "sufficient credible evidence."

On July 24, 2001, two years after Beechwood was closed, Shea sent another letter stating that, based on her review of a recent investigative report concerning one patient (DM) over a six day period in February 1999, "there is sufficient credible evidence that you have violated PHL 2803-d (patient abuse laws)."

On September 9, 2002, Statements of Charges were issued against the nurses regarding either committing or failing to report abuse or neglect. It was not until 2004 that the nurses, on advice of counsel, reluctantly entered into stipulations not admitting wrongdoing but paying fines of $300 each. Imagine what it was like for these two nurses worrying about their professional licenses and preserving their reputations while Altone pursued them simply for his own benefit.

On June 24, 2004, a second referral was sent to the Office of Professional Discipline (OPD), not with the information that was requested on March 15, 2000, but simply enclosing copies of the Stipulation and Order, "for whatever action, if any, is deemed appropriate." No action was ever taken by OPD.

***Physician licenses.*** On May 11, 1999, Altone wrote, "Consider PMC [Office of Professional Medical Conduct] input re physicians who submitted affidavits saying everything was OK," and specifically targeted Beechwood's medical director and his PA. He had no idea what issues could be created, but six months later requested that Abel and Shea send him citations to physician practice issues from the hearing transcript and decision, Altone sent an interoffice memorandum to Brian Murphy, chief counsel at the OPMC, with a copy of the ALJ report and references to the physician issues that he felt they should consider. He copied Colello, Greenberg, and Greenberg's deputy, Jerry Jasinski in on the memo.

Sometime after this, our medical director called me, markedly upset regarding inquiries about his hearing testimony. Ultimately, as with all the referrals to other agencies, OPMC never took any action. It is, however, important to note the OPMC connection here. ALJ Marc Zylberberg presided mainly at OPMC hearings; Dr. Roger M. Oskvig, who testified against Beechwood physicians, was on the OPMC board; Leeds had been an assistant director of OPMC; and Bill Comisky, who became Solomon's boss at the MFCU—and, in that capacity, would not let him close the Beechwood investigation—was the director of OPMC in 1999. The circle was unbroken.

## ELEVEN YEARS OF DOCUMENT CONTROL

At the DOH hearing, Altone stated, "We construed the scope of the subpoena duces tecum [a subpoena requiring production of documents without oral testimony] very broadly, and we requested and made it very clear [to staff] what we were looking for. We cannot turn over what does not exist." He claimed that he had made arrangements to identify and very expeditiously take steps that would be in compliance with the subpoena to the fullest extent possible. But, as it turned out, this is not at all what Altone actually had in mind.

On August 28, 2003, he wrote to Rosenthal that "the scope of the subpoena duces tecum did not comprehend all documents possibly relevant to Beechwood." Later, at his deposition, Altone stated that he made a "reasonable effort to comply" and considered his statement that he would produce everything to be "within reason," or "within the scope of the subpoena." He also said that he did not intend to "completely dispense with attorney/client privilege, or that they would turn over every scrap of attorney notes." Altone further acknowledged in his deposition that when privilege is being claimed on information otherwise responsive to a subpoena, the typical procedure would be to request an in-camera review or to produce a privilege log. However, typical privilege rules are not often used in administrative hearings, which are less formal.

*The Rochester file.* At the hearing, Darling stated that "The Department undertook a review of all the materials it had available regarding all ... at issue in this proceeding. We identified all of them and we have produced copies of everything, including personal notes of the various investigators and survey team personnel." Yet a review of the Rochester DOH file on April 19, 2010 revealed many drafts of deficiency statements and other documents that had not been turned over during the DOH hearing. These drafts demonstrated how facts from medical records were being deleted to suit DOH purposes, and they greatly expanded our knowledge of the number of edits involved, who was doing them, and when.

*Attorney-client privileged documents.* On June 24, 1999, the ALJ requested that Altone give him "everything that you think [Beechwood is] not entitled to ... then I'll review it and I'll decide whether they're entitled to it or not." DOH attorneys did not comply with the ALJ's instructions, however, and the ALJ did not enforce compliance. It would appear that the ALJ deliberately let Altone get away with noncompliance. On August 4, at the end of the hearing, he stated that "there are regulations ... extensively limit[ing] discovery ... in administrative proceedings ... so ... [DOH departments] don't have to deal with [subpoenas] a lot."

As covered in more detail in Chapter 14, it was not until April 23, 2007 that Altone, facing Beechwood's February 13, 2007 notice to compel, simply gave up his AC privilege claim concerning 1,700 pages of documents and turned them over to Beechwood. However, this left other documents for which he was still claiming AC privilege. In a subsequent hearing on April 30, 2007, regarding Altone's ridiculously constructed and wholly inadequate AC privilege logs on these still-outstanding documents, Magistrate Judge Feldman (p. 6) stated that both he and the plaintiffs were "obviously troubled" by the 1,700-page disclosure and its implication that the materials had been "improperly withheld" all along.

Judge Feldman (p.14) stated that, under the rules in Federal Court, "simply saying I assert ... attorney/client ... privilege is an insufficient indication of the privilege." He continued (p. 2): "The claim is to be made expressly ... and (p. 3) The burden is on the party asserting the privilege to establish each element of the privilege."

After given another opportunity to clean up his privilege log and failing again (September 4, 2007) to convince Judge Feldman of the need for any further privilege—or even of his command over what documents were even in the file—Altone agreed to let me review the complete Albany file and to request copies of whatever documents I had not seen before. The whole file was sent to Rochester, and I reviewed it on November 8, 2007 and March 8, 2008.

*Carlo's notes.* On June 29, 1999, Darling told the ALJ that, regarding Carlo's notes, he "reviewed the records, copied them, and redacted ... those determined to be attorney/client privilege, specific discussions with attorneys regarding litigation. Other than that, it's all been turned over."

Carlo testified falsely that "anything that is redacted [out of her notes] has to do with other facilities or other issues that don't pertain to Beechwood." It was not until March 13, 2008, after the motion to compel AC documents, two subpoenas (March 7, 2007 and April 9, 2007), and getting permission to review all DOH documents (November 8, 2007 and March 8, 2008) at the offices of their attorneys, that Beechwood finally obtained, without redactions, the notes Darling had sorted out of Carlo's notebooks. These documents proved that Carlo had testified falsely and demonstrated that Darling took great liberty with what he termed "litigation discussions." The notes contained crucial information about when these conferences with attorneys took place and what was being discussed at them. It is no wonder that the defendants' response to the 3rd Notice to Admit (Items #10 and #11) states that they are unable to produce Carlo's notebooks in their entirety for they were either lost or destroyed.

*Altone's failure to institute a litigation hold.* Defendants' response to the 3rd Notice to Produce (Item #50) admits that no litigation hold was ever issued to Department officials in either the program or legal divisions relating to the preservation of documents in the Beechwood matter.

*The missing Central Office (Colello's) file.* On May 18, 2001, senior Bureau of

Administrative Hearings attorney John Stefani told Colello that he had located OCC materials which he assumed had been gathered "to review in response" to the subpoena during the hearing. However, by June 26, 2007, Rosenthal wrote that, after going through the Beechwood file cabinet, he did "not see anything that would look like the old OCC file ... that I know once existed." Furthermore, Altone had "no idea" where it was.

On November 27, 2006, Altone verified that he knew that a file of Colello's was "placed in or next to the dedicated file cabinet in more recent years [after 2000]." However, by June 26, 2007, Rosenthal stated that Altone had no idea what happened to it.

*The missing enforcement file.* Colello stated that if an enforcement referral was made, an enforcement file would be opened. However, the defendants admitted at trial that there was no known "formal referral memo" or "enforcement file."

*Regarding Altone's emails.* At the DOH hearing, Altone often released parts of email strings but not others. A good example is release of the April 21 email about the "bigger picture" but not the April 23 email, which defined the components of the legal offensive. Altone also controlled when document searches and releases were done. By not searching for deleted emails on DOH backup tapes and playing for time, he allowed weeks of crucial material (prior to May 9, 1999) to be erased, supposedly without the ability of retrieval. This forced Rosenthal to acknowledge that "In some cases there may have been relevant e-mail notes, but such notes were deleted and are no longer retrievable."

On July 23, 1999, right after a discussion during the hearing about deleted emails, Altone was transferring 90 emails regarding Beechwood from one account to another. He had done nothing to reveal that he had these emails. In an affidavit dated August 25, 2003, he falsely verified that Rosenthal's affidavit was correct in claiming that there were no documents pertaining to the development and detailing of the enforcement plan.

In an email of November 27, 2006, Altone told his attorney, Gary Levine, that he both "saved and archived" Beechwood email, but Beechwood was never told about this. It was not until Altone's December 22, 2009 deposition, after being caught regarding the origin of one email, that Altone confessed that there was an "archived portion of Lotus Notes" that he used to send emails to himself. It took another year—December 18, 2010—before Beechwood received this archived tranche of emails, and that was only after a request to the court to compel, an oral argument on December 6, 2010, and a subsequent meeting between attorneys as to a production format that would be agreeable.

*Altone's control of responses to FOIL requests.* On September 7, 1999, one week after submitting Beechwood's legal summation to the ALJ after the DOH hearing, I was sending the first of what would eventually number 40 letters, comprising 174 separate requests for documents under the Freedom of Information Law (FOIL). The last request was made on July 5, 2005.

On October 1, 1999, Leeds received an email regarding the first FOIL request: "Brook has submitted a FOIL asking for NYSDOH policies, guidelines or other directives regarding complaint investigations, document retention and destruction; organizational charts regarding PAG and communications of PAG, etc. Please advise." A half hour later, Colello asked Altone to "please advise" regarding Beechwood's first FOIL request, and then states, "we don't act without you." Altone answered Colello (with copies to Greenberg, Jasinski, and Rosenthal) that "appropriate staff in DLA should have a look" at FOIL responses before they are sent.

On January 11, 2000, Altone asked Colello for responsive information regarding FOIL #00-01-111 so that he could decide what is "appropriately releasable." On April 11, 2000, Gene Therriault, the Public Records Access Officer, told John Signor (the DOH Public Information Officer) that Altone "has been coordinating much of the response to multiple FOIL requests." On October 2, 2000, with regard to FOIL 00-09-168, Therriault was told that all requests regarding Beechwood Nursing Home should be forwarded to legal to handle.

When Altone/DOH almost completely failed to comply with FOIL requests, Beechwood began filing petitions in State Supreme Court (June 2001, September 2001, and May 2002), which resulted in three court orders by Judge Evelyn Frazee for documents or affidavits as to why the requested material was not available. DOH produced over 800 documents, claimed various privileges on another 90 pages, and submitted 26 affidavits as to why documents were not available. Judge Frazee upheld the privilege claims after an in-camera review; however, DOH attorneys gave up these claims on April 23, 2007, and the 90 documents in question were included in the 1,700 AC documents turned over on April 23, 2007.

Affidavit responses to Judge Frazee, however, were less than truthfully made, as discovery made clear years later:

FOIL #00-09-168, #3, requested documentation of plans for termination, revocation, etc. as of May 11, 1999.

On December 26, 2001, without claiming any privilege on documents, Rosenthal stated that the DLA had nothing responsive. Yet DLA was in possession of notes by Altone, Shea, and Carlo, as well as various emails, such as Altone's April 23 email detailing a four-pronged offensive.

On December 31, 2001, Carlo stated that she had no responsive documents, when the previously redacted portions of her notes were responsive, and in her possession.

On April 9, 2002, Altone stated that his search of his records revealed no additional responsive documents and that, given the absence of records, it was impossible to say whether or not documents previously existed.

FOIL #01-01-048, #7, requested documentation of the decisions to charge Beechwood, and of subsequent decisions and approvals of these plans.

On December 26, 2001, Rosenthal stated that the only other document he could find in DLA was the May 11 email Altone had forwarded to himself on July 23, 1999 when he had Carlo's documents sent to him on May 31, 2001 and June 5, 2001.

On December 31, 2001, Carlo stated that "no documentation" could be located, yet her own previously redacted notes of May 26 and June 21, which she still possessed, addressed this issue.

Baker could also be seen to have perjured herself in her April 2002 affidavit by stating that she searched Western Regional Office records with Carlo and the search revealed no additional responsive documents.

DOH was better at complying with FOIL requests after the court orders, but FOIL requests only go so far. They are good at uncovering items the requester knows should be there, like policies and procedures, job descriptions, reports, or employee timecards; or items referred to by other documents and emails. But there was much more that still needed to be uncovered through the court-directed discovery process. Nevertheless, the FOILs helped pave the way.

On May 20, 2001, Colello wrote that "There is litigation pending regarding the failure to turn over certain documents pursuant to FOIL. The number of documents requested is an incredible burden now as it was when it was first prepared for the licensure revocation hearing. ... I have suggested that counsel's office be responsible for the materials that were originally reviewed for the hearing. I have already forwarded to you my response to John [Darling] asking for help as I work on getting the additional materials which were never reviewed by DLA."

Altone stated that at some point after the hearing, when FOIL requests "began coming to the division of legal affairs" and with the litigation pursued, an effort was made to centralize documents sent to, or otherwise accumulated by, the various attorneys involved in the case. The documents were placed in a multi-drawer locked file at the central office of Bureau of Administrative Hearings. He stated that the files were centralized to facilitate responding to these actions. As the years passed, documents that had existed in other places in the state eventually were housed in the Division of Legal Affairs, and for multi purposes: "to respond to foil requests and for purposes of this litigation." Carmel Camp, secretary in Rochester Office of Continuing Care, stated that besides the formal survey material, much of the material in the Rochester DOH file came as a result of the FOIL requests.

## THE DEPARTMENT OF LEGAL AFFAIRS
### WITHIN DOH WAS CONFLICTED

Conflicts of interest within DOH did not necessarily motivate the coordinated corrupt offensive against Beechwood, but they made it possible. The Administrative Procedure Act of 1946, which created (among other things) the very concept of administrative law, anticipated total separation of investigative and prosecutorial functions, the independence of administrative law judges, and fair and equitable adversarial processes in an administrative hearing. This proved either an unfulfilled, if noble, aspiration or just so much wishful thinking. The constitutional due process protections and the organizational firewalls are simply not present in administrative procedures. In all practicality, these things cannot be expected within agencies, especially when the department runs its own hearings and can depend on the complete deference of the judicial courts.

In Judge David Larimer's charge to the jury on June 26, 2012, he stated (p. 23): "Mr. Altone is a lawyer, and I instruct you on the law that an attorney must zealously and vigorously represent his client. The ability to zealously and vigorously represent his or her client is central to an attorney's profession." True enough. But inherent problems arise when government agencies have their own legal departments and the authority to make charges, conduct quasi-judicial hearings (with the force of law), and impose sanctions (with the force of law), especially sanctions that affect constitutional liberties. In-house legal departments are never truly independent. Firewalls simply do not exist between legal and program staff, especially with all the overlapping administrative functions that they have. As the ALJ stated in the DOH hearing, the attorneys are "generally ... hampered by their client, to wit, the program people." Such conflicts are bound to exist, no matter what policies and procedures may have been formally drawn up to prevent it, and without the rigor of needing to present a department's case in court, all structure breaks down. The stunning statements made in deposition testimony about what actually occurred in the Beechwood offensive stand in stark contrast with the safeguards neatly written into policies and procedures which, years earlier in interrogatory responses, Altone had claimed were rigidly followed.

> Greenberg testified that the Department of Legal Affairs was the in-house law firm of DOH. When a referral was made for an enforcement action, it was prosecuted without any independent analysis for legal sufficiency.
>
> Greenberg: "Program. They were the client. They would make the referral. We would prosecute the case in general."
>
> Steinhardt stated that he felt the role of House Counsel was to simply carry out directives from program. He never did a legal sufficiency review, nor did he believe that program officials could misstate the facts.
>
> Altone stated that almost every case referred would be pursued.
>
> Colello stated that, after receiving a referral, counsel was charged with the responsibility of preparing a statement of charges (SOC).
>
> Greenberg stated that when he signed an SOC, he just assumed the necessary approvals had been obtained. His signature was simply a ministerial signature, out of habit and practice that predated him.

It is virtually certain that none of this would happen if cases were required to be referred to the Attorney General's Office for prosecution. Under this requirement, cases would be independently reviewed regarding its ability to withstand judicial review.

In the Beechwood case, firewalls—such as they may have been—were totally absent. As we have seen, Mr. Altone, as Director of the Bureau of Hearings, was involved in advance planning and carrying out the offensive:

> Altone stated that, in Beechwood's case, things happened in a "different manner," there was a "preliminary determination" by program that they wanted legal folks involved. In short, the case began with a foregone conclusion, an effect in search of a cause.

> Altone testified that there was a "joint effort between legal and program" to develop the evidence and charges. Colello stated that "This enforcement was done in concert with DLA."

> Altone testified that he didn't know the basis for the April 16 discussions or what he meant by the "bigger picture" and had to admit that it was "not the norm" for his bureau to be discussing termination, revocation, a caretaker. and a fine on April 23, before there was any statement of deficiency (SOD) or any facts to justify an enforcement discussion.

> When, on May 13, Leeds stated that "the attorneys may not think we have sufficient report," Altone responded by telling Shea to work with Leeds, Carlo, and Baker to help "find more bad things" and to "show [serious violations of services regulations] more widespread than currently have."

Mr. Altone was also instrumental in gaining the advice and support of other agencies, such as HCFA:

> At "various points" before, during, and after the DOH hearing there were "several communications," primarily by phone, between HCFA and Bureau of Administrative Hearings attorneys, including John Gura and himself. These were for "cooperative information sharing" as well as for "coordination with HCFA."

As we have seen, for at least another decade, Altone was also instrumental in pursuing subsequent legal actions and obstructing justice with bogus privilege claims as he attempted to solidify positions and protect DOH officials, including himself, from liability. Recall that Steinman had warned, "they'll sue NYS for a billion $."

A lack of proper firewalls between program and legal, conflicting legal roles as advisor and prosecutor, and an intentionally vague or ill-defined client-attorney relationship led to serious abuses of power and blatant health care program administrative fraud. Without any evidence of non-compliance by the provider, or formal referral from program to legal, program requested advice regarding how to use state regulatory powers to close down Beechwood, what type of case they needed to build, and how it would be coordinated in the midst of conflicting federal law and regulation. Such actions amount to abuse of power and program fraud, as well as a violation of Disciplinary Rules (DR) in the New York Lawyer's Code of Professional Responsibility, which are "mandatory in character," and represent "the minimal level of conduct below which no lawyer can fall without being subject to disciplinary action."

DR7-102, 103: Instead of providing advice for the legal offensive, and participating in its advance planning (knowing full well that this would lead to fraudulent charges), Altone should have provided legal counsel against undertaking such activity.

DR1-101: Altone withheld or failed to disclose the evidence and material facts regarding the role of the Division of Legal Affairs in administrative and investigative events.

DR1-104: Even if they were directed by Greenberg, Altone and the others were responsible for obeying the law. Thorough knowledge of the law was Altone's responsibility, and he claimed that this knowledge is one of the reasons he was consulted.

DR 7-101: Altone and the other attorneys could have quit, rather than carry out the actions in which they participated. They had a responsibility to tell DOH officials that such actions were not the civic duty of the Department of health.

## HCFA WAS CONFLICTED

As the Second Circuit decided, HCFA supported DOH. This was a conflict of interest and violated Beechwood's right to due process because HCFA was required to independently review and certify that the state's certification of the survey results and sanctions desired were in accordance with federal requirements. HCFA's legal department, as with the state DOH and any agency with its own in-house legal department, was also conflicted as to who was its client.

## THE ATTORNEY GENERAL'S OFFICE (DAG) WAS CONFLICTED

New York Executive Law Section 63.1 states that the attorney general shall

"Prosecute ... all actions and proceedings in which the state is interested, and have charge and control of all the legal business of the departments and bureaus of the state ... in order to protect the interest of the state. No action or proceeding affecting ... the interests of the state shall be instituted ... by any department, bureau ... of the state, without a notice to the attorney-general ... so that he may participate or join therein if in his opinion the interest of the state so warrant."

When the attorney general was notified of and acquiesced to the Department of Health's intentions to use its own hearing to revoke Beechwood's operating certificate, at that point the AG's office was conflicted. First, the AG's office would be avoiding its own responsibilities, and looking the other way as the DOH went about charging Beechwood and its employees with abuse and neglect in its own administrative proceedings. Second, under Section 71 of the New York Executive Law, the AG would then be responsible to defend the officials for any challenge concerning the constitutionality of the administrative acts being undertaken.

This conflict was apparent in every action taken by the AG's office.

**First,** the AG's Office was not only aware of what DOH intended, its Medicaid Fraud Control Unit (MFCU) abstained from doing its duty, violated the Memorandum of Understanding (MOU) with the state DOH, and allowed DOH to administratively charge Beechwood with widespread abuse and neglect, and with imminent danger. The result? Millions of dollars in damages, ruined livelihoods, and thirteen years of legal work that would not otherwise have occurred.

Solomon stated that how he came to open the Beechwood investigation was not a "simple" question to answer. "Our office, after the success of Jim Sheehan, who was an AUSA [assistant United States attorney] at the time in Philadelphia, in bringing a fraud case against a nursing home for patient abuse and neglect, had decided that we wanted to look at nursing homes in general for possible fraud cases for not supplying services. Every region was looking to find someone to look at it, and when [Beechwood was] put in immediate jeopardy, I thought that would be a good home to take a look at."

There were meetings with Solomon about possibly investigating Beechwood for fraud, both before and after the immediate jeopardy was declared. Solomon was also aware of the media blitz about poor care and imminent danger to patients.

April 14, 1998: Francis noted in her calendar, "Meet with S.R. [Rubin] and Jerry Solomon re: Beechwood. 3hrs." This meeting was convened by Rubin.

April 17, 1999: Carlo wrote, "Sandy [Rubin] called re: Gerry Solomon - fraud for failure to deliver care." Solomon testified that DOH informed him in early April 1999 that Beechwood was going to be cited for IJ, and that he "called to ask about getting the deficiencies or the surveys and all the records."

April 19, 1999: Baker noted a discussion with Carlo: "Sandy/Jerry Solomon-re: DAG getting involved for Medicaid reimbursement when services were not provided: ie - SQC – IJ"

April 22, 1999: Carlo noted that she, Baker, HCFA counsel Annette Blum, and Jerry Solomon discussed "Directive fr NY - Mcd fraud unit across country - Make case with substd facil and tak back $. ... Reviewed Beechwood."

June 3, 1999: Baker emailed Carlo. "Subject: DAG mtg. Jerry Solomon would like to meet again, possibly on Monday regarding their project and facilities that might qualify for investigation related to Medicaid fraud. Beechwood comes to mind immediately."

June 14, 1999: Solomon and Davis attended the June exit conference at Beechwood. Solomon thus knew that Beechwood no longer had any IJ or SQC allegations and that DOH had served notices regarding its plans for revocation and caretaker proceedings, and that the civil division of his office was defending against Beechwood's request for an injunction the next day in an oral argument.

However, Solomon decided "to wait for the DOH proceeding to play out and I think once it did and they were terminated we decided to—I decided to open the investigation and to look at them." Solomon stated that he did call DOH to get informed as to when the hearing was taking place, and as a result attended one or two of the hearing sessions.

July 1, 1999: Solomon was identified by Carlo as being in the hearing room, just as Beechwood attorney Kevin Cooman was raising the issue of the references to Solomon in her notes. Solomon had come into the room just before that but had not yet been identified for the record.

There was no reason for Solomon to wait for DOH. Solomon's office had "jurisdiction" over supervision and administration of nursing homes, both criminally and civilly, and with matters such as widespread neglect and mistreatment, and immediate jeopardy; especially egregious allegations.

**Second,** the MFCU investigation itself was conflicted:

*The opening.* Solomon stated that how he came to open the investigation is not a "simple question to answer," but he first "got the transcript and read the transcript." The problem is, he wrote in his final investigative report that the testimony of Beechwood's witnesses would make it difficult indeed to prove Medicare or Medicaid fraud beyond a reasonable doubt. His auditor also wrote that testimony during the hearing refuted the DOH assertion that "poor care was given." This would make it appear there was no reason to open the criminal fraud investigation.

Solomon not only had read the transcript, he knew that Beechwood's quality stats and survey performance did not comport with the horror tale DOH had told. He testified that his unit tracked surveys of facilities, and he was thus familiar with Beechwood's survey history. Solomon concluded that the "handful of deficiencies" the facility received in the past was better performance than average. The Auditor's Report referred to the use of Quality Indicator reports in the audit and, so, the auditor was also aware that Beechwood's ranking was one of the best in the state. Solomon added that other than one complaint investigation resulting in no action, and a patient funds issue, which was not appropriate for his office, there had been no previous investigation of Beechwood since 1986, when he joined the Rochester office. He also knew "from newspaper accounts" that families were staging protests against DOH for closing a facility with which they were highly satisfied. To add to the confusion, Beechwood attorneys Paul Barden and David Rothenberg met with Solomon after the issuance of the first subpoena for documents. They were completely surprised when Solomon told them that "nothing will come of it" and that Brook Chambery does not need a criminal attorney, even though the audit would be tough. Barden wrote that Solomon seemed reluctant to take the case.

On August 3, 2001, Barden spoke to Solomon, who stated that New York City was driving the investigation forward. He said he had been trying to wrap it up for 18 months and had nothing on Brook. Eighteen months in wrap-up? That would mean that Solomon had been trying to end the investigation from its very beginning.

*The closing.* On August 6, 2001, after investigating 124 medical records, timecards, staffing records, financials, and the like, Solomon issued a fourth sub-poena for all the medical records of the residents involved in the DOH surveys leading to the termination, and he met with Francis and Carlo. On October 11, 2002, Solomon again told Beechwood attorneys that he wanted to drop the investigation into Brook Chambery but was having difficulty getting sign-off from the New York City office and needed to write a report justifying a case closure without any action being taken. On October 17, he told Beechwood attorneys that he was dropping the investigation.

On December 5, 2002, having heard no further word, Barden called Solomon to check on the progress of the wrap-up. Solomon was frustrated, stating that his New York City-based boss, Tom Staffa, would not take his word that there was nothing to the case. He demanded a very detailed report as to reasons for dropping it. Solomon was upset and irritated that Staffa put no stock in his position and years of experience. The man simply refused to accept his judgment. Solomon told Barden that Staffa was slated to retire very soon, and, at that point, he could deal directly with William Comiskey, who was, at the time, Deputy Attorney General for Medicaid Fraud. Solomon knew that Comiskey was familiar with the case and would be more sympathetic. Indeed, in 1999, Comiskey had worked for the New York DOH as head of the Office of Professional Medical Conduct, which had been involved in recommending Dr. Roger Oskvig for a rebuttal witness in the hearing. It was a small world.

On April 10, 2003, Solomon wrote his memorandum to George Quinlan, the upstate MFCU supervisor, and Patrick Lupinetti, who was in charge of the MFCU special projects unit explaining his rationale for closing the investigation of Beechwood without any action being taken. He stated that his office found "very good to excellent care" at the facility. On June 2, 2003, Lupinetti wrote to Comiskey, with a forward to Quinlan, stating that "For whatever it's worth, it doesn't look like there is much to work with here, but it is your call." On the same day, Quinlan replied to both Lupinetti and Comisky that "Beechwood was unique in its facts, and any criminal or civil prosecution would have been pointless. ... The owners essentially walked away from a half-million dollar annual profit, each, on principle over disagreements with DOH, and have a civil action pending against DOH for civil rights violations which is now on appeal from a summary judgment at the trial level." Finally, on June 4, Comiskey wrote to Quinlin: "Based on your note and Jerry's [Solomon's] memo, I concur in closure of this matter."

**Third,** charged with providing defense counsel for DOH officials, the DAG failed to disclose exculpatory materials from its own investigation of Beechwood as it filed for summary judgment in Beechwood's civil rights case, thus greatly prejudicing Beechwood's case. On August 3, 2001, Solomon was trying to wrap up the criminal investigation and discussing it with superiors in New York City. On April 26, 2002, Beechwood filed its "1983" civil rights suit, and on October 11, October 17, and December 5 of that year, Solomon told Beechwood attorneys that he wanted to close the investigation but could not get support to do so from the New York office, explaining that he needed to write a report justifying his reasons for closing the investigation.

On January 31, 2003, Darren Longo, the Assistant Attorney General of Counsel for the DOH defense, filed a motion for Summary Judgment.

On April 10, 2003, Solomon wrote his closing memorandum, stating that by all accounts, Beechwood gave "very good to excellent care," and on June 4, his boss, William Comiskey, wrote that he concurred in the closure of the investigation.

On June 23, 2003, Beechwood filed its opposition to the Summary Judgment motion.

On August 18, 2003, the MFCU Auditor filed his report, which directly contradicted the ALJ report from the DOH hearing. The auditor report stated: "testimony during the hearing and in our interviews refuted [the] contention" that "poor care" was given.

On September 5, Longo filed his reply memorandum of law in defense of his motion for summary judgment, stating (p. 10) that "If a facility fails to meet standards … then it may be shut down or otherwise sanctioned."

On September 19, 2003, Solomon returned all records subpoenaed from Beechwood, and informed Beechwood's attorneys that this represented the end of the investigation, but he provided no other information as to the results of the investigation.

On October 21, 2003, there was an oral argument before Judge Larimer regarding the defendants' move for Summary Judgment, which Judge Larimer granted on January 29, 2004, dismissing Beechwood's civil rights suit.

Continuing to obstruct justice, the MFCU resisted our attempts to obtain the documents in its files from the Beechwood investigation and further prejudiced our appeal of the civil rights case to the Second Circuit and our appeal of the

Medicare Termination to the Federal District Court. But we persisted. On December 22, 2004, Beechwood sent to the MFCU a FOIL for records. This was refused, mainly on a boilerplate claim of investigative work product, as was our subsequent appeal of the refusal. MFCU knew this would lead to legal action, so Solomon called me in an attempt to defuse the situation, inviting me to his office to see the file and to discuss it. I accepted and went to Solomon's office on June 21, 2005. But neither this meeting nor a subsequent appeal to the MFCU resulted in production of documents that were of any legal use.

On January 31, 2006, The Second Circuit overturned Judge Larimer and reinstated the "1983" case, but only on the First Amendment cause of action; however, on July 6, 2007, the indefatigable Judge Larimer dismissed our Medicare Termination case, stating (p. 10): "I find that to a great extent, Beechwood's claims in this action are moot. Beechwood is closed, its state operating license has been revoked by the State DOH."

*There was never any sufficient legal basis for MFCU to withhold crucial documents from Beechwood.* On June 21, 2007, Beechwood filed a motion to compel MFCU documents. Oral argument followed on September 4 before Magistrate Feldman. Special Assistant Attorney General Paul Mahoney, with the MFCU New York Office, and another MFCU attorney flew into Rochester for the proceeding. The MFCU had not even produced a privilege log to define the specific documents, or segments of documents, and its claims for withholding production. Magistrate Feldman began by asking Mahoney (p. 36), "Why did you wait until today to produce a privilege log?" The answer was incredible: "Because ... frankly part of our objection to the subpoena is the burden being placed on the State at this time, I mean on the Medicaid Fraud Control Unit at this time. This is a ... clearly a long standing and long churning litigation that has gone on."

Mr. Mahoney went on to make another flabbergasting statement as to why the documents had not yet been released—albeit one that he did not attempt to put in any brief as a formal position statement: "quite frankly this file is my agency's file on the matter, [and] the principle is important. ... there is a whole set of discovery rules under the Criminal Procedure Law that allows a Defendant to get access to that information. In this case, no action was taken. I'm not sure how in the civil litigation I heard described, that [it] is material or relevant, but that's not my brief here today." (p. 39)

Magistrate Feldman responded (p. 40): "This would be, as I understand it, the relevance. One of the issues here is whether the discretionary decisions by DOH in terms of the penalty to impose or in terms of the classification of the penalty, were reasonable or were justified and whether the actions of the defendants to try and close down the nursing home facility were justified by the nature of the complaints that were made. Your investigation may reveal witnesses who may have information on whether the Department of Health claims of patient neglect or patient abuse or lack of patient care were credible or not. If an investigator went out and interviewed one of the employees and the employee said, no, that didn't happen, or I told the Department of Health that that's not what happened, that conceivably could be relevant to the lawsuit here."

Mahoney (pp. 48, 49) stated that he was making a formal, but "general" work product privilege claim as to Solomon's closing memorandum, no matter whether Solomon was "review[ing]" fact information after "personally handling the investigation," or drawing conclusions of law for the Deputy Attorney General of the MFCU in determining whether or not to close out an investigation.

Feldman responded (pp. 51-52): "Let me make clear. Here you have a law enforcement agency that's conducted a thorough investigation and has made a decision not to prosecute. You've revealed the fact that interviews of staff, former staff, family members, and physicians were conducted and a vast majority of those interviewed indicated that the patient care at the facility was very good to excellent. Attorney General Solomon directed the case be closed based on insufficient evidence upon which to have a criminal prosecution. ... So, it's the position of your clients that where a public law enforcement agency investigates something and exonerates a person, that the person exonerated is not entitled to see the results of the investigation?"

Mahoney again chose to obfuscate (p. 53): "I would not characterize that document as an exoneration, I would characterize it as a decision not to prosecute." Feldman responded: "Based on insufficient evidence?" Mahoney answered: "Based on a review of that evidence ... I would characterize as a difference between a conclusion not to prosecute and a situation where there was a prosecution which an independent investigation established to be unfounded."

Even though his agency was providing the defense, Mahony continued with another staggering declaration (p. 57): "The substance of the investigation as revealed in those memoranda, I do not believe show any bearing on the allegations in this case such that this agency should be brought any further into it."

Feldman responded (p. 57): "I assume [Beechwood] counsel here would like to use that as the report of an official agency, which may be not hearsay under the Federal Rules of Evidence, as the results of an investigation conducted by an agency charged with that investigation, as evidence that the patients received good care, and therefore, the penalties that were imposed were unreasonable. One agency of the state of New York has investigated patient care and has determined there was very good care and another agency of the state has investigated patient care and come up with this finding that there is patient neglect. Why wouldn't that be something that would be helpful to a jury in deciding who's right?"

Feldman continued (p. 58): "Your agency has expertise in evaluating the raw material and determining whether there is probable cause to believe that a crime was committed and whether to prosecute that crime. ... And you determined there was no probable cause to prosecute someone for neglect or patient abuse, or substandard conditions, and another agency of your same governmental entity determined to take away somebody's license because of evidence of neglect, abuse, or lack of performance. Why wouldn't that be something that would be relevant to a jury's determination?"

Apparently back on his heels, Mahoney (p. 58) tried another tack that was not formally in his brief, namely that the two agencies had different burdens of proof. Feldman was quick to interrupt (p. 59), stating that was not unusual, and it was only one piece of evidence that a jury may deem relevant to a finding it has to make. Feldman could have added that the MFCU also had responsibility to look at matters from a civil standpoint before closing out an investigation. In addition, there was the MOU with the DOH, that had not been followed, providing the MFCU with the final decision-making authority on these matters to eliminate any difference in opinion that could otherwise arise.

Feldman did give Mahoney more time to perfect his claim to privilege on the documents, but he relented rather than risk an order to produce—which would have set a precedent MFCU did not want to set, and with the knowledge that he could raise arguments later, at trial, about admissibility. The whole investigative file was eventually produced but it involved much discussion and multiple document submissions over the next year.

When the attorney general, in pretrial maneuverings, tried to keep certain documents from jury consideration, Judge Larimer ruled:

Page 3: "Plaintiffs seek to introduce Solomon's memos, the Final Report, and certain other documents relating to the MFCU investigation, including handwritten notes, a subpoena, letters, and other materials.

"Defendants contend that these documents are inadmissible hearsay, and also are excludable under Rule 403 of the Federal Rules of Evidence, as unduly prejudicial. Plaintiffs contend that these documents are admissible as public records or reports under Rule 803(8), and that they are not *unfairly* prejudicial to defendants.

"I find that the [Auditor's] Final Report is admissible under Rule 803(8). ... It contains factual findings by a state agency, resulting from an investigation by that agency regarding a matter within that agency's jurisdiction."

Page 6: "Defendants' motion to preclude Solomon's memo from being admitted into evidence is granted, without prejudice to plaintiffs' offering excerpts from, or a redacted version of, the report at a later time."

We will never know what effect the proper production of these MFCU investigative materials would have had on influencing the various court decisions and the trajectory of the civil rights case or the Medicare termination appeal, but, had they been produced, I doubt that Judge Larimer's summary judgment decision of January 29, 2004 could have included these statements in dismissing Beechwood's retaliation claim:

Page 37: "The ALJ found 'Beechwood's claims of a conspiracy against it and/ or Mr. Chambery to be a total, complete, and ridiculous fabrication without a shred of evidence or support,' and that 'there [wa]s nothing in the record which indicate[d] to [the ALJ] that the actions taken and/or conduct of [DOH] was motivated by or taken in retaliation for Brook Chambery's exercise of any of his rights.' For the reasons already given, those findings are given preclusive effect here."

Page 38: "Defendants' conduct here was objectively reasonable and plaintiffs have not provided sufficient evidence to create an issue of fact about whether defendants acted out of retaliatory motives."

"I realize the Court's obligation, on a motion for summary judgment, to view the record in the light most favorable to the nonmoving parties, and to draw all inferences in their favor ... however, ... it is hardly surprising that there was 'some tension' between plaintiffs and defendants, and that defendants gave voice to that tension on occasion. In my view, that is not enough to give rise to an issue of fact about defendants' allegedly retaliatory motives."

Judge Larimer would have found it equally difficult to rely on cited case law (pg. 43) regarding the strong presumption to be given to state actors that they have properly discharged their official functions and draw the following conclusion when dismissing Beechwood's Equal Protection claim:

> Page 44: "The record demonstrates that defendants had valid, rational reasons for their actions, and there is no evidence of any individuals situated similarly to plaintiffs who were treated differently."

I also believe that Judge Larimer would have been profoundly shocked by the MFCU investigative outcome and thus unable to dismiss the Substantive Due Process Claim as he did using case law (p. 45), which cites the need to have conscience-shocking actions by government officials, and concludes:

> Page 45: I find no basis that defendants' conduct was arbitrary, malicious, had no legitimate purpose, and so on. Rather, defendants' conduct was rationally related to the state's legitimate interest in the regulation of nursing homes, and "it can hardly be doubted that the interest is of the highest order." Blue, 72 R.3d 1075, 1080 (2nd Cir. 1995).

I doubt the Second Circuit Court of Appeals would have been able to make the following statement in rejecting our appeal of Larimer's dismissal of the Equal Protection Claim:

> Page 21: "The partnership has adduced some evidence that the revocation of its operating certificate was an unusual measure, but, as the district court soundly observed, some sanctions may be imposed rarely because they are rarely justified. Id. at 276 ... (pg. 22) DOH might well decide that this particular facility presented the highly unusual instance in which harsher sanctions are needed because DOH could not rely on voluntary compliance and willing reforms. Conclusory assertions ... are not enough to show dissimilar treatment among those similarly situated, at least not at this stage of the proceedings."

As for Judge Larimer's July 6, 2007 decision in the Medicare Termination case, I believe production of the complete MFCU evidence file would have stopped him from beginning his decision by stating, as he did on page 1, that this "related action" was simply "another chapter in a contentious relationship between a nursing home and the governmental agencies." I also cannot see how he could have ruled as he did on the issue of mootness:

Page 10: "I find that to a great extent, Beechwood's claims in this action are moot. Beechwood is closed, its state operating license has been revoked by the State DOH, and the building where the nursing facility was operated has been sold."

Page 15: "As for the alleged 'name clearing' effect of a favorable ruling, 'reputational harm' does not rise to the level of the kinds of concrete disadvantages or disabilities that the Supreme Court has found constitute sufficiently adverse collateral consequences to render a case justiciable .... That is particularly so in light of the fact that Beechwood is no longer in business; any name-clearing effect would have no practical impact whatsoever."

I also doubt that, given the contrast between MFCU investigative results and the DOH hearing outcome that he would have continued to lend HCFA and its hearing the credibility that he did:

Page 45: "These alleged procedural irregularities, even if they occurred, were effectively cured by the extensive procedures afforded to Beechwood, which was allowed to and did present substantial evidence concerning the SODs. Since the ultimate factual findings of the ALJ and CMS are supported by substantial evidence, these alleged procedural errors caused Beechwood no harm or prejudice."

In other words, had all the MFCU documentation been available for production, I believe the legal landscape would have shifted dramatically. Not only would the time, expense, and risk of the whole ordeal have been greatly reduced, but we would have been permitted to present to the jury a full range of claims and slate of defendants (including HCFA officials) for liability resolution.

**Fourth,** the DAG could not perform its duty under NY Executive Law Section 63.12 to prosecute fraudulent or illegal acts by DOH officials in administration of the program, when it had already taken on responsibility to defend these officials. The conflict was apparent from the very beginning of the DOH hearing, when Altone argued that the DOH witnesses could not be questioned about bias because they were being represented by the DAG in a related civil rights case, and it could "jeopardize the Department's position ... in that proceeding."

At a meeting with AG Solomon on June 21, 2005, I was allowed to read his closing memo from the Beechwood investigation, which stated that everything we did demonstrated "very good to excellent care." I then asked him why he did not investigate the regulators who had caused the facility to be closed and referred to the statutes regarding fraud in the administration of healthcare programs. He responded that, as he interpreted the statutes, the duties of his office were narrowly defined and certainly did not extend to investigation of health care program fraud by DOH.

What else could he be expected to say? Yet, as discussed earlier, The New York Times reported that the MFCU was investigating improperly accepted gifts and expedited CONs by DOH senior officials, including Whalen, Leeds, and Robert Murphy, director of the Division of Health Facility Planning. Clearly, Solomon was anxious to steer clear of a dilemma that went like this:

*If:* The DOH allegations on the SOD and SOC allegations = Poor Care;

*And:* Poor care = Medicare/Medicaid fraud by the provider of services;

*But:* The MFCU investigation found no evidence of the poor care alleged on the SOD/SOC or any other poor care or fraudulent activity on the broader investigation,

Then: The DOH allegations set forth on the SOD and SOC regarding poor care = Medicare/Medicaid fraud in the administration of the program.

Because of his conflict of interest, Solomon did not formally interview or discuss the motivation for closing the facility with any DOH staff.

## THE DEPARTMENT OF JUSTICE (DOJ) WAS CONFLICTED

On June 7, 2005, after meeting with Colleen Balkin of the FBI, I wrote her to formally identify the reasons why the Bureau should pursue an investigation of the regulatory activity behind the actions taken against Beechwood. I referred to the federal criminal statutes and stated that "healthcare program fraud (1035, 1347) was committed against a provider of services by state and federal agency employees, who, depriving the owners, staff, patients, and community of the right to honest services (1346), conspired (371) to use the Medicaid and Medicare survey and enforcement process to create a basis for terminating the provider, in order to accomplish the ultimate objective of revoking the operating certificate and taking the property. False certifications (1018), false statements (1001), mail and wire fraud (1341, 1343), and obstruction of justice (1505) were all involved in carrying out the conspiracy."

Under Crimes: USC Title 18, Chapter 47 – Fraud and False Statements,

Section 1035: Health care fraud, the law states: "Whoever, in any matter involving a health care benefit program, knowingly and willfully- falsifies, conceals, or covers up ... a material fact, or makes any materially false, fictitious, or fraudulent statements ...in connection with the delivery of or payment for health care benefits, items, or services, shall be fined under this title or imprisoned not more than 5 years.

Under Crimes: Title 18, Chapter 63 – Mail Fraud, Section 1347: Health care fraud, the law states: "Whoever knowingly and willfully executes, or attempts to execute a scheme or artifice (1) to defraud any health care benefit program ... in connection with the delivery of or payment for health care benefits, items, or services, shall be fined under this title or imprisoned not more than 10 years or both. (If the violation results in serious bodily injury imprisonment can go up to 20 years, or life imprisonment if death is involved.) This includes violations of, or conspiracy to violate 1035, 371, 1001, 1341, 1343.

After my June 21, 2005 meeting with Solomon, I also asked that, at minimum, he support me in my request to the FBI for an investigation and cooperate with that bureau.

Colleen Balkin subsequently discussed the matter with the U.S. Department of Justice, which led to an early September call from Robert Trusiak, Esq. As soon as he heard that I had two federal suits in progress, he stated that he could not talk to me any further and hung up. Kevin Cooman wrote him on September 7, 2005, stating that he had no problem with Trusiak discussing matters directly with me, but that we recognized the conflict of interest posed by the fact that Christopher Taft, from the same office, was representing Sue Kelly and Michael Daniel in the civil rights case, and CMS in the federal court appeal of the administrative determination regarding the termination. Both of these cases were currently before Judge Larimer.

On October 5, 2005, Cooman formally requested that the DOJ appoint outside counsel or a special prosecutor to work with the FBI, due to the conflict of interest existing in Trusiak's office. This elicited a letter to Cooman on October 7, 2005, from Trusiak's office stating that just as it is important for citizens to bring complaints to them, "it is equally important for the federal government to conduct an investigation, if any, in a confidential manner and provide the complainant with neither confirmation of the investigation nor a status update."

That intriguing statement was the last we heard on the matter. We did not pursue it any further because, on January 31, 2006 we received the Second

Circuit Court decision and did not want a criminal investigation getting in the way of moving the civil rights lawsuit to court.

# CHAPTER 18

# Another New Year's Eve Present

I t was December 31, 2010, eleven and a half years since Beechwood was shuttered and seven years since Judge David Larimer granted the original summary judgment motion. We had just received Russel Altone's archive on
December 18, and five years of turbulent discovery was now over. We were hoping that we would finally be heading to trial.

That, however, was not to be, not without another summary judgment
motion, a phenomenal amount of work, and nine months of further delay. DOH
filed yet a new summary judgment motion with separate motion papers on why
each of the seventeen defendants should be dismissed from the lawsuit. It was
what it was meant to be: infuriating.

The Second Circuit had stated that "Beechwood produced sufficient evidence
of retaliatory motive to survive summary judgment. ... This is evidence from
which a jury could reasonably find that the DOH was campaigning against the
partnership as retaliation for the exercise of First Amendment rights. We therefore vacate and remand as to the First Amendment claim." That appeared to leave
all seventeen state defendants to face the jury. Yet here they were, trying to get
another chance to have a judge decide whether there was enough evidence to
allow them to go to trial prior to Beechwood being given the opportunity to fully
present its case. Was this just more running us through hoops, delaying the inevitable, and running up expenses?

There was a main brief, a declaration and memorandum of law, and a set of
Rule 56 Statements (allegations of fact) for each of the seventeen defendants. We
had to answer all the Rule 56 Statements with admissions or denials and provide

explanations. This was accompanied by a memorandum of law in opposition for each defendant, as well as the principle brief and accompanying affidavits. The strategy of the defendants was basically to take the emails, notes, and other documents that Beechwood had confronted them with in their depositions and try to put their own spin on them.

Burying our anger, we submitted our opposition material on April 29, 2011. An oral argument was heard before Judge Larimer on June 7.

## JUDGE LARIMER'S DECISION
### *BEECHWOOD RESTORATIVE CARE CENTER V. LEEDS*, 811 F. SUPP.2D 667, 02-CV-6235L (W.D.N.Y. 2011)

Judge Larimer handed down his decision on September 12, 2011. On page 5, he declared:

"This Court must comply with directives from the appellate court and must adhere to its mandate. Therefore, it indeed seems audacious, to say the least, for defendants to seek dismissal in favor of all the remaining defendants. ... I do, however, recognize that a party is not generally precluded from making successive motions for summary judgment, as long as the party is not simply asking the court to rethink its earlier decision.

"Defendants contend that their new motion for summary judgment is appropriate because it is based on evidence obtained through discovery following the Second Circuit's decision, as well as on new grounds. Defendants contend that 'extensive discovery, including numerous depositions, have been conducted and before the Court is a new summary judgment [motion] on a complete record.' Def. Mem. (Dkt. #187) at 3. Defendants also argue that whereas their prior motion, and this Court's and the Court of Appeals' previous decisions were based on the general legal principles of issue preclusion and absolute and qualified immunity, their present motion is based, in part, on the particular facts as to each individual defendant. It is also true, though, that defendants did not move previously on the primary ground raised here, i.e., that the evidence was lacking as to each individual defendant.

"Although I am not convinced that some of the grounds now asserted in support of defendants' current motion could not have been presented previously, there has been a significant amount of discovery since the Second Circuit issued its decision in 2006. Whether the evidence unearthed in that discovery helps or hurts defendants is one of the points of contention here, but since defendants are not simply seeking to reargue matters that they raised, or could have raised, on their prior motion, I conclude that they are not precluded from again seeking summary judgment.

"While the Second Circuit found plaintiffs' evidence sufficient to give rise to genuine issues of material fact as to plaintiffs' First Amendment claim, the court did not analyze the evidence as to each individual defendant, nor did the court intimate that its ruling was meant to apply across the board to all the defendants. The Court of Appeals determined, in summary fashion, that there was evidence that 'the Department of Health' engaged in retaliatory conduct against plaintiffs. The Court of Appeals did cite some evidence and referenced certain defendants but did not do a defendant-by-defendant analysis. Because it is necessary for plaintiffs to establish each defendant's personal involvement in the alleged constitutional violation, the task falls to this Court to determine whether any genuine issues of material fact exist as to each defendant's involvement in the alleged retaliatory action. The Court of Appeals has spoken as to some of the evidence, and this Court has no basis to second-guess the Court of Appeals' findings relative to those matters. The parties have referenced many additional items of evidence which they claim bear on whether defendants should defend their conduct at trial."

Judge Larimer turned to the subject of conspiracy, noting (p. 7) that "Defendants devote several pages of their brief to arguing that plaintiffs cannot establish that defendants conspired to violate their rights. They also argue that any conspiracy claims here are subject to dismissal pursuant to the intracorporate conspiracy doctrine, under which 'officers, agents and employees of a single corporate entity are legally incapable of conspiring together.'"

He continued: "In response, plaintiffs disavow any reliance on a conspiracy claim or theory. They contend instead that each defendant was personally involved in what they describe as DOH's 'offensive' against Beechwood, i.e., defendants' orchestrated campaign to put Beechwood out of business and to punish Chambery for his exercise of his First Amendment rights. Plaintiffs assert that defendants acted in concert, that defendants' actions caused plaintiffs to suffer one indivisible injury, and that all the defendants are therefore jointly and severally liable for plaintiffs' damages, but, they contend, such a claim does not require proof of the elements of a conspiracy.

"Although the complaint does make some references to defendants having conspired together, ... conspiracy and indivisible injury are distinct concepts.

"Plaintiffs have not asserted a civil rights conspiracy claim under § 1985, and in any event the only claim left, following the remand from the Second Circuit, is a First Amendment retaliation claim under § 1983."

Judge Larimer was insightful on the subject of qualified immunity, explaining on page 8, "With regard to qualified immunity, ... summary judgment on that ground is generally inappropriate with respect to First Amendment retaliation claims. If defendants acted with retaliatory intent, then no rational fact finder could conclude that they could have reasonably believed that their actions were lawful." He then went on to render a decision on the summary judgment motion on the retaliation claim with respect to each defendant.

> Page 9: "Defendants contend that there is no evidence of sufficient personal involvement on the part of any particular defendant to hold that defendant liable for unconstitutional retaliation against plaintiffs. By their motions, defendants appear to take the startling position that in spite of the Court of Appeals' clear statement as to the sufficiency of proof, no defendant should proceed to trial. If accepted, that argument would leave plaintiffs in the curious position of having stated a retaliation claim against defendants generally, which the Second Circuit has held should go to a jury, yet being unable to establish liability against any individual defendant. That cannot be the case."

> Page 10: "I have analyzed the evidence relating to retaliation as to each defendant. I have not, though, listed every piece of evidence and the permissible inferences from that evidence that could be considered by a jury as to any particular defendant. The Court of Appeals has already determined that issues of fact exist as to plaintiffs' First Amendment retaliation claim generally. It is not necessary, therefore, to go through the entire body of evidence before the Court. The only task left before me now is to decide whether enough evidence has been presented to give rise to issues of fact as to each individual defendant."

### Defendants Judge Larimer left in the suit:

#### *Sanford Rubin:*

> Page 10: "In holding that there was sufficient evidence to create a triable issue of fact as to plaintiffs' retaliation claim, the Second Circuit specifically cited the evidence concerning defendant Sanford Rubin, who at all relevant times was DOH's Regional Director. ...The Court of Appeals stated that "this is evidence from which a jury could reasonably find that the DOH was campaigning against the partnership as retaliation for the exercise of First Amendment rights."

> Page 11: "That statement by the court could hardly have made any clearer that the Court of Appeals believed there to be sufficient evidence to proceed on plaintiffs' claims against Rubin. While defendants have attempted to explain away those statements ... such inferences are not for the Court to draw on a motion for summary judgment."

### Laura Leeds:

Pages 11-12: "While there does not appear to be any direct evidence of retaliatory intent ... there is nonetheless evidence that Leeds was determined to see Beechwood closed, or at least that Chambery be removed as it operator, regardless of the actual situation at Beechwood in the Spring of 1999. For instance, ... Those statements are of course, subject to varying interpretations. ... It is not within the province of the Court, though, to draw such inferences on a motion for summary judgment."

Page 13: "In its 2006 decision in this case, the Second Circuit specifically cited Leeds's alleged "all the wrong reasons" statement as among the "evidence from which a jury could reasonably find that the DOH was campaigning against the partnership as retaliation for the exercise of First Amendment rights." 436 F.3d at 154.

"Again, more than one inference could be drawn ... While it would be surprising if Leeds had meant that as a public acknowledgment that DOH had closed Beechwood for unlawful reasons, ... it is evidence that a jury could consider in determining whether she acted with retaliatory intent."

### Russel Altone:

Page 20-21: "There is also evidence that as early as mid-April 1999, Altone was already discussing possible termination ... There is also some evidence that in May 1999, Altone gave Marie Shea ... instructions to "find ... bad things about Beechwood. ... Finally, I note that after the revocation proceedings ... Altone opined ... that "Chambery has nothing but bricks and mortar to sell."

"Viewing this evidence in the light most favorable to plaintiffs, then, I conclude that at least some of Altone's actions concerning Beechwood appear to have been non-prosecutorial in nature, and more a part of the investigative process. As to such actions, prosecutorial immunity would not apply."... Depending on the proof at trial, Altone may be entitled to judgment as a matter of law as to some or all of plaintiffs' claims against him, if the facts show that he was acting in a prosecutorial role. If not, then further factual findings will be required to determine whether he acted with retaliatory intent. Altone's motion for summary judgment is therefore denied."

### Susan Baker:

Pages 22-24: "As with many of the other defendants, the evidence concerning Baker is conflicting, and could be interpreted in different ways. On the motion before me, however, I must construe the record in the light most favorable to plaintiffs. ... Applying that standard here, I conclude that there are genuine issues of material fact that preclude the entry of summary judgment. ...

"The evidence also shows that Baker was closely involved with preparing the April 1999 Statement of Deficiencies ('SOD'), which ultimately led to the revocation of Beechwood's operating certificate. Just a few weeks after a complaint had been found to be 'unsubstantiated,' and after previous deficiencies had been corrected, DOH was moving ahead anyway with this SOD, alleging 'immediate jeopardy' to Beechwood residents and threatening termination of Beechwood's Medicare and Medicaid participation unless the alleged deficiencies were corrected within about two weeks. Curiously, those IJ allegations were apparently based on residents who had previously been discharged from Beechwood and were no longer there and thus could not be in immediate jeopardy. See HT 629, 630. The notice of that SOD, dated April 27, 1999, was signed by Baker. PL. Ex. 50.

"Baker also signed the May 18, 1999 letter from DOH to Chambery rejecting Chambery's proposed Plan of Correction ('POC'). Pl. Ex. 13. The record also shows, however, that on May 13, 1999, Baker reported to HCFA that no IJ still existed at Beechwood, although she also stated that '[n]one of the deficiencies [had been] corrected from the initial visit.' Pl. Ex. 78. Baker's handwritten notes from around this time indicate that there was a consensus or agreement to the effect that 'anything D or above still terminate,' (Pl. Ex. 80), in other words, if any deficiency still existed, DOH would proceed with termination proceedings, apparently with little regard for Chambery's efforts at remediation.

"To be sure, some of the evidence also suggests that Baker and her colleagues at DOH genuinely believed that Beechwood had serious problems with respect to patient care, and that their movement toward termination was entirely proper and justified. But certainly, some of this evidence could indicate that Baker shared in others' determination to put Beechwood out of business, for reasons that had little or nothing to do with any actual deficiencies regarding patient care.

"Which of those competing inferences should be drawn from this evidence is for a jury to decide. Suffice it to say at this point that there is evidence from which a jury could find that Baker was well aware of, and shared in, the animus toward Chambery on the part of some DOH officials, stemming from his First Amendment activity, and that she participated in the retaliatory 'offensive' against him. Baker's motion for summary judgment must therefore be denied."

### *Sharon Carlo:*

Page 27-28: "It is unnecessary to recite all of the evidence concerning Carlo here, but several items are worth mentioning. For one, it was Carlo who coined the term, 'DOH offensive' to describe DOH's proceedings against Beechwood. Dkt. #29 at A325. Though that term—which plaintiffs have missed no opportunity to recite in their papers—does not necessarily evince an unconstitutional motive, it is some evidence of her understanding and agreement that DOH was not simply seeking to correct the problems at Beechwood, but was engaged in a campaign to shut it down, for whatever reason."

"Carlo also stated in a May 14, 1999 email to Leeds that 'we're all on the same page' concerning Beechwood, explaining that 'the staff are working on the new deficiencies from Beechwood even as we speak.' Pl. Ex. 82. Again, those statements may simply reflect a shared belief that Beechwood was a substandard facility that needed to be shut down for the good of its residents, but to the extent that the evidence shows that some defendants were seeking to punish Chambery for exercising his First Amendment rights–and the Second Circuit has already held that there is enough evidence to support such a finding–Carlo's statement about being 'on the same page' as the other defendants is further evidence that she had such motives as well."

"I also note that in explaining its conclusion that Beechwood had 'produced sufficient evidence of retaliatory motive to survive summary judgment,' the Court of Appeals specifically cited an email authored by Carlo, in which–as the Second Circuit put it–she 'rejoiced with [the] exclamation ... 'HOT DIG-GITY DAWG' (followed by 50 exclamation marks).' Pl. Ex. 88;Beechwood, 436 F.3d at 154."

"Finally, it should be noted that Carlo took extensive and detailed notes from April through June 1999 concerning Beechwood and the more than forty conversations that she had with various persons referencing Beechwood over that period. At her deposition, Carlo stated that she could not remember what some of those notes (such as her reference at one point to the 'global picture' concerning Beechwood, Pl.Ex.29 at A288) meant, but she did acknowledge that the proceedings against Beechwood were a departure from the norm in some respects. See, e.g., Carlo Depo.Tr. (Dit.197-1) at 126-27,174, 229. That could, of course, reflect the extraordinarily poor conditions at Beechwood, which called for an unusually vigorous response from DOH, but it could also be taken as some evidence that Beechwood was singled out because of Chambery's unusually vociferous opposition to DOH practices. See, e.g., *Dillon v. Morano*,"

### Cynthia Francis:

Page 30-33: "Since the alleged wrong here–retaliation for the exercise of protected rights–is grounded in defendants' wrongful intent, it is not enough simply to show that defendants performed some acts that may have contributed to the harm suffered by plaintiffs. Plaintiffs must show that each defendant acted for constitutionally impermissible motives–specifically, in this case, for retaliatory reasons, or at least with an eye toward knowingly advancing others' retaliatory goals."

"There was testimony at the ALJ hearing that on one occasion, Francis made statements to a nurse working at Beechwood that indicated Francis's awareness or belief that the reason why Beechwood was being subjected to such exacting scrutiny was that there was some personal animus between Rubin and Chambery. The nurse, Gwendolyn Ann Westbrook, testified that Francis and other DOH surveyors were scrutinizing Beechwood so closely and persistently that at one point Westbrook said, either to Francis or in her presence, 'Oh, my God, what is this? Do I have to find another job or what?' HT at 2131. Westbrook testified that Francis 'leaned over to [her] ... and she goes, "You know, there are better places to work at than this and if you value our license, you wouldn't work here no longer." HT at 2132."

"Apparently, on another occasion, Westbrook testified, during a conversation with Francis, [that] Francis stated, 'You know, it's a personal thing.' When Westbrook asked her what she meant by that, Francis replied, 'Between my boss and your boss.' Westbrook again asked Francis to explain, and Francis allegedly 'told [Westbrook] about a lawsuit.' HT at 2132-33. When asked at the hearing for more details about what Francis said to her, Westbrook replied, 'A personal vendetta I don't know the correct word. A personal thing between her boss and my boss.' HT 2133-34. She also testified that Francis 'said they [i.e. DOH] [were] going to get him [ i.e. Chambery]. There [wasn't any] but. They weren't going to try to get him, they were going to get him.' HT at 2135."

"Westbrook's testimony, if believed by a jury, would certainly support an inference that Francis not only knew that Rubin and others within DOH were determined to 'get' Chambery because of his prior litigation against DOH, but that she understood that part of her mission was to come up with evidence that DOH could use for that purpose. The Second Circuit specifically cited this alleged exchange between Francis and Westbrook as part of the 'evidence from which a jury could reasonably find that the DOH was campaigning against the partnership as retaliation for the exercise of First Amendment rights.'436 F.3d at 154. I therefore conclude that there are genuine issues of fact as to whether Francis knowingly participated in the alleged plan to punish Chambery for his exercise of his First Amendment rights."

### Elisabeth Rich:

Page 33-34: "Francis and Rich also both signed a joint affidavit in June 1999, in support of the DOH caretaker petition in New York State Supreme Court. In that document, they stated that Chambery had 'demonstrated an inability and/or an unwillingness to correct deficiencies,' adding, 'In our opinion, it is imperative that this operator be replaced by a caretaker immediately.' Pl. Ex. 165 at 10, ¶ 10. That application was denied by Justice Francis Affronti, based on Justice Affronti's conclusion that there were 'seemingly inconsistent findings in the record as submitted ... by [DOH].'

"While that alone might not give rise to an issue of fact as to Rich, once again [third-floor nurse supervisor Charlene O'Connor's] testimony at the ALJ

ANOTHER NEW YEAR'S EVE PRESENT

hearing is relevant. She testified that Rich 'was very buddy, buddy, she was very informative.' HT at 2519. [O'Connor] testified, Rich 'told me [that Beechwood] was a very nice facility, she told me to be careful of what I say to her because we could end up on opposite sides of the courtroom.' [O'Connor] testified that she replied, 'Liz, I thought you were here investigating,' to which Rich replied, 'You never know.' HT at 2519. [O'Connor] also stated that on another occasion, she said to Rich, 'If we could meet on any other circumstances, I would like to get to know you better,' and that Rich replied, '[R]emember, you and I are just players in the greater scheme of things.'

"A reasonable factfinder could conclude, from this testimony, that Rich herself did not believe that there were significant problems at Beechwood, but that she nevertheless understood that her job, as a 'player in the greater scheme of things,' was simply to come up with identifiable problems at Beechwood. A factfinder could also conclude that Rich understood that her task had less to do with unearthing actual deficiencies than with supplying ammunition for eventual legal action by DOH against Beechwood and Chambery. I therefore deny defendants' motion for summary judgment as to the claim against Rich."

Although I don't believe that allowing the defendants another bite at the apple was in accordance with the Second Circuit's determination, and the jury might have come to different conclusions on some of the following individuals after hearing Beechwood's full presentation of the evidence, the fact that the number of defendants was dramatically reduced—and reduced to those who had the best audit trail for a finding of liability in a first amendment case—led to a trial that was definitely more manageable. To collect damages, Beechwood only needed to have two defendants found liable.

## DEFENDANTS JUDGE LARIMER DISMISSED FROM THE SUIT

### Antonia Novello:

Page 15: "Plaintiffs' claim against Novello mostly rests on certain alleged 'procedural irregularities' concerning the manner in which the decision was made to revoke Beechwood's operating certificate. ... Even if, as plaintiffs allege, 'Novello completely abdicated her responsibilities as the final decision maker and merely rubberstamped the order Greenberg had sent her,' Pl. Mem. of Law (Dkt. #243) at 4, that is not enough to show her personal involvement in the alleged constitutional deprivation."

### Arlene Gray:

Page 28: "Although Gray clearly took some actions with respect to Beechwood, there is scant evidence that she had any decision-making role in the investigation or proceedings against Beechwood, or that she harbored any retaliatory animus toward Beechwood or Chambery."

### Anna Colello:

Page 35-36: "What is lacking, however, is evidence from which a factfinder could conclude that Colello played any significant role in carrying out the so-called 'offensive' against Beechwood, or that she was aware of, or shared, any retaliatory animus toward plaintiffs. Plaintiffs' chief complaint about Colello seems to be simply that she knew that the usual DOH procedures were not being followed with respect to Beechwood, and that she did nothing to stop the 'offensive' or to call attention to those procedural improprieties. Even if true, however, that does not make out a retaliation claim.

"The most that the evidence shows with respect to Colello, however, is that she failed to do anything to stop the offensive from going forward. Plaintiffs repeatedly refer to conferences in which Colello took part, but they have shown no more than that she did not object to the plans to proceed with the enforcement action against Beechwood. Plaintiffs state, for example, that 'neither the absence of immediate jeopardy, nor any of the procedural irregularities, nor any of the "holes" in the latest SOD [in May 1999] caused any defendant, including Colello, to pause or reconsider the offensive underway against Beechwood.' Dkt. #241 at 12. Similarly, they state that Justice Affronti's decision denying the caretaker application gave Colello and the other defendants 'one last opportunity ... to reconsider their plans for revocation,' id. at 13, but that neither Colello nor the other defendants did so."

"There were due process claims (Fourth Claim) contained in the original complaint but those are gone now. In the wake of the Second Circuit's decision in this case, however, plaintiffs' remaining claim is not based simply on alleged procedural irregularities in connection with the enforcement proceedings, but on alleged retaliation for Chambery's First Amendment-protected activity. It is not enough, then, to show that DOH failed to follow its usual process or sequence of steps with respect to the enforcement proceedings against Beechwood, and that Colello stood by and did nothing; plaintiffs must show that she herself acted out of retaliatory animus, or at least that she knew of others' retaliatory motives, and that despite being in a position to intervene, she failed to do so."

### Dennis Whalen:

Page 37: "In short, plaintiffs' claims against Whalen rest on little more than a theory of *respondeat superior,* which is not applicable in § 1983 actions. Plaintiffs' argument that 'Whalen ... was where the buck stopped at DOH' does not set forth a legally sound basis for § 1983 liability."

ANOTHER NEW YEAR'S EVE PRESENT

To a layman, it seems incredibly unjust that in the first summary judgment motion, Judge Larimer would prematurely dismiss claims without looking at the evidence presented and before allowing the plaintiff to have any discovery, yet now he simply states that defendants like Colello can be dismissed because the original claim is gone. The constraints of the appeal process force plaintiffs to narrow the scope of their claims on appeal and focus on what are considered the most important. This is especially disconcerting when the Court of Appeals reinstated the defendant under a cause of action on which Judge Larimer got unanimously overturned.

One would also think that Judge Larimer would be a little more cautious about again dismissing high-level people like Colello, Novello, and Whalen on the improper motive claim that was still in play when the following demonstrate that something was desperately wrong within their organization and under their watch:

1. There isn't any decision-making document, signature or memory as to authorization to take the actions taken against Beechwood, or reasoning why.

2. Leeds stated that she could not provide the "specifics" of where the remedy decisions were made, but she had "to answer to a whole lot of other people."

3. The Statements of Admission confirmed the failure to institute a litigation hold, and that the OCC file disappeared.

4. The Statements of Admission revealed the lack of any "formal referral memo" or "enforcement file."

5. The actions being taken in the "offensive" against Beechwood had never been initiated previously.

As Judge Larimer stated in his jury instructions:

Page 19: "A wise and intelligent consideration of all the facts and circumstances shown by the evidence and the exhibits in this case should enable you to infer with a reasonable degree of accuracy what the defendants' state of mind was.

"Experience teaches us frequently that actions sometimes speak louder than spoken or written words. Therefore, you may rely on circumstantial evidence and inferences in determining what a person's state of mind was."

Page. 20: "In short, you may consider any act that the defendant performed or failed to do, and all the other facts and circumstances in the case which indicate what that person's state of mind was at the time of the events in question."

And it was precisely the defendants' "state of mind," especially in the all-encompassing toxic climate of personal animosity, that was at the heart and soul of this case.

# CHAPTER 19

# To the Jury

The official runup to the long-awaited liability trial began with a trial scheduling conference Judge David Larimer called together on September 26, 2011. As arduous as our journey had been to this point, we had reached not so much a destination as a new point of embarkation. Preparing for any trial is incredibly labor intensive, but when your opponents are government officials, the prospect is far heavier. This class of defendant has essentially unlimited funds and inherently enjoys favor with the court. We had to filter through many thousands of documents, refining this mountain down to the few hundred we considered crucial.

We finished this all-consuming project on October 26, just in time for me to head to my son's wedding the next morning.

We submitted our proposed trial exhibits to the court on November 1. Little more than a month later, on December 8, there was a court session with Judge Larimer concerning the failure of the Department of Health to respond to our proposed exhibits. It was not until January 6, 2012 that the defendants filed their response—an opposition to sixty percent or more of the exhibits Beechwood proposed. At the same time, they submitted their own exhibit proposals, to which we responded on January 26. We had no objection to most of the proposed exhibits, other than the ALJ decision from the federal administrative hearing. Many major issues had been raised by the defendants, including whether we could use Medicare Fraud Control Unit (MFCU) documents, OSCAR data (which showed the stellar performance of Beechwood), Judge Affronti's decision, and the federal ALJ report. Other objections touched on whose emails, notes, and other documents and communications could be used at trial and whether a decision on use should be delayed until a foundation can be established at trial. We also went on the offense. Beechwood moved to sanction the defendants for spoliation of evidence. All of these disputes were addressed in an oral argument before Judge Larimer February 17, 2012.

Judge Larimer's courtroom happened to be wired for electronic presentation of evidence, something less common then than it is today. Since we were the plaintiffs, it was our job to propose the presentation system to be used. At the time, the standard procedure was to hire IT contractors to do the job, and, typically, they deployed desktop computers with older software. Armed with an extensive background in developing software, I quickly set about finding a simple, cost-effective system, with great graphics, that the attorneys could operate themselves. I chose the Apple iPad 2, which had been released only the year before, and loaded it with a specialized software program called Trialpad. My brother, Dale, extensively tested this solution, so that we were fully confident in it. We still had to convince our own attorneys, the defense attorneys, and Judge Larimer that it was both failsafe and simple to use. We unveiled the proposed system in the courtroom on March 28, 2012. Our demonstration was greeted so positively that not only did all parties agree to its use, the Attorney General's Office and the Western New York federal court system purchased many of the devices and the Trialpad software.

On the same day, March 28, Judge Larimer also attempted to drive a settlement of the case. He tried to persuade all parties to agree to his serving not only as a mediator but also to holding confidential conferences with him, separately. He emphasized the risks to each party with moving to court and a jury trial. He admonished us to fully understand our "heavy burden" and the "thin reed" we had—with only a single claim left and the need to convince all the jurors. He warned that he intended to instruct the jurors to be especially careful in their deliberations and to seriously consider that he and two agencies had already ruled against us.

We took the first step toward a mediated settlement, which was valuing our lost business and laying out expenses. This, in fact, was the simple or at least straightforward part. The hard part was putting a value on the damage to my reputation, career, lost opportunities—the business ventures strangled in the cradle—and, not least of all, thirteen years of my life.

I soon learned and accepted that struggling to collect damages for these "hard part" matters was so much wishful thinking. Even the value of the business and expenses would involve heavy compromise in settlement discussions. In the end, we compromised significantly, but on April 19, 2012, we received a letter from Judge Larimer:

"I report that the gap between the [plaintiff's and defendants'] settlement numbers is quite significant. I presume that both sides made their best effort to advance a 'final' number and, therefore, it seems very doubtful that the gap can be 'bridged.' I therefore, see little benefit in my continuing in this settlement endeavor. ... So, we will continue to work toward trial which is fast approaching. We will then turn the matter over for resolution to the as-yet-unidentified members of the jury and the vagaries inherent in a jury trial."

### FINAL PREPARATIONS

After all the years of work and expense dedicated to getting our day in court, I spared no expense in ensuring that our trial attorneys, Kevin Cooman and David Rothenberg, had full confidence in what they were doing. We hired a jury consultant, Paulette Robinette, from a Kansas firm called Jury Sync, to run a focus group/mock jury, provide consultation on positioning at trial, and help with jury selection. Her expertise would prove invaluable.

We engaged Frank Torchio and Jim Canessa of Forensic Economics, a Rochester firm, to assemble and present the damages report. Torchio and Canessa brought extensive experience in expert testimony on valuations of companies, including very large public companies. Jim did a masterful job of presenting very complex financial matters to the jurors.

Finally, there was Sheldon Nahmod, our civil rights legal expert from Kent University Law School in Chicago, whose expertise and words of wisdom over the years had already been helpful in developing legal strategies.

On April 4, 2012, we ran the focus group/mock jury. Cooman presented the case for Beechwood, and Rothenberg presented the expected DOH case. Paulette Robinette led the discussion groups and decision making that followed. This exercise provided very valuable feedback, including what we took as the reassuring fact that our mock jurors had very little faith in both DOH actions and DOH claims, and were especially put off by the speed at which the agency had worked to close the facility.

## JUDGE LARIMER'S PRE-TRIAL DECISIONS

On April 13, 2012, we received Judge Larimer's decision on documents and issues for trial.

## Concerning Beechwood proposal to produce the MFCU documents at trial

Page 3: "Plaintiffs seek to introduce Solomon's memos, the Final Report, and certain other documents relating to the MFCU investigation, including hand-written notes, a subpoena, letters, and other materials.

"Defendants contend that these documents are inadmissible hearsay, and also are excludable under Rule 403 of the Federal Rules of Evidence, as unduly prejudicial. Plaintiffs contend that these documents are admissible as public records or reports under Rule 803(8), and that they are not unfairly prejudicial to defendants.

"I find that the [Auditor's] Final Report is admissible under Rule 803(8). ... It contains factual findings by a state agency, resulting from an investigation by that agency regarding a matter within that agency's jurisdiction."

Page 6: "Defendants' motion to preclude Solomon's memo from being admitted into evidence is granted, without prejudice to plaintiffs' offering excerpts from, or a redacted version of, the report at a later time."

Page 6: "Plaintiffs also apparently will seek to introduce a copy of what they describe as a 'work allocation agreement between DOH and MFCU ...' The Court does not preclude admission of this document at this time, but its admission at trial will be subject to a proper foundation being laid for its admission."

Page 7: "As to the remainder of this evidence relating to the MFCU investigation, the Court cannot issue a definitive ruling at this time. These various documents, which include personal notes and emails, may be admissible as admissions of defendants or their agents, or as background evidence concerning the MCFU investigation, but again a foundation must be laid, by way of testimony by defendants or the authors of the documents, subject to a showing of relevance."

## Concerning other matters

Page 8: "I ... deny defendants' motion to preclude the admission of Justice Affronti's decision, as well as related documents relating to DOH's state court petition for appointment of a caretaker."

Page 12: "Evidence regarding a proposed settlement that included a condition that Brook and Olive Chambery "shall never again jointly, individually or in combination with any other person" operate or own, or in any way be involved in the operation of a nursing home … could be viewed as punitive and retaliatory … [and] is not barred by Rule 408."

Pages 15-18: "Handwritten notes made by the defendants are admissible if plaintiffs lay the "proper foundation." The same is true for emails, letters from non-parties, and various reports taken from public databases."

Pages 22-24: "Tape recordings of conversations with defendants are admissible, as are time records and evidence regarding DHS commissioner Antonia Novello's criminal conviction."

Page 29: "At this point, the Court will not allow the federal administrative decisions to come into evidence, or are counsel to mention them during their opening statements. Depending on the proof at trial, the Court may revisit this issue. … It appears that the standards applied by the state and federal administrative authorities were not identical … and the risk of jury confusion that would be created … would likely outweigh whatever probative value it might have."

There were two more pre-trial conferences with Judge Larimer, on May 2 and May 8, before we finally reached the point of trial.

## THE LIABILITY TRIAL,
## MAY 14 – JUNE 26, 2012

*The Beechwood legal burden.* In his charge to the jury, Judge Larimer explained that, to prevail in its "1983" civil rights action, the plaintiff must prove, by the preponderance of the evidence, that:

1. Speech protected by the First Amendment was involved.

2. Government officials were acting under color of law.

3. Each defendant took the action he or she did with retaliatory animus or state of mind. That is, each either personally desired to retaliate or knew that others had that motive and took steps to further that cause.

4. The speech activities were a substantial motivating factor for the action taken.

5. The action taken was a cause of the damages claimed.

Proving that each defendant was sufficiently connected to the "adverse action" in order to be held personally liable under joint and several liability was a challenging task. Beechwood had the heavy burden of proving that each individual was retaliating in response to my exercise of free speech. The defense strategy opposing this was to depersonalize everything and argue that it was DOH, as a non-party "government agency," that took regulatory actions, not the individual defendants. Beechwood also had to prove that the defendants would not have taken the same actions absent their impermissible motives. In all practicality, we were also required to completely dispel the notion that there was any shred of evidence in the ALJ report pointing to poor care, failure to cooperate, or any other legitimate reason for the actions taken and sanctions applied against Beechwood.

Beechwood had the necessary emails, notes, timecards, policies and procedures, other documents, and deposition testimony to show the state of mind of each defendant. It had proof that the defendants predetermined their course of action and outcomes, never giving up, never changing course, and even pursuing us for years after the ALJ hearing—though not much of that aspect came into the liability trial. We had the necessary statements from the DOH defendants and other witnesses as experts on how departmental activity should be directed, coordinated, and documented, and admitting that standard procedure was not followed.

Other than attempting to spin their own written notes, emails, documents, and previous testimony, the primary basis of the defense was the ALJ report, which turned out to be the real 'thin reed' of the trial. Offsetting the ALJ report was the striking contrast provided by the MFCU investigation, Judge Affronti's decision not to order a caretaker, Beechwood's quality of care OSCAR data, the testimony of physicians and insurers regarding Beechwood's care, inconsistencies demonstrated within the defendants' past and present testimony, the inability of the defendants to explain their actions in the face of their own testimony regarding how things should work, and Novello's testimony that she had not looked at any Beechwood-related material before issuing the order to revoke the license. Novello's confirmation of her felony conviction for actions (unrelated to Beechwood) she took as NYS Commissioner of Health did not help the defendants' cause either, but their principal problem was that the jury simply could not believe them. The basis of this problem? The defendants were, in fact, not trustworthy.

### Judge Larimer's charge to the jury, June 26, 2012
In the wake of the Second Circuit's decision, "state of mind" took center stage, effectively creating a whole new world for us. Judge Larimer instructed the jury:

Page 7: "[The defendants] deny that they had any improper motive in reviewing the problems and deficiencies at Beechwood. ... The defendants also have raised a defense ... the essence of [which] is that they say that even if they had taken some action against Beechwood on account of his First Amendment rights, his complaints, they still would have taken the actions that they did.

"You are called upon to determine if these seven defendants, and you must consider each defendant separately, did in fact violate Mr. Chambery's protected rights under the First Amendment by taking severe, harsh, adverse action against Mr. Chambery and Beechwood for a reason: In retaliation for doing what a citizen has a right to do, that is, to complain."

Page 9: "1983 statute language reads as follows: 'Every person, who under color of any statute, regulation, custom or usage of any statute, regulation, custom or usage of any state, any person who subjects or causes a citizen of the United States to the deprivation of any rights and privileges secured by the Constitution, shall be liable to the party injured in an action at law.'"

Pages 9-10: "I don't think there's really too much dispute as the proof has developed that Mr. Chambery had the right to ... engage in speech that was protected by the First Amendment, ... and he did.

"In this case, there's no dispute that the defendants here were acting in the scope of their employment as Department of Health officials."

Page 11: "The plaintiff has the burden of establishing that his protected speech, his speech activities were a motivating factor, a substantial or motivating factor in the defendant's decision to take the adverse action against him. ... This is really the heart of the case."

Page 15: "Prior speech does not have to be the only reason the state defendants took the action they did. ... But if one of those reasons was on account of Mr. Chambery's protected speech, and if that reason played a substantial part in the decision, then the plaintiffs would have satisfied this aspect of the First Amendment claim."

Page 18: "You may find that some of the defendants took action against the plaintiffs, but that only some of them did so for retaliatory reasons. If you find that, then only those that acted with the retaliatory state of mind would be liable."

Page 19: "A wise and intelligent consideration of all the facts and circumstances shown by the evidence and the exhibits in this case should enable you to infer with a reasonable degree of accuracy what the defendants' state of mind was.

"Experience teaches us frequently that actions sometimes speak louder than spoken or written words. Therefore, you may rely on circumstantial evidence and inferences in determining what a person's state of mind was."

Page 20: "In short, you may consider any act that the defendant performed or failed to do, and all the other facts and circumstances in the case which indicate what that person's state of mind was at the time of the events in question."

Page 22: "If the defendant acted in good faith, seeking only to carry out his or her lawful duties as an employee of the DOH overseeing nursing homes, that defendant cannot be held liable. That's so even if a particular defendant was aware that maybe other people were motivated by some bad purpose or retaliation."

This is another example of the damage done by Judge Larimer's decision to grant the early summary judgment motion, forcing us to whittle down prematurely the number of claims in order to survive at the appeals level. Although the person described above may not be guilty of retaliation, he or she would be liable under other claims, such as due process. Such a participant could also be held accountable for participating in a fraudulent activity, or not fulfilling his or her professional duty to report such activity.

Page 23: "It's only if you find a defendant intentionally acted with a retaliatory purpose or that defendant had a knowing willingness to carry out and effectuate someone else's retaliatory aims can that defendant be held liable."

Page 23: "Mr. Altone is a lawyer, and I instruct you on the law that an attorney must zealously and vigorously represent his client. The ability to zealously and vigorously represent his or her client is central to an attorney's profession."

The point concerning Russel Altone is taken from Canon 7 of the New York Lawyers Code of Professional Responsibility, regarding Ethical Considerations. Unfortunately, Judge Larimer failed to add a qualifying phrase in Section EC7-1: "within the bounds of the law." He also failed to include another highly relevant section of this canon, which my attorneys also failed to address in response. Section EC 7-14 states that: "A government lawyer who has discretionary power relative to litigation should refrain from instituting or continuing litigation that is obviously unfair. A government lawyer not having such discretionary power who believes there is lack of merit in a controversy submitted to the lawyer should so advise his or her superiors and recommend the avoidance of unfair litigation. A government lawyer in a civil action or administrative proceeding has the responsibility to seek justice and to develop a full and fair record and should not use his or her position or the economic power of the government to harass parties or to bring about unjust settlements or results. The responsibilities of government lawyers with respect to the compulsion of testimony and other information are generally the same as those of public prosecutors."

Page 24: "Preponderance of the evidence means to prove that the fact is more likely true than not true. It means the greater weight of the evidence. It refers to the quality and persuasiveness of the evidence."

Pg. 25: "The burden is in this civil case a preponderance of the evidence standard."

Pg. 26: "The defendants have the burden of proving their affirmative defense, that 'by a preponderance of evidence that [they] would have taken the same action against Beechwood, regardless of whether there were free speech issues.'"

Pg. 27: "You must base your verdict upon ... the testimony of the witnesses who testified, and all the exhibits that have been received into evidence."

Pg. 29: "Administrative law is the branch of law governing the organization and operation of administrative agencies and the relations between administrative agencies, various branches of the government and with the public. ... An administrative law judge or ALJ is an official who presides at an administrative hearing. ... In this case Zylberberg was appointed ... to act in that capacity."

Pg. 30: "Following that hearing the ALJ ... issued a Report and Recommendation ... subject to review and possible modification by the NYS Commissioner of Health, at that time Antonia Novello."

Pg. 30: "I instruct you that the law of New York and the law here in federal court that I must apply is that the administrative law judge's findings that the Department of Health had proven violations at Beechwood are to be given preclusive effect by you. In other words, those findings by the administrative law judge were conducted—were made after a hearing, are binding on you, and you must accept the correctness of the ALJ's findings that there was sufficient evidence to show that the violations of the deficiencies at Beechwood existed."

Pg. 31: "But while existence at Beechwood of violations is of some relevance in this case certainly, it's not the ultimate issue in the litigation before you. What is chiefly at issue here and what you will be called upon to decide is why. Why the defendants took the actions they did.

"To answer that question, you need to examine the motivation and state of mind of each defendant. We've talked about that at some length already. The administrative law judge's decision does not dispose of that why question.

"Particularly, you must determine as to each defendant what that defendant's state of mind was when he or she took some action concerning Beechwood. Did the defendants scrutinize Beechwood's operations to an unusually significant or unwarranted degree because of Mr. Chambery's exercise of his First Amendment rights? Did they exaggerate or overstate the scope and severity of the deficiencies? Did they purposely target Beechwood for the ultimate sanction of revocation of its operating certificate?"

Pg. 32: "Retaliation need not have been the only reason, but if it was a substantial or motivating factor causing the defendants to take the action against Chambery and Beechwood, then plaintiff is entitled to your verdict. So while you're bound to accept the correctness of the administrative law judge's findings that there were violations, and you may consider those violations with regard to whether the defendants acted out of retaliatory intent or laudable intent, the findings of the ALJ are not alone dispositive. I repeat again: The plaintiff can prove a First Amendment violation for retaliation even if the measures taken by the defendant would have been otherwise justified. The question again comes down to each defendant's motive for acting as he or she did."

Pg. 33: "Now, while the administrative law judge's determination as to deficiencies is binding on you, he said other things in his Report and Recommendation which are not at all binding on you. For instance, he's made statements concerning his view of the credibility of the Department of Health's surveyors. He made statements rejecting plaintiffs' claim that the surveys were motivated by bias, animus or retaliation.

He [the ALJ] made other comments about his view of plaintiffs' claim relative to retaliation and conspiracy. He also made certain recommendations concerning penalties. None of those things are binding on you. The administrative law judge was charged with making a Report and Recommendation concerning deficiencies. He made that report, and those findings are binding on you."

Page 34: "I also instruct you that plaintiffs' claim here does not depend on, nor do plaintiffs allege any issues concerning legitimacy of the penalties and remedies recommended by the ALJ.

The ALJ recommended that Beechwood's operating certificate be revoked, and that recommendation was ultimately adopted by the commissioner. Given the ALJ's factual findings concerning violations, the penalty was permissible under New York State law. In other words, it was within the range of penalties permitted under state law. But, again, this does not dispose of the federal constitutional claim before you. That claim is separate and distinct from what the administrative law judge was called upon to decide. So even though the penalties imposed were lawful as a matter of state law, the imposition of those penalties could still have violated plaintiffs' constitutional rights if the proceedings which led to the imposition of the penalties were initiated, motivated for retaliatory reasons. This does not mean that the ALJ himself had to have acted out of retaliatory motives. If the defendants presented their application to revoke Beechwood's operating certificate for retaliatory reasons, that's enough for you to find [for] the plaintiffs, regardless of whether the ALJ, who is not a defendant here, had any retaliatory motives or whether he knew or believed that the defendants were acting out of retaliation."

Simply amazing!

It had taken Beechwood thirteen years to get around the mind-boggling limits on rational thought that had been allowed to develop under administrative law—and which Judge Larimer had been very eager to apply—and actually get to the point of being allowed to have someone consider all the facts and circumstances as well as the motivation and state of mind behind the actions taken by the defendants.

Although Judge Larimer had previously granted preclusive status to the ALJ's comments about the credibility of the defendants, the lack of retaliatory motive, and legitimacy of the penalties or remedies chosen, he now had to give instructions to the jury (pp. 33 and 34) explaining that these statements by the ALJ were not binding upon them.

And what a difference it made! The jury saw the evidence of the fraudulent use of the survey process; namely, preplanning the sanctions that would be used and the claims of immediate jeopardy and harm that would support it. They saw and heard the evidence of deficiencies being crafted and plans of correction being rejected without reason. They heard the inconsistent testimony and understood why there was a lack of proper documentation and the inability to explain actions. They were presented with evidence the court had been refusing to look at or consider for thirteen years.

Despite Judge Larimer's instruction to the jury (p. 33) that "the administrative law judge's determination as to deficiencies is binding on you" and that (p. 31) the chief issue before the jury was whether the defendants targeted Beechwood, overstated scope and severity, and scrutinized to an unwarranted extent, who was going to believe any part of the deficiencies when they couldn't believe any other part of the defense? The jury saw the ALJ report for what it was: an agency determination made in a kangaroo court. The defendants had no defense other than this report, and the more they brought it out and tried to rely on it, the more disgusted the jurors became.

Judge Larimer previously ruled (July 6, 2007, p. 45) that "procedural irregularities, even if they occurred, were effectively cured by the extensive [hearing] procedures afforded to Beechwood ... [and thus] caused no harm or prejudice."

But the jury again disagreed.

There is no need to document any particular trial events because the case was made before trial and sealed by deposition testimony. Our strategy was to use the defendants as our expert witnesses as part of our case in chief and to do it essentially on cross-examination. By the time we got to depositions, we had departmental policies and procedures, defendant work histories, and a good share of the emails and other documents necessary. We had the deponents verify and elaborate on standard policies and procedures, as well as on their own roles, and then we confronted them with what was done or not done regarding Beechwood. In effect, we led them to the slaughter—gently.

Our job at trial was to elicit the testimony and present the documents so that the jury could understand it. If testimonies changed at trial, there was always the deposition testimony to bring the defendants back into line. We had done our homework well.

# CHAPTER 20

# Truth's Long Arc

LIABILITY TRIAL

The eight-member jury got the "1983" case about eleven in the morning of June 26, 2012. Television and movies portray waiting for the jury verdict as an excruciating ordeal. Let me assure you, for once TV and film got it right. It is agony, especially after thirteen years. Fortunately, as these things go, the suspense did not last terribly long. After three-and-a-half hours of deliberation, the jury returned with a unanimous decision.

They found five of the seven defendants, Laura Leeds, Sanford Rubin, Sharon Carlo, Susan Baker and Cynthia Francis, liable. The wave of elation that swept over our team, my family, and me was overwhelming, one of those lifetime experiences that can never be forgotten. It was also a grand and glorious day for our friends and for all who had been connected with Beechwood, many of whom were also our friends.

The speed with which the jury returned its verdict demonstrated the issues, and especially the right and the wrong, were crystal clear to them. This is the beauty of trial by jury. It draws on something rare in the legal realm and almost nonexistent in closed administrative systems: ethical common sense. Jury trial is, of course, a basic constitutional right, and the fact that it resulted in justice makes dramatically apparent the urgent need to modify the Administrative Procedure Act and put an end to the unconstitutional constraints that deny access to due process in the judicial system. Speaking from a perspective both rational and moral, there was simply no uncorrupt, defensible reason for Beechwood, my family, and me to have been forced through thirteen years of expense and waste to obtain what, in the end, was a straightforward verdict. All was clear to a jury of laymen. This was precisely the kind of outcome foreseen by the framers of our Constitution. It should also have been clear to Judge Larimer from the very beginning.

## DAMAGES TRIAL

Leading up to the separate "damages" trial, on July 31, 2012, DOH moved "for an order limiting plaintiff damages to $1." The motion was denied, and on August 6, there was a conference with Judge Larimer. DOH Attorney Bernard Sheehan tried to deflect liability for damages. "What we ... intend to show," he said, "is that based on that evidence that's preclusive, HCFA—who is an independent decision maker, a totally separate agency—made a decision, made an independent decision to terminate Beechwood from the Medicare program, which is a completely federal program as well, and that that act constituted the intervening cause because Beechwood could not survive without Medicare funding" (p. 6). He went on: "The Medicare termination happened first" (p. 7).

The attempt to twist the story line was breathtaking. Regardless of what the evidence proved or what the Second Circuit ruled about HCFA's support for DOH, the defense was intent on claiming that HCFA was a totally independent player and decision maker, and all the damages should be allocated to the termination because, technically, it happened before DOH revoked the Beechwood license.

As if this nonsense were not enough, as the conference continued, Judge Larimer turned to our attorneys and stated, astoundingly: "Let's talk about the lost wages that Mr. Chambery seeks here. As I understand it, you seek to have the jury award Mr. Chambery lost wages from July of 1999 to the trial, which seems like an exceptionally long period of time here, and just seems sort of like asking for a lot here that, here again, this may not be as a matter of law, but it's over a decade. Are you still seeking to ask the jury to award him lost wages for a decade? You're going to try to convince the jury there's no other work in the healthcare field for a decade? He couldn't—I guess that's what you intend to argue?" (pp. 32.10-33.23)

Judge Larimer was responsible for much of the destruction our business and we, personally, had suffered over the years. He was also the cause of most of our unending labor. I estimate that, on average, there was a major event—a hearing day, trial day, motions filed or received, briefs and responding briefs, depositions, interrogatories sent and answers received, FOILs and FOIAs sent and answers received, and on and on—every week for thirteen years! The research, legal conferences, and writing necessary just to keep up with this was astounding and staggering. Holidays and vacations became a distant memory. During the thirteen-year period, there were perhaps three or four weeks of vacation with the family, usually long weekends in the nearby Adirondacks. In spite of all this, Larimer still managed to come out with the "lost wages" comment, which demonstrated his total absence of concern for the tremendous damage that can be inflicted by a regulatory agency, and the tremendous personal cost of that damage. Judge Larimer was oblivious.

## OFFERS TO SETTLE

On August 8, 2012, Debra Martin, who was in charge of the local AG's office, made a "good faith" settlement offer of $5 million. It did not take me long to turn it down.

On August. 15, the offer was doubled, to $10 million. I quickly rejected this as well, much to the demonstrated astonishment of David Larimer. Just four days later, on August 19, the Sunday evening immediately before trial, the offer was increased to $15 million. Again, I rejected it. The damages trial commenced.

## DAMAGES TRIAL AND SETTLEMENT, AUGUST 20–AUGUST 22, 2012

On Tuesday, August 21, Beechwood's expert witness testified about damages. The testimony was limited to the value of Beechwood as of June 1999, compensation for my time over the years as tabulated on the basis of the salary of an average administrator in the area, and expenses incurred other than legal fees. We also requested that the jury consider adding a value for my time beyond that of the average administrator because of what I had been previously making and because of the tremendous time and effort over the years to bring the matter to court. The legal fees and associated expenses and interest, which more than doubled the dollars we presented to the jury, are typically left for the judge to rule on.

One of the unfortunate aspects of being caught in a situation like this is the value of lost opportunities, such as the business expansion we had been about to undertake, the software rights we had negotiated as part of this anticipated expansion, and the new level of care we were about to initiate. These might-have-been elements are impossible to value concretely and thus are forever lost. The same was true of the value of intangible assets in the nursing home operation, such as databases, staff expertise, management expertise, market position, and so on—all of which would serve as a base for future expansion and be of great value in open-market negotiations. We knew these things had value but could not put definitive number on them.

We were also very conservative in the valuations that we did present to the jury. The value of the facility was very high from any angle, but we wanted to be seen as very reasonable in what we were asking the jury to award.

The defense, in contrast, was anything but reasonable. Their expert was due to testify the next day that the damages should be no greater than $1. This was the ludicrous position taken during opening statements and was not bound to go over well with a jury that had unanimously found five defendants liable for a violation of constitutional rights in closing the facility. Moreover, the jurors could not have been pleased by the eight-week defense-requested delay in the damages trial, which likely interfered with jurors' summer vacation plans. So, after our expert presented his valuation, Debra Martin told Beechwood attorneys that she would have another offer of settlement before trial the next morning. It would be presented to our attorneys in the judge's chambers at 8:45 a.m.

The next morning, I arrived at court about 8:45 and was told the attorneys were in chambers, as expected. Previously, we had wondered whether it was even possible to make a settlement offer of the nature we would entertain without its being subject to legislative approval. However, as Cooman relayed to me, the discussion included the state controller and staff from the offices of the governor and the state attorney general, all of whom were on the telephone and represented that they had the power to make the settlement happen. Cooman told me that Judge Larimer was astounded by the numbers being discussed, and when the number got to $25 million, which the state officials insisted was their limit, the judge reiterated repeatedly that he felt it definitely was. At that point, Cooman and Rothenberg came out into the courtroom to talk to me.

To put things in perspective, this settlement figure was about equal to the damages we had presented to the jury, with the addition of legal fees. To take it meant giving up the opportunity to collect thirteen years of interest on the value of the facility and the dollars invested over the years to maintain operations and pay the legal fees. These damages would have more than doubled the settlement amount being discussed. Settling is always a hard nut to swallow, but the uncertainties of further legal proceedings, which often lead to drastic discounts, prompted my attorneys to press me hard to take the current offer. They believed this figure was indeed as high as the settlement offer would go. Taking it would bring closure. Without it, we would roll the dice with the jury's determination of damages, Judge Larimer's award of interest and attorney fees, and the outcome of appeals. Given that appeals were virtually certain and the controlling case law vague—and the fact that Judge Larimer had voiced extreme surprise at the dollars already on the table, not to mention his demonstrated history of an absence of concern for Beechwood—the prospects for improving on $25 million did not look promising.

As it was, after thirteen years, I now had only a few minutes to make up my mind. The risks taken and resources spent over every one of those thirteen years rushed into those few minutes. In view of the time value of money and my aching desire to end this saga and move on with life, I decided to take the state's offer. I relayed the news to my family as they arrived in the courtroom. When Judge Larimer came in, he announced the settlement and asked that the jury be brought in.

The jury members looked very pleased when Larimer presented the details of the settlement. The speed at which the state made a settlement offer, together with its size, ratified the liability verdict they had rendered a few weeks earlier. Beechwood had been a valuable facility, and the defendants were fully liable for their improper motives in closing it.

### THE MEASURE OF VICTORY

It was finally done. It was a victory, though it could not make us whole. Nevertheless, I had met my goal, found five defendants liable, restored our reputation, and made "N.Y. State Pay," as the headline put it the next morning.

And it was a significant victory. We had to defeat the tactics and defenses mounted by the Department of Health and the Attorney General's Office, and we had to do it in spite of the bottomless pocketbook into which they could dip. Put it this way: we had to beat the state. That meant we also had to beat our way through both state and federal administrative proceedings, the federal court system and the principles of administrative law to which it defers, and lift the legal blinders and alter the bias toward government that administrative law fosters. As our consultant, Sheldon Nahmod, Esq. put it:

"Your victory is monumental in several respects.

"First, I have never encountered a section 1983 damages award to an individual or business remotely close to the size of the First Amendment damages award that you received.

"Second, many if not most First Amendment retaliation cases that are brought by individuals or small businesses turn out to be losers because of the difficulties for plaintiffs of showing both the impermissible motivation and the presence of but-for causation. You were able to overcome these difficulties.

"Third, few plaintiffs hang in the way you have and fight all the way to this kind of just result.

"Your victory also sent a strong message to the governmental entities sued and otherwise involved in your litigation. You therefore acted in the public interest as well as for yourself. These folks and others similarly situated will think long and hard (we hope) before pulling this sort of thing again.

"What a nightmare: a sound and successful business that helps people is put out of business permanently for spite, in an attempt to punish, by those who are supposed to be regulating and assisting them."

After court was dismissed, we waited outside the courtroom for the jury members to exit. We wanted to thank them personally for their service. Their response, however, was totally unexpected. There were hugs and tears of joy all around. The jurors were happy that it was over and probably relieved that they didn't have to decide on the damages award—though they were clearly pleased with the amount of the settlement. There were also a few comments that they felt the jury award would have been even higher.

## AFTER THE TRIAL

On December 31, 2012, we sold the office building that had been our base of operations since moving out of the nursing home. Three days later, on January 3, 2013, Beechwood received a wire transfer from the State of New York for $25 million. After some three months of effort devoted to getting the contact information and current addresses of employees who were at Beechwood in the spring of 1999, we were able to send out letters on February 12, inviting each of them and a guest to a party to be given on March 7, 2013. The RSVPs poured in.

On March 4, I send out another letter:

Dear _____,

One of the most trying times of my life was having to endure patients being moved, and staff being laid off due to the retaliatory actions being taken against me personally. It was made all the more difficult by the fact that the DOH hearing schedule prevented me from getting a chance to thank each one of you for your caring service and protection of the patients, right up until the end. On the day that we closed, by the time I got out of the hearing, the facility was empty and the lights were out. I walked the hallways shaking my head in disbelief.

It is hard to understand why government officials could abuse their authority to this extent and close a facility that had the track record and quality stats that we had (within the top few in the state). However, they had the unfettered power to do so, and decided to use it. A year later, the Medicaid/Medicare Fraud Control Unit of the Attorney General's office, which is equally charged with investigating patient care, began an investigation into just about every aspect of Beechwood's operations, and eventually reviewed the same patient records and issues cited by DOH. It was an exhaustive multi-year criminal investigation. I thank you for taking the time, often on multiple occasions, to answer questions posed by the investigators. The outcome was not surprising; the final investigative report stated that the care was "very good to excellent." What was particularly disturbing was that this conclusion was not made public. In fact, it took many years of legal maneuvers for us to even obtain this report and the accompanying investigative records.

My resolve to bring out the truth began on the first day of the hearing back in 1999. I knew the task would be rough but had no idea how rough. It took day and night work, six to seven days a week until we got to court in the summer of 2012. The legal actions and battles were too numerous to count, very intensive, and took an enormous amount of planning and detailed work to prevail. Just about all documents obtained took court orders. We began with very little proof and had to virtually build the case from scratch. We also had to endure major failures along the way. Two major cases were dismissed by the Court. One (challenging the federal termination) had to be let go after years of work simply because of time and money constraints. The other, the civil rights case that was just won, was successfully appealed and reinstated in 2006.

However, now that the jury found five DOH officials liable for violating my civil rights (first amendment right of free speech), and we have settled with the State of New York, we are able to do what we could not afford back in 1999, that is to provide a severance package in recognition of your service to Beechwood. Enclosed is a check ...

We also want to be sure to take this opportunity to thank you for your service at Beechwood, and remind you one last time (if we don't see you at the party): You were always, and remain simply the best! You helped accomplish great things at Beechwood, and many people will be forever grateful.

My mother and I, and the whole family hope to see you again at the upcoming party, and wish you all the best in your future endeavors.

Sincerely,
Brook Chambery

Running a single payroll thirteen years after shutting down all business functions was an incredibly difficult task. It necessitated research, obtaining legal opinions, and having discussions with state and federal officials. Was it a gift, or was it pay for work performed? If so, for what "ordinary and necessary" services were we paying? Did it have to be taxed and, if so, at what rate? Did FICA and unemployment have to be taken out? It was no longer feasible to set up the formal payroll system we had previously used. We had to set up a special program to figure the taxes, other deductions, and employer benefits, and to print the checks, stubs, and summary reports. Again, the computer savvy of my brother, Dale, came to the rescue. Amazingly, the payroll was run and taxes filed without a glitch.

## THE STAFF PARTY, MARCH 7, 2013

More than a hundred guests made it to the party that night. As the Rochester Democrat and Chronicle reported it, "co-workers reunited and shared joy instead of heartache. ... A few themes developed as attendees laughed, hugged, ate and drank. They spoke of how hard it was to see Beechwood close, and also said they loved working there and thanked the Chamberys for being so kind. ... In an extraordinary move last week, former employees were sent severance checks from the Chambery family, thanking them for their dedicated service."

## THE JURY PARTY, MAY 30, 2013

On January 27, 2013, I sent out the following letters:

Dear Juror:

Five months have now gone by since the Beechwood trial, and I wanted to take a moment to thank you from the bottom of my heart for the time you dedicated last year to being a juror at the trial. For my whole family, I can say that we truly appreciated it, and we have the greatest respect for you. Without people willing to do what you did, the system would not work properly, and justice might not be adequately served.

We (plaintiffs and plaintiffs' attorneys) would like the opportunity to get together with you and other members of the jury (and guests) within the next few weeks to dine, socialize, reflect, and otherwise just relax and enjoy each other's company. If that sounds of interest to you, would you please let me know by sending an email ... or calling ... You might also indicate preference for weekday or weekend. We will then set a place and a date, and see if that can work for all.

Sincerely,
Brook Chambery

It had taken some time to locate the jurors, obtain responses about interest, find common dates, and get it all coordinated, but on May 30, 2013, a full nine months from the damages trial, we finally got the opportunity to thank the jurors for their service. Five of the eight jurors, together with their partners, showed up that night, and, just as I had been overwhelmed by the hugs and tears with jury members after the trial ended, I was again engulfed in the warmth, friendliness, and bonds formed that evening. In fact, everyone was in favor of "doing it again some time."

The conversation that night made it clear that the jurors found their experience gratifying. People, ordinary people in a democratic nation, naturally want to do the right thing and to see that their government does the right thing as well. Those juror/party guests took satisfaction in the state's finally validating with its settlement offer *their* verdict and *their* assessment of Beechwood's value. They had been sickened by the government powerplay, reserved their greatest disdain for Leeds and Rubin, and were unreservedly happy for us.

# CHAPTER 21

# "A Government of Laws, Not of Men"

Administrative "law" engenders and enables a so-called quasi-judicial administrative process. The concept of law in a constitutional democracy is compatible only with a constitutionally defined judicial process. A "quasi" judicial process can result only, at the very best, in "quasi" justice, which, whatever it may be, is not justice.

For Beechwood, quasi-law, quasi-judicial process, and quasi-justice amounted to all-too-real injustice—expected in a totalitarian state, a corrupt state, but wholly incompatible with a healthy democracy. The two administrative hearings to which Beechwood was subjected, one federal, one state, were very different, but both demonstrated that, however structured, administrative hearings are not independent, reasonable, or able to provide a full and fair opportunity to litigate. They are proceedings brought by the commissioners for the benefit of the commissioners, without due process, and amounting to nothing other than kangaroo courts: mechanisms to rubber-stamp and enshrine whatever agency staff decree. While allowed by Administrative Procedure Acts at the state and federal level, these proceedings are not and can never be constitutional. The two hearings demonstrate different aspects of the problem.

### THE STATE ADMINISTRATIVE HEARING PROCESS

Beechwood was subjected to a state hearing brought under outdated and dysfunctional New York law. It allowed such a hearing to be used to revoke an operating certificate but, enacted before federalization of the Medicare/Medicaid certification process, it was in conflict with federal regulations as well as the New York State Department of Health' contract with the federal government as the federal survey agent. Indeed, the law also conflicted with a memorandum of understanding (MOU) between the DOH and the DAG outlining the typical process of referring egregious survey findings to the attorney general's office for further investigation. If warranted, the DAG would make application to the courts for adjudication and sanctioning of the operators. The two final dysfunctions of the state law were the absence of any established state hearing process for a license revocation and the absence of anything in state law or regulations defining either "efficiency" or "violation of code."

Thus, state law authorized a process in conflict with federal law and federal-state agreements, a process without established rules, and a process authorizing penalties for committing violations that exist only as words without legal definition in the state of New York. Remarkably, in practical terms, before the actions against Beechwood, none of this was ever outed as a grave problem—for the simple reason that no such revocation procedure had been carried out in New York state for at least a quarter-century. For all practical purposes, the proceeding brought against Beechwood was unprecedented, even sui generis.

Absent law and legal institutional context, the state hearing was run by a legal department that, as director of the DOH Division of Legal Affairs Henry Greenberg testified, was the in-house law firm of DOH and served at the pleasure of the program staff. There were no firewalls:

1. Greenberg stated that when a referral was made for an enforcement action, it was prosecuted without any independent analysis for legal sufficiency.

2. Russel Altone, director of the Bureau of Administrative Hearings (BAH), stated that the BAH represents the Department of Health in adjudicatory proceedings "initiated by the Department."

3. BAH house counsel Steve Steinhardt testified to his feeling that the role of house counsel was to simply carry out directives from the DOH program.

4. Statements by both the ALJ and BAH attorney Marie Shea made clear that the hearing was brought by the Commissioner, for the Commissioner.

As for the ALJ, he conducted an unprecedented proceeding untethered to law and ungoverned by any constitutionally mandated rights. He—

1. Had no experience in nursing home matters.

2. Was not an independent fact finder. ALJs received their formal designation from the Commissioner of Health; and Greenberg, as director of the legal division, reviewed and approved ALJ performance evaluations conducted by the supervising ALJ and met with the ALJs once a month to discuss issues.

3. Did not (10 NYCRR 51.9(d)(2)) have the authority to dismiss charges, or recommend alternative remedies. Beechwood could not challenge the appropriateness of the remedy.

4. Was only to make a recommendation to the commissioner as to the appropriateness of what the commissioner sought. The commissioner retained the right to make the ultimate decision.

5. Had "ALJ 1" on his vanity license plate, attesting to the unlikelihood of his ever questioning the party line.

Considering the gravity of the sanction being sought, the fifteen-day notice of the hearing, which met minimum requirements under the New York State APA, was unconscionably unreasonable. But it suited to a tee Altone's goal of "expediting" the process. Within fifteen days, we had to find an attorney, analyze the law, and prepare a defense, even as we were preparing a defense against the DOH application to the court for a caretaker to replace me. At the very same time, we were trying to comply with the directed plan of correction (DPOC) and gain certification on the final survey, which was to take place within this very time period. Moreover, per DOH regulations (10 NYCRR 51.8(b)), no prior discovery process was permitted, including access to survey notes. We thus had no way of verifying whether hearing testimony was truthful, accurate, and the product of firsthand knowledge.

From this legal and moral valley, deep as it was, everything continued downhill. The ALJ was "not inclined" to allow questioning of DOH witnesses to uncover potential bias and did not allow them to be questioned about bias either before or after we received the subpoena materials. Quite accurately, Altone stated that he didn't expect to abide by typical rules regarding privilege claims on documents being subpoenaed during the hearing, for such rules are rarely followed in administrative hearings. He also continued to withhold documents and make bogus privilege claims during the twelve years subsequent to the hearing.

Put it this way: the hearing was totally meaningless except to produce and control the outcome. On July 8, 1999, the ALJ asked Shea, "So, what is the point of the hearing?" She responded: "For revocation of the operating certificate." He then asked, "What if my recommendation is not to revoke the license? Then you are saying it doesn't matter?" Her answer was both odd and telling: "At this point, it has gone very far, Judge."

## THE FEDERAL ADMINISTRATIVE HEARING PROCESS

In contrast to the New York State DOH, the federal Healthcare Financing Administration (HCFA) had well-established hearing and internal appeals processes as well as expansive regulations regarding survey requirements, deficiency grading, and sanction applications. It appeared, therefore, that HCFA's responsibilities were clearly demarcated and that there were solid mechanisms for appeal.

Appearances, it turned out, were deceiving. The Beechwood case led to federal ALJ rulings interpreting a few vague and conflicting regulations in such a way that HCFA's responsibilities were largely nullified. Ultimately, the agencies had almost limitless latitude in writing and interpreting their own regulations, and the rest of the government deferred to these improvisations under administrative law. For instance—

*Survey protocol.* Although HCFA has published a very detailed survey protocol, it also provides vaguely worded escape clauses:

> 42 CFR 488.305(b): "The agency's failure to follow proper procedure will not invalidate otherwise legitimate deficiency determinations."

> 42 CFR 488.318(b)(2): "Inadequate survey performance does not invalidate adequately documented deficiencies."

These regulations, which are problematic to begin with, provided the means for both the ALJ and the Department of Appeal Board (DAB) to rule in a way that allowed HCFA to avoid responsibility for lack of compliance with its own regulations. Consider the DAB decision of April 11, 2002 (p. 13): "The ALJ understood his role clearly, and sustained his analysis that it was outside the scope of authority delegated to him to judge the 'lawfulness of processes or procedures that were used by a State survey agency.'" This effectively eliminated any incentive for HCFA administrators to provide the supervision of state agency procedures expected of them under the regulations.

*Remedy selection.* Although the law and regulations are very specific on types of sanctions and how the seriousness of deficiencies must be determined in order to select the appropriate remedy, the law contains a nullifying caveat, 42 USC 1395-i-3(h)(2)(a): "Nothing in this subparagraph shall be construed as restricting the remedies to the Secretary to remedy deficiencies." In addition, HCFA crafted regulations at 42 CFR 498.3 limiting challenges to its "initial determinations" to just three situations: 498.3(b)(7)—Termination remedy, 498.3(b)(12)—Findings of non-compliance leading to a remedy, and 498.3(b)(13)— Level of non-compliance leading to a civil monetary penalty (CMP remedy). Note that the regulation regarding termination does not use the same "level of non-compliance" wording as the CMP (monetary penalty) regulation does.

With these provisions in place, and again granting deference to the agency's interpretations of the law and ability to publish regulations, the Federal District Court in the Beverly Case (October 18, 2002, pg. 21), ruled that "under both the Act and regulations, HCFA has the authority to terminate immediately the participation of a deficient facility regardless of the level of the deficiencies." This caselaw precedent was followed in the Beechwood case:

DAB ruling on April 11, 2002 (p. 20): Endorsed the ALJ position taken in his October 3, 2001 decision, that (p .6) "Failure by Petitioner to comply substantially with even one of those requirements provides CMS with authority to terminate Petitioner's participation."

DAB ruling on January 26, 2004 (p. 32): "Nothing in those regulations suggests that a facility determined not to be compliant with participation requirements can preclude CMS from terminating its provider agreement on Beechwood's theory that some further "justification" is called for. The argument amounts to a back-door objection to CMS's discretion to select what remedy to impose."

DAB ruling on January 26, 2004 (p. 37): "We uphold the ALJ's conclusion that, in the posture of this case, he need not decide what level of scope and severity was shown for a given deficiency, so long as the proof supports a scope and severity level that exceeds the minimum required."

*CMS [HCFA] initial determinations.* Both the law and regulations are in alignment and clear about HCFA's responsibility to make "initial determinations" regarding non-compliance and remedies to be applied. Implementing a remedy is to be done only after certification materials are received from the state survey agency and reviewed by HCFA:

> SSA 1819 (h)(1) states "IN GENERAL -- If a State finds ... that a skilled nursing facility no longer meets a requirement ... (A) ... the State shall recommend to [HCFA] ..."

> 42 CFR 498.3(b)(7), (12), (13) states that HCFA is required to make "initial determinations" including findings of noncompliance resulting in remedies, the level of such noncompliance, and whether to terminate a provider.

> SOM (State Operations Manual) Section 2772 requires that the certification package (Forms 1539, 462L, as well as the 2567 and POC) must be sent to the RO [HCFA Regional Office] by the SA [survey agency, or DOH], by the state agency representative (SOM 2762, 2764(D)), and that the RO is to review that documentation before making its initial determination.

It could not be clearer; however, the DAB refused to be bound by these laws and regulations, as evidenced in the Beechwood DAB Decision, January 26, 2004:

> Page 30: "Beechwood cannot prevail by simply denying the existence of "official CMS [HCFA] action....It would defeat the existence of jurisdiction for any appeal under Part 498, since such jurisdiction arises only over an official CMS action in the form of a listed initial determination."

> Page 30: "We conclude that the question of whether CMS engaged in any particular decision-making process at all is equally outside the scope of this appeal process."

Through regulation and hearing decisions, CMS effectively peeled away all the structural layers that otherwise appeared to ensure reasoned decision-making on appeal.

## JUDICIAL DEFERENCE

The following actions and caselaw cited by Judge Larimer make clear that the judicial courts provide no source of oversight or restraint on operations under the APA:

*The refusal to issue an injunction:* The court's refusal to intervene with Beechwood's initial request for an injunction under Section 1983 (retaliation) to stop the irrational carnage was the product of Judge Larimer's bias toward the agency.

He failed to consider the constitutional issues or balance the private interests of Beechwood, its staff and residents against the need for the agency actions being taken. He stated (p. 5) that "a preliminary injunction for temporary relief is often described as an extraordinary and drastic remedy," especially when moving to (p. 7) stop "several agencies—the state agency on two fronts and the federal government—from carrying on its statutorily imposed obligations," but he did nothing to assess the reasonableness of the extraordinary and drastic remedies being levied on Beechwood.

Even though Beechwood was stunned by the unique and conflicting legal actions taken by DOH just a few days earlier, Judge Larimer maintained his irrational stance, stating (p. 5) that Beechwood had to show the likelihood of succeeding on the merits (p. 7) if it did get its "day in court," and establish (p. 7) "that the actions commenced by the State DOH were done in substantial part and motivating part to somehow punish or injure the operators and the facility." Not only would it be impossible for any party to meet such a burden at so early a stage and without any discovery, the burden he placed on the plaintiff was higher than expected to survive a summary judgment motion, and it was placed without referral to any case law to support him.

Judge Larimer went on to address the arguments raised by the federal and state defendants. The federal agency raised the exhaustion issue—namely, that the plaintiffs failed to exhaust administrative remedies. To fit the unique circumstances of this case into the case law he desired to use, Larimer stated (p.10) that "even though the complaint here is framed in constitutional terms," in his view "plaintiffs clearly seek to rescind the termination ... and halt the suspension of Medicare payments. Clearly, such relief is administrative in nature." He cited from:

Page 12: A Fifth Circuit case (*Affiliated Professional Home Health Care Agency v. Shalala*), which quoted from a US Supreme Court case, stating "the exhaustion requirement is applicable to a constitutionally based claim when that claim is inextricably intertwined with a substantive claim of administrative entitlement."

Page 13: *Ponce de Leon Health Care Inc. v. HCFA,* a Southern District of Florida case cited at 1997 Westlaw 419641, which quoted the United States Supreme Court's *Heckler v. Ringer* decision at 466 US 602, 622: "Section 405(h) (of the SSA) requires administrative exhaustion even for constitutional claims when the claims are inextricably intertwined with claims arising under the Medicare Act."

Page 13: *Western District of Texas Court in Northwest Health Care v. Sullivan* at 793 Fed. Supp. at 726: "To order the defendant agency to continue to allow plaintiff to participate in the Medicare program and thus bypassing the administrative appeal would mean that the Court would be circumventing Congress' express intent that a facility resort to a state or federal court only after it had exhausted its administrative remedies."

Judge Larimer then moved on to the abstention issue which was raised by the DOH defendants. In discussing this, he relied principally on the Younger doctrine, enunciated in *Younger v. Harris,* a 1971 Supreme Court case, and other related cases. He (p 15) stated that in the Second Circuit, in order to invoke the Younger abstention doctrine, three questions must be resolved:

1. Whether there is an ongoing state proceeding

2. Whether an important state interest is involved

3. Whether the federal plaintiffs have an adequate opportunity for judicial review of their constitutional claims during or after the state proceeding

He went on to state that (p. 16): "The Younger abstention doctrine derives from the recognition that a pending state [administrative] proceeding, in all but unusual cases, will provide federal plaintiffs with the necessary vehicle for vindicating their rights, constitutional or otherwise." He continued: "The Second Circuit has in numerous cases ... noted the well-established principle [that] 'state Courts have the solemn responsibility, equally with the federal courts to guard, enforce and protect every right guaranteed or secured by the Constitution of the United States.'" Here he was quoting from *Temple of the Lost Sheep v. Abrams,* 930 F. 2nd 178 at 183, and setting a state administrative process equal footing with a state court process.

Larimer continued (p. 17): "I believe that a further reason for me declining to grant injunctive relief here is that there is ample reason for this Court to stay its hand and abstain and let the state issues which predominate be decided by the state administrative and judicial proceedings." He then stated (p. 18): "Surely, the bias and animus of those bringing the charges would always be a matter of defense and could be raised appropriately in these state proceedings," continuing (p. 19): "There is no reason administratively that a state court cannot consider the retaliatory aspect of plaintiffs' defense here as it were to these very serious charges." However, he stated this without considering that state hearing officers are not authorized to decide motive or bias.

Judge Larimer concluded by stating (p. 20): ""The whole issue of abstention is a difficult one." He referred to a New Orleans Public Service versus Council of the City of New Orleans case, stating that "Justice Scalia noted that the mere assertion of substantial constitutional challenge will not alone compel the exercise of federal jurisdiction. What the Court looks to is the import of the generic proceedings to the state." He followed this by noting that "in fairness, I should state that in this particular case, Justice Scalia and the majority determined that abstention was not appropriate." However, his path was clear. Quoting from the *Schwartzberg v. Califano* case: (pg.20) "When [a provider's private] interest is weighed against the government interest in patient safety, the government interest must prevail." Larimer continued (Pg. 23) "The agencies do have broad discretion in the manner in which they undertake their tasks, and even though the Court may see a better way to do it, that does not necessarily mean that this Court is charged with some kind of a role of Ombudsman to oversee how the state agency carries out its very difficult tasks."

Government interest must prevail! The administrative law blinders were on. No matter that Judge Larimer found "significant conflicting evidence on the merits here on the entire issue concerning patient care and the reasons why the Department of Health got involved when it did, and to the extent it did," (p. 6). He knew DOH was moving for the ultimate sanction, license revocation, and he acknowledged there were actions on multiple state and federal fronts that would take years to sort out, if ever (pp. 10, 14). He knew that, at minimum, this meant the destruction of Beechwood's current business and asset values, as well as total disruption to the lives of the staff and residents. He knew that these types of actions had never been taken before and appeared to be problematic. He knew (p.. 23) that the future was uncertain as to whether the business could be resurrected after such an event. He knew all of this, yet he took the irrational stance that "The moving party must show irreparable harm should the injunction not be granted" (p. 5).

DOH certainly understood the magnitude of what it was doing. A couple of weeks later, on July 8, 1999, at the DOH hearing, Shea asked quality assurance coordinator Mary Jane Proschel, "Hasn't this situation gone on so long that restoring [Beechwood] to the point that it can truly function is at this point pretty doubtful?" Proschel answered, "I am afraid so."

It was incredible that Judge Larimer never questioned DOH about the basis for the actions being taken, and it was unconstitutional for Larimer to stay his hand and allow a "quasi-judicial" administrative hearing to determine whether a sanction of this magnitude was justified (p. 17) and to take the position that "surely, the bias and animus of those bringing the charges" could be raised and dealt with in this administrative hearing (p. 18). Judge Larimer should have known that hearing officers were not specifically authorized to assess bias or motive under the New York State APA, and he could have asked whether the DOH would allow that to happen. Of course, when the hearing took place, the ALJ refused to allow bias to be adjudicated.

***The refusal to look at the evidence before granting Summary Judgment.*** When the civil rights case was refiled, and this time with proof of retaliation three or four inches thick, Judge Larimer still could not subdue his bias in favor of the agencies and his distaste for suits against government officials, especially for constitutional violations and damages. He stated that Beechwood had its day in court (p. 26), even if "the DOH hearing may not have afforded plaintiffs the full panoply of procedures that are available to litigants in a civil action (p. 24)," and he was not about to let us get away with what he perceived as an end run around the results of the administrative hearing and a failure to pursue an Article 78, or a typical administrative appeal. As he expressed it, the constitutional issues were still window dressing, and the case was basically an appeal of an agency action, which deserved a great deal of deference by the court under the standards of administrative law. Thus, he gave great weight to the collateral estoppel or issue preclusion defense raised by DOH regarding the ALJ's decision.

Larimer (p. 13) quoted from *Leather v. Eyck,* 180 F.3d 420, 424 (2d Cir. 1999) that issue preclusion "means simply that when an issue of ultimate fact has once been determined by a valid and final judgment, that issue cannot again be litigated between the same parties in any future lawsuit," and (p. 14) from *University of Tennessee v. Elliott, 478 U.S. 788, 799 (1986)* that (p. 14) "[W]hen a state agency acting in a judicial capacity resolves disputed issues of fact properly before it which the parties have had an adequate opportunity to litigate ... federal courts must give the agency's fact finding the same preclusive effect to which it would be entitled in the State's courts." He also cited *Allied Chemical, an Operating Unit of Allied Corp. v. Niagara Mohawk Power Corp., 72 N.Y.2d 271, 276 (1988) (citations omitted), cert. denied, 488 U.S.* 1005 *(1989),* a New York Court of Appeals case stating that in the context of determinations of administrative agencies, "the doctrine [of collateral estoppel] is applied more flexibly, and additional factors must be considered by the court. These additional requirements are often summed up in the beguilingly simple prerequisite that the administrative decision be 'quasi-judicial' in character."

The administrative law blinders are dark indeed. Judge Larimer (p. 24) stated: "Plaintiff's contention that the ALJ was biased is entirely conclusory and speculative. The fact that he was employed by DOH is not enough in itself to show that his decision was predetermined. Referring to the case of *Stone v. City of New York, 240 A.D.2d 216, (1st Dep't 1997) (citing Matter of Children of Bedford v. Petromelis, 77 N.Y.2d 713, 723-724, vacated on other grounds, 502 U.S. 1025 (1992)),* he quoted that ALJs and investigators are employed by the same agency, *without more,* is insufficient as a matter of law to raise an inference of bias." He followed this, stating, "If it were, then adjudicative determinations of administrative agencies concerning charges brought by the agencies' investigators could almost never be given preclusive effect, which is clearly not the law in New York." According to him, (p. 17) "If the charges were true [per the ALJ determination], they couldn't have been 'spurious or concocted.'" Thus, the ALJ decision is all that he looked at from the record as a whole.

***Beechwood's First Amendment retaliation claim.*** Judge Larimer (p. 38) ignored "the Court's obligation, on a motion for summary judgment, to view the record in the light most favorable to the nonmoving parties, and draw all inferences in their favor," simply because this was a "highly regulated industry." He stated (pp. 17 and 23) that the plaintiffs were not prevented from litigating regarding improper motivation on the part of the defendants, thus demonstrating further that, as allowed by both the federal and state APAs, the only record he looked at was the ALJ's determination. He concluded (p. 37) that "The ALJ found "Beechwood's claims of a conspiracy against it and/or Mr. Chambery to be a total, complete, and ridiculous fabrication without a shred of evidence or support."

***Beechwood's equal protection claim.*** With full knowledge that DOH or HCFA had never taken such regulatory actions before, Judge Larimer demonstrated the deference to the agencies that is now well established under administrative law. He stated (p. 43) that he was "mindful" of the 'strong presumption that the state actors have that they properly discharged their official duties... ' citing from *Stemler v. City of Florence, 126 F.3d 856, 873 (6th Cir. 1997)*, cert. denied, 523 U.S. 1118 (1998). He added '[T]o overcome that presumption the plaintiff must present clear evidence to the contrary; 'the standard is a demanding one.' *Id.* (quoting *Armstrong, 517 U.S. at 463. See also Gavlak v. Town of Somers, 267 .Supp.2d 214, 225 (D.Conn. 2003)* ("Our determination ... is tempered by the policy of affording governmental decisions a strong presumption of validity, which directs us to uphold a governmental decision if there is 'any reasonably conceivable state of facts that could provide a rational basis for the classification'") (*quoting Heller v. Doe by Doe,509 U.S. 312, 319 (1993)'''*)' He concluded (p. 44), "The record demonstrates that defendants had valid, rational reasons for their actions, and there is no evidence of *any* individuals situated similarly to plaintiffs who were treated differently."

**The substantive due process claim.** Judge Larimer (p. 44) stated that this cause of action was "essentially a catch-all or umbrella claim, alleging that defendants' various acts alleged in the complaint constituted an "abuse of governmental power" and denied plaintiffs their right to substantive due process." He then (p.45) quoted from the following cases. 'Government conduct may be actionable under section 1983 as a substantive due process violation if it 'shocks the conscience,' *Spear v. Town of West Hartford, 954 F.2d 63, 68 (2d Cir.)* (*quoting Rochin v. California, 342 U.S. 165, 172 (1952), cert. denied, 506 U.S. 819 (1992)*). 'A substantive due process claim based on allegedly tortious conduct by a state actor therefore ordinarily requires evidence of conduct that 'can properly be characterized as arbitrary, or conscience-shocking, in a constitutional sense.' *Interport Pilots Agency, Inc. v. Sammis, 14 F.3d 133 (2d Cir. 1994)* (*quoting Collins v. City of Harker Heights, Texas, 503 U.S. 115, 128 (1992); see also Boyanowski v. Capital Area Intermediate Unit, 215 F.3d 396, 400 (3d Cir.)* (only the "most egregious official conduct can be said to be 'arbitrary in the constitutional sense'"), *cert. denied, 531 U.S. 1011 (2000)); Rosa R. v. Connelly, 889 F.2d 435, 439 (2d Cir. 1989)* (requiring evidence that official action was "arbitrary or irrational or motivated by bad faith"), *cert. denied, 496 U.S. 941 (1990); Chalfy v. Turoff, 804 F.2d 20, 23 (2d Cir. 1986)* (requiring proof of "systematic and intentional harassment" to transform official action causing economic injury into a constitutional violation) (per curiam).'

Larimer concluded: "I find no basis for plaintiffs' allegations that defendants' conduct was arbitrary, malicious, had no legitimate purpose, and so on. Rather, defendants' conduct was rationally related to the state's legitimate interest in the regulation of nursing homes, and 'it can hardly be doubted that the interest is of the highest order.' *Blue,* 72 F.3d 1075, 1080 (2d Cir. 1995)."

*The supremacy of federal law.* Regarding Beechwood's claim that federal law had supremacy in the survey and enforcement process, and without taking the time to analyze the structure of the state and federal regulations and how the system is designed to work, Judge Larimer granted further deference to agency interpretations of law and regulations and simply concluded (p. 47) that nothing in the regulations "expressly proscribe" the enforcement actions taken.

## THE SECOND CIRCUIT LOOKS AT THE EVIDENCE AND REVERSES THE DISTRICT COURT

To provide focus on appeal, Beechwood limited the issues presented to three of the original claims. Overturning Judge Larimer on the First Amendment claim was a crucial victory; however, the decisions on the Equal Protection and Due Process claims provide further insight into the impossible burdens the courts place on plaintiffs by providing too much deference to the agencies, especially before discovery.

### The First Amendment retaliation claim:

Page 10: "We review the district court's grant of summary judgment de novo, reviewing the evidence in the light most favorable to the Appellants [Beechwood]."

Page 15: "The ALJ's conscientious discussion of motive concerns the credibility of evidence presented by DOH; and while that may have impacted the ALJ's findings of violations, the State has not shown to us that the ALJ's credibility findings were so influential as to be actually decisive of the ultimate question concerning the quality of resident care."

Page 16: "The identification, characterization, and classification of the actual deficiencies found are within the state's discretion, and are therefore subject to a claim of improper motive."

Page 17: "Beechwood produced sufficient evidence of retaliatory motive to survive summary judgment," including a suspect chronology, close sequence of protest and scrutiny, preplanning, and that the hostile pursuit was motivated by an intent to punish for the exercise of First Amendment rights."

Page 18: "This is evidence from which a jury could reasonably find that the DOH was campaigning against the partnership as retaliation for the exercise of First Amendment rights."

Page 20: "Cooperation between state and federal bureaucracies acting in their regulatory spheres supports no inference that the federal actors acted with an improper motive. See *Hafner v. Brown*, 983 F.2d 570, 577 (4th Cir. 1992) (concluding that § 1983 civil conspiracy requires "a meeting of the minds to accomplish the *unlawful act*" ... There is no evidence suggesting that the federal defendants acted based on an unconstitutional animus as opposed to a spirit of cooperation."

### Concerning the Equal Protection claim:
Page 21: "An equal protection claim requires (inter alia) evidence from which a jury could find that the plaintiff was selectively treated as "compared with others similarly situated." *Lisa's Party City, Inc. v. Town of Henrietta*, 185 F.3d 12, 16 (2d Cir. 1999); see also *La Trieste Restaurant and Cabaret, Inc. v. Village of Port Chester*, 40 F.3d 587, 590 (2d Cir. 1994). As the district court observed, Appellants have failed to produce evidence of any "similarly situated" individual or institution treated more favorably than Appellants. Beechwood, 317 F. Supp. 2d at 276-78.

"The partnership has adduced some evidence that the revocation of its operating certificate was an unusual measure, but, as the district court soundly observed, some sanctions may be imposed rarely because they are rarely justified. Id. at 276 ... (pg. 22) DOH might well decide that this particular facility presented the highly unusual instance in which harsher sanctions are needed because DOH could not rely on voluntary compliance and willing reforms. Conclusory assertions ... are not enough to show dissimilar treatment among those similarly situated, at least not at this stage of the proceedings."

### Concerning a specific Due Process claim regarding taking the Certificate of Need [CON] without a hearing:
Pages 25-27: "We need not decide the issue because, even assuming that Beechwood was entitled under State law to notice and a hearing, there was no due process violation. We have previously held that where a due process violation results from a 'random unauthorized act' by state officials—as opposed to an 'established state procedure'—the availability of a 'meaningful post deprivation remedy' defeats the claim. An Article 78 proceeding therefore afforded a meaningful post-deprivation remedy for Appellants' claimed violation. ... 'An

Article 78 proceeding is adequate for due process purposes even though the petitioner may not be able to recover the same relief that he could in a § 1983 suit.' Hellenic, 101 F.3d at 881."

Not only do terms like "similarly situated" and "meaningful post-deprivation remedy" present a legal minefield, what good is a "post-deprivation" process that "may not" be able to provide the same relief or damages?

## THE DISTRICT COURT'S WHOLLY UNJUST MEDICARE TERMINATION RULING

The Second Circuit found that the subjective nature of deficiencies makes them subject to a claim of improper motive; that there was evidence of retaliatory conduct by the authors of the deficiencies (and the remedy recommendations); and that the federal agency officials acted in a spirit of cooperation with DOH. Yet, eighteen months later, on July 6, 2007, in handling Beechwood's appeal of the federal administrative determinations regarding the Medicare sanctions, Judge Larimer stated (p. 1) that this "related action" was simply "another chapter in a contentious relationship between a nursing home and the governmental agencies" and chose again to blindly apply the typical administrative law standards in making his determinations.

*Regarding the lack of proper survey protocol being followed:*
> Larimer ruled, page 45: "These alleged procedural irregularities, even if they occurred, were effectively cured by the extensive procedures afforded to Beechwood, which was allowed to and did present substantial evidence concerning the SODs. Since the ultimate factual findings of the ALJ and CMS are supported by substantial evidence, these alleged procedural errors caused Beechwood no harm or prejudice."

*Regarding remedy selection in general:*
> Judge Larimer ruled, page 46: "The gist of plaintiff's claim is that defendants acted arbitrarily and capriciously in imposing a DPNA (as well as in terminating Beechwood's Medicare and Medicaid provider status, a claim that is now moot). As stated though, there was substantial evidence supporting the factual findings that formed the basis for the DPNA. In light of the deferential standard of review applied by this Court, *see National Ass'n of Clean Air Agencies v. E.P.A.,* ___ F.3d ___, 2007 WL 1574609, at *6 (D.C. Cir. June 1, 2007) ("The arbitrary and capricious standard [under the APA] is '[h]ighly deferential,' and it 'presumes the validity of agency action'") (*quoting AT & T Corp. v. FCC,* 349

F.3d 692, 698 (D.C. Cir. 2003)); *Hilkemeyer v. Barnhart,* 380 F.3d 441, 445 (8th Cir. 2004) ("Our review [under § 405(g)] is deferential; we may not substitute our judgment for that of the ALJ"), I cannot agree with plaintiff's contention in this regard. *See Michigan Ass'n of Homes and Services for Aging, Inc. v. Sha-lala,* 127 F.3d 496, 501 (6th Cir. 1997) ("The regulations do allow for considerable discretion in determining the level of sanction to be applied" for noncompliance with program requirements); Northern Montana Care Center, 2006 WL 2700729, at *1 ("[B]ecause Defendants had a factual and regulatory basis for their imposition of the DPNA, this Court cannot conclude the Defendants' decision regarding the choice of penalty was arbitrary and capricious, an abuse of discretion, or otherwise not in accordance with the law"); *Beverly Health & Rehabilitation Services, Inc. v. Thompson,* 223 F.Supp.2d 73, 111 (D.D.C. 2002) ("there can be no question that the agency did not abuse its discretion by imposing termination, and it is not within this Court's province to substitute its judgment for the agency's decision that termination was appropriate given the scope and severity of the deficiencies found")." In Beverly, the Court also clarified that it felt that "under both the Act and regulations, HCFA has the authority to terminate immediately the participation of a deficient facility regardless of the level of the deficiencies."

CMS and the Federal Courts have thus isolated appeals from being able to deal with any of the layers of decision making leading to non-compliance and remedy determinations. CMS has in turn locked in the case law supporting the ridiculous position that it can terminate at any time, with just one deficiency, at a scope and severity of anywhere from "D" to "L," without the liability of being challenged on the rationality of this action.

Worse, as happened in Beechwood's case, HCFA can give the public one reason, such as wide spread imminent danger (L), for terminating a facility, and only have the burden at a post-deprivation hearing of having to prove one deficiency representing a potential for more than minimal harm (D) to allow the ALJ to support the termination decision. This is in spite of the fact that CMS has declared, and the Supreme Court of the United States has reiterated, that termination of a certified nursing facility from the Programs—which will necessarily mean the involuntary transfer of elderly and infirm residents, unemployment for health professionals, the demise of a community resource, and economic loss to its owners– is "rare and generally reserved for the most egregious and recidivist institutions" that violate Program requirements and are unable to correct them. *Illinois Council v. Shalala,* 529 U.S. 1, 22 (2000).

*Regarding the lack of CMS initial determinations:*
This issue arose after a unique request and hard-fought battle over a subpoena for HCFA's enforcement file. When HCFA finally complied, the response demonstrated that HCFA had no documentation of any decision making. As Beechwood wrote in its brief to the Court in support of a motion for partial summary judgment on December 30, 2005 (p.18), "The import of the disclosures finally extracted from CMS is profound: because CMS had no documentation showing that it ever actually made any 'initial determination' and certification review concerning the alleged noncompliance by Beechwood, or the remedies to be applied ... no legitimate CMS action ever took place. CMS therefore never met its obligations to review any recommendations made by its survey agent, engage in systematic decision making, and then make 'initial determinations' and issue any remedies. 42 U.S.C. § 1395i-3(h)(2)(A); 42 C.F.R. § 498.3(a) and (b)(7), (12), (13). In the absence of such CMS official action, all resident care findings alleged to support the deficiencies were nothing more than uncertified recommendations of the survey agency, and never acquired the imprimatur of CMS."

Beechwood continued: "This wholesale failure of CMS to actually engage in a deliberative oversight and enforcement process constitutes no less than a willful disregard of its statutory obligations, and its own rules, demonstrates that its enforcement actions were arbitrary, capricious and an abuse of discretion, and not in accordance with the statute or the CMS implementing regulations. CMS's actions and decisions must therefore be overturned. 5 U.S.C. § 706(2); *Chrysler Corp.*, 441 U.S. at 317; *Immigration and Naturalization Service v. Yueh-Shaio Yang*, 519 U.S. 26, 31(2002) (Overturning agency decision under the APA, observing that 'Though an agency's discretion is unfettered at the outset, if it announces and follows–by rule or by settled course of adjudication–a general policy by which its exercise of discretion will be governed, an irrational departure from that policy (as opposed to an avowed alteration of it) could constitute action that must be overturned.')."

Judge Larimer never ruled on this lack of CMS initial determinations. He avoided having to by determining (p. 10) "that to a great extent, Beechwood's claims in this action are moot. Beechwood is closed, its state operating license has been revoked by the State DOH, and the building where the nursing facility was operated has been sold." This was a wholly unjust ruling. In his Injunction Decision, Larimer stated (p.14): "Congress in its wisdom did not provide for a pre-deprivation proceeding, but rather a post-deprivation proceeding, and that process is in place. Plaintiffs have requested a hearing, and although it has not yet been scheduled, there is no indication one will not be provided." In his SJ#1 decision (p .49), he stated: "Plaintiffs had a right to a hearing before HCFA, but they were given such a hearing. Their vague, amorphous theory that DOH somehow interfered with the federal administrative process, or intruded into an area reserved for the federal authorities, by holding a 'premature' hearing of its own, finds no support in the applicable statutes, regulations, or case law." Here, however, Larimer was denying the right to an appeal in his court on the basis that the facility had its license revoked by the DOH hearing and thus was forced to close. Yet *he* was the one who allowed the state proceeding to move forward first. It is also very strange that a judge, who deferred to the agency so readily, did not flinch as that agency, which at first granted the right to the hearing (a proceeding that dragged on for years), was now suggesting that the proceeding was moot. Beechwood had also been closed and its state operating license revoked before the CMS appeal was even started at the administrative level.

### *Regarding the funding cutoff for new admissions (DPNA):*
Judge Larimer wrote (p. 16), "There is one respect, however, in which plaintiff's claims are not moot: plaintiff's claims for monetary relief." If the claim was not moot, he should have addressed, before addressing the survey issues, Beechwood's claim that without any proper initial determination by HCFA, the application of this remedy was an invalid action. However, he simply and unjustly decided to ignore the issue. In so doing and in choosing to call the termination a moot issue, he demonstrated his aversion to having to rule against an agency, especially when the issue got this significant.

### IN SUMMARY:
In his ruling on the defendants' first Summary Judgment motion, Judge Larimer did not hide his contempt of Beechwood's not having made an Article 78 appeal of the state hearing. However, the complete deference to the agencies that he demonstrated in his decision— especially in this decision, made after the Second Circuit ruling, demonstrates exactly why Beechwood discontinued the Article 78. In this portion of the book, I am looking back at years of retribution against Beechwood by members of the administrative government with the

objective of revealing how malicious and capricious administrative decisions can be yet still receive unthinking deference from judicial courts, which will abandon the law, morality, and common sense to follow the provisions of the APA. Essentially, the stewards of constitutional law look the other way.

The case law Judge Larimer cited was far from exhaustive, and his resorting and adding to it demonstrate how entrenched judicial deference to the agencies has become. Beechwood found an avenue of approach that was successful before the Second Circuit on one claim, but many other claims were lost along the way. In some measure, ultimately, after thirteen years and much devastation both personal and professional, we prevailed. But that also demonstrates how abysmal the chances of proper court review of administrative issues are. The practical effect of the APA and the case law established around it is the erosion or even absence of checks and balances on agency actions. This—quite understandably, though inexcusably—leads to officials believing and thus acting as if they are above the law. Well over two centuries ago, in 1780, John Adams recognized the most basic principle of democratic government when, in his draft of a constitution for Massachusetts, he explained his intention of creating a "government of laws, not of men." Until judicial courts, created in conformance with the United States Constitution, review without bias or deference the actions of everyone who comes before them, administrative agencies and agents included, we will not achieve what Adams and the other framers of American government sought. Courts must review the whole record of any matter that comes before them, deferring to no one and to nothing but the law. They must coolly cast a discerning eye on agency actions for signs of inappropriate action and failure to meet agency guidelines. And they must not shy away from the attempt to decipher the human, all too human, motives behind actions taken.

Although Judge Larimer was bound to follow the Second Circuit decision in running the Beechwood trial and providing instructions to the jury, his unwillingness to let that court's decision influence his decision in the appeal of the CMS sanctions, a closely related case, demonstrated how narrowly he viewed the scope of the Second Circuit decision and how hard it is to pry the courts away from the principles of administrative law, which have been built up over time.

By affording such a strong presumption of validity of the motives and judgment of government officials, of the decisions they made, and the actions they have taken; by allowing administrative law judges to determine a reasonably conceivable state of facts that can be construed as substantial evidence; and by deeming the ALJ decision a substitute for the whole record, judicial courts blind themselves to moral reality. They are rendered incapable of seeing anything that shocks the conscience. They can see only their blind, unquestioning faith in an assumption that, somehow, administrative agencies act only for reasons valid and rational. Neither humanity nor the institutions humanity creates are so inhumanly perfect.

# Reforms Urgently Needed

T he boldness of the defendants in making and prosecuting a fraudulent case against a facility of Beechwood's stature, the unique nature and breathtaking enormity of the sanctions applied, and the confidence exuded that they would prevail under the administrative law process demonstrate the urgent need for reform. The fullest scope of the dark side of administrative law is made plain before us by the fact that the defendants, facilitated by their in-house legal team, were able to use the regulatory process to commit unconstitutional acts and healthcare program fraud—and to do so, essentially, with impunity.

Judge David Larimer's breathtaking deference to the process, his refusal to look at the record as a whole, and his blind application of case law were not merely unjust and unconstitutional, they aided and abetted the continuation of the administrators' illegal activities, allowing the defendants to commit healthcare program fraud without any consequences.

We are left to derive five principal lessons from the malicious prosecution of Beechwood Restorative Center.

*First:* The judiciary must take care to balance public and private interests and to resist applying the unconscionably extreme level of deference to agency actions, which has developed under case law.

Administrative law assumes that agency officials and the agendas they establish are reasonable, that the legal proceedings they set in motion provide a full and fair opportunity to litigate, and that the courts provide a necessary constraint on improper activity. Unfortunately, reality is very different from these assumptions. Those standing accused need the judicial protections that are not only proper but their unalienable right under the Constitution. In the Beechwood case, the agency officials acted not only unreasonably, but unconstitutionally.

For agencies to earn the legitimacy to impose sanctions, the public must be assured that enforcement authority is being exercised properly. There must be well developed agency policies and procedures, along with a justified expectation that these will be followed. As the Beechwood case illustrates, the greater the degree of variance from standard procedure, the greater the likelihood of improper motive. The courts must inquire about and examine such novelties and improprieties, giving them the most deliberate attention on appeal of an administrative action. If the courts abandon this responsibility, agency officials are set free from all oversight, and private rights can be stampeded and trampled.

Instead of simply reviewing the "record" represented by the ALJ decision— and doing so under a highly deferential standard of review—courts must take care to look not through the lens of the ALJ but at the whole record in the context of the issues raised and the facts presented. A good example of the failure to do this is provided by Judge Larimer in the first Summary Judgment Decision when he stated: "I realize the Court's obligation, on a motion for summary judgment, to view the record in the light most favorable to the nonmoving parties, and to draw all inferences in their favor.... however, [n]ursing homes are a highly regulated industry, and some tension between operators of homes and regulators is to be expected." This was intended to mean "game over," and, in most cases, the accused would have no option but to swallow the injustice. Fortunately for Beechwood, we could afford to appeal, hire a great legal team, and, after years, obtain a favorable decision by the Second Circuit—which decided to do justice by reviewing "the district court's grant of summary judgment de novo, reviewing the evidence in the light most favorable to the Appellants" and reinstate the case.

The same must apply when a court evaluates particular claims or causes of action in deciding whether to grant a summary judgment motion. The court must recognize the tremendous difficulties of obtaining information from agencies and resist the temptation to avoid prematurely dismissing claims or the entire case, especially prior to an adequate discovery process. Consider the consequence of Judge Larimer's statement in his Second Summary Judgment decision to dismiss Anna Colello as a defendant: "There were due process claims contained in the original complaint but those are gone now." The Second Circuit provided another example when it ruled that "Conclusory assertions … are not enough to show dissimilar treatment among those similarly situated, at least not at this stage of the proceedings," and dismissed the cause of action *before* any discovery. As discussed earlier, the phrase "similarly situated" is a minefield when dealing with deficiencies issued by the regulatory agencies. By the end of discovery, Beechwood could have met this legal burden.

**Second:** The ability of any agency to run its own quasi-judicial process should be statutorily curtailed when the agency seeks to impose sanctions that impact constitutional rights and liberties. The party standing accused needs the constitutional protections of the judicial process and needs them most urgently at the initial stage of the proceedings. The agency should be required to assemble its case, send it to the attorney general or Justice Department for independent review. Only if it is found worthy of withstanding the rigors of the judicial process, should it be brought to court for trial and potential sentencing. Anything less deprives the accused of their constitutional rights and protections. Anything less leads to significant conflicts of interest with the law enforcement agency that must defend government officials against claims of constitutional violations. Anything less creates other incentives to improperly coordinate with other agency officials to protect personal interests.

As the federal Medicare Fraud Control Unit (MFCU) investigation of Beechwood proved, absent a never-before-used provision in the New York law allowing use of a Department of Health administrative hearing to revoke an operating license, DOH would have been forced to send a referral to the MFCU in compliance with the terms of the ruling memorandum of understanding. There would have been no civil or criminal action, no conflicts of interest, and Beechwood would still be in business today. In other words, my constitutional rights and those of Beechwood would have been protected, and the proper checks and balances would have been operative on the system.

That an agency should be allowed on its sole authority—through a kangaroo court hearing it entirely controls—to take licensing actions reducing a healthcare facility like Beechwood to "bricks and mortar," forcing patients to move against their will, and depriving staff of highly valued jobs is a complete abrogation of due process. The necessity of presenting and proving the case in a judicial court is, as Rochester MFCU director Jerry Solomon testified a "whole different ballgame," no matter what the standard of proof is. It reinstated the constitutional protection of those being accused.

It took Beechwood thirteen years and $4 million of capital to get its day in court. If it were not for the Second Circuit Court of Appeals removing the blinders of administrative law worn by the lower court, that day in court would have never come, and DOH would have had the first as well as the final word. As soon as Beechwood was allowed to proceed with its claim of improper motive against the DOH defendants, and the jury was allowed to hear all the evidence regarding that motive—the "state of mind" of the defendants—the pendulum swung 180 degrees. The state went from having its own ALJ declare that there was "not a shred of evidence" of improper motive, to offering $25 million to settle the case after a jury found the defendants liable for retaliation.

*Third:* The Administrative Procedure Act needs to be revisited. The APA had assumed separation of investigative and prosecutorial functions within the agencies, the independence of the ALJs, and fair and equitable adversarial process in administrative hearings. Time and again, and nowhere more than in the abuses heaped upon Beechwood, this assumption has been revealed as so much theoretical nonsense. The firewalls are simply not there and cannot in all practicality be expected to be there. Likewise, the hope that appeal to the courts will provide the due process protection and check on the agencies has proven to be a forlorn hope as judicial courts automatically defer to the agencies as parliaments once deferred to kings and queens.

The APA allows the court to substitute the record established by the ALJ as opposed to the record as a whole and then dictates that courts uphold ALJ factual findings when supported by substantial evidence. What constitutes *substantial* evidence? That is to be judged under an arbitrary and capricious standard of review, which is itself highly deferential, presuming the validity of agency action and limiting the ability of a court to substitute its judgment for that of the ALJ.

Problematic in itself, the highly deferential standard of review is made more damaging by the fact that agency regulations, policies, procedures, and actions need to be scrutinized very carefully—but are not. Agency regulations allow considerable discretion in determining violations and sanctions, limit their own liability for improper procedures, and dictate the rules of the quasi-judicial hearing process, including limits on due process protections and challenges to procedures used and decisions made by the agency. The result under the APA is no justice at all. Agency personnel understand that they operate without legal constraints as a law unto themselves. What incentive is there for agency personnel to run a fair and equitable hearing process under current APA dictates?

Beechwood was decertified by HCFA, a federal agency, and had its operating certificate revoked by DOH, a state agency, all without documentation in either agency as to the decisions and the decision makers. Beechwood had to endure both federal and state administrative proceedings, in which it was not permitted to challenge the appropriateness of the sanctions applied. Nor did the ALJs in either proceeding have authority to change the sanctions applied. As for the agencies, they were not required to defend the sanctions. Nor were the ALJs required to rule upon the scope and severity of the charges as originally alleged in deciding to uphold the sanctions imposed. When the ALJs upheld the sanctions, Judge Larimer duly upheld the ALJ decisions. Nowhere along this lockstep progression was either the state or federal agency obliged to defend the rationality of their decisions or the correctness of their procedures.

The U.S. Senate Report of 1945 (pp. 216-217), written as part of the debate over passage of the APA, states the legislative intent was to revisit the APA if problems arose. The report specifically noted: "The basic provision respecting [hearing] evidence in section 7(c) – requiring that any agency action must be supported by plainly "relevant, reliable, and probative evidence" – will require full compliance by agencies and diligent enforcement by reviewing courts. Should that language prove insufficient to fix and maintain the standards of proof, supplemental legislation will become necessary." It also stated that "The 'substantial evidence' rule set forth in section 10 (e) [judicial review] is exceedingly important. As a matter of language, substantial evidence would seem to be an adequate expression of law. The difficulty comes about in the practices of agencies to rely upon (and of courts to tacitly approve) something less – to rely upon suspicion, surmise, implications, or plainly incredible evidence. It will be the duty of the courts to determine in the final analysis and in the exercise of their independent judgment, whether on the whole record the evidence in a given instance is sufficiently substantial to support a finding, conclusion, or other agency action as a matter of law.... Should these objectives of the bill as worded fail, supplemental legislation will be required."

The report (p. 217) concluded: "The foregoing are by no means all the provisions which will require vigilant attention to assure their proper operation. Almost any provision of the bill, if wrongly interpreted or minimized, may present occasion for supplemental legislation." The Beechwood case illustrates that, indeed, the time has come to review every aspect of this legislation and case law that has built up around it.

*Fourth:* Agencies should not be allowed to use administrative proceedings as a means of interpreting their own regulations and limiting their liabilities, as was done by CMS in the Beechwood case. The current highly deferential treatment provided by the courts, which limits the ability to substitute constitutionally mandated judicial judgment for the "quasi-judicial" judgment of the ALJ, needs to be replaced with careful review measured against the intent of the laws. The CMS interpretations rendered, which Judge Larimer allowed to stand, permitted the agency not only to make a mockery of its own regulations and responsibilities but to eliminate any substantive grounds for appeal. That, in turn, eliminated the last degree of fairness in the system. These capricious and autocratic interpretations became precedent and were used in numerous subsequent hearings to suppress challenges to agency action.

*Fifth:* Public officials need to be held accountable for their actions. The inevitable question that arises after anyone is told the Beechwood story is: What happened to the defendants who were found liable?

The answer—well, the answer never fails to produce one effect: utter disgust. On March 28, 2016, the *Wall Street Journal* published an editorial arguing that Americans hate government because regulators who abuse their power are never held accountable. The editorial went on to say that even "gross abuses of power," such as "scheming to destroy a company based on falsehoods and then spending years trying to deny the victims due process under the law," go unpunished. "As government expands, so does its potential for abuse," and in this day of "gigantic and intrusive government," Americans "should know there will be some accountability for abuses of power." The *WSJ* editorial called for agency administrators to "set a better standard [and] show that there is some accountability." However, as the Beechwood case illustrates, the most egregious abuses of power, by their nature, not only involve agency administrators, they likely start with them.

Leeds, Rubin, Carlo, Baker, and Francis were all administrators within DOH, and it took every one of them to manage the tasks that had to be coordinated at the state and regional levels, to put on a united front to gain the cooperation of their staff and other departments and agencies, and to assemble and adjust the plans as necessary. According to Leeds, prosecuting Beechwood involved a "whole lot" of people at "all levels of DOH and HCFA," including the attorneys and the governor's office. An operation of this scale and complexity, and with the political risks involved, took authorization, cooperation, and assurances against reprisal at the highest levels. It was carried out, quite simply, because those who willed it had the administrative power to make it so.

The dark side of regulation is that there is currently nothing in place to regulate the regulators. They can make a case to justify any regulatory action desired and do so without a shred of evidence. They can use their investigative authority as a pretense to make a case, and then charge, prosecute, judge, and sentence, all within the confines of their own walls, using rules that they promulgate. Absent the need to go to court, all is permissible. Due process, discovery, rules of evidence, and burdens of proof that would be mandatory in the typical judicial process do not apply. Furthermore, the officials are protected by qualified and absolute immunities, taxpayer paid defense and indemnity, deference provided by the courts, and a law enforcement agency conflicted in its duty to provide for their defense. What more could one ask for? Administrative agencies are not so much above the law as beside and outside it.

If a plaintiff does make it to trial, the focus will be on proving liability and damages. Other than having the discomfort and temporary inconvenience of being deposed or even sitting for trial, those who end up as defendants continue to enjoy life without being disturbed in the least. When the judgment went against them, Leeds, Rubin, Carlo, Baker, and Francis simply walked away, keeping their jobs, pensions, assets, and reputations despite the finding of liability. In June of 2016, Carlo even received the 2016 NYSHFA Nurse Leadership Excellence Award for having an "illustrious career … championing the cause for the highest level of quality of care and life … [and an] ardent advocate for the staff in SNFs … and the residents they so proudly serve."

Years have passed since those thirteen years of Beechwood's agony. Public interest in the Beechwood case has died along with pertinent statutes of limitation on fraudulent activity. Such was the subject of a March 24, 2016 *Wall Street Journal* editorial discussing the NorCal Tea Party Patriots case against the IRS. The article quoted District Court Judge Susan Dlott, who wrote "the government is doing everything it possibly can to make this as complicated as it possibly can, to last as long as it possibly can, so that by the time there is a result, nobody is going to care except the plaintiffs." It also quoted Judge Raymond Kethledge, who wrote a Sixth Circuit Decision in the same case, noting that the agency's effort to obstruct the legal process was appalling and "only compounded the conduct that gave rise to it." Unfortunately, this type of activity is becoming all too familiar as the courts shrink from dealing with it. Judge Kethledge wrote that charges regarding an executive agency targeting citizens for their political views are "among the most serious allegations a federal court can address." This can be broadened further: charges of government agencies targeting citizens for any reason are very serious, and the courts need to take them seriously. Judge Larimer did not, and thus the case grew very complicated, very risky for the plaintiff, and very old.

Pursuit of punitive damages against public employees has its own set of legal problems, not least of which is that, typically, as under Article V, Section VII of the New York State Constitution, the pensions of public employees cannot be attached. In addition, pursuing such damages creates legal complications that can jeopardize government indemnification for general damages. In a case such as Beechwood's, where punitive damage awards and the chance of collecting them were minimal, it would have been foolish to pursue such awards.

The fact that the state of New York indemnified the defendants for their actions, and that it was a significant amount of money, may in the short term serve to deter future corruptly abusive actions by agency personnel. Yet by not having to bear any personal responsibility at all, and without changes in the laws dealing with public officers and administrative procedures, nothing will change.

# APPENDIX

Judge Larimer: Injunction; unpublished oral decision, June 17, 1999; *Beechwood v. Rubin,* WDNY #99-cv-6241.

Judge Affronti: Caretaker Application; unpublished oral decision, June 21, 1999; *Whalen v. Chambery,* New York Supreme Court, Monroe County Index #99/6020.

ALJ Zylberberg: Matter of *Whalen v. Chambery;* unpublished written decision, NY DOH Administrative Hearing (October 19, 1999).

Judge Frazee: Three unpublished orders to DOH for documents or affidavits under the NYS FOIL (June 2001, September 2001, and June 2002).

*Beechwood Sanitarium v. Centers for Medicare & Medicaid Services,* CR821, 2001 WL 1329831 (Oct. 3, 2001), Kessel, ALJ. [ALJ Decision #1].

*Chambery v. United States,* 54 Fed. Cl. 2 (2002). HUD reserve account funds.

*Beechwood Sanitarium v. Centers for Medicare & Medicaid Services,* DAB No. 1824, 2002 WL 848030 (April 11, 2002) [Board Decision #1].

*Beechwood Sanitarium v. Centers for Medicare & Medicaid Services,* CR966, 2002 WL 31599189 (October 28, 2002), Kessel, ALJ. [ALJ Decision #2].

Judge Frazee: *NY Beechwood and Brook Chambery v. John Signor and DOH:* Order Entered March 17, 2003 denying petitioners' application for FOI legal fees.

*Beechwood Sanitarium v. Centers for Medicare & Medicaid Services,* DAB 1906 (2004), 2004 WL 230866 (January 23, 2004) [Board Decision #2].

NY Appellate Division, Fourth Judicial Department: *Beechwood and Brook*

*Chambery v. John Signor and DOH*: 11 A.D.3d 987 (2004). Decision to uphold Judge Frazee's decision to deny FOI legal fees.

Judge Larimer: *Beechwood Restorative Care Center v. Leeds,* 317 F.Supp.2d 248 (W.D.N.Y. 2004) [Summary Judgment Decision #1].

*Beechwood Restorative Care Center v. Signor,* 5 N.Y.3d 435 (2005). NY Court of Appeals Decision upholding previous decisions to deny FOI legal fees.

*Beechwood Restorative Care Center v. Leeds,* 436 F. 3d 147 (2d Cir. 2006), reversing in part 317 F.Supp.2d 248 (W.D.N.Y.2004).

Judge Larimer: *Beechwood v. Thompson,* 494 F.Supp.2d 181 (W.D.N.Y. 2007). Appeal of the DAB decision.

*Beechwood v. Leeds,* WDNY 02-cv-6235, unpublished decisions and orders by Magistrate Jonathan W. Feldman (March, April, September 2008) (Docket entries #152, 154). Ordering DOH and the MFCU to turn over documents.

Judge Larimer: *Beechwood v. Leeds,* 811 F.Supp.2d 667 (W.D.N.Y. 2011). Summary Judgment Decision #2.

Judge Larimer: *Beechwood v. Leeds,* 856 F.Supp.2d 580 (W.D.N.Y. 2012). Concerning evidence the jury would be allowed to consider.


## MY PROTECTED SPEECH AS RULED BY THE SECOND CIRCUIT

### Appeals to HCFA regarding survey issues

12/03/98: Walsky at HCFA stated that he had worked with DOH central office on regulatory issues that I had raised.

12/09/98: Walsky stated that he had a "lengthy" conversation with DOH officials and directed them to look at "a few things."

1/7/99: After Walsky's acknowledgement on 1/5/99 that I had established an adequate pattern of problem survey procedures to justify an investigation by HCFA, I formally requested such an investigation.

To demonstrate how unique these responses from HCFA officials were, Leeds testified that every provider has the right to try every avenue of appeal that they choose, including going to HCFA; however, the position usually taken by HCFA was that the provider had to finish formal administrative appeals before they would consider any other provider requests. Beechwood had made valid complaints about survey procedure as opposed to specific survey findings, and thus HCFA was acting on its complaints.

### Certificate of Need (CON) request to provide certified home care services

8/16/96: Letter to DOH Commissioner DeBuono stating that "in the midst of tremendous need for home care services, and the tremendous need to try better and more efficient methods of delivering service, the State is not approving any more agencies to deliver certified home care services, and allowing the currently approved agencies to grow virtually unchecked and without competition.... Beechwood, as a certified skilled nursing facility, and because of its rehab program, is already directly providing a more extensive and comprehensive range of certified medical services than the code demands of the typical certified home health agency.... Why should we be prohibited from providing certified home care services and the continuum of care that the patient desires?"

> 2/14/97: Dougherty responded: "This is in response to your January 27, 1997 letter to Dr. DeBuono regarding the CON process for home care. The SHRPC has continued its review of the certified home health agency CON issues, and I will advise you of their final recommendation once these discussions have been concluded."

Beechwood never received any notification of resolution of this matter.

### Problems with State Regulations

11/26/96: Beechwood filed a petition with the New York Supreme Court regarding state discharge regulations that didn't comply with Federal regulations. This became known as the "Langeveld litigation."

> 1/3/97: Judge Fisher ordered and DOH stipulated that it would change its regulations to comply with federal regulations. It would take until September 23, 2015 for the regulatory changes to be implemented.

### Continuing Problems with State Regulations

5/28/97: Letter to DOH Commissioner DeBuono regarding state regulations that are both irreconcilable and out of compliance with federal regulations, and "hindering providers from carrying out their regulatory mandates" and leaving them

A COURT WITHOUT JUSTICE

"at risk for continuing receipt of Federal Financial Participation," The letter pointed out that the "State of New York is risking its own Federal Financial Participation if it does not get the policies and procedures in place to facilitate proper placement, work jointly with the providers, or institute quality control measures and safeguards against unnecessary utilization of care and services as outlined in" the federal regulations and mandated by the SSA.

6/23/97: Letter to DeBuono stating that "I received a letter from Laura Leeds (M8076) … In response to my citation to conflicting regulations, she simply states that 'I would like to thank you for sharing your thoughts … the points you raised will be shared with those working on the revision of the state's regulations.' Nothing was said about correcting Departmental policies and procedures to deal with the regulatory mandates cited, or the risks of losing Federal Financial Participation…. If problems exist, immediate attention should be given toward correction without forcing issues to court."

> 7/3/97: Leeds responded to my 6/23/07 letter to DeBuono: "There is no easy or quick fix to what you identified as conflicting regulations. Regulatory reform is a lengthy process at best. The changes ordered by the Court … have begun that process. …"

7/14/97: Letter to DeBuono stating that I couldn't accept the Leeds response, and that my "letter of May 28, 1997 put your Department on notice that serious irreconcilable regulatory conflicts exist which need to be resolved so that the system can operate according to basic Federal and State regulatory intent. I am sure that this notice and the response received will become very important at a later date."

## Trying to get HCFA to Force DOH Compliance with Federal Requirements

1/12/98: Letter to Walsky, in the HCFA regional office in New York City: "As you are aware, New York State is in the process of bringing discharge hearing regulations into compliance with Federal regulations as a result of legal action initiated by Beechwood…. However, … there are still problems to be faced within State law …. Enclosed is a position paper I wrote for the State of New York to make them aware of the extent of the problem. They have chosen to address only the issue forced upon them by the court, and seem to be waiting for other court

402

actions before they move any further.... Please review these issues and regulations and provide HCFA's perspective accordingly."

> 12/03/98: Walsky stated he reviewed the regulatory concerns from the letter of 1/12/98,and discussed them with DOH officials.

> 12/09/98: Walsky stated that he had a "lengthy" conversation with DOH officials and directed them to look at "a few things," and report back to him.

> 12/11/98: Walsky stated that he did not want to get more involved in the regulatory issues; he must let the State work it out itself. However, he would review the last three surveys complained about and provide formal comment. He would also have a federal surveyor at Beechwood on the next survey.

2/25/99: After a lengthy series of letters to HCFA's central office in Baltimore regarding issues presented by NYS State regulations, Mary Vienna, responded: "I apologize for the delay in responding, however many of the issues you raised were outside the purview of our center and we needed to consult with the experts on Medicaid hearings and appeals and the New York regional office to confirm our responses. ... While HCFA has broad guidelines requiring hearings, the actual procedures are left up to the individual States.... (This review of state regulations for consistency and compliance) is something that HCFA does not do. States are sovereign entities ..."

**Medicaid Access Provisions Mandated to Obtain a CON**
1/27/97: Letter to DOH Commissioner DeBuono stating that "I have had many telephone conversations with Ms. Linda Goudy regarding the CON enforcement problem. She has admitted the lack of enforcement mechanism ... However, no solution has been forthcoming ... The Department should either develop the enforcement mechanisms ... or eliminate these requirements as part of the CON process."

5/28/97: Letter to DeBuono: it "is very disturbing that absolutely nothing seems to be forthcoming concerning a formal Departmental response to the problems identified regarding the lack of enforcement of SF Certificate of Need provisions ... I have been bounced between divisions, and have waited eight months for a response.... This is an extremely important issue, and cannot wait for a response much longer."

8/1/97: DeBuono had a conference call with Leeds, Murphy and Testo regarding Chambery's 7/25/97 letter to DeBuono complaining of lack of response from Murphy regarding the Medicaid Access issues.

4/22/98: My fax to Pat Whitman in the Governor's Office of Regulatory Reform: "When we spoke a couple of weeks ago, you stated that "everyone seems to agree that Medicaid access quotas have outlived their usefulness. ... I would simply like to know: 1. Whether the State is going to enforce the access agreements currently in effect? 2. Whether I can pursue business interests without worrying about any further application of the Medicaid Access requirements?"

> 12/22/98: Pat Whitman is provided the list of Medicaid Access agreements being violated, and specifics on the degree of violation in each case.
>
> Leeds acknowledged that DOH had confirmed my figures, and that no penalty had ever been assessed regarding the violations, and that she would have been part of any decision regarding any penalty.
>
> 1/26/99: Call from Whitman stating that she faxed the documentation of Medicaid Access violations to C. Murphy, and suggested calling Murphy, and if that didn't work: "Next Step - Office of Attorney General."
>
> Note: Recall that at the same time, the DOH is being investigated by the AG for—
>
> 2/23/99: Whitman stated that "Murphy refuses to budge on his position" regarding enforcing Medicaid Access provisions to gain a CON.
>
> 4/2/99: Leeds, Testo, Murphy and others had a conference call regarding "Medicaid Access Agreements/Brook Chambery's letter to Pat Whitman."

4/6/99: Letter to Greenberg voicing frustration over the lack of movement on the Medicaid access issue and asking when the legal requirements are going to be changed.

4/6/99: Leeds told Pat Whitman that Medicaid Access had outlived its usefulness, if it ever needed to be there.

4/15/99: Murphy wrote to Whitman that "We clearly intend to apply the Medicaid admission requirements ..."

In her deposition, Leeds acknowledged their position was that DOH would not enforce agreement violations unless Medicaid Access became "an issue"; i.e.: Medicaid patients could not get placed.

# General Terminology

**AG:** Attorney General

**APA:** The federal Administrative Procedures Act

**Absolute Immunity:** Total immunity from suit for government prosecutors and adjudicators as long as they are acting within the scope of their duties.

**BAH:** Bureau of Administrative Hearing

**Burden of Proof levels:** Substantial Evidence, Preponderance of the Evidence, Clear and Convincing Evidence, and Evidence Beyond a Reasonable Doubt. *Substantial* means "such as a reasonable mind might accept as adequate." *Preponderance* is "more likely than not." *Clear and Convincing* is typically used in civil fraud cases and means "a firm belief, highly probable, or substantially more likely than not." *Beyond a Reasonable Doubt* is used in the criminal arena and means "being entirely convinced that evidence proves guilt."

**Certificate of Need (CON):** A certificate issued by the Department of Health, granting permission to create / operate a certain number of beds for certain levels of care, or to provide certain services.

**CFR:** Code of Federal Regulations

**CMS:** Centers for Medicaid/Medicare Services, a division of US Department of Health and Human Services. It was known as HCFA (Healthcare Financing Agency) before June of 2001.

**DOH:** NYS Department of Health

**DPOC:** Directed Plan of Correction. A POC in which the state survey agency directs the facility to take certain corrective measures as part of its own POC.

**Establishment:** A NYS DOH process involving a regulatory review of operators, their finances, and/or the proposed physical plant or project, and gaining approval to go forward.

**FOI:** Freedom of Information

**FOIA:** Federal FOI request

**FOIL:** State FOI request

**HCFA:** Health Care Financing Administration, a division of US Department of Health and Human Services. In June of 2001, the name was changed CMS, Centers for Medicare/Medicaid Services.

**MDS:** A federalized patient assessment form mandated by HCFA

**MFCU:** Medicaid Fraud Control Unit, a division of the New York State Attorney General's Office

**MR:** Medicare, the federal health insurance program for the elderly

**MD:** Medicaid, a joint state /federal program providing assistance for health care

**Medicaid/Medicare Certification:** Compliance with the federal regulations, enabling a provider to receive funds for providing services to Medicare and Medicaid patients.

**Medicaid Access Agreement:** An agreement between a nursing home provider and the NYS DOH regarding commitments to take certain types and percentages of Medicaid patients in return for a Certificate of Need (CON) to provide certain services.

**NYCRR:** New York Code of Rules and Regulations

**NYS PHL:** New York State Public Health Law

**OCC:** Office of Continuing Care

**Operating Certificate:** License to do business as a health care facility in NY. It is issued by the DOH. A condition of maintaining this license is to continue to be Medicare/Medicaid certified by HCFA/CMS.

**POC:** Plan of Correction. A document required by federal law, to be developed by a facility outlining what will be done to correct any cited survey deficiencies.

**Qualified Immunity:** "Government officials are shielded from civil liability under 42 U.S.C. § 1983 by the doctrine of qualified immunity so long as their conduct 'does not violate clearly established statutory or constitutional rights of which a reasonable person would have known.' *Harlow v. Fitzgerald*, 457 U.S. 800, 818 (1982)."

**SAP:** NY State Administrative Procedures act

**SOD:** Statement of Deficiency issued regarding any alleged conditions of non-compliance resulting from a survey.

**SOM:** State Operations Manual published by HCFA/CMS interpreting regulations for use by the state survey agency and providers.

**SSA:** Social Security Act

**Scope and Severity**: A system mandated by CMS for grading the deficiencies cited as the result of a survey.

**Substandard Quality Care (SQC):** There are certain deficiency tags, which if graded at a certain scope and severity level are considered substandard quality care.

**Summary Judgment:** A judgment entered by the court without a full trial, or on specific elements of the case. Typically, it is a request for a ruling that the other party has no case, for there are no facts at issue.

**Survey:** Process of determining compliance with federal Medicare/Medicaid standards of care.

**Survey Agency:** The state departments of health contract to do the survey activities for the federal government.

**Survey Cycle:** The series of survey visits beginning with the initial survey and ending with the final revisit. Each survey visit can result in a new statement of deficiencies.

**Survey Deficiency:** An allegation of noncompliance made by the survey team, as listed on the statement of deficiency (SOD)

**Survey Entrance Conference:** Surveyors announce themselves and the purpose for their visit, typically in a meeting with management officials of a healthcare facility.

**Survey Exit Conference:** Surveyors describe any noncompliance they have found on the survey visit, including providing examples.

**Survey Finding:** Facts cited in support of the deficiency alleged on the statement of deficiency.

**Surveyor:** Federally certified person working for either CMS or a state survey agency, and involved in surveying facilities.

# The Expertise of Those Who Regulated and Shaped the Industry

Both the Administrative Procedures Act (APA) and the case law that has developed around it are based on the assumption that agencies acquire a certain amount of in-house expertise and thus are a better and more efficient place to handle adjudicative matters than in the courts.

**Let's examine the healthcare "expertise" of the top officials at DOH in 1999**
The New York State Department of Health is a huge entity, with approximately 5,200 employees and consuming one third to one half of the State's operating budget. The department and the rules and policies promulgated determine how healthcare is delivered, who can deliver it, and (for the dollars DOH controls) how much the provider will be paid.

**Whalen: Acting Commissioner of Health**
Whalen began his career at DOH in 1974 in the Public Affairs Group, after just graduating from college. His father was the Deputy Commissioner of Health at the time. He moved through being Director of the Division of Health Systems Management, and then Director of the AIDs Institute, before becoming the Executive Deputy Commissioner in 1996, and Acting Commissioner from November of 1998 to June of 1999.

**Barnett: Director of the Office of Continuing Care**
Barnett had a bachelors and master's degree in economics, and another master's

degree in industrial administration. He only had one year at another job before joining DOH in 1979, and that was with Mechanical Technology Incorporated. He was never a surveyor or compliance officer and started at DOH as a research scientist coordinating a federal grant on hospital financial reporting. He was the assistant director of the division of health care financing for ten years before he was appointed by Commissioner DeBuono to be Director of the Office of Continuing Care (OCC), the second highest person in the DOH. Barnett left quality and enforcement issues up to Leeds.

**Leeds: Deputy Director of the Office of Continuing Care.**
Her highest degree was a Bachelor's in Arts, with an Education concentration. She had no healthcare degree, nursing experience, or nursing home administrator background, and had never been a certified surveyor. Leeds started employment at DOH in 1979 as an administrative analyst trainee and had training in administrative analysis, human resources, and especially budgets, which is what she "wound up" doing for her programs.

Leeds later worked for the Office of Professional Medical Malpractice (OPMC) for approximately ten years, including a role as Assistant Director, in which her job consisted of presenting cases to the board, training board members who were appointed to serve , and developing investigative materials.

After passing a civil service test for the payroll category Health Program Director II, which somehow she "held" permanently, Leeds received the political appointment as the northeast Regional Director and thus part of Commissioner DeBuono's executive staff. In January of 1995, she had to "roll back" into being the Assistant Director of OPMC, but later became Director of the Bureau of Long-Term Care. As Bureau Director, she did "policy direction for survey and surveillance and policy for long-term care," which, because of the federalization of the survey process, consisted of working with "HCFA regarding DOH's compliance with federal regulations around survey."

In December 1997 Leeds was appointed Deputy Director of the Office of Continuing Care, and reported directly to Whalen. As the Executive Deputy Director of the Office of Continuing care she had responsibility for three divisions and nine bureaus all related to post-acute care. Through the Division of Quality and Licensure, she controlled core functions of surveillance and enforcement, licensure and certification of facilities, and credentialing of facility staff.

Through the Bureau of Surveillance and Quality Assurance, Leeds was responsible for continuing facility licensure and certification, determining what cases got sent to DLA for enforcement, assuring compliance with federal requirements, and standardization of the survey process. Through the Bureau of licensure and Certification, Leeds was responsible for establishment of owners/operators; Certificates of Need (CON) for construction applications; and initial certification and licensure, and receiverships. To summarize, she was "The Program."

**Colello: Director of the Bureau of Long-Term Care and Quality Assurance.**
Colello graduated from law school in 1980 and went to work for the NYS Tax Department. She transferred to DOH in 1986, at first working for OPMC, and then moving to the Bureau of Administrative Hearings (BAH) in 1991 as an Associate Attorney, where she mainly prosecuted patient abuse cases (both as staff and supervising attorney). At trial, Colello stated that she was not even familiar with the NYS Adjudicative Plan.

Leeds appointed Colello to director of the Bureau of Quality Assurance in November of 1998, a newly created position. Leeds had worked with Colello previously in Colello's capacity as an attorney with the Bureau of Hearings (and most likely, also at the Office of Professional Medical Conduct [OPMC]). Colello believed Leeds appointed her to the bureau position because of her "knowledge of particularly the patient abuse law and the contributions I was making to that legal committee of that association." She stated that "the focus of this quality assurance bureau was to standardize the enforcement and inspection processes, … to assure that the inspections or surveys carried out by our field offices across the state were consistent," and legally sufficient.

**Rubin: Acting Director of the Western Region.**
Rubin had a bachelor's degree in Social Work, began his employment with DOH in 1974 "doing various functions regarding the Medicaid program, and stayed with DOH until he retired. Rubin was never certified or trained as a surveyor. Like Leeds, his payroll category was Health Program Director II.

Rubin began getting involved in long-term care about 1978 and worked in the long-term care program in various functions, the last of which was as the long-term care program director. However, at trial, he acknowledged that he knew nothing of the survey regulations, procedures, or quality indicator ratings.

In 1985, Rubin became the Rochester area administrator, which meant that he had administrative responsibilities for several programs in addition to long-term care. In this position, he was also the Deputy Director of the DOH Western Region. In January of 1999 he was appointed Acting Director of the Western Region, making him "responsible for regulation of (all) health care facilities in the 17 county area."

**Greenberg: General Counsel and Director of the Division of Legal Affairs.**
Greenberg was counselor to the Lieutenant Governor before moving to General Counsel at DOH in 1995. Before that, he was an Assistant United States Attorney, doing criminal trial work.

**Altone: Director of the Bureau of Administrative Hearings.** Altone began his employment with DOH in December of 1977 as a Senior Attorney and joined BAH in 1982. He became director of BAH in June of 1993. Sometime after the Beechwood matter in 2000, he was promoted to Assistant Counsel.

**Where Is the healthcare expertise?**
Being in a certain position within a department does not make one an industry expert, and this is where the APA and the courts are wrong in providing so much deference to what has been promulgated by agency officials. There was no healthcare industry experience or even a healthcare degree, such as public health management, in the management upper echelon of the Department. None.

The expertise these officials gain as they climb the management ranks is in the regulation of the industry and how to traverse the ever-growing complexities of the regulatory structure, which they themselves establish. Regulatory control instills power, resistance to change, and demand for their consultative services when they depart from the agency. It is this regulatory power that can easily lead to abuse of authority. The courts need to be vigilant at detecting such overreach, and not being too quick to provide complete deference to them as the experts.